W9-BUH-446

WITHDRAWN

JOSEPH POLANSKY

YOUR PERSONAL HOROSCOPE 2019

Month-by-month forecast for every sign

Thorsons

The author is grateful to the people
of STAR ★ DATA, who truly fathered
this book and without whom it
could not have been written.

Thorsons
An imprint of HarperCollins*Publishers*
1 London Bridge Street
London SE1 9GF

www.harpercollins.co.uk

First published by Thorsons 2018

18 19 20 21 22 LSCC 10 9 8 7 6 5 4 3 2 1

© Star ★ Data, Inc. 2018

Star ★ Data assert the moral right to
be identified as the authors of this work

A catalogue record for this book is
available from the British Library

ISBN 978-0-00-829881-4

Printed and bound in the United States of America
by LSC Communications

All rights reserved. No part of this publication may be
reproduced, stored in a retrieval system, or transmitted,
in any form, or by any means, electronic, mechanical,
photocopying, recording or otherwise, without the
prior permission of the publishers.

For more information visit www.harpercollins.co.uk/green

Contents

Introduction

Welcome to the fascinating and intricate world of astrology!

For thousands of years the movements of the planets and other heavenly bodies have intrigued the best minds of every generation. Life holds no greater challenge or joy than this: knowledge of ourselves and the universe we live in. Astrology is one of the keys to this knowledge.

Your Personal Horoscope 2019 gives you the fruits of astrological wisdom. In addition to general guidance on your character and the basic trends of your life, it shows you how to take advantage of planetary influences so you can make the most of the year ahead.

The section on each sign includes a Personality Profile, a look at general trends for 2019, and in-depth month-by-month forecasts. The Glossary (*page 5*) explains some of the astrological terms you may be unfamiliar with.

One of the many helpful features of this book is the 'Best' and 'Most Stressful' days listed at the beginning of each monthly forecast. Read these sections to learn which days in each month will be good overall, good for money, and good for love. Mark them on your calendar – these will be your best days. Similarly, make a note of the days that will be most stressful for you. It is best to avoid booking important meetings or taking major decisions on these days, as well as on those days when important planets in your horoscope are retrograde (moving backwards through the zodiac).

The Major Trends section for your sign lists those days when your vitality is strong or weak, or when relationships with your co-workers or loved ones may need a bit more effort on your part. If you are going through a difficult time, take a look at the colour, metal, gem and scent listed in the 'At a Glance' section of your Personality Profile. Wearing a piece of jewellery that contains your metal and/or gem will strengthen your vitality, just as wearing clothes or decorating your room or office in the colour ruled by your sign, drinking teas made from the herbs ruled by your sign or wearing the scents associated with your sign will sustain you.

Another important virtue of this book is that it will help you to know not only yourself but those around you: your friends, co-workers, partners and/or children. Reading the Personality Profile and forecasts for their signs will provide you with an insight into their behaviour that you won't get anywhere else. You will know when to be more tolerant of them and when they are liable to be difficult or irritable.

In this edition we have included foot reflexology charts as part of the health section. So many health problems could perhaps be avoided or alleviated if we understood which organs were most vulnerable and what we could do to protect them. Though there are many natural and drug-free ways to strengthen vulnerable organs, these charts show a valid way to proceed. The vulnerable organs for the year ahead are clearly marked in the charts. It's very good to massage the whole foot on a regular basis, as the feet contain reflexes to the entire body. Try to pay special attention to the specific areas marked in the charts. If this is done diligently, health problems can be avoided. And even if they can't be completely avoided, their impact can be softened considerably.

I consider you – the reader – my personal client. By studying your Solar Horoscope I gain an awareness of what is going on in your life – what you are feeling and striving for and the challenges you face. I then do my best to address these concerns. Consider this book the next best thing to having your own personal astrologer!

It is my sincere hope that *Your Personal Horoscope 2019* will enhance the quality of your life, make things easier, illuminate the way forward, banish obscurities and make you more aware of your personal connection to the universe. Understood properly and used wisely, astrology is a great guide to knowing yourself, the people around you and the events in your life – but remember that what you do with these insights – the final result – is up to you.

A Note on the 'New Zodiac'

Recently an article was published that postulated two things: the discovery of a new constellation – Ophiuchus – making a thirteenth constellation in the heavens and thus a thirteenth sign, and the statement that because the Earth has shifted relative to the constellations in the past few thousand years, all the signs have shifted backwards by one sign. This has caused much consternation, and I have received a stream of letters, emails and phone calls from people saying things like: 'I don't want to be a Taurus, I'm happy being a Gemini', 'What's my real sign?' or 'Now that I finally understand myself, I'm not who I think I am!'

All of this is 'much ado about nothing'. The article has some partial truth to it. Yes, in two thousand years the planets have shifted relative to the constellations in the heavens. This is old news. We know this and Hindu astrologers take this into account when casting charts. This shift doesn't affect Western astrologers in North America and Europe. We use what is called a 'tropical' zodiac. This zodiac has nothing to do with the constellations in the heavens. They have the same names, but that's about it. The tropical zodiac is based on the Earth's revolution around the Sun. Imagine the circle that this orbit makes, then divide this circle by twelve and you have our zodiac. The Spring Equinox is always 0 degrees (Aries), and the Autumn Equinox is always 0 degrees Libra (180 degrees from 0 Aries). At one time a few thousand years ago, these tropical signs coincided with the actual constellations; they were pretty much interchangeable, and it didn't matter what zodiac you used. But in the course of thousands of years the planets have shifted relative to these constellations. Here in the West it doesn't affect our practice one iota. You are still the sign you always were.

In North America and Europe there is a clear distinction between an astrological sign and a constellation in the heavens. This issue is more of a problem for Hindu astrologers. Their zodiac is based on the actual constellations – this is called the 'sidereal' zodiac. And Hindu astrologers have been accounting for this shift all the time. They keep close tabs on it. In two thousand years there is a shift of 23 degrees, and they subtract this from the Western calculations. So in their system many a Gemini would be a Taurus and this is true for all the signs. This is nothing new – it is all known and accounted for, so there is no bombshell here.

The so-called thirteenth constellation, Ophiuchus, is also not a problem for the Western astrologer. As we mentioned, our zodiac has nothing to do with the constellations. It could be more of a problem for the Hindus, but my feeling is that it's not a problem for them either. What these astronomers are calling a new constellation was probably considered a part of one of the existing constellations. I don't know this as a fact, but I presume it is so intuitively. I'm sure we will soon be getting articles by Hindu astrologers explaining this.

Glossary of Astrological Terms

Ascendant

We experience day and night because the Earth rotates on its axis once every 24 hours. It is because of this rotation that the Sun, Moon and planets seem to rise and set. The zodiac is a fixed belt (imaginary, but very real in spiritual terms) around the Earth. As the Earth rotates, the different signs of the zodiac seem to the observer to rise on the horizon. During a 24-hour period every sign of the zodiac will pass this horizon point at some time or another. The sign that is at the horizon point at any given time is called the Ascendant, or rising sign. The Ascendant is the sign denoting a person's self-image, body and self-concept – the personal ego, as opposed to the spiritual ego indicated by a person's Sun sign.

Aspects

Aspects are the angular relationships between planets, the way in which one planet stimulates or influences another. If a planet makes a harmonious aspect (connection) to another, it tends to stimulate that planet in a positive and helpful way. If, however, it makes a stressful aspect to another planet, this disrupts that planet's normal influence.

Astrological Qualities

There are three astrological qualities: *cardinal*, *fixed* and *mutable*. Each of the 12 signs of the zodiac falls into one of these three categories.

Cardinal Signs

Aries, Cancer, Libra and Capricorn

The cardinal quality is the active, initiating principle. Those born under these four signs are good at starting new projects.

Fixed Signs

Taurus, Leo, Scorpio and Aquarius

Fixed qualities include stability, persistence, endurance and perfectionism. People born under these four signs are good at seeing things through.

Mutable Signs

Gemini, Virgo, Sagittarius and Pisces

Mutable qualities are adaptability, changeability and balance. Those born under these four signs are creative, if not always practical.

Direct Motion

When the planets move forward through the zodiac – as they normally do – they are said to be going 'direct'.

Grand Square

A Grand Square differs from a normal Square (usually two planets separated by 90 degrees) in that four or more planets are involved. When you look at the pattern in a chart you will see a whole and complete square. This, though stressful, usually denotes a new manifestation in the life. There is much work and balancing involved in the manifestation.

Grand Trine

A Grand Trine differs from a normal Trine (where two planets are 120 degrees apart) in that three or more planets are involved. When you look at this pattern in a chart, it takes the form of a complete triangle – a Grand Trine. Usually (but not always) it occurs in one of the four elements: Fire, Earth, Air or Water. Thus the particular element in which it occurs will be highlighted. A Grand Trine in Water is not the same as a Grand Trine in Air or Fire, etc. This is a very fortunate and happy aspect, and quite rare.

Houses

There are 12 signs of the zodiac and 12 houses of experience. The 12 signs are personality types and ways in which a given planet expresses itself; the 12 houses show 'where' in your life this expression takes place. Each house has a different area of interest. A house can become potent and important – a house of power – in different ways: if it contains the Sun, the Moon or the 'ruler' of your chart; if it contains more than one planet; or if the ruler of that house is receiving unusual stimulation from other planets.

1st House
Personal Image and Sensual Delights

2nd House
Money/Finance

3rd House
Communication and Intellectual Interests

4th House
Home and Family

5th House
Children, Fun, Games, Creativity, Speculations and Love Affairs

6th House
Health and Work

7th House
Love, Marriage and Social Activities

8th House
Transformation and Regeneration

9th House
Religion, Foreign Travel, Higher Education and Philosophy

10th House
Career

11th House
Friends, Group Activities and Fondest Wishes

12th House
Spirituality

Karma

Karma is the law of cause and effect which governs all phenomena.
We are all where we find ourselves because of karma – because of
actions we have performed in the past. The universe is such a balanced
instrument that any act immediately sets corrective forces into motion
– karma.

Long-term Planets

The planets that take a long time to move through a sign show the long-term trends in a given area of life. They are important for fore-casting the prolonged view of things. Because these planets stay in one sign for so long, there are periods in the year when the faster-moving (short-term) planets will join them, further activating and enhancing the importance of a given house.

Jupiter
stays in a sign for about 1 year

Saturn
2½ years

Uranus
7 years

Neptune
14 years

Pluto
15 to 30 years

Lunar

Relating to the Moon. See also 'Phases of the Moon', below.

Natal

Literally means 'birth'. In astrology this term is used to distinguish between planetary positions that occurred at the time of a person's birth (natal) and those that are current (transiting). For example, Natal Sun refers to where the Sun was when you were born; transiting Sun refers to where the Sun's position is currently at any given moment – which usually doesn't coincide with your birth, or Natal, Sun.

Out of Bounds

The planets move through the zodiac at various angles relative to the celestial equator (if you were to draw an imaginary extension of the Earth's equator out into the universe, you would have an illustration of this celestial equator). The Sun – being the most dominant and powerful influence in the Solar system – is the measure astrologers use as a standard. The Sun never goes more than approximately 23 degrees north or south of the celestial equator. At the winter solstice the Sun reaches its maximum southern angle of orbit (declination); at the summer solstice it reaches its maximum northern angle. Any time a planet exceeds this Solar boundary – and occasionally planets do – it is said to be 'out of bounds'. This means that the planet exceeds or trespasses into strange territory – beyond the limits allowed by the Sun, the ruler of the Solar system. The planet in this condition becomes more emphasized and exceeds its authority, becoming an important influence in the forecast.

Phases of the Moon

After the full Moon, the Moon seems to shrink in size (as perceived from the Earth), gradually growing smaller until it is virtually invisible to the naked eye – at the time of the next new Moon. This is called the waning Moon phase, or the waning Moon.

After the new Moon, the Moon gradually gets bigger in size (as perceived from the Earth) until it reaches its maximum size at the time of the full Moon. This period is called the waxing Moon phase, or waxing Moon.

Retrogrades

The planets move around the Sun at different speeds. Mercury and Venus move much faster than the Earth, while Mars, Jupiter, Saturn, Uranus, Neptune and Pluto move more slowly. Thus there are times when, relative to the Earth, the planets appear to be going backwards. In reality they are always going forward, but relative to our vantage point on Earth they seem to go backwards through the zodiac for a period of time. This is called 'retrograde' motion and tends to weaken the normal influence of a given planet.

Short-term Planets

The fast-moving planets move so quickly through a sign that their effects are generally of a short-term nature. They reflect the immediate, day-to-day trends in a horoscope.

Moon
stays in a sign for only 2½ days

Mercury
20 to 30 days

Sun
30 days

Venus
approximately 1 month

Mars
approximately 2 months

T-square

A T-square differs from a Grand Square (see above) in that it is not a complete square. If you look at the pattern in a chart it appears as 'half a complete square', resembling the T-square tools used by architects and designers. If you cut a complete square in half, diagonally, you have a T-square. Many astrologers consider this more stressful than a Grand Square, as it creates tension that is difficult to resolve. T-squares bring learning experiences.

Transits

This term refers to the movements or motions of the planets at any given time. Astrologers use the word 'transit' to make the distinction between a birth, or Natal, planet (see 'Natal', above) and the planet's current movement in the heavens. For example, if at your birth Saturn was in the sign of Cancer in your 8th house, but is now moving through your 3rd house, it is said to be 'transiting' your 3rd house. Transits are one of the main tools with which astrologers forecast trends.

Aries

THE RAM

Birthdays from
21st March to
20th April

Personality Profile

ARIES AT A GLANCE

Element – Fire

Ruling Planet – Mars
   Career Planet – Saturn
   Love Planet – Venus
   Money Planet – Venus
   Planet of Fun, Entertainment, Creativity and Speculations – Sun
   Planet of Health and Work – Mercury
   Planet of Home and Family Life – Moon
   Planet of Spirituality – Neptune
   Planet of Travel, Education, Religion and Philosophy – Jupiter

Colours – carmine, red, scarlet

Colours that promote love, romance and social harmony – green, jade green

Colour that promotes earning power – green

Gem – amethyst

Metals – iron, steel

Scent – honeysuckle

Quality – cardinal (= activity)

Quality most needed for balance – caution

Strongest virtues – abundant physical energy, courage, honesty, independence, self-reliance

Deepest need – action

Characteristics to avoid – haste, impetuousness, over-aggression, rashness

Signs of greatest overall compatibility – Leo, Sagittarius

Signs of greatest overall incompatibility – Cancer, Libra, Capricorn

Sign most helpful to career – Capricorn

Sign most helpful for emotional support – Cancer

Sign most helpful financially – Taurus

Sign best for marriage and/or partnerships – Libra

Sign most helpful for creative projects – Leo

Best Sign to have fun with – Leo

Signs most helpful in spiritual matters – Sagittarius, Pisces

Best day of the week – Tuesday

Understanding an Aries

Aries is the activist *par excellence* of the zodiac. The Aries need for action is almost an addiction, and those who do not really understand the Aries personality would probably use this hard word to describe it. In reality 'action' is the essence of the Aries psychology – the more direct, blunt and to-the-point the action, the better. When you think about it, this is the ideal psychological makeup for the warrior, the pioneer, the athlete or the manager.

Aries likes to get things done, and in their passion and zeal often lose sight of the consequences for themselves and others. Yes, they often try to be diplomatic and tactful, but it is hard for them. When they do so they feel that they are being dishonest and phoney. It is hard for them even to understand the mindset of the diplomat, the consensus builder, the front office executive. These people are involved in endless meetings, discussions, talks and negotiations – all of which seem a great waste of time when there is so much work to be done, so many real achievements to be gained. An Aries can understand, once it is explained, that talk and negotiations – the social graces – lead ultimately to better, more effective actions. The interesting thing is that an Aries is rarely malicious or spiteful – even when waging war. Aries people fight without hate for their opponents. To them it is all good-natured fun, a grand adventure, a game.

When confronted with a problem many people will say, 'Well, let's think about it, let's analyse the situation.' But not an Aries. An Aries will think, 'Something must be done. Let's get on with it.' Of course neither response is the total answer. Sometimes action is called for, sometimes cool thought. But an Aries tends to err on the side of action.

Action and thought are radically different principles. Physical activity is the use of brute force. Thinking and deliberating require one not to use force – to be still. It is not good for the athlete to be deliberating the next move; this will only slow down his or her reaction time. The athlete must act instinctively and instantly. This is how Aries people tend to behave in life. They are quick, instinctive decision-makers and their decisions tend to be translated into action almost immediately. When their intuition is sharp and well tuned, their actions are powerful and successful. When their intuition is off, their actions can be disastrous.

Do not think this will scare an Aries. Just as a good warrior knows that in the course of combat he or she might acquire a few wounds, so too does an Aries realize – somewhere deep down – that in the course of being true to yourself you might get embroiled in a disaster or two. It is all part of the game. An Aries feels strong enough to weather any storm.

There are many Aries people who are intellectual. They make powerful and creative thinkers. But even in this realm they tend to be pioneers – outspoken and blunt. These types of Aries tend to elevate (or sublimate) their desire for physical combat in favour of intellectual, mental combat. And they are indeed powerful.

In general, Aries people have a faith in themselves that others could learn from. This basic, rock-solid faith carries them through the most tumultuous situations of life. Their courage and self-confidence make them natural leaders. Their leadership is more by way of example than by actually controlling others.

Finance

Aries people often excel as builders or estate agents. Money in and of itself is not as important as are other things – action, adventure, sport, etc. They are motivated by the need to support and be well-thought-of by their partners. Money as a way of attaining pleasure is another important motivation. Aries function best in their own businesses or as managers of their own departments within a large business or corporation. The fewer orders they have to take from higher up, the better. They also function better out in the field rather than behind a desk.

Aries people are hard workers with a lot of endurance; they can earn large sums of money due to the strength of their sheer physical energy.

Venus is their money planet, which means that Aries need to develop more of the social graces in order to realize their full earning potential. Just getting the job done – which is what an Aries excels at – is not enough to create financial success. The co-operation of others needs to be attained. Customers, clients and co-workers need to be made to feel comfortable; many people need to be treated properly in order for success to happen. When Aries people develop these abilities – or hire someone to do this for them – their financial potential is unlimited.

Career and Public Image

One would think that a pioneering type would want to break with the social and political conventions of society. But this is not so with the Aries-born. They are pioneers within conventional limits, in the sense that they like to start their own businesses within an established industry.

Capricorn is on the 10th house of career cusp of Aries' solar horoscope. Saturn is the planet that rules their life's work and professional aspirations. This tells us some interesting things about the Aries character. First off, it shows that, in order for Aries people to reach their full career potential, they need to develop some qualities that are a bit alien to their basic nature: they need to become better administrators and organizers; they need to be able to handle details better and to take a long-range view of their projects and their careers in general. No one can beat an Aries when it comes to achieving short-range objectives, but a career is long term, built over time. You cannot take a 'quickie' approach to it.

Some Aries people find it difficult to stick with a project until the end. Since they get bored quickly and are in constant pursuit of new adventures, they prefer to pass an old project or task on to somebody else in order to start something new. Those Aries who learn how to put off the search for something new until the old is completed will achieve great success in their careers and professional lives.

In general, Aries people like society to judge them on their own merits, on their real and actual achievements. A reputation acquired by 'hype' feels false to them.

Love and Relationships

In marriage and partnerships Aries like those who are more passive, gentle, tactful and diplomatic – people who have the social grace and skills they sometimes lack. Our partners always represent a hidden part of ourselves – a self that we cannot express personally.

An Aries tends to go after what he or she likes aggressively. The tendency is to jump into relationships and marriages. This is especially true if Venus is in Aries as well as the Sun. If an Aries likes you, he or she will have a hard time taking no for an answer; many attempts will be made to sweep you off your feet.

Though Aries can be exasperating in relationships – especially if they are not understood by their partners – they are never consciously or wilfully cruel or malicious. It is just that they are so independent and sure of themselves that they find it almost impossible to see somebody else's viewpoint or position. This is why an Aries needs as a partner someone with lots of social graces.

On the plus side, an Aries is honest, someone you can lean on, someone with whom you will always know where you stand. What he or she lacks in diplomacy is made up for in integrity.

Home and Domestic Life

An Aries is of course the ruler at home – the Boss. The male will tend to delegate domestic matters to the female. The female Aries will want to rule the roost. Both tend to be handy round the house. Both like large families and both believe in the sanctity and importance of the family. An Aries is a good family person, although he or she does not especially like being at home a lot, preferring instead to be roaming about.

Considering that they are by nature so combative and wilful, Aries people can be surprisingly soft, gentle and even vulnerable with their children and partners. The sign of Cancer, ruled by the Moon, is on the cusp of their solar 4th house of home and family. When the Moon is well aspected – under favourable influences – in the birth chart, an Aries will be tender towards the family and will want a family life that is nurturing and supportive. Aries likes to come home after a hard day on the battlefield of life to the understanding arms of their partner and the unconditional love and support of their family. An Aries feels that there is enough 'war' out in the world – and he or she enjoys participating in that. But when Aries comes home, comfort and nurturing are what's needed.

The good news is that there is much you can do to enhance your health and prevent problems from developing. Give more attention to the following – the vulnerable areas of your Horoscope (the reflexology points are shown in the chart above):

- The head, face and scalp. These are always important for Aries and this year is no exception. Regular scalp and face massage should be part of your health regime, and craniosacral therapy is said to be good for the head too.
- The musculature – another important area for you, Aries. While you don't need to be Arnold Schwarzenegger, you do need good muscle tone. Weak or flabby muscles can knock the spine and skeleton out of alignment and this will cause all kinds of other problems. So vigorous physical exercise (according to your age and stage in life) is a good thing.
- The adrenals. With the adrenals it is important to avoid anger and fear, the two emotions that stress them out. Ginseng is said to be good for the adrenals.
- The heart has become important in recent years, and will become even more so after December 3. Most spiritual healers affirm that worry and anxiety are the major root causes of heart problems. So try to avoid these; replace them with faith.
- The lungs, arms, shoulders, small intestine and respiratory system. These are always important for you, Aries, as Mercury, the planet that rules these areas, is your health planet. (The reflexes to the lungs are shown above.) Regular arm and shoulder massage, especially the shoulders, is beneficial as tension tends to collect there and needs to be released.

With Mercury as your health planet, good health also means good mental health. It is good to exercise your body, as was mentioned above, but it's just as important to exercise your mind and to give it proper care and feeding. The intellect needs food – ideas of wisdom and truth – exercise, digestion and expression. So read good books by good writers. Digest them and then express them – either by the spoken or written word. Keeping a journal is good for mental health.

Intellectual purity is a good thing in its own right, but with you, Aries, it can be a health issue. The best cure for error is light. Invoke it often. Learn to turn the mind off when not in use. A hyperactive mind burns energy that the body needs for other things. Meditation is a big help for this.

As our regular readers know, the first line of defence is always high energy – a strong auric field. This is our spiritual immune system. A strong aura will repel germs, microbes and other opportunistic invaders. So make sure to get enough rest.

Mercury is a very fast-moving planet, and in a given year will move through all the signs and houses of your chart (this year he will visit some twice). So there are therapies that will work that depend on where he is at a given time. These things are best discussed in the monthly reports.

Home and Family

Normally when the 4th house is not strong, there's not much going on on the home or family front: they tend to the status quo. But with you things are different. There will be two lunar eclipses this year, each of which will shake up things at home in various ways. In addition there will be a solar eclipse on July 2 that will occur in your 4th house. This too is going to shake things up. Often there are dramas in the lives of family members, and often hidden flaws in the home come to light and repairs are needed. We will deal with this in more detail in the monthly reports.

A move is not very likely this year – though there's nothing in your Horoscope that signals against it.

This is much more a career year than a family year. Most of the long-term planets are in the upper, day side of your Horoscope, and the night side of your Horoscope will never totally dominate your chart (though there will be periods where it is stronger than it normally is this year). Thus if problems arise they will be due to inattention – lack of focus. If problems arise pay more attention here.

There will be dramas in the lives of parents and parent figures this year. If they are married, the marriage is being severely tested. If they are in a relationship, this too will get tested. They could also be having surgery or near-death kinds of experiences. There are three eclipses in your 10th house, which rules one of your parent figures. (If you are a woman, it rules the mother; if you are a man, the father.) So there is a lot of drama going on in their lives. The overall health of this parent or parent figure needs watching too.

One of the parents or parent figures in your life has excellent job prospects in the year ahead. And, towards the end of the year, will have a better social life. Moves don't seem likely for either of them.

Children or children figures are having multiple career changes. They are being more experimental in this area. A move is not likely. They seem more focused on love than on the career, but they can find love through pursuing their career goals. They are working hard – they have many job opportunities – but they're also having fun. They work hard and play hard. Children or children figures of childbearing age are more fertile than usual this year.

If you have grandchildren of the appropriate age, they too seem more fertile. A move will work better for them after December 3. They will have a prosperous year.

If you're planning major repairs or renovations (or building a home), May 16 to July 23 will be a good time to do them. If you're beautifying the home in a cosmetic kind of way, or buying objects of beauty for the home, July 3–27 will be a good time.

The Moon is your family planet – the best possible one to have as this is her natural domain. But the Moon is the fastest of all the planets and will traverse *all* your houses in any given month. So there are many short-term family trends that are best discussed in the monthly reports.

Finance and Career

Very important financial things are happening now. You had a fore-taste of this last year as Uranus flirted with your money house. Now, on March 7, he is moving in there for the long haul. So, in finance, expect the unexpected. By the time Uranus is finished with you, in seven years' time, you will be in completely different financial conditions than you are now – radically different. They will also be much better. However, in order for your financial prayers to be answered, things need to be shaken up. Obstructions need to be blasted away. There is a need to learn to handle the insecurities that change brings.

Uranus is the planet of innovation and experimentation. So you are throwing out all the old financial rule books – all the old tried and true methods – and discovering what works for you personally. Experiments sometimes fail but these are temporary setbacks and you learn from them. Often, however, experiments succeed, and when they do earnings will skyrocket beyond belief. Money and earning opportunities can come in unexpected ways, out of the blue, and often when things seem darkest.

Uranus is a planet of extremes. The financial highs will be super-high, but the lows can be super-low too. Make sure you set aside money from the good times to cover the bad periods.

Uranus favours the new, and thus you're attracted to start-up companies and even start-up industries. He rules the high-tech world – computers, software, the online world. He rules companies that are involved with new inventions and innovations. These are all alluring and you have a good feeling for them. You can even be involved in radically new technologies. In fact, whatever you're actually doing, your technological expertise is important. By all means invest in technology – get the latest software, apps and computers.

Uranus also rules science and astrology. So astrology can be important in earnings – perhaps through consultations or investment. Your friends seems rich and seem supportive and provide financial opportunity too.

Venus, your financial planet, is a fast-moving planet (not as fast as the Moon or Mercury, but faster than all the others). In a given year she will move through all the signs and houses of your chart. (This year, indeed, she will make one-and-a-third turns around your chart – she moves faster than usual.) Thus earnings and earnings opportunities can come in many different ways, depending on where Venus is and the aspects she is receiving. These short-term trends are best dealt with in the monthly reports. The good news is that Venus will move forward all year – a financial plus, showing forward progress.

The career is unusually active this year. Your 10th house is not only the strongest in the Horoscope, but will be the scene of three eclipses in the year ahead. So there is much change happening there. With

Saturn and Pluto in your 10th house all year, you're working hard and methodically. There is a beautiful, single-minded concentration on your goals, which is 90 per cent of success. This is not the chart of 'overnight' success, but of success that happens methodically and through steady, persistent work. It shows success earned through sheer merit and for no other reason. You simply must be the best at what you do. It might seem slow and boring, but the eclipses will come and blast away any obstructions and, suddenly, you'll be where you want to be.

With Saturn in your career house bosses can be more exacting and demanding, and difficult to please. The cosmic way to handle this is to give them even more than they ask for. Pick up the burdens and go the extra mile. By the end of the year, as Jupiter moves into your career house, you can expect promotions (official or unofficial) and recognition. It shows success.

Love and Social Life

This is not an especially strong love and social year. Some years are like that. Money and career seem far more important this year. The empty 7th house indicates the lack of focus. Usually this tends to the status quo: you're more or less satisfied with things as they are and have no compelling need to make changes.

There's nothing in your chart against love and romance, but nothing especially favouring them either. Those who are married will tend to stay married. Singles will tend to stay single.

In your chart Venus does double duty. She is both your financial planet and your love planet. Thus love and money tend to go together with you. When finances are going well, love tends to go well; when love goes well, finances tend to go well. And vice versa. Problems in love will often show problems in finance.

The good news here is that your love planet is moving unusually fast this year. Usually Venus will move through all 12 houses in a year. This year she will move through your 12 houses and then repeat the cycle for four more houses. (In effect she is moving (approximately) a third faster than usual.) This indicates social confidence – it shows someone who covers a lot of social territory. For singles it indicates a kind of fickleness in love. The love needs and desires change constantly. Someone who attracted you one month might not attract you the next.

Thus for singles I see a lot of dating in 2019, but not long-term, serious relationships. Enjoy the love life for what it is. It seems about gaining experiences.

Because Venus is moving so fast there will be a lot of short-term love trends, depending on where she is in the Heavens and the aspects that she receives. These are best dealt with in the monthly reports.

The other important development is that with Uranus moving out of your sign, you are going to be more stable in love. There is less rebellion, less need for change. This will bode well for love later on, in the future. You're becoming a more 'settled' kind of person.

Friendship – a different kind of social activity – seems more active. Friendships are not only good in their own right; they will help the bottom line. Your taste in friends seems more stable than your taste in romantic partners. You like them rich and dependable. Being involved with friends and group activities definitely helps the finances. It will be good also to get involved with professional or trade organizations. They are not only helpful financially but seem to boost the career too (especially after March 7). New and significant friends will come into the picture after December 3, as Jupiter starts to make beautiful aspects to Uranus (your planet of friends).

As was mentioned earlier, parents and parent figures are having their relationships severely tested. There will be improvement at the end of year though, after December 3. There is serious love this year for siblings or sibling figures in your life – marriage would not be a surprise. Children and children figures are very focused on love, and this is 90 per cent of the secret of success. They have love opportunities as they pursue their career path or with people involved in their career. Serious love is likely from December 3 onwards (and next year too). Grandchildren (if you have them) are having a stable kind of love year – but they seem very happy.

Self-improvement

The spiritual life, as we've mentioned, is very active and strong these days. Neptune has been in your spiritual 12th house for many years now and will be there for many more. Most of you are now on a spiritual path – and if it hasn't happened yet (unlikely!) it will happen. Those of you on that path are making very good progress.

Neptune is the planet of transcendence. He gives an ability to 'rise above' all earthly conditions and circumstances and see things from a higher, broader perspective. This might not seem like much, but it's very powerful. It is like looking at things from a satellite orbiting the Earth rather than from a car. We see much more. We see the broad scope of things. We measure and judge things differently. Things that seem 'bad' in the short term (usually something unpleasant) are seen as good when the whole, wider picture is understood.

Much of what we have discussed in recent years still applies this year. The transit of a long-term planet such as Neptune is not really an 'event' but a process. It is a string of many events, all leading to one thing. So, the dream life is very active – and you should pay attention to it as the dreams will be significant and revelatory. Your ESP (extra-sensory perception) faculties are getting stronger and stronger. Your intuition is much more reliable this year than in previous years, as Neptune is receiving better aspects from the other planets. (You will see even greater improvement after December 3.) Without this intuitive element, sacred literature doesn't yield much insight. This must be read as much by the heart as by the mind. Often the intellect can't understand certain passages, but intuition reveals the true intent. There will be many supernatural kinds of experiences this year. (Some call these synchronistic experiences – meaningful coincidences.)

One of the spiritual challenges this year comes from the power in your 10th house of career. This will tend to pull you in a worldly direction. There is a need to succeed in the world and in your outer goals. And, often, this will conflict with spiritual values. In the world it's 'dog eat dog': get to the top any way that you can. So this internal struggle will need to be resolved. There are no rules for this. Some people marry the two urges by pursuing a worldly career and doing charity and *pro bono* work on the side. Some people actually choose a spiritual-type career – either ministry or working for a non-profit organization or a company that caters to these things. Some people pursue their worldly career but work to do it in a spiritual way. Each person finds their own solution.

The other spiritual challenge you face has to do with Uranus's move into your money house. This, as we've said, brings sudden changes to the financial life and the ups and downs can be very extreme. There is a need to handle financial instability in a spiritually correct way. Eventually you will learn this; Uranus is a genius who knows how to do his job.

Meditating on the affluence of God will be a great help. In the midst of all the changes and challenges, the Divine flow of affluence never ceases and never wavers. Concentrating on that – developing faith – will get you through with flying colours. Faith is a muscle that needs building up, just like every other muscle.

Month-by-month Forecasts

January

Best Days Overall: 2, 3, 12, 13, 21, 22, 30, 31
Most Stressful Days Overall: 5, 6, 19, 20, 25, 26
Best Days for Love: 1, 12, 13, 21, 22, 25, 26, 30, 31
Best Days for Money: 1, 2, 3, 12, 13, 15, 16, 21, 22, 30, 31
Best Days for Career: 5, 6, 15, 16, 23, 24

A wild and challenging month is ahead, with never a dull moment. Nevertheless, the month seems successful. You're just working harder. You begin your year in the midst of a yearly career peak. Your 10th house of career is very powerful, with half the planets either in it or moving through. Not only that, a solar eclipse on the 6th (in America it's on the 5th) also occurs in your 10th house. This is the first of three eclipses that will happen in your career house this year. You can't be bothered with home and family issues right now. You've got to focus on the career – the demands here are powerful.

The solar eclipse brings career changes, which can take many forms. In some cases people actually change their career paths; usually though, the eclipse indicates changes in your company or industry. Sometimes the government changes the laws or the rules and regulations. The rules of the game change. Often this will bring personal dramas in the lives of parents, parent figures, bosses and authority figures. The change is not usually very comfortable while it's happening, but with hindsight it can be seen as beneficial. A parent or parent figure in your life has to make important financial changes. Every solar eclipse affects the children and children figures in your life and this one is no different. It will be a good idea to reduce your schedule until the 20th, and especially this period. The children should avoid risky kinds of activities over the eclipse period.

We will also have a lunar eclipse on the 21st, which also affects children and children figures as it occurs in your 5th house. So let them take it easy over this period too. Like the previous eclipse, this one affects the finances of a parent or parent figure. He or she needs a course correction as their financial thinking and strategy have not been realistic, as the events of the eclipse will show. Every lunar eclipse impacts on the home and family. So there can be some crisis at home – perhaps a major repair or a personal drama with a family member. The lunar eclipse will reveal flaws in the home that you didn't know were there, giving you an opportunity to correct them. The dream life will tend to be hyperactive this period, but shouldn't be given much weight. The emotional plane of the whole planet is roiled up and disturbed (even animals are more edgy), and your dreams are more like 'psychic waste products' stirred up by the eclipse. Get them out of your system and go on with your life. Family members need more of your patience. Emotions are running high.

The other headline this month is health. This needs more attention until the 20th. Make sure you get enough rest. Keep your focus on the essentials and don't fret the trivialities. From the 5th to the 24th, back and knee massages will be very helpful.

February

Best Days Overall: 8, 9, 10, 17, 18, 26, 27
Most Stressful Days Overall: 1, 2, 15, 16, 21, 22, 28
Best Days for Love: 11, 19, 20, 21, 22, 28
Best Days for Money: 9, 10, 11, 12, 17, 18, 19, 20, 26, 27, 28
Best Days for Career: 1, 2, 11, 12, 19, 20, 28

Health is much improved this month, but still needs some attention. Enhance the health through calf and ankle massage until the 10th, and with foot massage afterwards. Mars, the ruler of your Horoscope, has been in your sign since January 1 and will still be there until February 14. Aries tend always to be in a rush, but more so now. Haste can lead to arguments and accidents, so be mindful on the physical plane. Be especially mindful from the 11th to the 14th as Mars travels with Uranus. Friends should also be more mindful.

There are interesting and happy financial developments this month. On the 3rd Venus, your financial and love planet, crosses the Mid-heaven. The Mid-heaven is the highest point in the chart and perhaps the most powerful point in the Horoscope. Thus she is exercising more influence. This spells increased earnings. In addition, your ruling planet Mars moves into your money house on the 14th, indicating great personal focus here. You have the financial favour of bosses, elders, parents and parent figures. Pay rises, official or unofficial, can happen. You spend more on yourself. You adopt an image of prosperity – people see you this way. Your good career and professional reputation enhance your earnings. What I also like here is that the financial planet, Venus, is in Capricorn from the 3rd onwards. This shows sound financial judgement and a prudent approach. Your financial decisions should be good, and it's a very good time to set up budgets, savings and investment plans (and stick to them). This is a time to build up wealth for the long term.

Venus crossing your Mid-heaven is good for the love life too. It shows that love and social opportunity will come as you pursue your career goals (and, in many cases, with people involved in your career). Love is high on your agenda this month. Just as in finance, you're more prudent in affairs of the heart. You favour successful and powerful people, people who can help you careerwise – and you're meeting these kinds of people too. Singles could be tempted by relationships of convenience these days. Love seems very practical. There is a romantic or social opportunity with a boss or authority figure in your life on the 17th or 18th.

Stern Saturn has been in your 10th house of career since last year. So, your career advances through sheer merit. However, this month it won't hurt to increase the 'likeability' factor. It's not a substitute for merit, but it does help it along.

On the 19th the Sun enters your spiritual 12th house and stays there for the rest of the month – a good time to focus more on your spiritual practice. This is a period where spiritual breakthroughs are more likely. Your personal creativity is also very inspired these days.

March

Best Days Overall: 8, 9, 17, 18, 25, 26
Most Stressful Days Overall: 1, 2, 15, 16, 21, 22, 27, 28, 29
Best Days for Love: 3, 4, 15, 16, 21, 22, 23, 24
Best Days for Money: 3, 4, 8, 9, 10, 11, 15, 16, 17, 18, 23, 24, 25, 26
Best Days for Career: 1, 2, 10, 11, 19, 20, 27, 28, 29

A happy month ahead, Aries. Enjoy! This is a month for making progress on whatever spiritual path you're on. Spiritual growth and a sound intuition are not only good in their own right, but will pay off creatively in your ability to handle your children, your ability to enjoy life and, after the 26th, in a financial and social way too.

Spiritual breakthroughs and revelations can happen all month, but especially on the 15th and 16th, and from the 24th onwards. Those of you working in the creative arts are especially inspired on the 15th and 16th. Mercury, your health planet, makes a station – he 'camps out' – right on your spiritual planet, Neptune, from the 24th to the 31st. This is a wonderful aspect for spiritual healing. If you feel under the weather during this time, you should consider seeing some sort of spiritual healer.

Health is good this month (but keep in mind that two long-term planets are still in stressful alignment with you). And compared to January, it is excellent! Like last month, enhance the health through foot massage and through spiritual techniques such as meditation, prayer, reiki, the laying on of hands and the manipulation of subtle energies. Your health planet is travelling backward from the 5th to the 25th, so avoid making important changes to the health regime then. Any such changes will need more study and research.

Students below college level need more focus. They are too apt to get dreamy and go off into 'other worlds'.

The planetary power is approaching its maximum Eastern position for the year. As our regular readers know, this means that the planetary power is flowing towards you rather than away from you. You are in a period of maximum independence (and this becomes even stronger after the 20th), so it is time to take responsibility for your own happiness and conditions of life. If those conditions are irksome, make any changes that need to be made (before the 5th and after the 25th are the best times for this). There's no need to please the world at the moment. If you are happy there is that much less suffering in the world. Self-interest is not evil, and self-sacrifice is not necessarily saintly. It all depends on the cycle you're in.

Your love planet, Venus, spends most of the month in Aquarius and your 11th house. Thus this is more of a 'friendship' period than a romantic one. Many of you are more captivated by the 'idea' of love than actual love itself. (And in many cases you attract those kinds of people.) This position favours groups, organizations and the online social media world. And romantic opportunities can happen in these venues. The financial life is also helped by these activities. You need more of an online presence in whatever you're doing.

On the 26th Venus will enter Pisces, your 12th house. This is Venus's strongest position (on the celestial level), so the social and financial magnetism are greatly enhanced. Intuition will guide you in both love and finances.

April

Best Days Overall: 4, 5, 13, 14, 22, 23
Most Stressful Days Overall: 11, 12, 17, 18, 24, 25
Best Days for Love: 2, 3, 11, 12, 17, 18, 21
Best Days for Money: 2, 3, 4, 5, 6, 7, 8, 11, 12, 13, 14, 21, 22, 23
Best Days for Career: 7, 8, 15, 16, 24, 25

Another happy month, Aries. Last month, on March 20, the Sun entered your sign and you began one of your yearly personal pleasure peaks. You're still very much in this peak this month, until the 20th. A lot of leisure opportunities have come already and more are on the way. You're closer to your children (or children figures in your life), and they seem devoted to you. You are a bit of a child yourself these days and this is why you get on with them. Women of childbearing age are more fertile until the 20th, too. You look great. There is a star quality to your image. Aries generally do not lack self-confidence, but these days it is stronger than ever.

On the 20th Venus enters your sign, and this brings happiness in both love and finances. Love and romantic opportunities seek you out. You can't escape them. Singles only need to go about their daily business – and enjoy life: love will find them. Those who are married or in a serious relationship receive more devotion from the beloved. Similar things are happening financially. Money seeks you out rather than the other way around. Financial windfalls occur. The money people in your life are devoted to you.

Health is excellent this month. Yes, there are still two long-term planets in stressful alignment with you, but they are out-powered by the short-term planets. The feet and spiritual healing techniques are still important until the 17th of this month, but afterwards focus on the normal areas important for Aries – the head and scalp, the muscles, the arms and shoulders and the adrenals. Physical exercise is very beneficial, and craniosacral therapy is especially good after the 17th. Review our discussion of health in the yearly report.

Last month was a strong 'independent' kind of month, and this month even more so. So, exercise your independence and make those changes that need to be made. Later on, as the power in the Eastern sector weakens, it will become more difficult to alter things.

Children and children figures in your life have excellent social and romantic opportunities from the 21st to the 23rd.

On the 20th the Sun moves into your money house and you begin a yearly financial peak. This will be a beauty – it happens with your financial planet, Venus, in your 1st house. This creates a lot of financial energy. Friends and social contacts seem very helpful, and money is earned in happy ways and spent in happy ways.

Career is important all year and this month is no exception. Only now, from the 20th onwards, the lower, night side of your chart is stronger than it has been all year. It is not dominant, but is at its strongest yearly level. So spend more time with the family, and strive towards emotional wellness.

May

Best Days Overall: 1, 2, 3, 10, 11, 19, 20, 29, 30
Most Stressful Days Overall: 8, 9, 15, 16, 21, 22
Best Days for Love: 2, 3, 14, 15, 16, 21, 31
Best Days for Money: 2, 3, 4, 5, 10, 11, 14, 19, 20, 21, 29, 30, 31
Best Days for Career: 4, 5, 13, 14, 21, 22, 31

This month there is another reason to de-emphasize the career a little: your career planet, Saturn, goes retrograde on the 2nd. Thus many issues here will only be resolved with time. Career is still going well this month, but slower than usual. In the meantime it is good to get the home, family and emotional life in order – and you seem to be doing this. Mars moves into your 4th house of home and family on the 16th and spends the rest of the month there. This will be a good time for doing renovations or major repairs on the house.

Mars, the ruler of your Horoscope, has been 'out of bounds' since April 21 and will remain that way all this month. This means that you are venturing outside your normal 'comfort zone' of life. Probably the solutions you seek are not available in the usual places and you have to go 'far afield' to find them. This a more adventurous kind of period for you (but Aries likes adventure).

Another important planet in your chart, Mercury, will be briefly 'out of bounds' from the 28th to the 31st. This can indicate various things: the books you're reading are outside the norm; your job can take you outside your normal sphere. In some cases you are seeing therapists or alternative health practitioners who are off the beaten track.

The month ahead is unusually prosperous. Money is rolling in. You're still in the midst of a yearly financial peak, until the 21st, and children, children figures, bosses and authority figures are all supportive of your financial goals. Career might be slowing down, but not the financial life. On the 15th Venus moves into your money house and spends the rest of the month there. She is in her own sign and house and is therefore more powerful on your behalf. This spells extra earnings – stronger earning power. From the 17th to the 19th Venus travels with Uranus. This transit often brings sudden and unexpected financial benefit. Sometimes it doesn't bring physical money, but expensive material objects instead. Your spouse, partner or current love – friends in general – are supportive financially and are bringing opportunity. You're still in a very independent period (although it's becoming less so day by day), but in finance the social graces are very important.

The love life is happy this month too. Venus, who does double duty in your chart as both the love planet and financial planet, is still in your 1st house until the 15th. Thus, as we mentioned last month, there's no need for any special effort in the love department. Venus in your sign signals instant love – impetuous love – someone who falls in love quickly. But after the 15th this changes. You slow things down. You favour wealthy people. Material things – material gifts – attract you. You find love opportunities as you pursue your financial goals and often with people involved in your finances. The money people in your life like matchmaking these days.

June

> Best Days Overall: 7, 8, 15, 16, 25, 26
> Most Stressful Days Overall: 5, 6, 11, 12, 18, 19
> Best Days for Love: 1, 11, 12, 20, 21
> Best Days for Money: 1, 7, 8, 11, 15, 16, 20, 21, 25, 26, 27, 28, 29
> Best Days for Career: 1, 9, 10, 18, 19, 27, 28, 29

Mercury remains 'out of bounds' until the 16th, so review our discussion of this last month. Mars, which has been 'out of bounds' since April 21, returns to his normal borders on the 12th. Your days of 'wondering and wandering' are winding down.

You're leaving behind two very strong financial months. By the 9th, as Venus leaves your money house, finance becomes less important. Financial goals, the short-term ones at least, have been attained and you can shift your attention elsewhere. Your 3rd house of communication and intellectual interests became strong on May 21, and this month it is even stronger. So the mind is sharp and your communication skills are stronger than usual. Students below college level might want to take advantage of this and attend summer school – learning will be quicker and easier. But even non-students should become students this month. It is a very good time to attend lectures and seminars and to take classes in subjects that interest you. A good time to catch up on your reading as well. Your gift of the gab and intellectual knowledge will help the bottom line. You're probably spending more on intellectual pursuits, too.

Until the 9th love is still materialistic and down to earth. You are the 'material girl' or 'material boy' these days. Love and social opportunities still happen as you pursue your financial goals and with people involved in your finances. But after the 9th, the venue for romance shifts. Now it happens in your neighbourhood and perhaps with neighbours. School and educational-type functions – lectures and seminars, the bookstore and the library – become venues for romance. A romantic date might be a lecture or class, rather than a night out on the town. While Venus was in Taurus (May 15 to June 9) wealth was a turn on. Now it is a person's mind and speech that attract you. You like people who are easy to talk to, people you can share ideas with. In astrology we would say, people with whom there is harmony in the mental bodies.

Health is still good, but after the 21st it needs more attention. As always, make sure to get enough rest. Never allow yourself to get over-tired. Low energy is the primal disease. After the 21st half of the planets are in stressful alignment with you, so focus more on health – and especially your emotional health. Diet seems an issue from the 4th to the 27th. Simple dietary changes can produce much wellness, but these things should be checked with a professional. Water-based therapies are powerful during this period. Swim in the ocean or river or lake. Spend more time around water. If this is not practical, take long soaks in the bath. You have a good connection to the healing powers of water from the 4th to the 27th.

Retrograde activity among the planets is heating up this month. We're not yet at the pinnacle of it for the year (that will happen next month), but we're close. This is hard for an Aries to take. The fast way, the short cut, might not really be the fastest way. Patience, patience, patience.

July

Best Days Overall: 4, 5, 13, 14, 22, 23, 24, 31
Most Stressful Days Overall: 2, 3, 8, 9, 15, 16, 29, 30
Best Days for Love: 1, 8, 9, 10, 11, 20, 21, 31
Best Days for Money: 1, 4, 5, 10, 11, 13, 14, 20, 21, 22, 23, 24, 25, 26, 31
Best Days for Career: 6, 7, 15, 16, 25, 26

Health is an important issue this month. Not only do we have at least half (and at times more) of the planets in stressful alignment with you, but we also have two eclipses that impact on you in a stressful way. So focus on health this month. Make sure (as always) to get enough rest. If possible, spend more time at a health spa, or schedule more massages or health treatments. Keep the mind focused on the essentials and don't waste time and energy on trivia. Enhance the health in the ways mentioned in the yearly report. Chest massage is powerful all month, but especially until the 19th. After the 19th be more careful in dietary matters. Health will start to improve after the 21st, but will still need watching.

The two eclipses this month are replays (although not quite exact replays) of the eclipses of January. The solar eclipse of the 2nd occurs in your 4th house of home and family. So, there can be dramas at home – perhaps repairs are needed. There are dramas in the lives of family members (especially a parent or parent figure). This parent or parent figure has some financial crisis and dramatic change is needed (which will happen over the next six months). The family finances, as a whole, need to be changed. The strategy and thinking have been unrealistic, as the events of the eclipse will show. Children and children figures (ruled by the Sun in your chart) are always affected by every solar eclipse. So they need reduce their schedules over this period. Do your best to keep them out of harm's way.

The lunar eclipse of the 16th occurs in your 10th house of career and is the second of three eclipses that happen here this year. So, there are more career changes and shake-ups. There are shake-ups in the corporate hierarchy and in your industry. Bosses, parents and parent figures – authority figures in your life – have personal dramas. Their marriages are being tested (this happened during the solar eclipse of the 2nd too). Again, repairs can be needed at home. Emotions are volatile in the family – perhaps there is some sort of crisis going on. Siblings and sibling figures in your life have a financial crisis, and dramatic changes will be needed in this area.

Retrograde activity is at its maximum for the year. Half of the planets are moving in reverse from the 7th onwards. Changes and decisions need to be made, but study things more carefully first.

Once the dust settles from the eclipses, you begin a yearly personal pleasure peak from the 21st onwards. Enjoy your life. Handle your challenges, but make time for some fun.

August

Best Days Overall: 1, 9, 10, 19, 20, 28, 29
Most Stressful Days Overall: 4, 5, 11, 12, 26, 27
Best Days for Love: 1, 4, 5, 9, 10, 20, 21, 30, 31
Best Days for Money: 1, 9, 10, 19, 20, 21, 22, 28, 29, 30, 31
Best Days for Career: 2, 3, 11, 12, 21, 22, 30, 31

Retrograde activity among the planets is still intense this month, but less so than in July. On the 2nd, Mercury starts moving forward, and on the 11th Jupiter moves forward. But on the 12th Uranus starts to go backward. Again, patience, patience, patience. With this many planets retrograde, the cosmos is urging you to be more perfect in all that you do. Little mistakes can delay things even further. Go slow, steady and perfectly. This is, ultimately, the fastest way to your goals.

You have been in one of your yearly personal pleasure peaks since July 21, and this continues until August 23. It is not irresponsible to have fun now. It will actually increase earnings and lead to love. It will also have a positive impact on your health and well-being. The cosmos is often counter-intuitive.

The month ahead looks to be prosperous. It is a good kind of prosperity. A happy prosperity. Venus, your financial planet, will be in your 5th house until the 21st. This shows luck in speculations (I especially like the 8th and 9th for this). The 8th and 9th are days of very strong financial increase. It shows money that is earned in happy, joyful ways and that you're enjoying the wealth you have, spending on fun and leisure and joyful activities. Those of you in the creative arts will find your work more marketable. Children and children figures seem supportive (and you could be spending more on them too). One of the problems here can be overspending. You earn easily and you spend easily. You're an impulse spender. However, this will change after the 21st as Venus moves into Virgo, your 6th house of health and work. You will have more financial caution. You will seek value for money. You will be less speculative and down to earth. You will earn from work and productive service. Job seekers should have good success from the 23rd onwards as there are many job opportunities happening – even those of you already employed will have opportunities for overtime or second jobs.

Love is happy this month too. The 8th and 9th not only bring financial increase, but happy love opportunities and meetings. Love doesn't seem too serious these days. Love affairs rather than serious, committed relationships are indicated. You just want to have fun and you're probably attracting these kinds of people too. Love opportunities happen in the usual sorts of places this month (until the 21st) – at parties, resorts, the theatre and places of entertainment. After the 21st the workplace becomes a venue for love. But love can also happen as you pursue your health goals or with people involved in your health. One of the problems with Venus in Virgo is hyper-perfectionism and hyper-criticism. Do your best to avoid this – even in your thoughts.

September

Best Days Overall: 5, 6, 15, 16, 24, 25
Most Stressful Days Overall: 1, 2, 7, 8, 9, 22, 23, 28, 29
Best Days for Love: 1, 2, 8, 9, 20, 28, 29
Best Days for Money: 5, 6, 8, 9, 15, 16, 17, 18, 19, 20, 24, 25, 28, 29
Best Days for Career: 7, 8, 9, 17, 18, 19, 26, 27

On July 3 the Western social sector of your chart started to become powerful. This means that the planetary power has been moving away from you and towards others. This month the planets are approaching their maximum Western (social) positions. Thus, since July 3, there has been less personal independence. There has been a need to develop the social graces and to get things done by consensus rather than by direct action. It is a time to let others have their way (so long as it isn't destructive), and to allow your good to come to you through others. It is a time to take a vacation from yourself, and put others first. This, as we have said before, is not especially saintly; it's just the cycle you're in. Changing conditions that irk you is more complicated now. Best to make a note of them and make the changes later on, when you're back in a more independent cycle. While this period brings a lessening of independence, it is wonderful for your love and social life.

(Independence is a wonderful quality, but not such a good thing for love.) On the 23rd, as the Sun enters Libra, your 7th house of love and romance, you enter a yearly love and social peak. So romance is in the air, and you're in the mood for it – open to it.

Venus's solstice, from the 15th to the 18th, is the announcement of the coming social shift. She pauses in the Heavens (in her latitudinal motion) and then changes direction. And so it is with you. There is a social pause and then a change of direction.

In the meantime, with your 6th house of health and work very strong, it is a good time to do all those boring, detailed jobs that you normally hate to do. You're more in the mood for this type of work and they should go easier and faster. It is good that you're very focused on health this month as the care you take now will stand you in good stead after the 23rd, when health becomes an issue.

After the 23rd, up to 60 per cent of the planets will be in stressful alignment with you at times. Your normal superabundant energy is not up to its usual standard. If you feel tired, take a nap. Recharge. No vehicle can run with no fuel in the tank. Work more calmly and shift activities. Don't fret over trivia. Focus on what's really important. Until the 14th enhance the health by massaging the reflex point to the small intestine. After the 14th, enhance the health in the ways mentioned in the yearly report. Pay more attention to the kidneys and hips. Massage the hips regularly. A herbal kidney cleanse might also be a good idea. The good news is that good social health (which you seem to have) will reflect positively on your energetic health.

Venus moves into your 7th house of love on the 14th, where she is powerful in her own sign and house. So your finances should be good. Social grace and likeability are always important in your financial life, but this period even more so than normal. Joint ventures and partnerships could also happen.

October

> Best Days Overall: 2, 3, 4, 12, 13, 21, 22, 30, 31
> Most Stressful Days Overall: 5, 6, 19, 20, 26, 27
> Best Days for Love: 10, 11, 19, 20, 26, 27, 28, 29
> Best Days for Money: 2, 3, 4, 10, 11, 12, 13, 15, 16, 19, 20, 21,
>   22, 28, 29, 30, 31
> Best Days for Career: 5, 6, 15, 16, 23, 24

This month your 7th house of love becomes even stronger, with Mars's move into there on the 4th. He joins the Sun and Venus, meaning that two out of the three most important planets in your chart – the Sun and the ruler of your Horoscope – will be in your 7th house. This signals a *lot* of social power. Your yearly love and social peak is even stronger. Your personal popularity is at its height. You're there for others and they feel this and appreciate it. You're a good friend to have these days. You're also personally more romantic. Singles will have many love opportunities.

Health is still very much an issue this month – especially until the 23rd. Keep in mind our discussion of this last month. The problem this month is that your 6th house of health is empty after the 4th, and so you might not be paying enough attention here – and you should. Enhance the health in the ways mentioned in the yearly report. After the 3rd pay more attention to the colon, bladder and sexual organs. Most of you will tend to be overactive sexually – best to keep it in moderation. Don't deprive yourself, but don't overdo it either. A herbal colon cleanse might be a good idea, and you will respond well to detox regimes. Health and energy will improve after the 23rd, when the planetary stress is greatly reduced.

Mars, the ruler of your Horoscope, has his solstice from the 4th to the 11th. He pauses in the Heavens in his latitudinal motion, and then changes direction. It is interesting that this happens as he is changing signs and houses – leaving your 6th house and entering your 7th. So there is a personal shift of gears for you. You become more social.

But there is another shift that Mars is announcing. He is crossing from the lower (night side) of your chart to the upper (day) side. Thus, the upper half of the chart is now totally dominant: 80 per cent (and sometimes 90 per cent) of the planets will be in the upper half of the chart. Now the career becomes all consuming. Last month (on the 18th) your career planet, Saturn, started to move forward after many months of retrograde motion. Things are starting to move forward in your career and you're ready to take advantage. All systems are go. You are successful now, but you haven't even touched your peak.

November

Best Days Overall: 8, 9, 10, 18, 19, 26, 27
Most Stressful Days Overall: 1, 2, 16, 17, 22, 23, 28, 29, 30
Best Days for Love: 8, 9, 18, 19, 22, 23, 29
Best Days for Money: 8, 9, 10, 11, 12, 18, 19, 26, 27, 29
Best Days for Career: 1, 2, 11, 12, 20, 21, 28, 29, 30

The upper (day) side of your Horoscope is not only strong quantitatively – at least 80 per cent of the planets are there – but qualitatively as well. The Sun and Mars, two of the three most important planets in your chart, spend all month here. And there are periods where even the Moon (the other most important planet) will also be here (from the 1st to the 7th and from the 22nd to the end of the month). Your 10th house of career, strong all year, becomes even stronger on the 26th as Venus, enters. Your 4th house of home and family, by contrast, is basically empty. Only the Moon moves through there on the 16th and 17th. So the power and might of the cosmos is in your career and outer goals. Pursue them actively. You have a lot of help.

Your 8th house of regeneration became powerful on October 23 and is still strong this month. Thus the libido is stronger than usual and, as long as you don't overdo it, things will be OK. The spouse, partner or current love is having a banner financial month. You seem very involved here – especially from the 19th onwards. A strong 8th house favours detox regimes of all kinds – and not only physical detoxing. It favours the detoxing of the mind and emotions, too – the purging of negative habits of thought and feeling – as well as the detoxing of possessions. There is a need to de-clutter your environment, to get rid of possessions that you don't need or use. Sell them or give them to charity. A strong 8th house is also good for weight-loss regimes, if you need them. Good physical health is often a matter of getting rid of things in the body that don't belong there (and not so much about adding things to the body). The same is true for mental and emotional health. This is a good month for tax and estate planning (if you are of appropriate age). Good for paying down debt or refinancing existing debt.

The month ahead is prosperous. Venus spends almost all month – until the 26th – in Sagittarius, your 9th house. This is a fortunate place. Earnings are increasing. There is boundless financial optimism. Foreigners might be playing an important role in the financial life. There is business-related foreign travel.

Venus will go 'out of bounds' from the 15th to the 30th. This signals that you're more adventurous in both love and finance. The solutions you seek are not in your normal spheres and you must go outside them to find what you want. And it seems you're successful. Venus travels with Jupiter from the 22nd to the 24th, indicating a nice payday. For singles this indicates an important romantic meeting as well.

On the 26th Venus crosses your Mid-heaven for the second time this year. On the terrestrial level, the Mid-heaven is the most powerful position for any planet. This is another good signal for prosperity. It should bring a nice payday.

Health is much improved compared to last month. Continue to enhance the health through detox regimes, through more care of the colon and bladder and by sexual moderation.

December

Best Days Overall: 6, 7, 15, 16, 24, 25
Most Stressful Days Overall: 13, 14, 19, 20, 26, 27
Best Days for Love: 8, 9, 17, 18, 19, 20, 28, 29
Best Days for Money: 8, 9, 17, 18, 26, 28, 29
Best Days for Career: 8, 9, 17, 18, 26, 27

Your career is the main headline this month. And, what a headline it is! You've been working hard and diligently for the past two years. You progressed inch by inch, slowly and methodically. Now, the payoff happens. Jupiter moves into your career house on the 3rd and suddenly you are the hottest ticket in town. But this is not all. Your 10th house has been strong all year, but this month at least 60 per cent, and at times 70 per cent, of the planets are in or moving through your 10th house. Mighty cosmic geniuses are supporting your rise and success. If you can manage to keep your health (a challenge from the 22nd onwards) you're on top of the world. Many people in your life are also succeeding this month and they seem helpful to your own career.

On the 22nd you begin a yearly career peak. For many of you it will be a lifetime career peak. The message of the Horoscope is: do your duty, achieve what you came here to achieve, get your outer goals right and everything else in life will sort itself out. You will have prosperity, creativity, love and even health.

Keep in mind our health discussions of the past few months. You won't be able to avoid working hard or avoid the demands of your career, but you can pace yourself better. Rest when tired. Drop the inessentials from your life or delegate them to others. Get more massages or health treatments. Spend more spare time at a health spa. Until the 9th continue with detox regimes. From the 9th to the 24th enhance your health through thigh massage and more care of the liver. Prayer is potent medicine too. After the 24th, back and knee massage will be powerful. It will also be useful to review the yearly report on health.

A solar eclipse on the 26th occurs in your career house, the third eclipse of the year in this house. It seems to me that, though the eclipse is disruptive, it is positive. (Good things can be just as disruptive as bad things.) It takes time to adjust to the disruption, and you should definitely reduce your schedule over this period. The good news is that the eclipse happens just after Christmas, so many will not be working that day. Travelling, though, wouldn't be advisable then. Instead, spend some quiet time at home. The same advice goes for children, children figures, parents and parent figures in your life. This eclipse occurs very near Jupiter, so college-level (or college-bound) students are affected. They could change schools, courses or other educational plans.

Venus, your love and financial planet, is still 'out of bounds' until the 13th. This indicates, as was mentioned last month, that you feel a need to go outside your normal haunts in order to fulfil your financial and love goals.

Taurus

THE BULL

Birthdays from
21st April to
20th May

Personality Profile

TAURUS AT A GLANCE

Element – Earth

Ruling Planet – Venus
  Career Planet – Uranus
  Love Planet – Pluto
  Money Planet – Mercury
  Planet of Health and Work – Venus
  Planet of Home and Family Life – Sun
  Planet of Spirituality – Mars
  Planet of Travel, Education, Religion and Philosophy – Saturn

Colours – earth tones, green, orange, yellow

Colours that promote love, romance and social harmony – red-violet, violet

Colours that promote earning power – yellow, yellow-orange

Gems – coral, emerald

Metal – copper

Scents – bitter almond, rose, vanilla, violet

Quality – fixed (= stability)

Quality most needed for balance – flexibility

Strongest virtues – endurance, loyalty, patience, stability,
a harmonious disposition

Deepest needs – comfort, material ease, wealth

Characteristics to avoid – rigidity, stubbornness, tendency to be overly
possessive and materialistic

Signs of greatest overall compatibility – Virgo, Capricorn

Signs of greatest overall incompatibility – Leo, Scorpio, Aquarius

Sign most helpful to career – Aquarius

Sign most helpful for emotional support – Leo

Sign most helpful financially – Gemini

Sign best for marriage and/or partnerships – Scorpio

Sign most helpful for creative projects – Virgo

Best Sign to have fun with – Virgo

Signs most helpful in spiritual matters – Aries, Capricorn

Best day of the week – Friday

Understanding a Taurus

Taurus is the most earthy of all the Earth signs. If you understand that Earth is more than just a physical element, that it is a psychological attitude as well, you will get a better understanding of the Taurus personality.

A Taurus has all the power of action that an Aries has. But Taurus is not satisfied with action for its own sake. Their actions must be productive, practical and wealth-producing. If Taurus cannot see a practical value in an action they will not bother taking it.

Taurus's forte lies in their power to make real their own or other people's ideas. They are generally not very inventive but they can take another's invention and perfect it, making it more practical and useful. The same is true for all projects. Taurus is not especially keen on starting new projects, but once they get involved they bring things to completion. They are finishers and will go the distance, so long as no unavoidable calamity intervenes.

Many people find Taurus too stubborn, conservative, fixed and immovable. This is understandable, because Taurus dislikes change – in the environment or in their routine. This is their virtue. It is not good for a wheel's axle to waver. The axle must be fixed, stable and unmovable. Taurus is the axle of society and the heavens. Without their stability and so-called stubbornness, the wheels of the world (and especially the wheels of commerce) would not turn.

Taurus loves routine. A routine, if it is good, has many virtues. It is a fixed – and, ideally, perfect – way of taking care of things. Mistakes can happen when spontaneity comes into the equation, and mistakes cause discomfort and uneasiness – something almost unacceptable to a Taurus. Meddling with Taurus's comfort and security is a sure way to irritate and anger them.

While an Aries loves speed, a Taurus likes things slow. They are slow thinkers – but do not make the mistake of assuming they lack intelligence. On the contrary, Taurus people are very intelligent. It is just that they like to chew on ideas, to deliberate and weigh them up. Only after due deliberation is an idea accepted or a decision taken. Taurus is slow to anger – but once aroused, take care!

Finance

Taurus is very money-conscious. Wealth is more important to them than to many other signs. Wealth to a Taurus means comfort and security. Wealth means stability. Where some zodiac signs feel that they are spiritually rich if they have ideas, talents or skills, Taurus only feels wealth when they can see and touch it. Taurus's way of thinking is, 'What good is a talent if it has not been translated into a home, furniture, car and holidays?'

These are all reasons why Taurus excels in estate agency and agricultural industries. Usually a Taurus will end up owning land. They love to feel their connection to the Earth. Material wealth began with agriculture, the tilling of the soil. Owning a piece of land was humanity's earliest form of wealth: Taurus still feels that primeval connection.

It is in the pursuit of wealth that Taurus develops intellectual and communication ability. Also, in this pursuit Taurus is forced to develop some flexibility. It is in the quest for wealth that they learn the practical value of the intellect and come to admire it. If it were not for the search for wealth and material things, Taurus people might not try to reach a higher intellect.

Some Taurus people are 'born lucky' – the type who win any gamble or speculation. This luck is due to other factors in their horoscope; it is not part of their essential nature. By nature they are not gamblers. They are hard workers and like to earn what they get. Taurus's innate conservatism makes them abhor unnecessary risks in finance and in other areas of their lives.

Career and Public Image

Being essentially down-to-earth people, simple and uncomplicated, Taurus tends to look up to those who are original, unconventional and inventive. Taurus people like their bosses to be creative and original – since they themselves are content to perfect their superiors' brainwaves. They admire people who have a wider social or political consciousness and they feel that someday (when they have all the comfort and security they need) they too would like to be involved in these big issues.

In business affairs Taurus can be very shrewd – and that makes them valuable to their employers. They are never lazy; they enjoy working and getting good results. Taurus does not like taking unnecessary risks and they do well in positions of authority, which makes them good managers and supervisors. Their managerial skills are reinforced by their natural talents for organization and handling details, their patience and thoroughness. As mentioned, through their connection with the earth, Taurus people also do well in farming and agriculture.

In general a Taurus will choose money and earning power over public esteem and prestige. A position that pays more – though it has less prestige – is preferred to a position with a lot of prestige but lower earnings. Many other signs do not feel this way, but a Taurus does, especially if there is nothing in his or her personal birth chart that modifies this. Taurus will pursue glory and prestige only if it can be shown that these things have a direct and immediate impact on their wallet.

Love and Relationships

In love, the Taurus-born likes to have and to hold. They are the marrying kind. They like commitment and they like the terms of a relationship to be clearly defined. More importantly, Taurus likes to be faithful to one lover, and they expect that lover to reciprocate this fidelity. When this doesn't happen, their whole world comes crashing down. When they are in love Taurus people are loyal, but they are also very possessive. They are capable of great fits of jealousy if they are hurt in love.

Taurus is satisfied with the simple things in a relationship. If you are involved romantically with a Taurus there is no need for lavish entertainments and constant courtship. Give them enough love, food and comfortable shelter and they will be quite content to stay home and enjoy your company. They will be loyal to you for life. Make a Taurus feel comfortable and – above all – secure in the relationship, and you will rarely have a problem.

In love, Taurus can sometimes make the mistake of trying to control their partners, which can cause great pain on both sides. The reasoning behind their actions is basically simple: Taurus people feel a sense of ownership over their partners and will want to make changes that will increase their own general comfort and security. This attitude is OK when it comes to inanimate, material things – but is dangerous when applied to people. Taurus needs to be careful and attentive to this possible trait within themselves.

Home and Domestic Life

Home and family are vitally important to Taurus. They like children. They also like a comfortable and perhaps glamorous home – something they can show off. They tend to buy heavy, ponderous furniture – usually of the best quality. This is because Taurus likes a feeling of substance in their environment. Their house is not only their home but their place of creativity and entertainment. The Taurus' home tends to be truly their castle. If they could choose, Taurus people would prefer living in the countryside to being city-dwellers. If they cannot do so during their working lives, many Taurus individuals like to holiday in or even retire to the country, away from the city and closer to the land.

At home a Taurus is like a country squire – lord (or lady) of the manor. They love to entertain lavishly, to make others feel secure in their home and to encourage others to derive the same sense of satisfaction as they do from it. If you are invited for dinner at the home of a Taurus you can expect the best food and best entertainment. Be prepared for a tour of the house and expect to see your Taurus friend exhibit a lot of pride and satisfaction in his or her possessions.

Taurus people like children but they are usually strict with them. The reason for this is they tend to treat their children – as they do most things in life – as their possessions. The positive side to this is that their children will be well cared for and well supervised. They will get every material thing they need to grow up properly. On the down side, Taurus can get too repressive with their children. If a child dares to upset the daily routine – which Taurus loves to follow – he or she will have a problem with a Taurus parent.

Horoscope for 2019

Major Trends

Last year Uranus, the planet of sudden revolutionary change, made a brief foray into your sign and then retreated. It was a quick foreshadowing of what was to come. Those of you born early in the sign of Taurus felt it most strongly (those born from April 20 to April 24). This year, on March 7, Uranus enters your sign and will stay for the next seven years or so. All of you will be affected eventually, but again, those of you born early in the sign will feel it strongest. Fasten your seat belts, it's going to be a wild ride for the next seven years! Change will be the order of the day. Your lesson will be how to handle (and be comfortable with) sudden change and personal instability. Not so easy for a Taurus.

You are coming out of an excellent love and social year. This year, because of Uranus in your sign, these relationships will get tested.

Jupiter will spend almost the whole year (until December 3) in your 8th house of regeneration. This indicates 2019 will be a sexually active kind of year and a year where projects involving personal transformation and reinvention go well.

Both Saturn and Pluto spend the year in your 9th house of religion, philosophy and higher education. This will impact foreign travel as well, and so this is not an especially great year for foreign travel – go only if you must. College students will have to work harder and be more disciplined in their studies. There will be three eclipses in your 9th house in the coming year, signalling much change and disruption in these areas. Religious and philosophical beliefs will get tested – reality checked. Some will have to be tossed out; some will get revised.

Neptune has been in your 11th house for many years now, and remains here all this year too. This transit shows you're attracting spiritual friends, and are perhaps involved in spiritual or charitable groups.

The career should be very successful this year. It seems important to you – more important than mere money. Many happy career opportunities will come to you. There are more details on this later.

Your most important interests in the year ahead will be spirituality (until March 7); the body and image (from March 7 onwards); sex, death and rebirth, personal transformation and reinvention (until December 3); religion, philosophy, higher education and foreign travel; and friends, groups and group activities.

Your paths of greatest fulfilment this year will be communication and intellectual interests; sex, death and rebirth, personal transformation and reinvention (until December 3); and religion, philosophy, higher education and foreign travel (after December 3).

Health

(Please note that this is an astrological perspective on health and not a medical one. In days of yore there was no difference, both of these perspectives were identical. But now there could be quite a difference. For a medical perspective, please consult your doctor or health practitioner.)

There's very good news on the health front this year. There are no long-term planets in stressful alignment with you, so the health will be good. Sure, there will be periods in the year where health is less easy than usual, because of the transits of the short-term planets. However, these are temporary and not trends for the year. When they pass your naturally good health and energy return.

Uranus will be in your sign from March 7 onwards this year. This doesn't show health problems per se, but there will be a tendency to test the limits of the body, to be experimental with the body. If this is done unthinkingly it can lead to injury. So, while it is good to test the body's limits (we often set arbitrary limits that are not warranted), it should be done in a safe, supervised way. Martial arts, yoga and tai chi are all safe ways to experiment and to push your body.

Your empty 6th house is another positive health signal. It shows that you're not paying too much attention here. You sort of take good health for granted, and you don't need to focus overly much here.

Because the aspects are so good and there is more cosmic energy available to you, many of you with pre-existing conditions should notice improvements.

Good though your health is, you can make it even better. Give special attention to the following – the more vulnerable areas for Taurus (the reflexology points are shown in the chart above):

- The neck and throat are always important areas for Taurus. Regular neck massage should be part of your regular health regime. Tension tends to collect in the neck and needs to be released (craniosacral therapy is excellent for this).
- The hips and kidneys. These areas are also always important for Taurus. Regular hip massage will be very beneficial; this will not only strengthen the hips and kidneys but the lower back as well. A herbal kidney cleanse every now and then (if you feel under the weather) might be a good idea too.

Venus serves double duty in your Horoscope. She is both the ruler of your Horoscope and of your 6th health house. The ruler of your Horoscope can be compared to your 'personal trainer', while the ruler of your 6th house can be compared to your personal physician. Their roles are similar but distinct. The personal trainer is more concerned with cosmetic issues – the physique and personal appearance. The personal physician is concerned with overall health. The fact that the

Important foot reflexology points for the year ahead

Try to massage all of the foot on a regular basis – the top of the foot as well as the bottom – but pay extra attention to the points highlighted on the chart. When you massage, be aware of 'sore spots' as these need special attention. It's also a good idea to massage the ankles and below them.

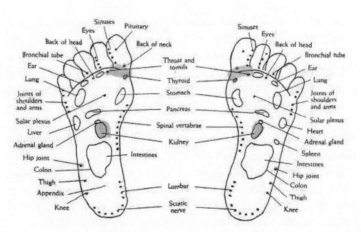

same planet serves both functions shows that for you, good health also means 'looking good'. It shows that the state of your health (more than hosts of lotions and potions) determines the physical appearance. Stay healthy, Taurus, and you will look good.

Venus, as our regular readers know, is a fast-moving planet, and in any given year she will move through all the sectors of your chart. This year, however, she will move even faster than usual, going through some sectors twice. So there are going to be many short-term health trends, depending on where she is and the aspects she receives. These are best covered in the monthly reports.

Home and Family

Your 4th house of home and family is not a house of power this year. This tends to the status quo: you seem basically content with things as they are and have no need to make major changes.

Yet, in spite of this, there will be changes and disruptions. Every year there are two solar eclipses which impact on home and family (because the Sun is the ruler of your 4th house). This year – highly unusually – there will be three. Not only that, but there is a lunar eclipse on January 21 that occurs in your 4th house, bringing more disturbance. So there will be dramas in the family and in the lives of family members. Sometimes repairs are needed to the home – major ones. We will deal with this more fully in the monthly reports.

Uranus in your sign doesn't necessarily show a move, although it signals great personal restlessness. A need for personal freedom. We could say that you have a passion for personal freedom, and some want no personal responsibility whatsoever. This often indicates someone who travels around a lot, someone who lives in different places for long periods of time, someone who is nomadic. You could still officially be living in your residence, but you're a nomad.

Your family planet, the Sun, is one of the faster-moving planets. He changes signs and houses every month, so there are many short-term family trends that depend on where he is and the aspects he receives. These are best dealt with in the monthly reports.

With the Sun as your family planet you like a home that is beautiful and prestigious. You like the home to express your star quality.

One of the parents or parent figures in your life seems unusually devoted this year. He or she could be coming to visit for a long time. A move could happen for this parent or parent figure later on in the year – after December 3. Before then a move is not advisable. He or she seems more temperamental this year, more subject to mood swings.

Siblings and sibling figures in your life are having a great social year – and singles could marry – but a move is not likely. (There's nothing against it, however.) Children and children figures are likely to move, and it looks happy. If they are of childbearing age, they are more fertile than usual. Grandchildren (if you have them) have been moving around quite a lot in recent years; this year they seem more settled.

If you're planning major repairs or renovations (or if you plan to build a house), July 1 to August 23 would be a good time for this. If you're redecorating on a more cosmetic level, or buying objects of beauty for the home, July 27 to August 21 seems a good time. Your taste will be excellent. (Mercury will be retrograde from July 7 to August 1, however, so avoid that period.)

Finance and Career

Though, Taurus, you are always interested in finance, it has become less important than usual over the past few years. Your money house is not a house of power. Generally this shows a basic contentment with things as they are. You have no pressing need to make dramatic changes or overly focus here. It should be a stable, quiet financial year.

However, if financial problems do arise, the empty money house could be the reason. You're probably not paying enough attention here, and you need to focus more.

Mercury, one of the fastest moving of the planets (only the Moon moves faster than him) is your financial planet. In any given year he will move through all the houses and sectors of your chart. Further, his motion is often erratic: sometimes he races across the Heavens, sometimes he moves at a moderate pace, sometimes he is basically motionless and sometimes he's going backward. This pretty much describes your financial life. It signals a need to be flexible and agile if you are to attain your financial goals. There is a need (and you have this ability) to take advantage of the short-term trends in the market-

place and profit from them. It favours trading, retailing, sales, marketing, advertising and PR. Teaching and journalism are also favoured
here – but the business side of these things, rather than being a
practitioner.

Because Mercury moves so fast there are many short-term financial
trends that depend on where he is and the aspects he receives. These
will be dealt with in the monthly reports.

Jupiter, as we mentioned earlier, spends almost all year in your 8th
house. This gives many messages. Money can come through insurance
payments or tax refunds. In general, good tax planning – tax efficiency
– will boost the bottom line and you need to pay attention here. It
shows that the spouse, partner or current love is having a banner
financial year. He or she should be more generous with you. Often this
position indicates inheritance. Hopefully no one has to die, but you
could be named in someone's will or be appointed to some administrative position in an estate. People involved with estates can be important in your financial life. Those of you of appropriate age are probably
doing estate planning now, or making changes here. This position is
also excellent for borrowing or paying down debt (according to your
need). It shows good access to 'outside capital'. If you have good ideas
there are investors willing to back you.

Career is the main headline this year, however – and it looks very
good. Uranus, your career planet, moves into your own sign on March
7. Thus, happy career opportunities are coming to you and there's not
much you need to do to attract them. They will find you. Just go about
your daily business. This aspect signals that you have the favour of the
'higher ups' in your life – bosses, elders, parents and parent figures. It
is true that this devotion can be a double-edged sword: they favour you
but also want to exercise more control. But still they are providing
opportunity.

Your career planet in your own sign gives other messages as well.
You have the image of success. You dress the part. People see you as
successful. It also shows that your personal appearance and overall
demeanour are big factors in your career. (This is probably why you are
dressing and accessorizing this way.)

The whole year looks successful, but especially after December 3 as
Jupiter moves into beautiful aspect with your career planet. You can

expect promotions (official or unofficial), more honour and more recognition. Your professional status is increased. (This will continue next year too.)

Usually career success comes with financial success. This doesn't seem the case this year; financial fruits will probably happen later.

The career planet in your own sign favours a career in real estate, agriculture or agricultural products, copper or copper mining (or industries involved with copper), or companies involved with personal accessories. You seem much more personally comfortable in your career path than you have been for many years.

Love and Social Life

As we mentioned earlier, the love and social life are not prominent in this year's Horoscope. Generally this tends to the status quo. Probably you are satisfied with things as they are, the question is whether your spouse, partner or current love is too?

This complication is not really your fault. You're under Uranus's influence (especially those of you born early in the sign), and the influence of a planet can be likened to that of a drug. It's as if you have taken 'freedom' pills, or 'rebellion' pills. You might be quite unaware of what you're projecting, but your beloved will be very aware.

Freedom is a wonderful thing. It's exhilarating. But generally it's not helpful for committed kinds of relationship, which, by definition, means a limitation on personal freedom. Does this mean that the current relationship will end? Not necessarily. But it can get severely tested. You and the current love will have to work harder to keep things together. Those of you involved with a Taurus romantically should understand what's going on and give your Taurean other half maximum freedom and space (so long as it isn't destructive). This is the first step. Step two is to do unconventional, 'outside the box' activities together as a couple. This will assuage Taurus's need for change and freedom. Inject more excitement and change into the current relationship.

For unattached Taureans marriage is not advisable these days. For a start, you're probably meeting people who are not interested in long-term relationships. Secondly, you're better off having serial love affairs

– where you can have the change you crave – rather than a committed relationship, which might not last.

Saturn is travelling with your love planet, Pluto, this year, which also indicates the testing of love relationships.

The final complication in love again relates to Uranus's position in your own sign, which signals a constant, never-ending redefinition of the self and image. You and your image get upgraded the way you upgrade software. As soon as you settle on one image or one definition of yourself, another idea or refinement comes along and you morph into that. If you are different then, by definition, you have different likes and tastes. A person that satisfied the 'old you' might not satisfy the 'new you'. The same is true in reverse. Your lover fell in love with Taurus 1; now he or she is dealing with Taurus 2 or Taurus 3. Does he or she still feel the same way?

In my practice I have seen these things sometimes work out. This doesn't happen often, but when it does a lot of work went into it.

Your love planet Pluto has been in Capricorn, your 9th house, for many years now, and he will remain there for the next few years too. So, romantic opportunities happen in foreign lands or with foreigners, or in religious or educational-type settings. The place of worship is as much a venue of romance (perhaps more) as the local night club. The same is true with college functions and gatherings. A part of you likes the traditional kind of relationship, but another part likes to be unconventional. So you are of two minds when it comes to love – and these two minds argue with each other. It's very difficult to satisfy both.

Self-improvement

Taureans are conservative people by their nature. People who don't like them would call them stubborn. People who like them will say they have tenacity. They have the quality of perseverance and they have it in spades. Often this quality spells the difference between the success or failure of a project. Change and flexibility are not their strong points. They love routine. A Taurean will say, 'Why should I try this new restaurant or new dish when I know my normal place will be good? Why gamble?'

Now Uranus is moving into your sign for the next seven or so years, meaning that change, the upending of routine, will be the order of the day. How will you handle this? This is going to be the spiritual lesson. Other signs handle this better; for you it is a challenge.

The first step is to embrace change rather than fight it. Recognize that it is for your ultimate good – which it is – and flow with it. When you give up your resistance, you will find that things flow more smoothly. Change doesn't have the terrible consequences that you fear. Make change your friend and ally, not your opponent.

It is normal that when sudden changes happen that there are feelings of insecurity – even outright fear. Write down your feelings on a piece of paper. Write a short phrase that captures your feelings. Then touch the paper and let it go, touch it and let it go. Do this for about 15 minutes. This will discharge any negative feelings that you have. You will find that you start to feel much better and the mind will be clearer. Solutions will start to come to you. (The solutions were always there, only you couldn't receive them because of the emotional disturbance.) Make a regular practice of this and things will go much easier for you.*

Some people like to write out what they feel. Set a timer for 15 minutes and write out your negative feelings as they come to you. Don't hold back. After 15 minutes, tear the paper into shreds and throw it in the bin. As you do this say: 'These negative feelings are now thrown out.'

Uranus has been in your spiritual 12th house for the past seven years and you have been experimental in your spiritual life. Many of you have been like the wandering holy men of old – wandering from one teacher and teaching to the next, from one book to the next, from one philosophy to the next. This is a natural stage on the spiritual path. But now you're more settled spiritually. By now, you have a settled path, it just remains for you to walk it.

Neptune, as we mentioned earlier, has been in your 11th house for many years now. This shows much involvement with spiritual groups and spiritual friends. (In fact the friendships you make now should be spiritual-type people – there's no need even to waste time on others.) These spiritual groups can be a great help and support in the coming years.

---

* This technique is discussed in more detail in my book *A Technique For Meditation* (Mantra Books, 2011).

Month-by-month Forecasts

January

Best Days Overall: 5, 6, 15, 16, 23, 24
Most Stressful Days Overall: 7, 8, 21, 22, 27, 28
Best Days for Love: 1, 5, 6, 12, 13, 15, 16, 21, 22, 23, 24, 27, 28, 30, 31
Best Days for Money: 2, 3, 4, 5, 12, 13, 15, 16, 17, 18, 21, 22, 25
Best Days for Career: 3, 4, 7, 8, 13, 14, 22, 31

Your year starts with a bang. The fireworks didn't end on New Year's Eve. Two eclipses shake things up this month in a foreshadowing of things to come in the year ahead.

The solar eclipse of the 6th (in America it's on the 5th) occurs in your 9th house. Your 9th house is very strong this month and you would have a natural urge for foreign travel, but it's probably wiser to reschedule this. If you must travel, then you must; the eclipse shouldn't deter you. But if you can, schedule your trip around the eclipse period. This eclipse is not only in your 9th house but it affects the ruler of that house, Saturn, too. So its impact is more powerful than usual. It impacts very strongly on college-level (or college-bound) students. It signals shake-ups in their school, shake-ups in educational plans, changes of courses and perhaps even changes of schools. The good news here is that with the 9th house so powerful this month, there is success here. The changes are helpful.

Every solar eclipse affects the home and family (the Sun is your family planet), so there are dramas at home and in the lives of family members – parents or parent figures seem especially affected. Repairs could be needed in the home. Imperfections or hidden problems come to light and need to be fixed. Often this doesn't happen quickly (they can sometimes take months to fully resolve). Siblings and sibling figures in your life are forced to make important financial changes – this usually comes about through some shock. This is the first of three eclipses that will happen in your 9th house this year.

The lunar eclipse of the 21st is almost (but not quite) a replay of the solar eclipse. It occurs in your 4th house of home and family and it reveals that the problems in the home, with family members and a parent or parent figure, are not yet resolved. They are still experiencing personal dramas. Every lunar eclipse affects siblings and sibling figures, and this one is no different. Again, they need to make important financial changes. This eclipse affects students below college level, bringing changes in schools or educational plans. Often this kind of eclipse shows changes in your neighbourhood, such as heavy construction. There are dramas in the lives of your neighbours.

In spite of all the drama going on, the month ahead is still prosperous and successful. The Sun will enter your 10th house of career on the 20th and you'll begin a yearly career peak. This seems stronger than the usual career peak. Almost all of the planets are above the horizon this month. The planetary power – almost the whole Horoscope – is supporting your outer life and activities. Even your family is supportive. They see your success as a 'family project'.

February

Best Days Overall: 1, 2, 11, 12, 19, 20, 28
Most Stressful Days Overall: 3, 4, 5, 17, 18, 24, 25
Best Days for Love: 1, 2, 11, 12, 19, 20, 24, 25, 28
Best Days for Money: 3, 4, 9, 10, 13, 14, 15, 16, 17, 18, 24, 25, 26, 27
Best Days for Career: 3, 4, 5, 10, 18, 27

Last month was prosperous and so is the month ahead. Your financial planet, Mercury, entered Aquarius on January 24 and he will be there until the 10th. In this position Mercury is strong celestially (he is in the sign of his exaltation) and terrestrially (at the top of chart, the 10th house). Thus earning power, the financial magnetism, is unusually strong. Money is earned rather easily, and financial goals happen quickly and with relative ease. (All the planets are moving forward this month too, so general progress is fast.)

On the 10th Mercury enters the spiritual sign of Pisces. Thus your financial intuition is very sharp – especially on the 18th and 19th. (Be aware of the dream life those days, as it will tend to contain important financial guidance.) Mercury likes the 11th house and is comfortable there, so your finances seem comfortable. Online activities, being involved with groups and organizations, are financially helpful. Your social connections likewise. It's a good time to spend on high-tech equipment now – it seems like a good investment and you can earn from it. Mercury will make nice aspects to Jupiter on the 2nd and 3rd and this should also produce financial opportunities.

Health is basically good this month, but needs a bit of attention until the 19th. Nothing serious is afoot – just lower energy than usual. Enhance the health through back and knee massage from the 3rd onwards. A spinal adjustment by a chiropractor every now and then might also be a good idea.

Mars moves into your sign on the 14th, giving many messages. On the positive side you're more active, bolder and achieve things much faster than usual. And since Mars is your spiritual planet, it signals an ability to mould and shape the body through spiritual means – meditation, visualization and affirmation. Keep in the mind that the body has no will of its own; it has appetites and habits (karmic momentums) but no independent will. It is totally amenable to the spirit – and this month, you will learn how this works. Techniques will be shown. The downside of this transit by Mars is haste and aggression. Haste can lead to accidents and injury. Aggression (even unconsciously) can lead to fights. So be more mindful on the physical level.

Love seems happy this month. Venus, your ruling planet, spends the month from the 3rd onwards in the happy 9th house. On the 22nd and 23rd she starts to travel with your personal love planet, Pluto. This will bring happy romantic opportunities for singles.

March

Best Days Overall: 1, 2, 10, 11, 19, 20, 27, 28, 29
Most Stressful Days Overall: 3, 4, 17, 18, 23, 24, 30, 31
Best Days for Love: 1, 2, 3, 4, 10, 11, 15, 16, 19, 20, 23, 24, 28, 29
Best Days for Money: 5, 6, 7, 8, 9, 13, 14, 15, 16, 17, 18, 23, 24, 25, 26
Best Days for Career: 1, 3, 4, 10, 19, 27, 30, 31

The main headline this month, and we mentioned it in the yearly report, is Uranus's move into your sign on the 7th. Fasten your seat belts and get ready for dynamic and sudden changes. This month, only those of you born very early in Taurus (April 20–22) will feel the effect of this, but as time goes on (and in future years) all of you will feel it. There are many positive things to Uranus in your sign. You are a more interesting and exciting person to be around. You're not the usual conservative Taurus; you're more a 'free spirit'. You are seen as successful by those around you, as someone powerful and prominent. Career opportunities come to you and there's nothing much you need to do to attract them. These opportunities will find you wherever you are. (You can't hide from the planets). There are many image and personality changes happening now – a long-term trend.

Love could be a problem now, however. You might not feel it, but the spouse, partner or current love will notice: you seem more rebellious and unpredictable to them. They are not sure of your loyalty. You will have to make special efforts to assuage their doubts.

Health is basically good now. But with Uranus in your sign you seem more experimental with your body, testing its limits. Mars in your sign all month reinforces this. It is good to experiment, but do it in a conscious, mindful way, not in a careless, daredevil-type way. You can enhance your already good health with calf and ankle massage. You seem to be exercising more these days and this could be putting a strain on the calf muscles. On the 26th your health planet moves into Pisces, so give more attention to the feet. Foot massages will be very beneficial, and spiritual-healing techniques too.

Finances are good, but more complicated and perhaps slower than usual. Mercury is in retrograde motion from the 5th to the 28th. As our regular readers know, this is not the time for making major purchases or financial decisions. Instead, it's a time to review options and to take stock. Gaining mental clarity on finance is the most important thing this period. Mercury makes a very unusual station (he 'camps out') on Neptune from the 24th to the 31st. Spirit is delivering important financial messages then. Pay attention to the dream life during this time. Financial information can also come through psychics, tarot readers, astrologers and other spiritual channels. (Sometimes a phrase from a newspaper can leap out at you and send a message.)

April

Best Days Overall: 6, 7, 8, 15, 16, 24, 25
Most Stressful Days Overall: 13, 14, 19, 20, 26, 27
Best Days for Love: 2, 3, 7, 8, 11, 12, 15, 16, 19, 20, 21, 24, 25
Best Days for Money: 2, 3, 4, 5, 9, 10, 13, 14, 22, 23
Best Days for Career: 6, 15, 24, 26, 27

The planets are kind to you this month. With the exception of the Moon – and then only sometimes – there are no planets in stressful aspect with you in April. Health and energy will be good. With good health all kinds of things that seemed impossible before are now possible. And, with the planetary momentum basically forward this month, you should see fast progress towards your goals.

Venus has one of her solstices from the 22nd to the 25th. She pauses in the heavens and then changes direction (in her latitudinal motion). This is a pause that refreshes. You will probably find a pause in your own affairs during that period. There's nothing to worry about. Enjoy it.

Your spiritual 12th house is powerful until the 20th. This is a period for internal growth, for meditation, spiritual practice, the study of sacred scripture and for involvement in idealistic pursuits. Taurus will never forget worldly things, but at this time it is good to downplay them a bit. A little vacation from the mundane world is a healthy thing. Internal growth always precedes external growth. Things – good or bad – have to happen through you before they happen to you. Once this period is over, the party begins. The Sun enters your 1st house on the 20th and you begin one of your yearly personal pleasure peaks. Time to pamper the body and indulge its lawful cravings. Time to give it the good food, wine and desserts.

This is the period to get the body and image into the shape you want them to be. More important than the physical pleasures are the self-confidence, self-esteem and self-appreciation (which is not narcissism) that occur when the Sun enters your sign. The body glows and has a 'star quality' to it. Personal appearance shines (personal appearance has a lot to do with one's energy levels). Thus it is generally good for the love life.

The family (and especially the parents or parent figures in your life) are unusually devoted to you. They also seem in better harmony with each other this month. You have good family support now. If the parents or parent figures are single, they have good romantic opportunities from the 21st to the 23rd.

Mars, your spiritual planet, spends the month in your money house. This indicates good financial intuition. Intuition is the short cut to wealth. One millisecond of real intuition is worth many years of hard graft. Intuition will not negate the need for work, but the work will be the side effect and not the cause of wealth. Your financial planet Mercury will be in your spiritual 12th house from the 17th onwards, which reinforces all this.

May

Best Days Overall: 4, 5, 13, 14, 21, 22, 31
Most Stressful Days Overall: 10, 11, 17, 18, 24, 25
Best Days for Love: 2, 3, 4, 5, 13, 14, 17, 18, 21, 22, 31
Best Days for Money: 2, 3, 6, 7, 10, 11, 13, 14, 19, 20, 23, 24, 29, 30
Best Days for Career: 4, 13, 21, 24, 25, 31

Mars went 'out of bounds' on April 21 and will be 'out of bounds' this whole month. This signals, first, that in your spiritual life and practice you're outside your normal comfort zone. Perhaps you're exploring exotic or alien teachings. (There's nothing wrong with this, by the way. Truth is truth and we should welcome it from whatever source.) Generally this happens when the answers you're seeking are not to be found where you usually seek them and you must go outside that sphere. It takes courage and daring. This aspect would also show that you're outside your normal sphere in your financial life too – at least partly.

You're still in the midst of one of your yearly personal pleasure peaks until the 21st. On the 21st, the Sun enters your money house and you begin a yearly financial peak. Now, finances were good last month, and they're good this month even before the 21st. But after then they get even better. Your financial planet Mercury enters your own sign on the

6th and stays there until the 21st, bringing financial windfalls and almost effortless financial opportunity. Nothing much needs to be done – except to go to the bank! On the 21st Mercury will join the Sun in your money house. Mercury in his own sign and house is more powerful on your behalf and all of this spells increased earnings. There is good family support and you're probably spending more on the home and family too. Your financial judgement is sound.

Love is good this month, and will get even better after the 15th as Venus enters your sign. This transit produces another mini personal pleasure period. It enhances the physical appearance. It adds beauty and grace – a sense of style – to the image. The overall social magnetism is increased. Venus travels with Uranus from the 17th to the 19th. This can bring you a sudden, unexpected career or job opportunity. Venus in your sign is a good time to buy clothing and personal accessories. Your taste will be spot on. The only problem with love is the retrograde of your love planet, Pluto, which began on April 24. It doesn't stop love from happening, only slows things down a bit.

Health is still excellent. Like last month, there are no planets in stressful alignment with you (highly unusually). Only the Moon will make stressful aspects, and then only for short periods. You can enhance your already good health with scalp and face massage until the 15th, and with neck massage after then.

June

Best Days Overall: 1, 9, 10, 18, 19, 27, 28, 29
Most Stressful Days Overall: 7, 8, 13, 14, 20, 21
Best Days for Love: 1, 9, 10, 11, 13, 14, 18, 19, 20, 21, 28, 29
Best Days for Money: 2, 3, 4, 7, 8, 13, 14, 15, 16, 24, 25, 26, 30
Best Days for Career: 1, 9, 17, 18, 20, 21, 27

Things are slowing down in the world – 40 per cent of the planets are retrograde this month – but for you things are mostly moving on time and in good order.

Health is still wonderful. Only after the 27th is there any planet in stressful alignment with you – Mercury. And he is not a major hitter. So, you have plenty of energy and drive. You can enhance your already good health through neck massage until the 9th, and then through arm and shoulder massage.

Finance is the major headline this month. You're still well into a yearly financial peak until the 21st. Your financial planet Mercury is moving speedily this month, through three signs and houses of your chart. This denotes confidence and fast progress. You make financial decisions quickly and they tend to be good. Money and financial opportunity will come through various people and in various ways. You will tend to spend differently too – it just depends on where Mercury is. Up until the 27th, money is earned through good sales, marketing and PR. Buying, selling, trading and retailing are also favoured. You could be spending more on sales and marketing too – and it seems like a good investment. Family support is strong all month. Family connections are also playing an important role in finances. Residential real estate and earning money from your home are also favoured.

Mercury goes 'out of bounds' from the 1st to the 16th. This makes you more adventurous in finance. You're thinking 'outside the box'. You're going outside your normal areas in the pursuit of wealth.

Love doesn't seem a big issue this month. Your 7th house is empty and Pluto, your love planet, is retrograde and not receiving any especially good aspects. After the 21st you will have to work harder on your current relationship.

Mars is still 'out of bounds' until the 12th. This not only affects your spiritual life, as we discussed last month, but now that he is in your 3rd house Mars is affecting your reading tastes – they are outside your usual norm. (You could have experienced this last month too – after May 16.)

Your 3rd house of communication is strong all month, but especially after the 21st. This is an excellent transit for students, signalling focus and success. This might be a good time for students to attend summer school. And even non-students can benefit from taking courses in subjects that interest them. Investors will experience an increase in investment income.

July

Best Days Overall: 6, 7, 15, 16, 25, 26
Most Stressful Days Overall: 4, 5, 10, 11, 17, 18, 19
Best Days for Love: 1, 6, 7, 10, 11, 15, 16, 20, 21, 25, 26, 31
Best Days for Money: 1, 4, 5, 13, 14, 21, 22, 23, 24, 27, 28, 29, 30, 31
Best Days for Career: 6, 15, 17, 18, 19, 25

Things have gone rather easily for you these past few months. It's been a placid kind of period. To prevent any lethargy, however, the cosmos throws some excitement and challenge at you this month. First off, there are two eclipses. This almost guarantees change and excitement. But also we see, for the first time since February, a raft of planets (short-term ones) in stressful aspect with you. So health will need attention this month – especially from the 23rd onwards. Until the 3rd enhance the health with arm and shoulder massage. From the 3rd to the 28th pay more attention to the stomach – diet will be an issue this period. After the 28th give more attention to the heart. The most important thing, as our regular readers know, is to maintain high energy levels. Make sure you get enough rest.

The solar eclipse of the 2nd occurs in your 3rd house and affects students below college level. They could change schools or educational plans. There are personal dramas in the lives of siblings and sibling figures – and also in those of neighbours. There can be disruptions in your neighbourhood. Communication equipment will get tested and sometimes will need replacement. The money people in your life are forced to make important financial changes. Every solar eclipse impacts on the home and family, and this one is no different. Thus there are dramas in the lives of family members. Repairs might be needed in the home. The good news is that your home and family are major priorities this month and you seem on the case. The results will be successful. Siblings and sibling figures are also forced to make important financial changes. There is disruption in their financial lives.

The lunar eclipse of the 16th occurs in your 9th house – the second one of the year in this house. This also impacts on students, both at college and pre-college levels. It indicates shake-ups and disturbances in their schools – in the administration, and changes in subjects, courses or educational plans. There are shake-ups in your place of worship too. Again siblings and sibling figures are having personal dramas. The money people in your life still need to make financial changes. This eclipse affects your love planet, Pluto, so there are dramas in the life of the current love. Your relationship gets tested.

Career is important all year – after all, your career planet, Uranus, is in your sign. But these days it can be de-emphasized a bit, and more focus given to the home and family. Emotional wellness will pay career dividends later on.

August

Best Days Overall: 2, 3, 11, 12, 21, 22, 30, 31
Most Stressful Days Overall: 1, 7, 8, 14, 15, 28, 29
Best Days for Love: 1, 2, 3, 7, 8, 9, 10, 11, 12, 20, 21, 22, 30, 31
Best Days for Money: 1, 8, 9, 10, 19, 20, 23, 24, 25, 28, 29, 30
Best Days for Career: 2, 11, 14, 15, 21, 30

Health still needs watching this month. However, you will see major improvements from the 23rd onwards. This is just a temporary spell of low energy caused by short-term transits: by the 23rd *all* the planets will be in harmonious alignment with you. In the meantime, enhance the health through right diet and cultivating good emotional health. It would be good to have some fun too. Avoid depression (another name for low energy) like the plague. Meditation is one of the best natural ways to manage the emotional life.

The night side (the lower half) of your Horoscope is dominant this month, so career issues can be downplayed. It is good, when the night side of your chart is strong, to pursue career goals by the methods of night – by dreaming, visualization and meditation. Later, as the planetary power shifts, these visualizations and dreams will start to become realities. You will see major improvements in the career from the 23rd onwards, but most of your focus should still be on your family (and especially on children and children figures) for a while.

With the 4th house so strong these days (it was very strong last month too), it is a good time for psychological therapies. Those of you already in therapy will see much progress – more so than usual. Breakthroughs will happen.

There is another shift underway. On July 23 the planetary power began to shift from the Eastern to the Western sector of your chart, from the sector of self to the sector of others. This month that shift is in full swing. There is less independence now – and perhaps less of a need for it. It is time to adapt to situations rather than change them. Your good comes through others and their good graces and not so much from your personal initiative. The planetary power is moving away from you and towards others. And so should you. Put others first, provided that doing so isn't destructive. Your way might not be the best way these days.

Finances, always important for you, Taurus, are good this month. Mercury moves speedily and financial confidence is good. There is fast progress. Things are slower in the world (40 per cent of the planets are retrograde) but you don't seem affected financially. Family and family connections are still a major factor in finances. After the 28th, money comes in fun kinds of ways and you're likely to spend more on leisure. Taureans are not especially speculative, but after the 28th you are a bit more so than usual.

There is big improvement in the love life from the 23rd onwards.

September

Best Days Overall: 7, 8, 9, 17, 18, 19, 26, 27
Most Stressful Days Overall: 3, 4, 10, 11, 24, 25, 30
Best Days for Love: 3, 4, 8, 9, 18, 19, 20, 26, 27, 28, 29, 30
Best Days for Money: 5, 6, 8, 9, 15, 16, 20, 21, 24, 25, 28, 29
Best Days for Career: 7, 10, 11, 17, 26

Last month, on the 23rd, you began one of your yearly personal pleasure peaks. This goes on until September 23. Your 5th house of fun, children and creativity is chock-full of planets – and most of them are beneficent, friendly planets. So it's time to have some fun and enjoy life. As you do, you will find that health and finances also improve. Spiritual gurus all talk about the importance of 'letting go'. Take a vacation from your cares and personal goals and just enjoy the wonderful life that has been given. When you go back to your worries and issues, you will find many of them have been solved or are less severe. You are in one of those 'letting go' times.

Since August 18 there has been a beautiful Grand Trine in the Earth signs. Earth is your native element, so things are very comfortable for you. Your financial and management judgement (always good) are super these days. You sense and feel what will work on the physical and material plane. You have a special ability to make dreams and ideas 'real' – to materialize them. The Grand Trine in Earth tends to prosperity. This Grand Trine will be in effect all month, although it gets a bit weaker after the 23rd.

Your love planet, Pluto, is still retrograde, but the love life is wonderful this month. Perhaps it is slower than usual. There's no need to arrange a wedding or make important love decisions, but it seems happy as it is. Love is good all month, but after the 14th it might need more work and effort.

Health is wonderful all month. There are no planets in any stressful kind of aspect with you (except the Moon, and then only occasionally). Health is another form of wealth and should be considered a prosperity factor. You can enhance your already good health by having fun until the 14th, and then by giving more attention to the hips and kidneys after then. A happy love life will do much to enhance the health too. Regular hip massage and an occasional herbal kidney cleanse will also be good. If health problems occur (unlikely), restore harmony to the love life as soon as possible.

Mercury, your financial planet, is moving forward but a bit slower than last month. So finances are moving forward. Until the 14th there is happy money – money that is earned (and spent) in happy ways. There is luck in speculations too. The health field (a huge field) seems attractive to investors. But money will come from solid work after the 14th. This is not a problem for Taurus, though. Taureans like work.

October

Best Days Overall: 5, 6, 15, 16, 23, 24
Most Stressful Days Overall: 1, 7, 8, 21, 22, 28, 29
Best Days for Love: 1, 5, 6, 10, 11, 15, 16, 19, 20, 23, 24, 28, 29
Best Days for Money: 2, 3, 4, 10, 11, 12, 13, 17, 18, 19, 20, 21, 22, 28, 29, 30, 31
Best Days for Career: 5, 7, 8, 14, 15, 23

Your 6th house of health and work became powerful on September 23 and is still powerful until the 23rd. Thus, in the unlikely event that you are unemployed (rare for a Taurus) there are many job opportunities happening – and good ones. Even if you are already employed there are opportunities for overtime and second jobs. You're in the mood for work these days and employers pick up on this.

There is also a great focus on health since September 23. With no planets in stressful alignment with you, this can be a kind of 'over focus'. Be careful not to magnify little things into big things. On the positive side, it's a good time to get into daily health regimes of a preventative nature. This will stand you in good stead for later in the month when health and energy are a bit more stressful. After the 23rd make sure to get enough rest. Things that you did with no problem over the past few months might be harder now. Until the 8th enhance the health with hip massage and more attention on the kidneys (like last month). After the 8th you will respond well to detox regimes. Give more attention to the colon, bladder and sexual organs. Safe sex and sexual moderation become more important after the 8th.

Love is really the main headline this month. There are a few nice developments happening. First of all, your love planet, Pluto, starts to move forward on the 3rd after many months of retrograde motion. By now you'll have greater clarity about love, your relationship, and what your needs are. By the 23rd your 7th house of love becomes powerful for the first time this year. It happens little by little. On the 3rd Mercury enters the 7th house; on the 8th, Venus does; and on the 23rd, the Sun. You begin a yearly love and social peak. The love life and social life become very active. There is a lot of socializing that relates to business and work. You have the aspects of someone who likes to do business with friends and someone who likes to socialize with people you do business with. The distinctions between friendship and business are blurred. One merges into the other. There is also more socializing with family members. Family likes to play Cupid these days. You find an allurement to health professionals or to those who are involved in your health. If you focus on your financial, health and family goals, the love life will take care of itself.

Career is more stressful after the 23rd. You just have to put in more work. Part of the problem is the focus on the social life, which seems to distract you. But this is a good distraction this month.

November

Best Days Overall: 1, 2, 11, 12, 20, 21, 28, 29, 30
Most Stressful Days Overall: 3, 4, 5, 18, 19, 24, 25
Best Days for Love: 1, 2, 8, 9, 11, 12, 18, 19, 20, 21, 24, 25, 28, 29, 30
Best Days for Money: 6, 7, 8, 9, 10, 13, 14, 16, 17, 18, 19, 26, 27
Best Days for Career: 1, 3, 4, 5, 11, 20, 28

Health is improving but still needs a bit of watching until the 22nd. Mars in your 6th house of health until the 19th indicates that you get good results from spiritual therapies, such as meditation, the laying on of hands, reiki and the manipulation of subtle energies. If you feel under the weather see a spiritual healer. Spiritual-type exercises also seem good – yoga, tai chi, chi gong, etc. And give more attention to the liver and thighs until the 26th. Regular thigh massage is beneficial. After the 26th back and knee massage will be powerful.

Your health planet goes 'out of bounds' from the 15th to the 30th. Thus in health matters you're exploring things outside your normal experience. There are no answers in your normal sphere and you must go beyond for what you seek. Your job could also be taking you outside your usual haunts.

Venus travels with Jupiter almost all month, and especially from the 22nd to the 24th. This is a happy transit. It brings success at the job and perhaps a happy job opportunity. It also brings love and sexual opportunity. It brings good news on the health front.

You're still in a yearly love and social peak until the 22nd. And you will still be active socially after that date. Mercury will be in your 7th house all month and on the 19th Mars enters here. Mars's entrance into your house of love indicates socializing with spiritual-type people. Wealth and family connections are important, but there is a yearning for spiritual connection. Being on the same page spiritually – in your ideals and practice – will be a big help in love. Spiritual-type venues or charity events will also be places of romantic opportunity.

The upper, day side of your Horoscope is very dominant now. At least 80 per cent (and sometimes 90 per cent) of the planets are in the upper half of the chart. So, this is a time for moving forward in your career and outer ambitions. Your career planet is still retrograde, but it won't stop your progress, only slow things down a bit.

Finances are more complicated this month. Mercury, your financial planet, is retrograde from the 2nd to the 20th. So more care is needed when making important purchases or investments. (You shop for groceries and minor items, obviously, but we're talking about the big things.) Your normally good financial judgement is not up to its usual standards. So, use Mercury's retrograde period to attain mental clarity on your finances. When this happens, you'll be ready to move forward with confidence.

December

Best Days Overall: 8, 9, 17, 18, 26, 27
Most Stressful Days Overall: 1, 2, 15, 16, 21, 22, 28, 29
Best Days for Love: 8, 9, 17, 18, 21, 22, 26, 27, 28, 29
Best Days for Money: 6, 7, 8, 11, 12, 15, 16, 17, 25, 26
Best Days for Career: 1, 2, 8, 17, 26, 28, 29

In spite of the solar eclipse on the 26th the month ahead seems happy and eventful. This eclipse, the third of the year in your 9th house (it has really taken a pounding) once again affects college-level students. There are more shake-ups in their schools and more changes in educational plans. (The eclipses will not leave you alone until you get it right.) There are more shake-ups in your place of worship too. Religious beliefs have been severely tested by the previous two eclipses and this continues. This is basically good – though not pleasant. Some of these things are little more than superstitions and should be ditched. Others might just need some modification. Changes in the belief system will have dramatic effects on every other aspect of life. Our lives are controlled by our beliefs. Jupiter, the planet of religion and philosophy, is also directly impacted here, reinforcing all the above.

It will not be sensible to travel during this period – though the urge is strong. If you can avoid it, wonderful. If not, schedule your flights around the eclipse period (a few days before or after it). The impact on Jupiter signals that the spouse, partner or current love is having a financial disturbance and this will lead to important changes. Siblings and sibling figures also have to make important financial changes. Every solar eclipse affects the home, family and one of the parents or parent figures in your life. So there are dramas happening here too. The good news is that health is good. You have plenty of energy to handle the challenges.

Jupiter makes an important move into your 9th house on the 3rd, and he will remain here well into next year. College students might make changes in their subjects and courses, but the changes will be fortunate. There is success in their studies.

Your powerful 9th house this month (and it's been strong all year) gives an intense interest in religion, philosophy, theology and higher education. You will find a juicy theological discussion more interesting than a night out on the town; a sermon more interesting than a rock concert. This will be the trend for 2020 as well. This month well over half of the planets are either in the 9th house or moving through there. So these interests are unusually strong.

The career is also going well. Yes, you need to tread carefully and there are many things that are not yet clear, but good progress is happening. Venus crosses your Mid-heaven, for the second time this year on the 20th. This indicates personal success. You are at the top of your world. Everyone else looks up to you. It also shows that your good work ethic is appreciated by your superiors.

Your spiritual planet, Mars, is still in the 7th house of love this month. So, you need someone spiritual in your life. Good spiritual compatibility is ultra-important.

Gemini

Ⅱ

THE TWINS

Birthdays from
21st May to
20th June

Personality Profile

GEMINI AT A GLANCE

Element – Air

Ruling Planet – Mercury
  Career Planet – Neptune
  Love Planet – Jupiter
  Money Planet – Moon
  Planet of Health and Work – Pluto
  Planet of Home and Family Life – Mercury

Colours – blue, yellow, yellow-orange

Colour that promotes love, romance and social harmony – sky blue

Colours that promote earning power – grey, silver

Gems – agate, aquamarine

Metal – quicksilver

Scents – lavender, lilac, lily of the valley, storax

Quality – mutable (= flexibility)

Quality most needed for balance – thought that is deep rather than superficial

Strongest virtues – great communication skills, quickness and agility of thought, ability to learn quickly

Deepest need – communication

Characteristics to avoid – gossiping, hurting others with harsh speech, superficiality, using words to mislead or misinform

Signs of greatest overall compatibility – Libra, Aquarius

Signs of greatest overall incompatibility – Virgo, Sagittarius, Pisces

Sign most helpful to career – Pisces

Sign most helpful for emotional support – Virgo

Sign most helpful financially – Cancer

Sign best for marriage and/or partnerships – Sagittarius

Sign most helpful for creative projects – Libra

Best Sign to have fun with – Libra

Signs most helpful in spiritual matters – Taurus, Aquarius

Best day of the week – Wednesday

Understanding a Gemini

Gemini is to society what the nervous system is to the body. It does not introduce any new information but is a vital transmitter of impulses from the senses to the brain and vice versa. The nervous system does not judge or weigh these impulses – it only conveys information. And it does so perfectly.

This analogy should give you an indication of a Gemini's role in society. Geminis are the communicators and conveyors of information. To Geminis the truth or falsehood of information is irrelevant, they only transmit what they see, hear or read about. Thus they are capable of spreading the most outrageous rumours as well as conveying truth and light. Geminis sometimes tend to be unscrupulous in their communications and can do both great good or great evil with their power. This is why the sign of Gemini is symbolized by twins: Geminis have a dual nature.

Their ability to convey a message – to communicate with such ease – makes Geminis ideal teachers, writers and media and marketing people. This is helped by the fact that Mercury, the ruling planet of Gemini, also rules these activities.

Geminis have the gift of the gab. And what a gift this is! They can make conversation about anything, anywhere, at any time. There is almost nothing that is more fun to Geminis than a good conversation – especially if they can learn something new as well. They love to learn and they love to teach. To deprive a Gemini of conversation, or of books and magazines, is cruel and unusual punishment.

Geminis are almost always excellent students and take well to education. Their minds are generally stocked with all kinds of information, trivia, anecdotes, stories, news items, rarities, facts and statistics. Thus they can support any intellectual position that they care to take. They are awesome debaters and, if involved in politics, make good orators. Geminis are so verbally smooth that even if they do not know what they are talking about, they can make you think that they do. They will always dazzle you with their brilliance.

Finance

Geminis tend to be more concerned with the wealth of learning and ideas than actual material wealth. As mentioned, they excel in professions that involve writing, teaching, sales and journalism – and not all of these professions pay very well. But to sacrifice intellectual needs merely for money is unthinkable to a Gemini. Geminis strive to combine the two. Cancer is on Gemini's solar 2nd house of money cusp, indicating that Geminis can earn extra income (in a harmonious and natural way) from investments in residential property, restaurants and hotels. Given their verbal skills, Geminis love to bargain and negotiate in any situation, and especially when it has to do with money.

The Moon rules Gemini's 2nd solar house. The Moon is not only the fastest-moving planet in the zodiac but actually moves through every sign and house every 28 days. No other heavenly body matches the Moon for swiftness or the ability to change quickly. An analysis of the Moon – and lunar phenomena in general – describes Gemini's financial attitudes very well. Geminis are financially versatile and flexible; they can earn money in many different ways. Their financial attitudes and needs seem to change daily, as do their feelings about money: sometimes they're very enthusiastic about it, at other times they couldn't care less.

For a Gemini, financial goals and money are often seen only as means of supporting a family; these things have little meaning otherwise.

The Moon, as Gemini's money planet, has another important message for Gemini financially: in order for Geminis to realize their financial potential they need a greater understanding of the emotional side of life. They need to combine their awesome powers of logic with an understanding of human psychology. Feelings have their own logic; Geminis need to learn this and apply it to financial matters.

Career and Public Image

Geminis know that they have been given the gift of communication for a reason, that it is a power that can achieve great good or cause unthinkable distress. They long to put this power at the service of the highest and most transcendental truths. This is their primary goal, to communicate the eternal verities and prove them logically. They look up to people who can transcend the intellect – to poets, artists, musicians and mystics. They may be awed by stories of religious saints and martyrs. A Gemini's highest achievement is to teach the truth, whether it is scientific, inspirational or historical. Those who can transcend the intellect are Gemini's natural superiors – and a Gemini realizes this.

The sign of Pisces is in Gemini's solar 10th house of career. Neptune, the planet of spirituality and altruism, is Gemini's career planet. If Geminis are to realize their highest career potential they need to develop their transcendental – their spiritual and altruistic – side. They need to understand the larger cosmic picture, the vast flow of human evolution – where it came from and where it is heading. Only then can a Gemini's intellectual powers take their true position and he or she can become the 'messenger of the gods'. Geminis need to cultivate a facility for 'inspiration', which is something that does not originate in the intellect but which comes through the intellect. This will further enrich and empower a Gemini's mind.

Love and Relationships

Geminis bring their natural garrulousness and brilliance into their love life and social life as well. A good talk or a verbal joust is an interesting prelude to romance. Their only problem in love is that their intellect is too cool and passionless to incite ardour in others. Emotions sometimes disturb them, and their partners tend to complain about this. If you are in love with a Gemini you must understand why this is so. Geminis avoid deep passions because these would interfere with their ability to think and communicate. If they are cool towards you, understand that this is their nature.

Nevertheless, Geminis must understand that it is one thing to talk about love and another actually to love – to feel it and radiate it. Talking about love glibly will get them nowhere. They need to feel it and act on it. Love is not of the intellect but of the heart. If you want to know how a Gemini feels about love you should not listen to what he or she says, but rather, observe what he or she does. Geminis can be quite generous to those they love.

Geminis like their partners to be refined, well educated and well travelled. If their partners are wealthier than them, that's all the better. If you're in love with a Gemini you had better be a good listener as well.

The ideal relationship for the Gemini is a relationship of the mind. They enjoy the physical and emotional aspects, of course, but if the intellectual communion is not there they will suffer.

Home and Domestic Life

At home the Gemini can be uncharacteristically neat and meticulous. They tend to want their children and partner to live up to their idealistic standards. When these standards are not met they moan and criticize. However, Geminis are good family people and like to serve their families in practical and useful ways.

The Gemini home is comfortable and pleasant. They like to invite people over and they make great hosts. Geminis are also good at repairs and improvements around the house – all fuelled by their need to stay active and occupied with something they like to do. Geminis have many hobbies and interests that keep them busy when they are home alone.

Geminis understand and get along well with their children, mainly because they are very youthful people themselves. As great communicators, Geminis know how to explain things to children; in this way they gain their children's love and respect. Geminis also encourage children to be creative and talkative, just like they are.

Horoscope for 2019

Major Trends

Very interesting developments are happening this year, Gemini. One of the major headlines is the love and social life. This looks very happy and active. Jupiter will be in your 7th house of love for almost the entire year, until December 3. Romance is definitely in the air for singles. More on this later.

Uranus, your religious and philosophical planet, is making a major move from your 11th house into your 12th house of spirituality this year. Last year he flirted with your 12th house and you got a bit of an inkling of what is to come; this year, on March 7, he will move in properly and will stay for the next seven years. This is going to bring great change to your spiritual life. It's going to bring major changes in spiritual or charitable organizations that you're involved with. More details later.

Your 8th house of regeneration has been powerful for many years, and since last year, as Saturn entered, it has become even more powerful. Thus for some years now many of you have been dealing with death and death issues. In some cases it was literal death. In other cases, only encounters with it. The dark angel has been hovering around you, letting you know that he's around. These trends continue in the year ahead. You can cooperate with this energy in a positive way by getting involved in personal transformation and re-invention. This is a form of death and will satisfy the angel. It is not physical death but a kind of psychological death – we die to our old selves.

Neptune, your career planet, has been in your 10th house of career for many years now, and he remains there for many more. This shows a need – an urge – for a spiritual-type career – something that is idealistic. More on this later.

There is another interesting observation about the year ahead. The upper half of your Horoscope – the day side – contains *all* the long-term planets. This means that the lower side of the Horoscope will never dominate this year. There will be times when it is relatively stronger than usual (and we will discuss this in the monthly reports), but it will never dominate. Thus in general 2019 is a more career-oriented kind of year. Insomnia could be a problem for some people.

Your most important interests in the year ahead will be love and romance (until December 3); sex, life and death issues, personal transformation and reinvention; career; friends, groups and group activities (until March 7); and spirituality (from March 7 onwards).

Your paths of greatest fulfilment this year are finance; love and romance (until December 3); and sex, death and death issues, personal transformation and reinvention.

Health

(Please note that this is an astrological perspective on health and not a medical one. In days of yore there was no difference, both of these perspectives were identical. But now there could be quite a difference. For a medical perspective, please consult your doctor or health practitioner.)

Health should be good this year. There are only two long-term planets – Jupiter and Neptune – in stressful alignment with you, which is a big improvement over previous years. And by the end of the year, as Jupiter moves into Capricorn in December, there will be only one long-term planet stressing you. There is much improvement happening in health and energy. Furthermore, your empty 6th house indicates that you're not that focused on health, which I read as a good sign. You have no need to concentrate on it – health is basically good.

Sure, there will be periods in the year where health is less easy than usual, and we will discuss this in the monthly reports, but these are

Important foot reflexology points for the year ahead

Try to massage all of the foot on a regular basis – the top of the foot as well as the bottom – but pay extra attention to the points highlighted on the chart. When you massage, be aware of 'sore spots' as these need special attention. It's also a good idea to massage the ankles, and especially below them.

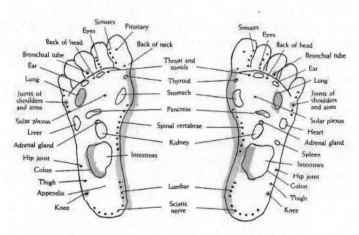

temporary things caused by short-term transits. They are not trends for the year.

You can make your good health even better. Pay attention to the following – the vulnerable areas of your Horoscope (the reflexology points are shown in the chart above):

- The lungs, arms, shoulders and respiratory system. These are always important areas for you, Gemini. Regular arm and shoulder massage should be an integral part of your health regime. Tension tends to collect in the shoulders and needs to be released.
- The colon, bladder and sexual organs are also always important. There are some spiritual healers who say that all disease begins in the colon, so keeping it healthy is a very good idea. Herbal colonics would be good if you feel under the weather. Safe sex and sexual moderation are always important for you.
- The spine, knees, teeth, skin and overall skeletal alignment have become important in recent years, ever since Pluto, your health planet, moved into Capricorn, and this has been reinforced by Saturn (the planet that rules these areas) travelling with Pluto since last year. So regular back and knee massage is good. If you're out in the sun use a good sunscreen. Get regular dental check-ups. Give the knees more support when you exercise.
- The gall bladder, which has only become important in recent years.

Your health planet Pluto rules surgery generically, and has been in your 8th house of surgery for many years now. Not only that, the planet that actually rules surgery in your chart – Saturn – is also there, travelling next to Pluto. So you have probably had some surgery in recent years. There is a strong tendency to it, and it will probably be recommended to you. Sometimes these things are necessary. But it is good to explore detox regimes too – these same planets signal that you respond well to them. In many cases detox will do the same thing, but it will take longer.

Your health planet in the conservative sign of Capricorn shows that in health matters you're conservative. You gravitate to orthodox medicine. And, even if you opt for alternative therapies, you tend to choose old and established therapies – the ones that have stood the test of time.

Saturn and Pluto both rule sex in your Horoscope. (Pluto is the generic ruler; Saturn is your actual ruler.) The presence of both in the sign of Capricorn, your 8th house, suggests a need to reduce extraneous sex – to focus more on quality rather than quantity. Less but of a higher quality is preferable to more of lesser quality. If you stay alert to your body you will know when enough is enough.

Home and Family

Though it is not generally known, home and family are always important to Gemini. They're not really famous for this. They're more famous for their brilliant minds and communication skills. Keep in mind that the ruler of their Horoscope, a very important planet, is also the family planet – the ruler of the 4th house.

Important though home and family are, this year they are less so than usual. The 4th house is not a house of power – love and career are much more of a focus. As our regular readers know, this tends to the status quo. You seem more or less content with things as they are and have no need to make major changes.

But this aspect can also show other things. If family problems arise (God forbid) it's probably due to lack of attention. To correct the issues, you'll have to pay more attention.

A parent or parent figure is likely to move or renovate the existing home in the coming year. There can also be the fortunate sale or purchase of a home. It looks happy. If this parent figure is of childbearing age, she is more fertile than usual. The other parent figure needs to be more careful about alcohol and drugs. The body is more sensitive than usual – it is becoming more spiritualized – and could overreact to these things. One of the parents or parent figures will benefit from spiritual-healing techniques this year, particularly from March 7 onwards. He or she should read as much as possible on this subject.

Children or children figures in your life seem involved in major repairs in the home. A move could happen late in the year – from December 3 onwards. This, though, seems stressful and complicated and there could be many delays.

Siblings and sibling figures are having a quiet, stable kind of year. There's nothing against a move, but nothing especially supporting one either; 2020 seems better for a move than this year. Siblings and sibling figures have many job opportunities all year, and especially after December 3.

Grandchildren (if you have them) can have many moves this year. They seem unsettled – nomadic. This trend will continue for many more years.

If you're planning major repairs or construction work to the home (or of a home), August 13 to October 4 is a good time. If you're redecorating or planning minor repairs, or buying art objects for the home, August 21 to September 14 is a good time.

The family finances seem stable and more or less the way they were last year. The finances of one of the parents or parent figures in your life will start to stabilize this year after being erratic for many years.

Your family planet, Mercury, is a fast-moving and often erratic planet (it is no accident that the word 'mercurial' has this meaning). Sometimes he races through the heavens, sometimes his pace is leisurely. Sometimes he stands still (makes a station) and sometimes he goes backward. This is a good description of your family and emotional life. It is full of twists and turns. Because of this, there are many short-term trends that affect the family life, depending on where Mercury is and the aspects he receives. These trends are best dealt with in the monthly reports.

Finance and Career

The money house is empty this year. This tends to the status quo and I see it as a good thing. There is more or less contentment with things as they are and you have no need to pay too much attention here.

But with two lunar eclipses in the year ahead – one on January 21 and the other on July 16 – there will be financial changes, disruptions and course corrections. It is always a good thing to make periodic course corrections and the eclipses provide that opportunity. The changes will be good, but generally not so pleasant while they're happening.

The lack of power in the money house can indicate lack of attention and focus. Thus, if financial problems arise, they are probably due to this. The solution is to pay more attention to your finances.

Having said all of that, I feel the year ahead will be prosperous. The North Node of the Moon (this is not a planet, but an important abstract point) spends the year in your money house. The North Node denotes excess. So your problem (and it's a good one to have) could be an excess of money – not a lack.

Saturn and Pluto will spend the year in your 8th house. This shows various things. The spouse, partner or current love seems to be having financial difficulties. He or she has taken on (or it was forced on him or her) extra financial burdens. So there is a feeling of lack there. There is a need to rearrange the finances, to shift things around and reorganize them. And, if this is done, he or she will find that all the resources needed are there. His or her financial situation will improve greatly after December 3, as Jupiter moves into the money house.

If you are involved in estates or insurance issues, they seem very complicated, with many delays involved. Tax issues can be burdensome too. Borrowing and accessing outside capital also seems more complicated this year. There are many delays. It's probably best not to borrow money – unless it's an emergency. Accessing outside capital will get much easier after December 3. If you're looking for outside investors for your projects, this will also be easier after December 3.

The Moon is your financial planet and is the fastest-moving of all the planets. Whereas the other fast-moving planets (the Sun, Mercury and Venus) will move through all the houses in your Horoscope in a year, the Moon does this every month. Thus there are many short-term trends in finance that are best dealt with in the monthly reports.

In general we can say that earning power will be strongest on the new and full moons and when the Moon is waxing (growing in strength).

Career has been important for many years now, and remains so this year. Many of the career trends that we've written about in past years are still very much in effect. Neptune, the most spiritual of all the planets, is your career planet and he occupies your 10th house of career. Thus he is in his own sign and house. He is powerful here and this tends to success, but there are complications.

Neptune in the 10th house signals a need for more idealism in the career path. It favours working for charities, spiritual organizations, or organizations involved in altruistic kinds of activities. In many cases this has already happened, but if not it can still happen. You need to feel that your career is 'blessed from on high', that it is 'divinely ordained' and is your real mission in life. Just being successful for the sake of being successful – for ego-gratification purposes – will not satisfy you. You need to feel that you are 'saving the planet' or 'saving the world' – that you are improving conditions for all people.

It also shows that your bosses are like this too. They seem more altruistic and idealistic (or they portray themselves this way).

On a more mundane level, this indicates a lot of hidden things – hidden machinations – going on in the career. There can be some unpleasant revelations here. It would also show a need to do more homework on career matters, for what seems obvious is not the reality.

Love and Social Life

Here we have one of the main headlines of the year ahead. Jupiter, your love planet, moved into your 7th house of love last year on November 9 and will be there for almost the whole year ahead – until December 3. This is a classic signal for love, romance and serious relationship.

But this Jupiter transit is stronger than usual. Jupiter is in his own sign and house where he is most comfortable and powerful. He is basically well aspected. And, as he is also your love planet, social grace and magnetism are unusually powerful right now. For singles this indicates serious romance – a serious kind of relationship. It might not mean a literal marriage (though this is likely) but a relationship that is 'like' a marriage.

After two years of having Saturn in your 7th house of love, when relationships were severely tested and the social life in general was restricted, this is a welcome change. Love is doubly happy these days. You deserve it.

For those who are married, for those whose marriages have survived the past two years, this transit shows more romance in the marriage and more socializing in general. As a couple you're meeting new and significant people. You're attending more weddings and parties. Your social sphere is enlarged.

Singles will also experience some of this. Aside from romance, the general social sphere will be enlarged.

Jupiter moving through the 7th house can also indicate business kinds of partnerships – these too are 'like a marriage'.

Many a marriage dissolved in the past two and a half years, and this year the prospects for a second marriage are excellent. For those of you working on a third marriage, the prospects improve after March 7. But even if marriage doesn't happen you will have a happy social life.

With Jupiter in his own sign and house this year (until December 3), many of your natural love tendencies are greatly magnified. You're attracted to foreign partners, and highly educated and refined kinds of people. You always have a tendency to fall in love with the professor, minister or mentor, and this year even more so. You like people you can learn from.

Religious and philosophical compatibility is even more important than usual. Even if everything else is good, if there are problems here the relationship will be in trouble. You don't need to agree philosophically on every little detail, but you need to be on the same page – to agree the basics.

Love and social opportunities happen in foreign lands, at your place of worship, at religious functions or at educational-type functions (college or university functions). A trip to an exotic place can not only lead to romance, but will enhance an already existing one.

Children and children figures in your life have had unstable love lives for many years. There have probably been divorces. After March 7 their love lives start to stabilize. Siblings or sibling figures are having a good social period until March 7.

Self-improvement

Neptune, the most spiritual of all the planets and your career planet, in his own sign and house is more powerful than usual. This has been the case for many years now and will be so for many more. We have discussed the mundane ramifications of this, but the real message here is 'get right spiritually and your career will fall into place' – it will be something satisfying and harmonious. It might not be easy – it seldom is – but it will give you fulfilment and be something you're capable of doing. The best thing you can do for your career is to get into right alignment with the Divine within you (under whatever name or concept you have). We could say that your spiritual practice, your spiritual path, *is* the real career these days – everything will flow from that.

There are other things – important things – happening in the spiritual life this year. Uranus is making a major move from your 11th house into your spiritual 12th house on March 7. Your spiritual life and spiritual activities are going to become very exciting now – and for many years to come. It will be full of change and experimentation. Spiritual experiences – even peak experiences – can happen suddenly and out of the blue. A lot of your old concepts and attitudes about spirit will get challenged and many will have to be revised or discarded. Spirit itself will show you what is what.

Beginners on the path will be like the *sannyasin* of old – the wandering seeker who travelled from one guru and holy man to another seeking wisdom and enlightenment. I wouldn't take this too literally though. Times are different today. Rarely do people wander the forests in search of gurus. Today, they wander bookshops, workshops and seminars. They join different spiritual groups for short periods of time, searching, searching, searching. There's nothing wrong with this, by the way. It's a natural stage on the path.

For more advanced students it shows taking a more scientific, rational approach to spirituality. There is a science to it. In the years to come it is advisable to explore this. Understanding the science will help you keep stability, regardless of your mood or outer circumstance. Paths such as gnosis, hermetic science, kabbalah, jnana yoga and esoteric astrology (the spiritual side of astrology) will be interesting and helpful. In many cases all the old rules will get thrown out and you will see what works for you through trial and error. It is said that 'every person is their own unique path to the Divine'. And, this is certainly so for you these days.

Uranus is your planet of religion. His position in your 12th house (and for many years to come) shows a need to explore the mystical paths of your own native religion. Every religion has its mystical side. Yours is no exception. In fact, every religion is merely the outgrowth of the mystical experience of its founder. This will be fruitful for you.

There's no need to travel far and wide in search of mystical experience and Higher Knowledge. Just go deeper into what you already have.

Month-by-month Forecasts

January

Best Days Overall: 7, 8, 17, 18, 25, 26
Most Stressful Days Overall: 2, 3, 10, 11, 23, 24, 30, 31
Best Days for Love: 1, 2, 3, 12, 13, 21, 22, 30, 31
Best Days for Money: 2, 3, 5, 6, 12, 13, 16, 19, 20, 21, 22, 25
Best Days for Career: 1, 10, 11, 19, 20, 27, 28

You're just coming off a very strong love and social month. But the social life is still active this month. The planetary power is still very much in the Western, social sector of your chart – the sector of 'others'. Your 7th house of love is still very strong, and the ruler of your Horoscope, Mercury, is there until the 5th. On the 7th Venus will move there and start to travel with your love planet, Jupiter. So love is still very happy. Singles have powerful romantic opportunities (especially from the 21st to the 23rd). Personal independence is weak these days – probably a good thing. Your way is unlikely to be the best way. Besides, it's much more fun to be popular (which you are) than to be alone and self-reliant. Let others have their way as long as it isn't destructive. Self-reliance is a good thing, but not right now. The time for that will come later on. Right now, it's best to adapt to conditions. Make a note of what irks, and in the coming months, when the planetary power shifts, you'll be able to make the appropriate changes.

We have two eclipses this month. The solar eclipse of the 6th (in America it's on the 5th) occurs in your 8th house, and affects the ruler of that house too. This gives many messages. The spouse, partner or current love has some financial disturbance – some shock – and has to make changes. He or she will have more of this to deal with in the year ahead as there are two more eclipses in this house. There can be shocks involving taxes, estates or insurance payments. The 8th house is the house of death, so there is much involvement with this (generally on a psychological level). You must confront death in some way. Sometimes people have dreams of death. There is a need for a deeper understanding of it. Every solar eclipse affects siblings and sibling figures in your life, so they are having personal dramas. Cars and

communication equipment will get tested and often repairs or replacements are needed. The 8th-house connection suggests you should
reduce your schedule around this time, and avoid taking risks.

The lunar eclipse of the 21st also impacts on siblings, sibling figures,
cars and communication equipment. It is almost a replay (but not
quite) of the solar eclipse. Both eclipses affect students below college
level. There can be shake-ups and disturbances at their schools and
changes in educational plans. Every lunar eclipse affects your finances.
This is because the Moon, the eclipsed planet, is your financial planet.
You go through these things twice a year. The eclipse forces you to
make the appropriate financial changes, the course corrections that are
needed. It's usually not pleasant while it's going on, but the end result
will be good. Financial change – generally through a disturbance – is
happening with the money people in your life too. Both eclipses are
showing this.

February

Best Days Overall: 3, 4, 5, 13, 14, 21, 22
Most Stressful Days Overall: 6, 7, 19, 20, 26, 27
Best Days for Love: 9, 10, 11, 17, 18, 19, 20, 26, 27, 28
Best Days for Money: 3, 4, 9, 10, 14, 15, 16, 17, 18, 24, 26, 27
Best Days for Career: 6, 7, 15, 16, 24, 25

All the planets are above the horizon of your chart this month; only the
Moon will occupy the night side (the lower half), and then only from
the 13th to the 25th. This is highly unusual. The planetary powers are
supporting your career and outer goals and here is where you should
be focused. On the 10th, the ruler of your Horoscope, Mercury, moves
into your career house, signalling success and personal elevation. On
the 18th and 19th Mercury travels with Neptune, your career planet,
bringing even more elevation. It also brings a happy career opportunity
to you. Your intuition is right on the money now. On the 19th the Sun
enters the 10th house and you begin a yearly career peak. And so this
should be a very successful month! If you have an issue with your boss
or any government departments or agencies, the 18th and 19th will be
good days to handle it.

Health is good this month, but after the 19th it does need a bit more attention. There is nothing serious afoot, just a period of low energy. Perhaps the demands of the career are draining. As always make sure to get enough rest. Enhance the health in the ways mentioned in the yearly report.

Love is still happy this month – especially until the 19th. Your love planet is receiving very nice aspects. After the 19th you'll have to work harder on it. You and the beloved don't seem in agreement and compromises will be necessary. This is a short-term issue. Overall, for the year ahead, the love life is super.

Finance is not a big issue. The money house is empty this month, with only the Moon moving through there on the 13th and 14th. This tends to the status quo. You probably won't see the financial results of your career success just yet, but it will happen. In general your earning power will be strongest from the 4th to the 19th, as your financial planet waxes (grows). The full Moon of the 19th looks like an especially good financial day: it is a 'super Moon' – a full Moon that occurs when the Moon is her closest distance to Earth. The new Moon of the 4th will also be a strong financial day.

Computer and technology equipment can be erratic from the 11th to the 14th. Keep all your electronic files safe and backed up.

Be more patient with children or children figures in your life on the 17th and 18th – they seem disappointed and pessimistic.

March

Best Days Overall: 3, 4, 13, 14, 21, 22, 30, 31
Most Stressful Days Overall: 5, 6, 7, 19, 20, 25, 26
Best Days for Love: 3, 4, 8, 9, 15, 16, 17, 18, 23, 24, 25, 26
Best Days for Money: 8, 9, 15, 16, 17, 18, 25, 26
Best Days for Career: 5, 6, 7, 15, 16, 23, 24

Career is the main headline this month. Your 10th house of career is chock-full of planets: 40 per cent (and sometimes 50 per cent) of the planets are either there or moving through there. Your 4th house of home and family, by contrast, is empty; only the Moon will move through there on the 21st and 22nd. So home and family issues don't need much attention now. A very successful (and profitable) month ahead, Gemini. Mercury, the ruler of your Horoscope, spends the month in your 10th house, showing personal elevation and success. The new Moon of the 6th is not only in your house of career, but happens right on Neptune, your career planet. This also brings elevation and success to you. It will also clarify career matters as the month progresses. It will bring – naturally and normally – all the information you need to make good career decisions.

But there's more here. Mercury makes a station right on Neptune, your career planet. This means he 'camps out' on this planet. This happens from the 24th to the 31st. So some major development (and it looks positive) is happening here.

The only complication is Mercury's retrograde, from the 5th to the 28th, indicating that there is some uncertainty in the career. Use this period to gain more clarity on matters. Things are not as they seem to be.

Health needs more watching this month – especially until the 20th. You're busy in your career, as you should be, but allow some time for rest and rejuvenation. Trivial things should be dropped. Keep your energy on the things that are important. Enhance the health in the ways mentioned in the yearly report.

Your focus on career, which is right and proper, is complicating the love life. Singles might be dating less. Those of you who are married might not be paying enough attention to the beloved. Perhaps there are subtle resentments about this. This is a short-term problem and will resolve itself next month. The beloved can be having his or her own personal emotional dramas.

The new Moon of the 6th and the full Moon of the 21st (in America this happens on the 20th) are excellent financial days, but you probably will have to work harder for it. The full Moon is especially significant as it is close to being a super Moon – the Moon's perigee (her closest distance to earth) is on the 19th. Earning power will be strongest (and you'll have the most enthusiasm for finance) from the 6th to the 21st, when the Moon is waxing.

April

Best Days Overall: 9, 10, 17, 18, 26, 27
Most Stressful Days Overall: 1, 2, 3, 15, 16, 22, 23, 29, 30
Best Days for Love: 2, 3, 4, 5, 11, 12, 13, 14, 21, 22, 23
Best Days for Money: 4, 5, 11, 12, 13, 14, 22, 23, 24
Best Days for Career: 1, 2, 3, 11, 12, 19, 20, 29, 30

Some interesting developments happen this month. On March 26, as Venus moved into your 10th house, the planetary power shifted from the Western, social sector to the Eastern sector of your chart – the sector of self. This month, Mars enters your sign and stays there for the whole month. So personal independence and self-reliance are getting much stronger now. Other people are always important, but you're less dependent on them. Your personal initiative is the way things get done. Personal independence will get even stronger in the coming months, but it is strong enough now to make the changes in your life that need to be made. No need to adapt yourself to irksome conditions. If they trouble you, change them.

There are other improvements happening too. Short-term career goals are more or less achieved by now, and you have more time for the social life – especially friendships. Love and romance are much better than last month, especially after the 17th. The spouse, partner or current love is also feeling much better and this makes a big difference. Your love planet, Jupiter, will start to go into reverse on the 10th. This doesn't stop love from happening but slows things down a bit. Singles are more cautious now in love, which can be a good thing. Your tendency has been to jump into relationships much too quickly.

As far as friends are concerned, there's nothing much you need to do. They seek you out. You just have to go about your daily business.

Health is vastly improved over last month. Most of the planets are in harmonious alignment with you. Mars in your sign gives energy, courage and an ability to get things done quickly. You're more fearless these days. With Mars in your sign, as our regular readers know, there is a tendency to belligerence. Anger can flare too quickly and conflicts can happen as a result. So, be strong, brave and active, but tone down the anger.

Finances are not a big deal this month. The money house is basically empty, with only the Moon moving through there on the 11th and 12th. The new Moon of 5th and the full Moon of 19th are good financial days. Earning power tends to be strongest from the 5th to the 19th as the Moon, your financial planet, grows and waxes. This gives more enthusiasm for finance.

On the 20th the Sun enters your spiritual 12th house and travels with Uranus for a time (from the 21st to the 23rd). This brings happy social experiences for siblings and sibling figures. They can be a wilful (and often unwitting) source of spiritual information. They can spark your intuition.

May

Best Days Overall: 6, 7, 15, 16, 24, 25
Most Stressful Days Overall: 13, 14, 19, 20, 26, 27
Best Days for Love: 2, 3, 10, 11, 14, 19, 20, 21, 29, 30, 31
Best Days for Money: 2, 3, 4, 5, 8, 9, 10, 11, 13, 14, 19, 20, 24, 29, 30
Best Days for Career: 8, 9, 17, 18, 26, 27

Mars went 'out of bounds' (this doesn't happen very often) on April 21, and will be 'out of bounds' for the entire month ahead. This has a few interpretations. You're meeting friends from outside your normal social circle – outside your normal haunts. These people can be pulling you out of your normal sphere too. You're exploring technologies that are outside your norm. Parents or parent figures are going outside their normal spheres in the search for profits and earnings. You could be experimenting with your body in unusual kinds of ways.

You're entering your period of maximum personal independence this month, which will last into next month too. So keep in mind our discussion of this in April. This is a time for taking responsibility for your own happiness. It's up to you. There's no one else to blame: if conditions irk you, change them. You have the power now to do so. The planetary power is supporting you – the cosmos cares about your personal welfare. Your self-interest is as important as any other's – and this month it is more important (at least to you).

The month ahead is happy and prosperous. On the 21st, two of the three most important planets in your chart – the Sun and Mercury – enter your 1st house and you begin one of your yearly personal pleasure peaks. The body gets indulged now. You look great and have star quality. Self-confidence and self-esteem are strong. You can do anything you set your mind to.

Mars is still in your sign and remains there until the 16th. So use his energy positively. Get things done. Exercise more (which you are probably doing anyway). Experiment with the limits of your body in mindful ways. Avoid temper tantrums, haste and irritation. Make haste but in a mindful kind of way. On the 16th Mars moves into your money house and stays there for the rest of the month. This would favour the high tech and online worlds. Whatever you're doing, good use of technology and online activities boost finances. Friends seem helpful financially too. The only problem here is that Mars in your 2nd house can make you too speculative – too reckless – in money matters. You could be too quick to jump into investments or to spend money. Sleep on things more. It might be 'boring' but it's safer. In general, earning power should be strongest from the 4th to the 18th as the Moon waxes. The new Moon of the 4th and the full Moon of the 18th should be strong financial days. The Moon's perigee on the 13th is also good.

Health is excellent all month, but especially from the 21st onwards.

June

Best Days Overall: 2, 3, 11, 12, 20, 21, 30
Most Stressful Days Overall: 9, 10, 15, 16, 23, 24
Best Days for Love: 1, 7, 8, 11, 15, 16, 20, 21, 25, 26
Best Days for Money: 2, 3, 5, 6, 7, 8, 11, 12, 15, 16, 22, 25, 26
Best Days for Career: 5, 6, 18, 19, 23, 24

Another happy and profitable month ahead. Enjoy.

You remain in one of your yearly personal pleasure peaks until the 21st, and you're still in a period of maximum independence for the year. Personal appearance shines (a little known fact is that when there is more energy, the personal appearance improves). The Sun illuminates your body until the 21st. On the 9th Venus enters your sign and sheds her grace and beauty on you. One would think that this would foster love, but this year, not so much. All these planets are opposing your love planet, Jupiter. You and the beloved are seeing things in opposite ways. You seem more distant. He or she is doing their thing; you're doing yours. The challenge will be to bridge your differences. If this can be done the relationship can be stronger than ever. In astrology, it is your opposite who is the natural marriage partner. One's opposite is considered the 'complement' – the completion. The partner is strong where you are weak and you are strong where he or she is weak. This was the challenge last month too. The spouse, partner or current love should rest and relax more these days. Energy is not what it should be.

Career is a bit more stressful this month. You just have to work harder. Perhaps all the fun you're having is distracting you. You need to work harder on your relationship with a parent or parent figure (and perhaps your boss). This is a short-term problem and passes after the 21st.

In general, the career is becoming less important this month. On the 9th, as Venus crosses from the upper half to the lower half of your Horoscope, the lower, night side of your chart becomes powerful. It's time to focus on the home, family and your emotional wellness. Besides, your career planet, Neptune, starts to retrograde on the 21st, so things are slowing down there. Many career issues will only be resolved by time – not so much by your direct action.

Prosperity is ultra-strong this month. On the 21st you begin a yearly financial peak, but you will be feeling this even before that date. Mars is in your money house all month, and on the 4th, Mercury, the ruler of your Horoscope, moves in too. So earnings will be strong. You're personally more focused. You're spending on yourself. Sales and marketing projects (and writing projects in general) go well. And, like last month, the online world seems kind to you.

Health is excellent. You can always enhance it further in the ways mentioned in the yearly report.

July

Best Days Overall: 1, 8, 9, 17, 18, 19, 27, 28
Most Stressful Days Overall: 6, 7, 13, 14, 20, 21
Best Days for Love: 1, 4, 5, 10, 11, 13, 14, 20, 21, 22, 23, 24, 31
Best Days for Money: 2, 3, 4, 5, 10, 11, 13, 14, 21, 22, 23, 24, 29, 30, 31
Best Days for Career: 2, 3, 10, 11, 20, 21, 29, 30

Two eclipses in the coming month will test how well you've used your power of free will and independence. It is OK to veer a few degrees from your orbit. But if you veer too far off, along comes an eclipse and brings you back in line. If you are in line with what the cosmos wants you to do there is little to fear from an eclipse. It will shake things up and actually help you in so doing.

The solar eclipse of the 2nd occurs in your money house. Your financial thinking and strategy are amiss and need to be changed. The events of the eclipse will show you what's wrong. This eclipse brings dramas in the lives of siblings and sibling figures. It impacts on students, shaking up their schools and educational plans. Often there is a change of schools. Cars and communication equipment will get tested. Sometimes there is need for repair or replacement.

The lunar eclipse of the 16th occurs in your 8th house – the second eclipse of the year in this house. This causes more financial change both for you and your spouse, partner or current love. Your health and work planet, Pluto, is affected by this eclipse, so there might be job changes or disruptions at work. If you hire others there could be some employee turnover now. Sometimes there is a health scare and a need to change the health regime. Again, as in January, there are confrontations with death – usually on the psychological level. There is a need to understand this better.

Yes, there will be financial changes – dramatic ones – but the month ahead is prosperous. You're still in the midst of a yearly financial peak until the 23rd. Venus enters your money house on the 3rd and stays there until the 28th. This shows the importance of social connections and children to finances. They seem supportive.

Health is good this month – not perfect, but good. Thus the lunar eclipse of the 16th can produce a scare but not much more. You can enhance the health further in the ways mentioned in the yearly report.

Retrograde activity hits its maximum for the year after the 7th. Half the planets are travelling in reverse. Things are slowing down in the world. You can minimize delays and glitches (you won't avoid them altogether) by being more perfect in all that you do. The slow, steady way is really the fast way.

August

Best Days Overall: 4, 5, 14, 15, 23, 24, 25
Most Stressful Days Overall: 2, 3, 9, 10, 16, 17, 30, 31
Best Days for Love: 1, 9, 10, 19, 20, 21, 28, 29, 30, 31
Best Days for Money: 1, 9, 10, 19, 20, 26, 27, 28, 29, 30
Best Days for Career: 7, 8, 16, 17, 26, 27

The action and focus this month happens in your 3rd and 4th houses – those of communication, the home and family. Until the 23rd, the 3rd house is easily the most powerful in your Horoscope. This is happy. The 3rd house is your favourite, Gemini, all about communication and intellectual interests. Your naturally strong skills get even better and sharper. You absorb information like a sponge. And, you're able to communicate better than usual. It is a wonderful aspect for students, teachers, writers, bloggers, sales and marketing people. These people (and many Geminis are involved in these things) should have a very successful month. The money people in your life grow even richer.

Finances are good this month. Mercury, the ruler of your Horoscope (and always friendly to you), is in the money house until the 11th. This indicates focus, and focus is 90 per cent of success. We get what we focus on in life. After the 11th, the money house is basically empty. Only the Moon moves through there on the 26th and 27th. I read this as a good thing. Short-term financial goals have been achieved and you can focus on your first love – communication and intellectual interests.

There are other indicators that show prosperity too. First off, there are two new Moons this month – one on the 1st and the other on the 30th. This is a rare occurrence. The new Moon tends to be a powerful financial day for you. The first new Moon is especially significant as it is a 'super new Moon' – it occurs almost exactly when the Moon is in perigee and closest to the Earth. She is much more powerful than usual. The full Moon of the 15th will be another good financial day. In general, earning power will be strongest from the 1st to the 15th and on the 30th and 31st – as the Moon waxes.

Love is happy early in the month. Your love planet, Jupiter, starts moving forward on the 11th. Mercury moves into Leo on the 11th and starts to make nice aspects to your love planet. Those of you already in relationships have more harmony with the beloved. Singles have nice romantic opportunities. The 20th to the 22nd is especially good for romance. Later on in the month (from the 23rd onwards), as short-term planets move into stressful aspect with Jupiter, you will have to work harder on your relationship. It doesn't stop love, but there is more effort involved.

The short-term planets are now at their maximum night position (and will remain so next month too). Your career planet, Neptune, is still retrograde. So, focus on the home, family and your emotional wellness for now. Career goals are better pursued by the methods of night, rather than the methods of day – visualize, dream and put yourself in the 'feeling' of where you want to be.

September

Best Days Overall: 1, 2, 10, 11, 20, 21, 28, 29
Most Stressful Days Overall: 5, 6, 12, 13, 14, 26, 27
Best Days for Love: 5, 6, 8, 9, 15, 16, 20, 24, 25, 28, 29
Best Days for Money: 5, 6, 7, 8, 15, 16, 18, 19, 22, 23, 24, 25, 28
Best Days for Career: 3, 4, 12, 13, 14, 22, 23, 30

Health became more delicate last month, from the 23rd, and this is the situation until the 23rd of this month. So, as always, rest and relax more. Try to include more massages or other health treatments in your schedule. Enhance the health in the ways mentioned in the yearly report. You will see dramatic improvement after the 23rd.

The love life will also improve after that date. It's OK before then, but seems more stormy than usual. It needs more effort. Mercury and

Venus are travelling together for much of this month. This shows that you have much social grace and magnetism. Personal appearance is much improved and you seem more in the mood for love.

Your 4th house of home and family was very powerful last month, and is still powerful until the 23rd. Family passions seem to run high. A lot of this has to do with old baggage – old events that were never fully resolved. This complicates communication with family members.

If you're planning renovations or repairs to the home, this is a good time to do it.

When the 4th house is strong, people become more nostalgic. They remember the 'good old days' and the 'bad old days'. There is a stronger interest in history in general – personal and collective. You tend to meet people from your past and reconnect for a time. There will be dreams of past experiences that happen spontaneously. This is not random or haphazard. This is nature's therapeutic system, urging you to review past events from your present state of consciousness and understanding. You don't rewrite history – the facts are still the facts – but you will interpret the events in another way. They will have a different meaning now than they did when they happened.

Once your quota of the past is redeemed, you begin one of your yearly personal pleasure peaks. This begins on the 23rd. This is a time for recreation and leisure. A time to enjoy your life. It is interesting that the word 'recreation' comes from 're-creation'. You re-create your life on better terms through fun kinds of activities. Many seemingly insoluble problems get sorted out in this way.

Finances are not a big issue these days. The money house is basically empty. Only the Moon moves through there on the 22nd and 23rd. However, the new Moon of the 28th is another 'super new Moon', occurring with the Moon at her perigee. This is a powerful financial day. The full Moon of 14th is another good financial day. In general earning power is strongest from the 1st to the 14th and from the 28th to the 30th – as the Moon waxes and grows.

October

Best Days Overall: 7, 8, 17, 18, 26, 27
Most Stressful Days Overall: 2, 3, 4, 10, 11, 23, 24, 30, 31
Best Days for Love: 2, 3, 4, 10, 11, 12, 13, 19, 20, 21, 22, 28, 29, 30, 31
Best Days for Money: 2, 3, 4, 7, 8, 12, 13, 17, 18, 19, 20, 21, 22, 28, 30, 31
Best Days for Career: 1, 10, 11, 19, 20, 28, 29

You're still in the midst of a strong party month, perhaps even stronger than last month. You need not worry about being 'irresponsible', however; the time for work will come later on. In the philosophy of astrology, the 5th house of fun, creativity and children is just as important as the 2nd house (finance) or the 10th house (career). It is part of life. Things wouldn't be complete without it. Enjoying your life will bring many side benefits. It makes you more popular socially. It will enhance your spirituality. You'll feel better and have better family relationships. And, it will enhance your intellectual abilities. Perhaps the most important benefit is that when we are enjoying ourselves we are temporarily free of 'worry'. Worry (which everyone seems to indulge in) will not take you into hell, but it will take you to its gates. Dropping worry, in and of itself, is the solution to many problems.

Health is good this month. There is a lot of the element of Air in the Horoscope early in the month and this is comfortable for you. You do need to be careful about an over-stimulated mind – it can go round and round and round achieving nothing. Good to turn it off when not in use. You can enhance your already good health in the ways mentioned in the yearly report.

Little by little the party winds down. On the 3rd Mercury enters your 6th house. On the 8th Venus enters and on the 23rd so does the Sun. It is time to get down to work. No one will need to urge you: you feel it on your own. Your health and work planet, Pluto, will start moving forward on the 3rd and your 6th house of work becomes ultra-powerful from the 23rd onwards. Jobseekers have good fortune now. And even if you're already employed, you will have opportunities for overtime or a second job. One job doesn't seem enough for you these days.

Love is happy. Jupiter, your love planet, is moving forward and receiving nice aspects. The Moon will spend more than twice as long as usual moving through your 7th house this month – she will spend five days in Sagittarius. (And these are also good days financially.) Love is good this month, and will get even better in November.

The planetary power is now in the Western, social sector of your chart. This began last month and is even stronger now. Personal independence is much weaker, but the cosmos compensates you with increased popularity and social grace. It is time to put others first and take a vacation from personal desires. If conditions irk you, adapt to them as best you can. The time to change them will come next year, when the planets move through your Eastern sector once more.

November

Best Days Overall: 3, 4, 13, 14, 22, 23
Most Stressful Days Overall: 6, 7, 20, 21, 26, 27
Best Days for Love: 8, 9, 10, 18, 19, 26, 27, 29
Best Days for Money: 6, 7, 8, 9, 10, 16, 17, 18, 19, 26, 27
Best Days for Career: 6, 7, 16, 17, 24, 25

Jobseekers still have nice opportunities this month, but job offers (or new employees) need to be checked carefully. Things are not as they seem. Get all the details and resolve your doubts. It is still a great month to do those boring, detail-oriented jobs that need to be done. You're more in the mood for them and they will go more smoothly.

Mercury is retrograde from the 2nd to the 20th. Thus self-esteem and confidence are not up to their usual standards. In a way this is a good thing. It isn't necessary for you to be overly strong or confident. With the Western, social sector of your chart getting stronger and stronger it is good to downplay the self. You can let others have their way, so long as it isn't destructive. Your social grace is what counts now. Good comes to you through others.

The love life has been good all year. Many of you are already in serious, committed relationships. And, this month it gets even better. If you're still unattached, this is a good period to change things. Jupiter has been in your 7th house all year. Venus is there until the 26th. On the 22nd, the Sun moves in and you begin a yearly love and social peak. Venus will travel with Jupiter from the 22nd to the 24th – particularly good days for romance. Love is romantic these days, but also playful. You are attracted to people you can have fun with.

Venus goes 'out of bounds' from the 15th to the 30th, indicated that in your spiritual life you're exploring exotic kinds of teachings. The answers you seek are not to be found in the usual places and you're forced to look elsewhere. This would also show that children and children figures in your life are also moving outside their usual haunts.

Health needs more attention from the 23rd onwards. The good news is that your 6th house of health is strong and you are paying attention here. Enhance the health in the ways mentioned in the yearly report, but this month also give attention to the head, face and scalp (from the 19th onwards), the heart (all month), and the adrenals (from the 19th onwards). Physical exercise seems helpful after the 19th too.

Finance doesn't seem a major issue this month. The money house is empty. Only the Moon moves through there on the 16th and 17th. The new Moon of the 26th and the full Moon of the 12th are strong financial days. Earning power should be stronger from the 1st to the 12th and from the 26th to the 30th, as the Moon waxes in strength.

December

Best Days Overall: 1, 2, 11, 12, 19, 20, 28, 29
Most Stressful Days Overall: 3, 4, 5, 17, 18, 24, 25, 31
Best Days for Love: 8, 9, 17, 18, 24, 25, 26, 28, 29
Best Days for Money: 6, 7, 8, 13, 14, 15, 16, 17, 26
Best Days for Career: 3, 4, 5, 13, 14, 21, 22, 31

Jupiter has done his job in your love life and he can now move on to bless other areas of your life – he moves into Capricorn, your 8th house, on the 3rd. Nevertheless, you're still in the midst of a yearly love and social peak this month (and for some of you it is a lifetime love and social peak).

Jupiter's move into conservative Capricorn signals important changes in your love attitudes. Up until now it's been passion and fun. It's been spontaneous. Now love is more practical. For those of you already in relationships, the honeymoon period is about over with and you enter the more practical side of love: arranging the relationship in practical ways, dividing up responsibilities, etc. For singles (if there are any of you still out there) it shows more caution in love. You're not apt to fall in love at first sight, as you were liable to do before. This is probably a good thing.

Love is going well, and Jupiter in your 8th house is showing an active sex life. No more need be said.

We have a solar eclipse on the 26th – the third one of the year, and the third eclipse of the year in the 8th house. The spouse, partner or current love is prospering now, but needs to make important financial changes. The strategy and thinking are not realistic. Since this eclipse impacts on Jupiter, he or she should take things easy over this period, and avoid travel then. Students are again affected by the eclipse. There can be more disturbances or shake-ups at schools, changes of educational plans, changes in subjects or courses. Siblings, sibling figures and neighbours are also affected. There can be personal dramas going on. There could be disruptions in the neighbourhood. Cars and communication equipment get tested for the third time this year. And, once again, you have confrontations with death. There is still a need for deeper understanding here. When we understand death, we understand life better. This is the whole point.

Health and energy will improve after the 22nd. Physical exercise is still advisable this month. Face and scalp massage will also be good.

Finance, as has been the case for many months now, is not a big issue. The finances of the spouse, partner or current love seem more important to you than your own. The full Moon of the 12th and the Moon's perigee on the 18th are good financial days. Also, earnings will be stronger (you have more enthusiasm and zeal for finance) from the 1st to the 12th and from the 26th onwards, as the Moon waxes.

Cancer

THE CRAB

Birthdays from
21st June to
20th July

Personality Profile

CANCER AT A GLANCE

Element – Water

Ruling Planet – Moon
   Career Planet – Mars
   Love Planet – Saturn
   Money Planet – Sun
   Planet of Fun and Games – Pluto
   Planet of Good Fortune – Neptune
   Planet of Health and Work – Jupiter
   Planet of Home and Family Life – Venus
   Planet of Spirituality – Mercury

Colours – blue, puce, silver

Colours that promote love, romance and social harmony – black, indigo

Colours that promote earning power – gold, orange

Gems – moonstone, pearl

Metal – silver

Scents – jasmine, sandalwood

Quality – cardinal (= activity)

Quality most needed for balance – mood control

Strongest virtues – emotional sensitivity, tenacity, the urge to nurture

Deepest need – a harmonious home and family life

Characteristics to avoid – over-sensitivity, negative moods

Signs of greatest overall compatibility – Scorpio, Pisces

Signs of greatest overall incompatibility – Aries, Libra, Capricorn

Sign most helpful to career – Aries

Sign most helpful for emotional support – Libra

Sign most helpful financially – Leo

Sign best for marriage and/or partnerships – Capricorn

Sign most helpful for creative projects – Scorpio

Best Sign to have fun with – Scorpio

Signs most helpful in spiritual matters – Gemini, Pisces

Best day of the week – Monday

Understanding a Cancer

In the sign of Cancer the heavens are developing the feeling side of things. This is what a true Cancerian is all about – feelings. Where Aries will tend to err on the side of action, Taurus on the side of inaction and Gemini on the side of thought, Cancer will tend to err on the side of feeling.

Cancerians tend to mistrust logic. Perhaps rightfully so. For them it is not enough for an argument or a project to be logical – it must feel right as well. If it does not feel right a Cancerian will reject it or chafe against it. The phrase 'follow your heart' could have been coined by a Cancerian, because it describes exactly the Cancerian attitude to life.

The power to feel is a more direct – more immediate – method of knowing than thinking is. Thinking is indirect. Thinking about a thing never touches the thing itself. Feeling is a faculty that touches directly the thing or issue in question. We actually experience it. Emotional feeling is almost like another sense which humans possess – a psychic sense. Since the realities we come in contact with during our lifetime are often painful and even destructive, it is not surprising that the Cancerian chooses to erect barriers – a shell – to protect his or her vulnerable, sensitive nature. To a Cancerian this is only common sense.

If Cancerians are in the presence of people they do not know, or find themselves in a hostile environment, up goes the shell and they feel protected. Other people often complain about this, but one must question these people's motives. Why does this shell disturb them? Is it perhaps because they would like to sting, and feel frustrated that they cannot? If your intentions are honourable and you are patient, have no fear. The shell will open up and you will be accepted as part of the Cancerian's circle of family and friends.

Thought-processes are generally analytic and dissociating. In order to think clearly we must make distinctions, comparisons and the like. But feeling is unifying and integrative.

To think clearly about something you have to distance yourself from it. To feel something you must get close to it. Once a Cancerian has accepted you as a friend he or she will hang on to you. You have to be really bad to lose their friendship. If you're related to Cancerians they'll never let you go no matter what you do, always trying to maintain some kind of connection even in the most extreme circumstances.

Finance

The Cancer-born has a deep sense of what other people feel about things and why they feel as they do. This faculty is a great asset in the workplace and in the business world. Of course it is also indispensable in raising a family and building a home, but it has its uses in business. Cancerians often attain great wealth in a family business. Even if the business is not a family operation, they will treat it as one. If the Cancerian works for somebody else, then the boss is the parental figure and the co-workers are brothers and sisters. If a Cancerian is the boss, then all the workers are his or her children. Cancerians like the feeling of being providers for others. They enjoy knowing that others derive their sustenance because of what they do. It is another form of nurturing.

With Leo on their solar 2nd money house cusp, Cancerians are often lucky speculators, especially with residential property or hotels and restaurants. Resort hotels and nightclubs are also profitable for the Cancerian. Waterside properties attract them. Though they are basically conventional people, they sometimes like to earn their livelihood in glamorous ways.

The Sun, Cancer's money planet, represents an important financial message: in financial matters Cancerians need to be less moody, more stable and fixed. They cannot allow their moods – which are here today and gone tomorrow – to get in the way of their business lives. They need to develop their self-esteem and feelings of self-worth if they are to realize their greatest financial potential.

Career and Public Image

Aries rules the 10th solar career house cusp of Cancer, which indicates that Cancerians long to start their own business, to be more active publicly and politically and to be more independent. Family responsibilities and a fear of hurting other people's feelings – or getting hurt themselves – often inhibit them from attaining these goals. However, this is what they want and long to do.

Cancerians like their bosses and leaders to act freely and to be a bit self-willed. They can deal with that in a superior. They expect their leaders to be fierce on their behalf. When the Cancerian is in the position of boss or superior he or she behaves very much like a 'warlord'. Of course the wars they wage are not egocentric but in defence of those under their care. If they lack some of this fighting instinct – independence and pioneering spirit – Cancerians will have extreme difficulty in attaining their highest career goals. They will be hampered in their attempts to lead others.

Since they are so parental, Cancerians like to work with children and make great educators and teachers.

Love and Relationships

Like Taurus, Cancer likes committed relationships, functioning best when the relationship is clearly defined and everyone knows their role. When they marry it is usually for life. They are extremely loyal to their beloved. But there's a deep little secret that most Cancerians will never admit to: commitment or partnership is really a chore and a duty to them. They enter into it because they know of no other way to create the family that they desire. Union is just a way – a means to an end – rather than an end in itself. The family is the ultimate end for them.

If you are in love with a Cancerian you must tread lightly on his or her feelings. It will take you a good deal of time to realize how deep and sensitive Cancerians can be. The smallest negativity upsets them. Your tone of voice, your irritation, a look in your eye or an expression on your face can cause great distress for the Cancerian. Your slightest gesture is registered by them and reacted to. This can be hard to get used to, but stick by your love – Cancerians make great partners once you learn how to deal with them. Your Cancerian lover will react not so much to what you say but to the way you are actually feeling at the moment.

Home and Domestic Life

This is where Cancerians really excel. The home environment and the family are their personal works of art. They strive to make things of beauty that will outlast them. Very often they succeed.

Cancerians feel very close to their family, their relatives and especially their mothers. These bonds last throughout their lives and mature as they grow older. They are very fond of those members of their family who become successful, and they are also quite attached to family heirlooms and mementos. Cancerians also love children and like to provide them with all the things they need and want. With their nurturing, feeling nature, Cancerians make very good parents – especially the Cancerian woman, who is the mother *par excellence* of the zodiac.

As a parent the Cancerian's attitude is 'my children right or wrong'. Unconditional devotion is the order of the day. No matter what a family member does, the Cancerian will eventually forgive him or her, because 'you are, after all, family'. The preservation of the institution – the tradition – of the family is one of the Cancerian's main reasons for living. They have many lessons to teach others about this.

Being so family-orientated, the Cancerian's home is always clean, orderly and comfortable. They like old-fashioned furnishings but they also like to have all the modern comforts. Cancerians love to have family and friends over, to organize parties and to entertain at home – they make great hosts.

Horoscope for 2019

Major Trends

A challenging year ahead, Cancer, but you've been through even more challenging times; 2016 was arguably more challenging than the coming year. You got through that, and you will get through the year ahead. It's important to understand that the universe never gives us more than we can handle. If challenges are given it means that you can handle them. The challenge itself is the measure of your abilities. Also understand that challenges – difficulties – are not bad. They're perhaps not pleasant, but they bring growth and strength.

There is good news here too this year. Things will get easier after March 7, as Uranus leaves his stressful aspect with you.

Health needs more watching this year and we will discuss this later.

The love life is very challenging this year. Complicated. Serious relationships will get tested. Singles are not likely to marry. Things will improve in this department, however, after December 3 when benevolent Jupiter moves into your 7th house of love.

Jupiter spends most of the year in your 6th house. Thus you are a hot item in the job market. Happy opportunities are coming your way.

Usually we get two solar eclipses in a year, but this year we will have three. This signals that there is more financial change and disruption than usual. You will need to make more course corrections than usual.

Uranus has been in your 10th house for the past seven years, causing great instability in the career and producing many career changes. On March 7 he leaves this house and moves into the 11th. The career should thus become more stable, with fewer shocks and surprises.

Neptune has been in your 9th house for some years now and he will be there for many more to come. Thus your religious, theological and philosophical beliefs are becoming 'spiritualized' – more refined. You are approaching religion in a whole different way.

Your most important interests this year are health and work (until December 3); love and romance; religion, theology, higher education and foreign travel; career (until March 7); and friends, groups and group activities (from March 7 onwards).

Your paths of greatest fulfilment this year will be health and work (until December 3); love and romance (from December 3 onwards); and the body and image.

Health

(Please note that this is an astrological perspective on health and not a medical one. In days of yore there was no difference, both of these perspectives were identical. But now there could be quite a difference. For a medical perspective, please consult your doctor or health practitioner.)

Health, as we mentioned, needs watching this year. Three powerful planets are in stressful aspect with you at the start of the year; after March 7 there will be two. But these two – Saturn and Pluto – are powerful planets – not powers to be trifled with.

The good news here is that your 6th house of health is strong and this indicates focus. You're on the case. You're taking care of things. You're open to healthy lifestyles and regimes. It would be much more dangerous if the 6th house was empty. That would show lack of attention.

Stressful aspects don't mean sickness per se. It only means greater vulnerability. More work and effort is needed to maintain good health. If you put in the work - and it seems that you will - you should avoid most problems.

As always, the first line of defence is high energy levels. Make sure to get enough rest. Keep your focus on the essentials in your life and let go of trivialities and side issues. Take a business-like approach to your energy. Invest it for greatest return and don't fritter it away.

There is more good news. Health can be enhanced by giving more attention to the following areas - the vulnerable areas in the Horoscope (reflexology points are shown in the chart above):

- The heart has been important for some years now and is even more important in the year ahead. The important thing with the heart is to avoid worry and anxiety - the two emotions that stress it out. Cultivate faith. (Worry can be defined as lack of faith.)

Important foot reflexology points for the year ahead

Try to massage all of the foot on a regular basis - the top of the foot as well as the bottom - but pay extra attention to the points highlighted on the chart. When you massage, be aware of 'sore spots' as these need special attention. It's also a good idea to massage the ankles and below them.

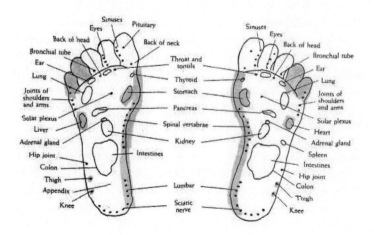

- The stomach and breasts are always important for you, Cancer, as is diet. *What* you eat is important, but *how* you eat is perhaps just as important. Do your best to elevate the act of eating – to elevate it in vibration. Make it an act of worship. Express thanks for the food. Bless it. Both the food and your digestive system will respond.
- The liver and thighs are two other important areas for the Cancerian. Regular thigh massage should be part of your normal health regime, and a herbal liver cleanse every now and then – especially when you feel under the weather – might be a good idea.
- The spine, knees, teeth, skin and overall skeletal alignment will become important later on in the year – after December 3. Your health planet, Jupiter, will move into Capricorn which rules these areas. Regular back and knee massage will be good (the lower back will be strengthened by thigh massage, as well as liver). Good dental hygiene becomes more important than usual. Therapies such as Alexander Technique, Rolfing and Feldenkrais will be beneficial, and yoga and Pilates are also good for the spine.

When overall energy is lowered – because of planetary stress – pre-existing conditions often flare up and seem to get worse. The body lacks the energy to control them. So, as we mentioned, make sure to get enough rest.

Jupiter, your health planet, spends almost all year in a Fire sign. Thus you have a good connection to the healing powers of the Fire element. Plain old sunshine is a healing tonic. If you feel under the weather, get out in the Sun and absorb the rays. Heat-oriented therapies are powerful this year – things like saunas, steam rooms and hot baths (as hot as you can take them). The hotter climates are better healthwise than the colder ones.

It is one thing to have a few long-term planets arrayed against you, but if they are joined by the short-term planets, the stress is greatly magnified. Those periods require more rest and more attention to health than usual. This year these vulnerable periods are: January 1 to January 20; March 20 to April 19; and September 23 to October 22. We will discuss this more fully in the monthly reports.

Home and Family

Home and family are always important to the Cancerian. That's what life is all about – creating, nurturing and protecting the family. This is still the case this year (and will always be), but to a lesser extent than usual. Even the strongest interests have their rhythms. They wax and wane like the Moon, your planetary ruler. This year, with your 4th house of home and family basically empty (only short-term planets will move through there), you're in a waning home and family phase. The marriage, love life, friendships seem far more important these days.

The empty 4th house can be read as a good thing. It often indicates contentment with the status quo. You have no need to make dramatic changes. You can, if you like, but there's no pressing need. It tends towards stability. However, if family problems do arise, lack of attention can be the cause and you'll have to start paying more attention here.

Venus, a fast-moving planet, is your family planet. During the year she moves through all the signs and houses of your chart, and in fact this year she will move through some signs twice – she is moving faster than usual this year. Thus there are many short-term family trends depending on where Venus is and the aspects she receives. These are best dealt with in the monthly reports.

With Venus as your family planet, the home tends to be a social centre as well as a home. You tend to entertain a lot from your home and with family. Venus is not only your family planet, but also the ruler of your 11th house of friends; thus there is a tendency to consider friends as part of the family and to treat them that way.

If you're planning major renovations or repairs (or planning to build a house) October 4 to November 19 is a good time. If you're planning cosmetic kinds of decoration – painting the house or buying art objects for the home – September 14 to October 23 will be a good time.

A parent or parent figure in your life can move later in the year. (It can also happen next year.) He or she will be very prosperous in 2020. The other parent or parent figure will enjoy good career success after December 3. He or she has been restless for some years now and seems to be settling down. The marriage of the parents or parent figures – if it survived the past seven years – will become more stable.

Siblings or sibling figures in your life are likely to move this year. They also have good fortune in the purchase or sale of a home. If siblings or sibling figures are of childbearing age, they will be more fertile than usual.

Children and children figures are prospering this year. A move is more likely after December 3 (or next year) than earlier in the year.

Finance and Career

Though this is not well known, Cancer tends to wealth. Some of the richest people have been Cancerians (John D. Rockefeller, the first billionaire, comes to mind but there are many others). This is because the financial planet, the Sun, occupies your sign at birth. Cancerians have excellent financial skills and instincts. So this area is always important to you, but this year less so than normal – your money house is basically empty.

Generally the empty money house is a sign of contentment. There's no need to make financial changes. The tendency is to the status quo. But this year could be different. As was mentioned, three solar eclipses this year will shake up the financial life and produce dramatic changes. In addition there will a lunar eclipse on January 21 that occurs in your money house, and also affects finance. The financial life is subject to four eclipses this year. This is twice as many as usual.

In a way this is good (but not necessarily pleasant). The financial landscape is a constantly shifting and changing thing. Hot companies can cool down very quickly. Booming industries can go bust rather quickly. Technology, government regulations and the like can change things. Strategies that were good under one set of circumstances are not good under a different set. So, having periodic course corrections in the financial life is good and necessary. In your case the cosmos – through its tough love – forces the issue. This year, course correction is an ongoing thing.

With the Sun as your financial planet, you have a natural affinity for residential real estate, hotels, restaurants, the food business and family businesses. You also have an affinity for both gold and silver, the commodities. Electric utilities, power companies, entertainment companies – industries that cater to youth – are all interesting to you.

Since the Sun is a fast-moving planet, in the course of the year moving through every sector of your Horoscope, there are many short-term trends in finance that depend on where the Sun is and the aspects he receives. These are best dealt with in the monthly reports.

In general you will have strong financial periods from March 20 to April 19; July 23 to August 22; and December 22 to December 31.

With Uranus moving out of your 10th house on March 7, the career is going to be less hectic and more stable. Perhaps a bit more boring. But boring is the price we pay for stability. Authority figures in your life also seem more stable. This year their instability happens in their financial lives.

With the relatively fast-moving Mars as your career planet there are many short-term trends in the career that are best dealt with in the monthly reports.

Love and Social Life

A complicated and challenging area this year, Cancer. Last year was the same story and the saga is continuing. Saturn has been in your 7th house of love since December 21, 2017 and he will remain there for all the year ahead. In addition, Pluto, the planet of death and rebirth, has also been in your 7th house for many years.

Cancerians by nature don't like divorce. Family is sacrosanct. If you see a Cancerian who has been divorced you can rest assured that things were *very* bad. Extremely bad. They will do almost anything to hang on to a marriage and keep things together. Yet, there have probably been divorces (and widowings) over the past ten years. And this year there is more testing going on.

There are various scenarios shown in the Horoscope. Existing relationships seem the most threatened. They are getting 'stress tested' to reveal hidden flaws that can then be corrected. If the relationship is fundamentally sound, it can actually get better when the flaws are seen and corrected. But the unsound ones are likely to fail.

Stress testing has other benefits. When things are good, when harmony prevails, we don't know if love is real. Love is just natural in those conditions. It is only under difficult conditions that we learn the depth of our love.

Since the cosmos wants the best for you, it tests you.

As we mentioned, relationships were tested last year too, but this year the stress testing seems even more severe. This year, in addition to Saturn in your 7th house, there will also be three eclipses in that house, to add to the drama. Saturn in a sign can be considered like a long-drawn-out two-year eclipse. But now three short-term eclipses add more intensity.

For singles, marriage is not advisable this year. Singles will be dating, but not as much as usual. Saturn is urging quality over quantity. Better fewer dates but good ones than hosts of mediocre dates. Singles will have relationships, but they don't seem very happy or romantic. There are at least three this year. The third one, which will happen late in the year, has possibilities.

One of the problems with Saturn in the 7th house is that one is tempted to relationships of convenience, rather than real love. Singles will certainly have these kinds of opportunities.

Social and romantic opportunities happen in the usual places this year - at parties, gatherings, resorts and places of entertainment. Singles are attracted to older, more settled kinds of people; people who can provide security and steadiness. Business people seem most alluring.

Those involved with Cancer romantically need to be careful of being over-controlling. Cancerians can see you this way even if you're not trying to be. You need to bend over backwards to avoid this. Also, work to show more love and warmth.

We see a similar story with your friendships - though not as severe. Uranus is moving into your 11th house of friends on March 7 and will be there for many years. So, friendships are getting tested. There is much social instability. A lot of this instability is not your fault. Friends are undergoing dramatic, life-changing events of their own. Some are having surgery or near-death kinds of experiences. The testing is coming from that - not you. The good news here is that you can meet new friends suddenly and unexpectedly. It can happen anytime, in any place. The friends that you do make are unconventional, interesting and exciting: scientists, technology geeks, astronomers, astrologers and inventors.Run-of-the-mill is a social turn-off these days.

Those of you in or working on the second marriage have an easier time. But romance will really improve after December 3.

Self-improvement

Neptune, the most spiritual of planets, has been in your 9th house for many years now, and will be there for many more years to come. So, you are undergoing a long-term process with regard to your religious and philosophical beliefs: they are being spiritualized, elevated. This kind of thing can never happen overnight. It takes time – and this is what is going on here.

The 9th house can be considered the most important house in the Horoscope. It shows our personal religion, our personal philosophy of life.

It is our philosophy that determines our world view, and which will determine our emotional reactions. Emotional reactions – moods and feelings – are caused by a person's interpretation of an event. And what determines a given interpretation? Philosophy.

People experience problems in life. Sometimes they are related to love or finances or health. But these problems are only masks for the real problem, which is always theological. Here is the root. These problems are revealing a theological deficiency, and to correct them at their root an adjustment to the theology is needed.

So events in the 9th house – which is happening for you – will have profound effects on every department of life. You are being called to elevate and correct your theology.

Neptune in the 9th house shows a need to explore the mystical traditions of your native religion. Every religion has a mystical tradition (often now buried under masses of humanly created rules and regulations), and yours is no different. Getting in touch with this is an important interest these days. It will pay dividends in many areas of your life.

The other important spiritual lesson this year is learning to deal with social instability – and not just to deal with it but to be comfortable with it. Uranus will be in your 11th house for many years to come. Embrace the instability. Learn to enjoy it.

Month-by-month Forecasts

January

Best Days Overall: 1, 10, 11, 19, 20, 27, 28
Most Stressful Days Overall: 5, 6, 12, 13, 25, 26
Best Days for Love: 1, 5, 6, 12, 13, 15, 16, 21, 22, 23, 24, 30, 31
Best Days for Money: 2, 3, 5, 6, 12, 13, 16, 21, 22, 25
Best Days for Career: 2, 12, 13, 21, 30, 31

Your marriage or current relationship has been tested for over a year, and gets tested again this month by the solar eclipse of the 6th (in America it happens on the 5th). This is a very strong eclipse affecting you and your spouse, partner or current love. So both of you should take it easy during this period. You need to be taking it easier anyway – this is not your best health period – but it's especially necessary during the eclipse period. This testing of your partnership might not be due to the relationship itself, but due to the personal dramas going on in the life of the beloved.

This solar eclipse (as does every one of them) forces important financial changes. This is not something to fear. You go through these twice a year (although this year it happens three times). So course corrections in finance are in order. The events of the eclipse will show you where your thinking and planning have been amiss.

Health needs much care this month. At least 60 per cent (and sometimes 70 per cent) of the planets are in stressful alignment with you. This is no joke. Your career and social life are both hyperactive and require much attention. It's stressful. Make sure to get enough rest. Keep your mind focused on the important things and let the lesser things go. Trivialities shouldn't even be considered – not now. Enhance the health in the ways mentioned in the yearly report. Try to schedule more massages or natural health treatments. Health will improve after the 20th but will still need care.

The lunar eclipse of the 21st occurs in your money house and brings more financial changes. Also, as does every lunar eclipse, it affects you personally. It forces a re-evaluation and redefinition of yourself and the image you want to project to others. This too is nothing to fear as you go through this twice a year. It's healthy to redefine yourself. We are growing, ever-changing beings. Our self-concept should reflect this.

Mars spends the month in your 10th house, indicating much activity – and perhaps aggressiveness – in your career. You could be fighting a war there – against your competitors.

Your financial planet, the Sun, is in your 7th house of love until the 20th. A lot of your socializing this month is business-related. Singles are attracted to the wealthy, the good providers. You spend more on social matters but can earn from socializing too. On the 20th your financial planet moves into your 8th house. Use any spare cash to pay down debt. This transit is also good for refinancing existing debt and for tax planning.

February

Best Days Overall: 6, 7, 15, 16, 24, 25
Most Stressful Days Overall: 1, 2, 8, 9, 10, 21, 22, 28
Best Days for Love: 1, 2, 11, 12, 19, 20, 28
Best Days for Money: 3, 4, 9, 10, 14, 17, 18, 24, 26, 27
Best Days for Career: 8, 9, 10, 19, 28

Health is improved compared with last month, and will get better after the 14th as Mars moves away from his stressful aspect to you. It is further improved after the 19th. Enhance the health further in the ways mentioned in the yearly report.

The planetary power is still mostly in the Western, social sector of your chart. So, you're still in a social period. Social grace will get you further than personal initiative. This is a time for cultivating your social skills. Venus's move into your 7th house on the 3rd reinforces this. Adapt to conditions as best you can. The time will come – and it's not far off – when changes will be easier to make. Venus in your 7th house is a positive for love, but Saturn's continued presence in that house suggests a need for caution – a go-slow attitude. Most of you have a practical concept of love these days, but this month even more so. It's not so much about passion but is utilitarian. This is especially so on the 17th and 18th. You and the beloved need to inject some passion, some fire into your relationship. It looks like you're both just going through the motions.

Your financial planet is still in your 8th house until the 19th. As was the case last month, it is a good aspect for tax planning and debt reduction, and to refinance existing debt on more favourable terms. If you have good ideas for projects, this is a good month to approach outside investors. Also good to get rid of possessions that you don't use, and reduce waste and other redundancies. Do you have more than one bank account? Investment account? Slim things down. It's also good to put the financial interest of others ahead of your own. Your job is to make other people rich. As you do this, your own prosperity will happen naturally and normally – by the karmic law.

On the 19th your financial planet enters your 9th house and spiritual Pisces. This indicates good financial intuition. It favours investments in foreign companies and foreign lands. It also favours water utilities, shipping and shipbuilders, oil and natural gas. People in these industries can be important in your financial life these days.

More important than the above is a need and ability to explore the spiritual dimensions of wealth. This is the road to true financial independence. With this understanding we are not concerned with the overall economy or stock market or material conditions. One accesses the supernatural, rather than the natural, wealth supply.

The dream life is particularly active on the 18th and 19th. Pay attention as these dreams have spiritual significance.

March

Best Days Overall: 5, 6, 7, 15, 16, 23, 24
Most Stressful Days Overall: 1, 2, 8, 9, 21, 22, 27, 28, 29
Best Days for Love: 1, 2, 3, 4, 10, 11, 15, 16, 19, 20, 23, 24, 27, 28, 29
Best Days for Money: 8, 9, 17, 18, 25, 26
Best Days for Career: 1, 2, 8, 9, 10, 11, 19, 20, 28, 29

The planetary power is all in the upper half of your Horoscope this month; only the Moon will move through the lower half of the chart (from the 15th to the 26th). This is a lot of power favouring your career and outer goals. Home and family can take a back seat for a while – though they too seem supportive of the career. On the 20th the Sun enters your 10th house and you begin a yearly career peak. With 90 per cent of the planets moving forward (and at times it's all of them) you should see fast progress to your career goals. The financial planet in the 10th house signals prosperity. The Sun is in his 'high noon' position, blazing brightly. It shows pay rises, official or unofficial. It shows the financial favour of the 'higher ups' in your life – bosses, parents, parent figures and authority figures. It's important to maintain a good career reputation as this promotes earnings. Money can come from government payments too. Your career planet, Mars, will be in your 11th house of friends all month, so it will be beneficial to be involved with professional and trade organizations. Friends and networking with friends will also help the career.

But before all this happens, your 9th house of religion, philosophy, theology and higher education is powerful – until the 20th. Financial intuition is still important. The 15th and 16th bring spiritual guidance on finance. This can come in dreams or through psychics, tarot readers, spiritual channels or other religious types. As our regular readers know, a millisecond of a true intuition is worth many years of hard labour. This is a wonderful period for college students. They are focused on their studies and seem successful. If you're involved in legal issues, these too seem successful.

Health needs more attention after the 20th. The aspects are not as severe as they were in January, but there's still more stress to your health than earlier in the month. So, as always, make sure to rest. Enhance the health in the ways mentioned in the yearly report.

Love still needs work. Keep in mind our discussion of last month. There is a need to 'warm things up' a bit.

This is a month for spiritual and religious breakthroughs. You have many planets in your 9th house and Mercury, your spiritual planet, Cancer, will make a rare station on Neptune, the most spiritual of the planets, from the 24th to the 31st. So, pay attention to the dream life this period – it is significant. The invisible worlds and their denizens are letting you know that they are around. They have their ways of doing this.

April

Best Days Overall: 1, 2, 3, 11, 12, 19, 20, 29, 30
Most Stressful Days Overall: 4, 5, 17, 18, 24, 25
Best Days for Love: 2, 3, 7, 8, 11, 12, 15, 16, 21, 24, 25
Best Days for Money: 4, 5, 13, 14, 22, 23, 24
Best Days for Career: 1, 2, 4, 5, 10, 11, 19, 20, 28, 29

The power is still very much in the upper half of your Horoscope this month, and your 10th house of career is even stronger than it was in March. In contrast, your 4th house of home and family is basically empty, with only the Moon moving through there on the 17th and 18th. So, like last month, the focus is on your career and outer goals. You pursue your career by the methods of day – by direct action. If you have visualized your goals in the previous night cycle, now is the time to act on them. You're not really ignoring your family now (a Cancerian never ignores the family), as they seem supportive of your goals and are probably active participants. The family as a whole is elevated in status this month.

Your career planet, Mars, spends the month in your spiritual 12th house. This gives various messages. You advance your career through charitable and altruistic kinds of activities. You make important connections in this way. Your spiritual understanding – which comes from your spiritual practice – aids the career. Career guidance comes in dreams and intuition. Psychics, tarot readers, astrologers, spiritual channels and ministers have important career information for you. On a deeper level, your spiritual practice *is* the career – the mission – this month. Get right spiritually, and finance and career will take care of themselves.

Health is stressful this month – until the 20th. This doesn't mean sickness, just low energy and greater vulnerability. You have to focus more on it. This is not so easy with a busy career and social agenda, but you can do it. As always, make sure to get enough rest – this is always the first line of defence. Enhance the health in the ways mentioned in the yearly report. Schedule more massages and health treatments. Don't waste time and energy on unimportant things. Stick to what is important to you.

Finances will be good. The Sun is still in your 10th house until the 20th, so keep in mind our discussion of this last month. On the 20th the Sun will enter Taurus, your 11th house. This is good. You are less of a risk-taker now, more conservative. Financial judgement is much better than when the Sun was in impulsive Aries. The Sun travels with Uranus from the 21st to the 23rd. This can bring a sudden, unexpected expense, but also the money needed to cover it. It is a good period to pay down debt or to attract outside investors to your projects. You and the beloved seem in financial synch during this time. There is good cooperation between you.

May

Best Days Overall: 8, 9, 17, 18, 26, 27
Most Stressful Days Overall: 1, 2, 3, 15, 16, 21, 22, 29, 30
Best Days for Love: 2, 3, 4, 5, 13, 14, 21, 22, 31
Best Days for Money: 2, 3, 4, 5, 10, 11, 13, 14, 19, 20, 24, 29, 30
Best Days for Career: 1, 2, 3, 6, 7, 17, 26, 27, 29, 30

Health is improving day by day. It's not perfect yet, but improving. It's amazing how mere shifts in planetary energy can have such an impact. Pre-existing conditions should be improved. Mars moving into your sign on the 16th is akin to taking high doses of amphetamines. It boosts energy. You do more. You get things done faster and, in general, are more independent.

Mars is not the only factor boosting independence. The planetary power has now shifted – it began last month – from the social Western sector to the independent Eastern sector of the chart. It is not yet at its maximum point – that will happen in the next few months – but it's a factor now. Thus, you have more power (and willingness) to change conditions to the way you want them. You have more power to create your own happiness. You're not so dependent on the grace of other people. You can go solo if you choose.

Mars in your own sign signals other things too. Mars is your career planet. Thus career opportunities are seeking you out, effortlessly. You have the image of a successful person and are probably dressing the part. Bosses, parents and parent figures seem devoted to you. You have their favour. (However, this devotion needs to be looked at more carefully – it can show a desire for a degree of control over you.)

Your financial planet, the Sun, is still in harmonious aspect with you, which is good for the cash flow. The Sun is in Taurus until the 21st, indicating that the financial judgement is very sound and conservative. Your social connections – especially friends – are helpful in finances. It will be very good to be involved with groups, professional and trade organizations as this will lead to profit opportunities. Online activities are also very helpful. This is a good month to buy high tech equipment or to upgrade what you do have.

On the 21st the Sun moves into your 12th house of spirituality. Thus, your financial intuition becomes all important. You will be more charitable this period too. You will spend on spiritual things – spiritual books, CDs, DVDs and the like. Being involved in charities or altruistic causes will boost your bottom line, generally through the connections you make there. Financial information will come to you in dreams and through psychics, astrologers, tarot readers and spiritual channels. Spirit is very concerned about your financial health. It has its ways of helping – usually through intuition.

Mars in your own sign is not the best signal for love. Watch the temper. Too much self-assertion – which is happening now – can complicate the love life. Self-confidence and self-assertion are wonderful things, but not so wonderful socially or romantically.

June

Best Days Overall: 5, 6, 13, 14, 23, 24
Most Stressful Days Overall: 11, 12, 18, 19, 25, 26
Best Days for Love: 1, 9, 10, 11, 18, 19, 20, 21, 28, 29
Best Days for Money: 2, 3, 7, 8, 11, 12, 15, 16, 22, 25, 26
Best Days for Career: 4, 5, 13, 14, 23, 24, 25, 26

The planets are now approaching their maximum Eastern position of independence for the year. (Next month will be more or less the same.) This is definitely the time to make the changes that need to be made. The planets are supporting you. The cosmos desires your personal happiness. When you are happy there is that much less misery in the world. So, it's time to focus on your personal interests. A time to have things your way. You know what's best for you. If others don't go along with your ideas (and it looks that way) you can go it alone. This doesn't mean riding roughshod over others. It only means that you tend to your own interests and fulfil them. Later on, in the coming months when the planets start to shift to the West again, it will be more difficult to make the changes that you want. So seize the moment.

Mars is still in your sign all month. On the 4th Mercury joins him, and on the 21st, the Sun. From the 21st onwards you are in one of your yearly personal pleasure peaks. This is a time to enjoy all the pleasures of the body – to fulfil your sensual desires. But it's also good for getting the body and image into shape.

Personal independence is complicating the love life. Though you look good and have much star quality, love seems challenging. It's not about looks: you and the beloved seem on opposite sides of the universe. You're not seeing eye-to-eye. This creates tension. The beloved is focused on his or her interests and you're focused on yours. Somewhere there is middle ground. You'll have to find it. It's a challenging time for singles as well. You're not really in the mood for love. You don't seem willing to go out of your way for it. Besides, your love planet, Saturn, went retrograde on May 2 and will be retrograde for a few more months. Your love goals aren't clear.

Mars, your career planet, went 'out of bounds' on April 21 and is still 'out of bounds' until the 12th of this month, so you've been going outside your normal haunts in pursuit of your career goals. This can also show that your career – the demands of the career – has sent you to unfamiliar places. A parent or parent figure has also been outside his or her normal sphere.

Health is good this month. Not perfect but good. You still have two powerful long-term planets – Saturn and Pluto – in stressful alignment, but you have a lot of help from the short-term planets.

Finances are excellent this month, and even better after the 21st than before. The financial planet in your own sign brings financial windfalls and opportunities your way.

July

Best Days Overall: 2, 3, 10, 11, 20, 21, 29, 30
Most Stressful Days Overall: 8, 9, 15, 16, 22, 23, 24
Best Days for Love: 1, 6, 7, 10, 11, 15, 16, 20, 21, 25, 26, 31
Best Days for Money: 4, 5, 13, 14, 21, 22, 23, 24, 29, 30, 31
Best Days for Career: 4, 13, 14, 22, 23, 24, 31

Two eclipses this month impact on you very strongly. However, the good news is that you have plenty of energy to handle them.

The solar eclipse of the 2nd occurs in your own sign, and shows a need to redefine yourself and your image. Often with this kind of eclipse one is subject to slanders or innuendos from others. Thus it becomes imperative to define yourself for yourself. Otherwise others will define you and it won't be pleasant. Every solar eclipse forces financial changes on you. Your thinking and strategies are not realistic – as the events of the eclipse will show. In this particular case, you might be too pessimistic in your planning. Your earnings and earning power are greater than you think. You're in a very prosperous month. The eclipse will probably make it even more prosperous – but perhaps through some shocks.

The lunar eclipse of the 16th also has a strong effect on you, as not only does it impact on the Moon, the ruler of your Horoscope, but it occurs in stressful alignment with you. So be sure to really reduce your schedule during both eclipses. This eclipse occurs in your 7th house of love and once again (as happened in January) tests love and the current relationship, which have been undergoing a testing period for some time now. So, be more patient with the beloved (who is also having personal dramas) and avoid making important love decisions one way or another. Your love planet Saturn is still retrograde. Usually long-repressed grievances (real or imagined) come up for cleansing. The good news is that now you can see the problem and can deal with it better. Before, it was hidden.

In the case of singles an eclipse in the 7th house often shows a change in the marital status. It doesn't mean that you marry (and that's not advisable now anyway), but you make certain decisions about it that will manifest later on down the road.

Every lunar eclipse impacts on you personally – especially your body, image and self-concept. So, in a way, this is a repeat of the solar eclipse of the 2nd. There's no way of getting around it – you need to redefine yourself for yourself. In the coming months you will be presenting a 'new look' to the world.

The lunar eclipse will also affect children and children figures in your life. They have personal dramas too. They too should take it easy over this eclipse period. There's no need to take risks.

August

Best Days Overall: 7, 8, 16, 17, 26, 27
Most Stressful Days Overall: 4, 5, 11, 12, 19, 20
Best Days for Love: 1, 2, 3, 9, 10, 11, 12, 20, 21, 22, 30, 31
Best Days for Money: 1, 9, 10, 19, 20, 28, 29, 30
Best Days for Career: 1, 9, 10, 19, 20, 21, 30, 31

The planetary power is still mostly in the independent Eastern sector, although that begins to change next month. So, if there are changes you need to make, now is the time to do so: later on it will be more difficult.

Retrograde activity is less intense than last month, but is still strong with 40 per cent of the planets in reverse gear most of the month. Many of the phenomena we mentioned last month can have delayed reactions.

You're still in the midst of a yearly financial peak. Your money house is easily the strongest in your chart until the 23rd. So the focus is on finance as it should be. Mars has been in your money house since July 1 and will be here until the 18th. This shows the financial favour of the authority figures in your life – they seem directly and actively involved in your finances. (A parent or parent figure too.) Venus in the money house until the 21st shows good family and social support. Mercury in your money house from the 11th to the 29th signals good financial intuition, charitable giving and the importance of good sales, marketing and PR.

Sales, marketing and PR – letting people know about your product or service – is important later in the month too, as the Sun moves into your 3rd house of communication. This transit also favours trading, buying, selling and retailing. Your gift of the gab is a big financial asset. The money people in your life are having a banner financial month from the 23rd onwards. The rich get richer. The Sun makes nice aspects to Uranus on the 29th and 30th. This shows good financial cooperation with the spouse, partner or current love. It shows sudden, unexpected money coming to you.

The power in the 3rd house from the 23rd onwards is good for students, indicating focus on studies and thus success. But even non students should become students during this period. Take courses, attend lectures, seminars and workshops in subjects that interest you. The mind is sharper now and information is absorbed better.

The love life is still stressful but you should see improvement from the 18th onwards. Saturn starts to receive harmonious aspects. The beloved is in a better mood and things should go easier.

Drive more carefully from the 15th to the 17th.

September

Best Days Overall: 3, 4, 12, 13, 14, 22, 23, 30
Most Stressful Days Overall: 1, 2, 7, 8, 9, 15, 16, 28, 29
Best Days for Love: 7, 8, 9, 17, 18, 19, 20, 26, 27, 28, 29
Best Days for Money: 5, 6, 7, 8, 15, 16, 18, 19, 24, 25, 28
Best Days for Career: 7, 8, 9, 15, 16, 17, 18, 19, 26, 27

Health is definitely an issue this month, especially after the 23rd. At least half of the planets will be in stressful alignment with you (and sometimes more). So take it nice and easy. Make sure to get enough rest. Spend more time at health spas if you can, and try to schedule more massages and health treatments. Hot baths will relax and rejuvenate the body. Spend more time outside in the sunshine. Enhance the health in the ways mentioned in the yearly report.

If you take care of your health the month ahead looks happy. The planetary power is nearing its maximum position in the lower half of the Horoscope – your favourite half. Career can be downplayed for a while. The cosmos urges you to do what you most love to do – handle the family, focus on your home and, most importantly, on your emotional wellness.

This is still an excellent month for students. Your 3rd house is powerful all month, but especially until the 23rd. The mind is sharp and the communication faculties are enhanced. There will be success in your studies. This is a great time for all of you to catch up on your reading and to take classes in subjects that interest you. This is not only fun in its own right, but will help the career. Your communication skills further the career.

Venus, your family planet, has her solstice from the 15th to the 18th. This means that she pauses in the heavens (in her latitudinal motion) and changes direction. So there is a pause in your family life and then a change of direction.

On the 23rd the Sun enters your 4th house of home and family. Mercury and Venus enter on the 14th, so the home is the natural focus. Those of you undergoing professional therapy will make good progress. Even if you're not involved in formal therapy, the Inner Therapist is hard at work. You will be confronted with many old memories that will now get resolved – reinterpreted and understood in a better way. This is Nature's emotional healing. The dream life is likely to be more active from the 23rd onwards too. These dreams will have psychological significance. This is a time for building up the forces for your next career push at the end of the year (and into 2020).

Love is OK until the 23rd (everything is relative; you still have Saturn in your 7th house). After the 23rd love becomes more complicated. It's most likely not you; the beloved is having personal challenges and this affects things. The good news here is that your love planet, Saturn, starts moving forward on the 18th. By now you'll have more clarity in love matters. Your decisions will be much better.

October

Best Days Overall: 1, 10, 11, 19, 20, 28, 29
Most Stressful Days Overall: 5, 6, 12, 13, 26, 27
Best Days for Love: 5, 6, 10, 11, 15, 16, 19, 20, 23, 24, 28, 29
Best Days for Money: 2, 3, 4, 7, 8, 12, 13, 17, 18, 21, 22, 28, 30, 31
Best Days for Career: 7, 12, 13, 17, 18, 26, 27

Health is still an important issue this month. Review our discussion of this last month. You should see some improvement after the 23rd, but it still needs monitoring.

Your 4th house of home and family is still powerful this month. Mars, your career planet, moves into this house on the 4th, indicating that the home and family *is* the career – the mission – for the month ahead. If you get the home base in order, if you're in a place of emotional harmony, the career will take care of itself.

Mars will have his solstice from the 4th to the 11th. This means that he pauses in the heavens (in his latitudinal motion) and then changes direction. He sort of 'camps out' in one place during that period. So a pause in the outer career is called for. It is pause that refreshes. Then there will be a change of direction.

Mars in your 4th house signals an excellent time for making repairs or renovations in the home. It is also a good time (for some of you) for building a home. It also shows that career should be pursued by the hidden methods of night, rather than the overt methods of day. Visualize your career goals. Put yourself in the mood and feeling of where you want to be and what you want to achieve. Live, as much as possible, in that feeling. We could call this 'controlled day-dreaming' or meditation. When the planets shift to the upper half of your chart, you can take the overt steps to achieve your dreams. But right now it is not necessary to concern yourself about the 'hows'. Live in the finished idea. The 'how' will reveal itself later on.

Your financial planet, the Sun, will be in your 4th house until the 23rd. Thus you're spending more on the home and family. You can also earn through them. Family and family connections are important financially. It favours earning money from home too. On the 23rd the financial planet moves into your 5th house – a very fortunate position. It shows 'happy money'. You earn in happy ways – perhaps as you're out at a party or sports event. Perhaps as you're wining and dining clients or prospective customers. You tend to be more speculative and lucky in that department. You're spending more on the children or children figures in your life, but can also earn from them. Much depends on their age and stage. If they are young they can inspire you with ideas. Often they are the motivating force behind earnings. And, equally often, they can be a direct source of supply.

When the Sun moves into your 5th house on the 23rd you begin the second of your yearly personal pleasure peaks. Time to enjoy your life and re-create yourself. Personal creativity will be unusually strong – and those who have experienced the creative flow know what a joy that is. You get on especially well with the children and children figures in your life.

November

Best Days Overall: 6, 7, 16, 17, 24, 25
Most Stressful Days Overall: 1, 2, 8, 9, 10, 22, 23, 28, 29, 30
Best Days for Love: 1, 2, 8, 9, 11, 12, 18, 19, 20, 21, 28, 29, 30
Best Days for Money: 6, 7, 8, 9, 10, 16, 17, 18, 19, 26, 27
Best Days for Career: 3, 4, 5, 8, 9, 10, 17, 26

The love life began to improve after October 23. And it will improve further after the 19th of this month. There is still a need to 'warm things up' in your relationship – to keep the spark of romance alive – but it's easier now. Singles are not likely to marry just yet (next year will be a different story) but they have better opportunities. Any relationship that has lasted this far will probably last through anything. It is basically healthy. Venus's move into your 7th house on the 26th makes the beloved a bit softer, less stern and more romantic.

Health is also much improved, and after the 19th will improve even further. It is still far from perfect, but much improved. Continue to enhance the health in the ways mentioned in the yearly report. The good news is that you're paying attention to your health.

You're still very much in a yearly personal pleasure peak until the 22nd. Having fun, letting go of worries and care is not only healthy, but helps you financially and in the career.

Jupiter has been in your 6th house of work all year. Venus is there until the 26th, and on the 23rd, the Sun moves here. So this is an excellent period for jobseekers. You've had great job aspects all year, but this month they are especially good. Most of you are probably employed and the power in the 6th house shows extra jobs or overtime work. It is also a good time to hire people. You will have plenty of applicants. Children and children figures have been prosperous all year, but now (and especially after the 23rd) they prosper even more.

Your personal prosperity seems strong this month too. Until the 22nd your financial planet is in the happy-go-lucky 5th house. You're spending on leisure and can earn through that too. It favours investments that cater to youth – music and entertainment. Financial opportunities come at resorts or places of entertainment. On the 22nd the financial planet moves into Sagittarius – a sign of expansion. Financial goals are very high now. Financial horizons get expanded. You should see an increase in earnings. Over-spending could be an issue. The financial planet in the 6th house shows earning from work – and probably, as was mentioned, you will have extra jobs or overtime.

Venus, your family planet (also your planet of friends) goes 'out of bounds' from the 15th to the 30th. Thus family members are going outside their normal haunts. Friends too. In psychological issues you're venturing into unknown territory too.

December

Best Days Overall: 3, 4, 5, 13, 14, 21, 22, 31
Most Stressful Days Overall: 6, 7, 19, 20, 26, 27
Best Days for Love: 8, 9, 17, 18, 26, 27, 28, 29
Best Days for Money: 6, 7, 8, 15, 16, 17, 26
Best Days for Career: 3, 4, 5, 6, 7, 13, 14, 21, 22, 31

The love and social life has taken quite a pounding this past year. Saturn and Pluto in your 7th house was problematic enough. You've also had many eclipses here (and there's still one more to come, on the 26th). Yet, you're turning a corner now. The worst is over with. On the 3rd Jupiter, benevolent and expansive, moves into your house of love. There is more optimism now. There is light at the end of the tunnel. There is an upturn in the social life. You're meeting new and significant people. Your circle of friends expands. For singles this signals romance on the horizon, perhaps even marriage or a serious relationship. (Although marriage is more likely next year, when Saturn moves out of your 7th house.)

The solar eclipse of the 26th affects you strongly, so take it easy during this period. There's no need for risk-taking activities. This eclipse, combined with Jupiter's move into your 7th house, signals a crucial shift in your love life. Important decisions are being made. The love attitudes change. This eclipse also impacts on the spouse, partner or current love. He or she should also take it easy at this time. There are more personal dramas happening in his or her life. There are also personal dramas in the lives of your friends (the friends of the heart). Your work planet, Jupiter, is affected by this eclipse, so job changes are afoot. There is a need to change your health regime too. If you employ others there are dramas with employees, and perhaps some staff turnover. And, as with every solar eclipse, financial changes are happening. This is the third eclipse of the year that impacts on finance.

Health is an issue this month, especially from the 22nd onwards. If you take the right precautions – get enough rest, focus on essentials and enhance the health in the ways mentioned in the yearly report – you should get through OK.

Though the eclipse will shake up the financial life, finances are basically good this month. Until the 22nd your financial planet is in expansive Sagittarius. This gives *big* wealth ideas – larger-than-life goals. Whether one reaches them or not, it tends to prosperity. You could be more speculative and risk-taking this period. There would be a tendency to over-spend. After the 22nd, as the financial planet moves into conservative Capricorn, the financial judgement becomes sounder and more realistic. The solar eclipse of the 26th can cause some financial shocks, but you will have the wherewithal to handle them. Your financial planet is travelling with Jupiter from the 26th to the 28th. This is basically a prosperity period. The social connections are playing an important role in finances from the 22nd onwards. You spend more on your social life, but it seems like a good investment. This is a good period to set up budgets and long-term savings and investment plans.

Leo

♌

THE LION

Birthdays from
21st July to
21st August

Personality Profile

LEO AT A GLANCE

Element – Fire

Ruling Planet – Sun
   Career Planet – Venus
   Love Planet – Uranus
   Money Planet – Mercury
   Planet of Health and Work – Saturn
   Planet of Home and Family Life – Pluto

Colours – gold, orange, red

Colours that promote love, romance and social harmony – black, indigo, ultramarine blue

Colours that promote earning power – yellow, yellow-orange

Gems – amber, chrysolite, yellow diamond

Metal – gold

Scents – bergamot, frankincense, musk, neroli

Quality – fixed (= stability)

Quality most needed for balance – humility

Strongest virtues – leadership ability, self-esteem and confidence, generosity, creativity, love of joy

Deepest needs – fun, elation, the need to shine

Characteristics to avoid – arrogance, vanity, bossiness

Signs of greatest overall compatibility – Aries, Sagittarius

Signs of greatest overall incompatibility – Taurus, Scorpio, Aquarius

Sign most helpful to career – Taurus

Sign most helpful for emotional support – Scorpio

Sign most helpful financially – Virgo

Sign best for marriage and/or partnerships – Aquarius

Sign most helpful for creative projects – Sagittarius

Best Sign to have fun with – Sagittarius

Signs most helpful in spiritual matters – Aries, Cancer

Best day of the week – Sunday

Understanding a Leo

When you think of Leo, think of royalty – then you'll get the idea of what the Leo character is all about and why Leos are the way they are. It is true that, for various reasons, some Leo-born do not always express this quality – but even if not they should like to do so.

A monarch rules not by example (as does Aries) nor by consensus (as do Capricorn and Aquarius) but by personal will. Will is law. Personal taste becomes the style that is imitated by all subjects. A monarch is somehow larger than life. This is how a Leo desires to be.

When you dispute the personal will of a Leo it is serious business. He or she takes it as a personal affront, an insult. Leos will let you know that their will carries authority and that to disobey is demeaning and disrespectful.

A Leo is king (or queen) of their personal domain. Subordinates, friends and family are loyal and trusted subjects. Leos rule with benevolent grace and in the best interests of others. They have a powerful presence; indeed, they are powerful people. They seem to attract attention in any social gathering, standing out because they are stars in their domain. Leos feel that, like the Sun, they are made to shine and rule. Leos feel that they were born to special privilege and royal prerogatives – most of them attain this status, at least to some degree.

The Sun is the ruler of this sign, and when you think of sunshine it is very difficult to feel unhealthy or depressed. Somehow the light of the Sun is the very antithesis of illness and apathy. Leos love life. They also love to have fun; they love drama, music, the theatre and amusements of all sorts. These are the things that give joy to life. If – even in their best interests – you try to deprive Leos of their pleasures, good food, drink and entertainment, you run the serious risk of depriving them of the will to live. To them life without joy is no life at all.

Leos epitomize humanity's will to power. But power in and of itself – regardless of what some people say – is neither good nor evil. Only when power is abused does it become evil. Without power even good things cannot come to pass. Leos realize this and are uniquely qualified to wield power. Of all the signs, they do it most naturally. Capricorn, the other power sign of the zodiac, is a better manager and administrator than Leo – much better. But Leo outshines Capricorn in personal grace and presence. Leo loves power, whereas Capricorn assumes power out of a sense of duty.

Finance

Leos are great leaders but not necessarily good managers. They are better at handling the overall picture than the nitty-gritty details of business. If they have good managers working for them they can become exceptional executives. They have vision and a lot of creativity.

Leos love wealth for the pleasures it can bring. They love an opulent lifestyle, pomp and glamour. Even when they are not wealthy they live as if they are. This is why many fall into debt, from which it is sometimes difficult to emerge.

Leos, like Pisceans, are generous to a fault. Very often they want to acquire wealth just to help others economically. Wealth to Leo buys services and managerial ability. It creates jobs for others and improves the general well-being of those around them. Therefore – to a Leo – wealth is good. Wealth is to be enjoyed to the fullest. Money is not to be left to gather dust in a mouldy bank vault but to be enjoyed, spread around, used. So Leos can be quite reckless in their spending.

With the sign of Virgo on Leo's 2nd money house cusp, Leo needs to develop some of Virgo's traits of analysis, discrimination and purity when it comes to money matters. They must learn to be more careful with the details of finance (or to hire people to do this for them). They have to be more cost-conscious in their spending habits. Generally, they need to manage their money better. Leos tend to chafe under financial constraints, yet these constraints can help Leos to reach their highest financial potential.

Leos like it when their friends and family know that they can depend on them for financial support. They do not mind – and even enjoy – lending money, but they are careful that they are not taken advantage of. From their 'regal throne' Leos like to bestow gifts upon their family and friends and then enjoy the good feelings these gifts bring to everybody. Leos love financial speculations and – when the celestial influences are right – are often lucky.

Career and Public Image

Leos like to be perceived as wealthy, for in today's world wealth often equals power. When they attain wealth they love having a large house with lots of land and animals.

At their jobs Leos excel in positions of authority and power. They are good at making decisions – on a grand level – but they prefer to leave the details to others. Leos are well respected by their colleagues and subordinates, mainly because they have a knack for understanding and relating to those around them. Leos usually strive for the top positions even if they have to start at the bottom and work hard to get there. As might be expected of such a charismatic sign, Leos are always trying to improve their work situation. They do so in order to have a better chance of advancing to the top.

On the other hand, Leos do not like to be bossed around or told what to do. Perhaps this is why they aspire for the top – where they can be the decision-makers and need not take orders from others.

Leos never doubt their success and focus all their attention and efforts on achieving it. Another great Leo characteristic is that – just like good monarchs – they do not attempt to abuse the power or success they achieve. If they do so this is not wilful or intentional. Usually they like to share their wealth and try to make everyone around them join in their success.

Leos are – and like to be perceived as – hard-working, well-established individuals. It is definitely true that they are capable of hard work and often manage great things. But do not forget that, deep down inside, Leos really are fun-lovers.

Love and Relationships

Generally, Leos are not the marrying kind. To them relationships are good while they are pleasurable. When the relationship ceases to be pleasurable a true Leo will want out. They always want to have the freedom to leave. That is why Leos excel at love affairs rather than commitment. Once married, however, Leo is faithful – even if some Leos have a tendency to marry more than once in their lifetime. If you are in love with a Leo, just show him or her a good time – travel, go to casinos and clubs, the theatre and discos. Wine and dine your Leo love – it is expensive but worth it and you will have fun.

Leos generally have an active love life and are demonstrative in their affections. They love to be with other optimistic and fun-loving types like themselves, but wind up settling with someone more serious, intellectual and unconventional. The partner of a Leo tends to be more political and socially conscious than he or she is, and more libertarian. When you marry a Leo, mastering the freedom-loving tendencies of your partner will definitely become a life-long challenge – and be careful that Leo does not master you.

Aquarius sits on Leo's 7th house of love cusp. Thus if Leos want to realize their highest love and social potential they need to develop a more egalitarian, Aquarian perspective on others. This is not easy for Leo, for 'the king' finds his equals only among other 'kings'. But perhaps this is the solution to Leo's social challenge – to be 'a king among kings'. It is all right to be regal, but recognize the nobility in others.

Home and Domestic Life

Although Leos are great entertainers and love having people over, sometimes this is all show. Only very few close friends will get to see the real side of a Leo's day-to-day life. To a Leo the home is a place of comfort, recreation and transformation; a secret, private retreat – a castle. Leos like to spend money, show off a bit, entertain and have fun. They enjoy the latest furnishings, clothes and gadgets – all things fit for kings.

Leos are fiercely loyal to their family and, of course, expect the same from them. They love their children almost to a fault; they have to be careful not to spoil them too much. They also must try to avoid attempting to make individual family members over in their own image. Leos should keep in mind that others also have the need to be their own people. That is why Leos have to be extra careful about being over-bossy or over-domineering in the home.

Horoscope for 2019

Major Trends

There's a lot of change happening for you this year, Leo, but you will get through it, as always. This year there are three solar eclipses, instead of the normal two; because the Sun is your ruling planet, you are very much affected by them. Also there will be a lunar eclipse on January 21 that occurs in your sign. So, four of the five eclipses this year will impact on you. You will be making serial changes to your personality, wardrobe and image. You will be redefining yourself multiple times. Reinventing yourself. We will deal with these eclipses in more detail in the monthly reports.

The job situation seems difficult – a burden. You don't seem to be enjoying work as much as you would like. Job changes seem in the cards: there are three eclipses in your 6th house of work. More later.

Overall health and energy seem basically good this year, but you will be making major changes – and probably multiple times – to your health regime. There's more on this later.

The main headline this year is Uranus's move (after seven years) from your 9th house to your 10th house of career. Major career change is happening – more details later on. As Uranus is your love planet, this move also has implications for the love life – big changes in attitude will be happening. Again, we say more on this later.

With Jupiter spending almost all year in your 5th house there is going to be fun in your life. True you are working hard, but you're managing to have fun too. Leos of childbearing age are more fertile than usual.

Neptune has been in your 8th house of regeneration for many years now, and he will be there for many more. This shows that the sex life is becoming more spiritualized. There is a need (and this will continue) to elevate it above lust into an act of worship. More on this later.

Your most important interests this year will be children, fun and creativity (until December 3); health and work; sex, personal transformation and reinvention, occult studies; religion, philosophy, higher education and foreign travel (until March 7); and career (from March 7 onwards and for many years to come).

Your paths of greatest fulfilment this year are children, fun and creativity (until December 3); health and work (from December 3 onwards); and spirituality.

Health

(Please note that this is an astrological perspective on health and not a medical one. In days of yore there was no difference, both of these perspectives were identical. But now there could be quite a difference. For a medical perspective, please consult your doctor or health practitioner.)

Health, as we mentioned, is good this year. Until March 7 there are no long-term planets in stressful alignment with you. And even after March 7, there will only be one in such an alignment. So, health and energy are good. Yet, in spite of this, we see a very powerful 6th house – easily the strongest in the Horoscope. There is great focus here, and in this case I'm not so sure it is a good thing. While it's good to pay attention to your health, the danger here is 'too much of a good thing'. Little things can be magnified into big things. Needless procedures are undertaken which can actually cause health problems. It would be wise to keep in mind the old dictum: 'If it ain't broke, don't fix it.'

Three eclipses in your 6th house indicate dramatic changes – multiple changes – to your health regime. Sometimes eclipses signal health scares, but since your overall energy is good these are likely to be only scares.

Your health is good, but you can make it even better. Give more attention to the following – the vulnerable areas of your Horoscope this year (the reflexology points are shown in the chart above):

- The heart. This is always important for a Leo, as Leo rules the heart. The important thing with the heart (as our regular readers know) is to avoid worry and anxiety. These are the two emotions that stress the heart. Instead, develop more faith.
- The spine, knees, teeth, skin and overall skeletal alignment. These are also very important for you, Leo, as Saturn, your health planet, rules these areas. And since 2018 and Saturn's move into your 6th house of health, they have become even more important than normal. So, as always, regular back and knee massage should be

part of your regular health regime. There are chairs and mats that give back massages and one of them might be a good investment these days. Give the knees more support when exercising. Maintain good dental hygiene. If you're out in the sun use a good sunscreen.

- The colon, bladder and sexual organs have become important since 2008, when Pluto entered your 6th house (and they will remain important for many more years to come). Safe sex and sexual moderation are crucial (Leo can definitely overdo these things). A herbal colon cleanse every now and then would be a good idea – especially if you feel sluggish or under the weather.
- The liver and thighs will become important after December 3 when Jupiter, the planet that rules these areas, enters your 6th house. Thigh massage will be powerful then; it will not only strengthen the liver, but the lower back as well. A herbal liver cleanse every now and then will also be good.

Important foot reflexology points for the year ahead

Try to massage all of the foot on a regular basis – the top of the foot as well as the bottom – but pay extra attention to the points highlighted on the chart. When you massage, be aware of 'sore spots' as these need special attention. It's also a good idea to massage the ankles, and especially below them.

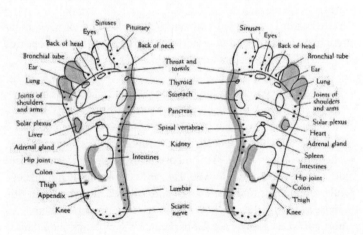

These are the most vulnerable areas in the coming year. Problems, if they happened (God forbid) would most likely begin here. Thus, keeping them healthy and fit is sound preventive medicine. Most of the time problems can actually be prevented. But even in cases where they can't (due to strong karmic momentum) they can be softened to a great extent and need not be devastating.

Saturn as the health planet shows someone who undertakes disciplined daily health regimes (even Spartan-type regimes). It shows someone who willingly changes their lifestyle around health.

Pluto in your 6th house of health and work indicates a few things. It shows the power of detox regimes. Often it indicates surgery (either actual or recommended), but detoxing should be explored first. And, since Pluto is the ruler of your 4th house of home and family, it shows the importance of good emotional health. Your mood needs to be kept positive and constructive. Meditation will be a help here too.

Though overall your health is good, there will be periods in the year when it is less good. These are not trends for the year ahead, but short-term things caused by the transiting planets. This year, those periods will be January 20 to February 18; April 20 to May 20; and October 23 to November 22. Make sure to get more rest during these times.

Home and Family

Your 4th house of home and family is not a house of power this year – not a major interest or focus. This, as our regular readers know, tends to the status quo. It shows basic contentment with things as they are. There is no pressing need to make major changes.

This empty 4th house gives you more freedom at home and in family matters. You can move or renovate your home if you like, but there's no pressing need for it. (Many of you moved or made important renovations to the home last year. This year, the need has passed.)

Pluto, your family planet, has been in your 6th house since 2008, so you have been working to make the home a healthier kind of place. In some cases mould, lead or other toxic materials have been removed from the home. In other cases the home is filled with health equipment and products: the home is more like a health spa than a home. This trend continues in the year ahead.

This transit also shows that you are very involved in the health of family members – perhaps more so than with your own health.

Your family planet in the 6th house also indicates someone who is working more from home. Many of you are (and have been) creating home offices and the like. The home is as much a workplace as a home.

Jupiter was in your 4th house last year. Thus the family circle expanded – usually through birth or marriage. Leos of childbearing age were unusually fertile last year, and the trend continues in the year ahead. If pregnancy didn't happen last year it can happen in the year ahead. (And even if it did, it can happen again.)

Parents and parent figures will be getting along better with their spouses after March 7. One of them seems very restless. He or she wants to explore personal freedom and chafes under any kind of commitment or responsibility. This person is ready for major change. Moves are not likely for either parent or parent figures this year. (It's probably not advisable either.) One of the parents or parent figures is having a banner financial year. In general the family as a whole seems more prosperous.

Siblings and sibling figures can move later in the year – from December 3 onwards. But it can happen next year too. They benefit from spiritual-healing techniques these days, and if they feel under the weather they should see a spiritual-type healer. Their love and social life is becoming more stable after many years of instability.

Children and children figures are prospering this year. They are living the good life and travelling more. They prosper next year too. A move is not indicated though.

If you're planning major repairs (or building a home), November 19 to the end of the year would be a good time. If you're planning more cosmetic redecoration work, or buying objects of beauty for the home, January 1 to January 7 and October 8 to November 23 seem good times.

Finance and Career

Money doesn't seem a big issue this year. The money house is basically empty, with only short-term planets moving through there. Their effect is temporary. As our regular readers know, this tends to the status quo. Earnings will be more or less as they were last year. It is true that you have the freedom to make changes and improve things, but you seem to lack the interest. Contentment is good. But if financial problems arise, lack of interest – lack of attention – is the probable cause. You will have to force yourself to pay more attention here.

With Mercury as your financial planet you excel at trading, buying, selling, communications, sales, marketing and PR. You also have a good affinity for the entertainment and music industries, also gaming and resorts. Industries that give 'pleasure' to people are interesting to you. And industries that cater to younger people.

Mercury is a fast-moving planet and in a given year he will move through all the sectors of your Horoscope and make aspects (positive or negative) to every planet in your chart. So, there are many short-term financial trends that depend on where Mercury is and the aspects he receives. These will be dealt with in the monthly reports.

Those of you who are unemployed have job opportunities this year. There are at least three. Those already employed will have opportunities for overtime or second jobs. However, these don't look very happy – they're jobs, full stop. They seem demanding and you're working very hard. Later in the year – from December 3 onwards – the situation changes. From then on, and well into next year, you will have very happy job opportunities – dream jobs. In the meantime just do your best.

The career is becoming very interesting. On March 7, as we mentioned, Uranus will move into your 10th house of career and will remain there for many years. This signals many dramatic kinds of changes in the career – and these happen suddenly and unexpectedly. The career becomes exciting as anything can happen at any time. The expression 'expect nothing but be ready for everything' applies to you now (and for years to come). Many of you will actually change the career path. Some of you will change the way you approach things. There is a need for more freedom in the career, and this position favours a freelance kind of career. It favours careers in technology, the online world and in the electronic media. Good use of these media (and networking skills) will boost the career in whatever you're doing.

Uranus also happens to be your love planet. This shows various things. It shows good support from the spouse, partner or current love. He or she seems very involved in the career. Friends are succeeding and helping out too – providing opportunity. It indicates someone who advances the career by social means – by attending or hosting the right kinds of parties and gatherings. It shows an ability to meet on a social level just the right people who can help you. Your personal likeability and social skills are very important careerwise. Merit on its own doesn't seem enough.

This can also be read another way. Your mission (your real career) is your marriage partner and friends. To be there for them.

Venus is your career planet and this year she is moving very fast. Usually she goes through the twelve signs and houses in your chart in the year, but this year she will move through some signs and houses (four of them) twice. Her speedy motion suggests faster progress and good confidence. It suggests someone who covers a lot of territory. This would show success.

Because Venus is so fast moving, there are many short-term career trends that depend on where she is and the aspects she receives. These are best discussed in the monthly reports.

Love and Social Life

Your love planet will spend most of the year (from March 7 onwards) near your Mid-heaven, making him the most elevated planet in the Horoscope. The Mid-heaven point (the top of the chart) is where any planet is most powerful (of course, the sign it's in also plays a role, but given equivalent signs, the Mid-heaven is the most powerful position). It's common sense. The Sun at noon (when he is at the Mid-heaven – his highest point in the sky) is where he is hottest. He is exerting his strongest influence. Now, this same reasoning can be applied to all the other planets. Mercury will be more mercurial when he is on the Mid-heaven; Venus will be more magnetic and charming at the Mid-heaven; and so on for all the other planets.

So your personal love magnetism, your social grace is ultra, ultra-strong these days (and for years to come). Uranus's position at the top of your chart also shows that love and romance are high on your agenda. Very important. It shows your aspiration. This focus, the importance that you give it, tends to success.

For singles this signals important changes in the love attitudes and needs. You are always a love-at-first-sight kind of person. This is your nature. But over the past seven years, with your love planet in Aries, this has been accentuated. And, this haste hasn't always worked out for you. Now with the love planet in Taurus, an element of caution is being introduced. I read this as a good thing. You take more time than you used to. You check things out more deeply. (You're still quick on the trigger, but less so.)

For the past seven years only the passion of love mattered. Only the feeling. Only the desire. Now, other things start to matter. You are attracted to the high and mighty, to people of power, prestige and success. You like people who can help you careerwise – people who have achieved something. The feeling of love is still important, but now these other qualities are also important, perhaps equally so.

With Uranus as your love planet you're always attracted to unconventional types, to people who are breaking barriers whether it be in science, technology or the media. This doesn't change. But if these people are also highly successful, it's even better.

For singles this can signal a romantic relationship with a boss or authority figure. The opportunities are certainly there. You have the aspects of someone who falls in love with the boss.

You find love and romantic opportunities as you pursue your normal career goals or with people involved in your career. In fact, much of your socializing this year (and over the years to come) is career-related.

Uranus is receiving very nice aspects this year. So love is going to be happy. It gets even better after December 3, as Jupiter moves into good aspect with Uranus. You might not actually marry, but you will have love and you will meet people who are 'marriage material'.

With Jupiter spending almost all year in your 5th house, there are many opportunities for love affairs. But these aren't serious things. Just entertainment.

Self-improvement

The sex drive of Leo is legendary. Only Scorpio can compare with it. Even so, Leo and Scorpio approach sex in different ways. For Leo, sex is entertainment and creativity (the way we make babies); for Scorpio it is more about power.

There is nothing evil about sex. It is the most sacred of the forces. And it is precisely this sacredness that makes it so dangerous when abused or misused. The stronger the force, the greater the negativity when abused. So, it is fitting that you're in a cycle of spiritualizing the sex force and the act itself, with Neptune the most spiritual of all the planets, in your 8th house of regeneration for some years.

With most people sex is an act of lust. But for you – especially in the past few years – you're learning other approaches to it. It can be an act of worship, a path to the Divine. Thus you are a candidate for disciplines such as Kundalini or Tantra yoga. Rightly used, sex can heal the body and even outer negative conditions. Learn as much as you can. This is a long-term trend.

We discussed the many career changes going on this year (and for the next several years). Spiritually speaking, the lesson here is to become comfortable with career instability and change, to embrace it and enjoy it. Consider it fun rather than a problem. Lose the fear about it. Meditation will be a big help.

Saturn and Pluto travel together this year. They will always be 'neighbours' but at times they will be much closer than that. This indicates a need to 'manage' the emotions (Pluto rules your 4th house of emotions and moods). You will have special power over them. However this needs to be used properly. Generally, people will repress their negative emotions, but this can only go on for so long. It's like trying to repress a cough. There is a need for a positive way to have psychic cleansings without repression (which can also damage the health). In my book *A Technique For Meditation* (chapters 2 and 3)* methods are given for this. The feeling nature is not to be repressed but directed in positive ways. We were never meant to be 'victims' of our feelings, but managers of them.

With the Moon as your spiritual planet, moods and emotions play a huge role in your spiritual life. It's very difficult to make contact with the Divine within when you're in a bad mood. Clear away the psychic debris and watch how much better your prayers and meditations go.

---

* Mantra Books, 2011.

Month-by-month Forecasts

January

Best Days Overall: 2, 3, 12, 13, 21, 22, 30, 31
Most Stressful Days Overall: 7, 8, 15, 16, 27, 28
Best Days for Love: 1, 3, 4, 7, 8, 12, 13, 14, 21, 22, 30, 31
Best Days for Money: 2, 3, 4, 5, 12, 13, 15, 16, 21, 22, 23, 24, 25
Best Days for Career: 1, 12, 13, 15, 16, 21, 22, 30, 31

You did plenty of partying last month, now it's time to get down to work. Whether you're employed or looking for work, there are lots of job opportunities for you this month. The Sun's conjunction with Saturn on the 1st and 2nd is an especially good time for jobseekers, but the whole month is good.

We have two eclipses this month – both of them will affect you strongly, so take it easy over those periods. The solar eclipse of the 6th (in America it happens on the 5th) occurs in your 6th house of health and work. This is the first of three eclipses that will occur in this house this year. This indicates job changes – this can be with your present company or with another one. Also, the conditions of the workplace can change. Over the coming months you'll be making dramatic changes to the health regime. Every solar eclipse forces you to redefine yourself – to redefine how you think of yourself and how you want others to think of you. This is a healthy thing. We are constantly changing and it's good, periodically, to upgrade our view of ourselves. This year the need seems greater than usual. Sometimes impurities in the body come up for cleansing.

The lunar eclipse of the 21st is almost (but not quite) a replay of the solar eclipse. It occurs in your own sign. Those of you born early in the sign of Leo (July 23–25) will feel this most strongly – but all of you will feel it to some degree. Again, it forces a redefinition of your self, your self-concept and the image that you present to others. If you haven't been careful in dietary matters, it can bring a detox of the body. Since the Moon is your spiritual planet, it signals upheavals and disturbances in spiritual organizations that you're involved with. There are dramas in the lives of gurus and guru figures in your life. You're making course corrections in your spiritual life – in your teachings and practice.

On the 20th, as the Sun (the ruler of your Horoscope) enters your 7th house, you begin a yearly love and social peak. Your personal popularity is unusually strong. You go out of your way for others and they appreciate this. You're there for your friends. With your love planet, Uranus, moving forward on the 6th, social confidence is good and love should be happy.

Health needs watching after the 20th. This doesn't seem serious, just a period of lower energy. Enhance the health in the ways mentioned in the yearly report.

February

Best Days Overall: 8, 9, 10, 17, 18, 26, 27
Most Stressful Days Overall: 3, 4, 5, 11, 12, 24, 25
Best Days for Love: 3, 4, 5, 10, 11, 18, 19, 20, 27, 28
Best Days for Money: 3, 4, 9, 10, 15, 16, 17, 18, 19, 20, 24, 25, 26, 27
Best Days for Career: 11, 12, 19, 20, 28

The planetary power is now mostly in the upper (day) side of your chart. On the 14th Mars will move into your 10th house, indicating much career activity and a need for aggressiveness, and next month Uranus will also move into your 10th house of career. So it is time to focus on the career and your outer goals and to attain them by the methods of day – by overt, physical actions.

Mars travels with Uranus, your love planet, from the 11th to the 14th. This can bring some disturbance or dramatic turn in the love life. Friends, children and children figures in your life should be more mindful on the physical level. Happily this transit is a short-term thing. You're still in the midst of a yearly love and social peak until the 19th, and still seem very popular. The new Moon of the 4th occurs in your 7th house of love and will illuminate relationship issues as the month progresses.

The planetary momentum is overwhelmingly forward this month, with *all* the planets moving forward (very unusually). This shows a fast-paced month and rapid forward progress to your goals. (There is a faster pace to world events as well.)

Your financial planet, Mercury, is in your 7th house until the 10th, signalling the importance of social connections in finance. Friends (and the current love) seem favourable to your financial goals. You'll probably spend more on socializing during this time, but it seems like a good use of money. On the 10th Mercury will move into your 8th house of regeneration and the sign of Pisces. This gives many messages. Intuition becomes important (especially on the 18th and 19th). This is a period for accessing the supernatural rather than the natural supply. It's a period for 'miracle money' rather than natural money. Natural money will, of course, happen, but it's the miracle money that is more interesting. The financial planet in the 8th house suggests a need for a financial detox. Get rid of waste or redundancies. Prosper by cutting back. Don't cut things that you need or enjoy, only the waste and the unneeded. It would be good to go through your physical possessions and get rid of things that you don't use or need. Sell them or give them to charity. It is a period for 'decluttering' (de-complicating) your environment. If you have good ideas for future projects, it is a good time to approach potential investors or banks. A good period to pay down debt or to apply for a loan – depending on your need. Good for tax planning and, for those of you who are older, estate planning.

The Sun will enter your 8th house (joining Mercury) on the 19th. So it is a good period for losing weight (if you need it) and a physical detox. The libido will be stronger than usual.

March

Best Days Overall: 8, 9, 17, 18, 25, 26
Most Stressful Days Overall: 3, 4, 10, 11, 23, 24, 30, 31
Best Days for Love: 1, 3, 4, 10, 15, 16, 19, 27, 23, 24, 27, 30, 31
Best Days for Money: 5, 6, 7, 8, 9, 15, 16, 17, 18, 19, 20, 23, 24, 25, 26
Best Days for Career: 3, 4, 10, 11, 15, 16, 23, 24

Love and career are the main headlines this month. Venus will be in your 7th house of love until the 26th, while, on the 7th, Uranus, your love planet, crosses your Mid-heaven and enters your 10th house. Venus and Uranus are now in 'mutual reception'. Each is a guest in the house of the other. The career planet, Venus, is in Uranus's house and Uranus is in Venus's house. This is a positive. It indicates good cooperation between the two planets. They are not likely to offend each other while they are guests in each other's house. This gives many messages. First off it shows the importance of love this month (this will be the case for many years to come, but especially now). It is high on the agenda – your mission and career for the month. It shows someone whose love and social life is career-related. You're attending gatherings and functions involved with your career and business. It shows someone who furthers the career by social means. You mix with the high and mighty in your life. You meet just the right people who can help you careerwise. Love too becomes more practical – a bit unusual for Leo. You gravitate to successful and powerful people. Power and status are romantic turn-ons. Singles find love opportunities as they pursue their career goals and with people involved in their career. This is an aspect of someone who marries or dates 'up'. Love and career go together these days. If love is going well, the career will go well. If career is going well, love will tend to go well.

In addition, Mars is still in your 10th house this month. Thus you're very active in the career. You have competition. You need to defend your turf, your brand or your position. There is need to be a 'career warrior'.

Finances are more complicated this month, however, as your financial planet, Mercury, is retrograde from the 5th to the 28th. This will slow down earnings, but won't stop them. There can be all kinds of glitches and delays in finance. Do your best to minimize these things by being particularly careful in all details of your financial dealings. Avoid major purchases or investments this period. Of course shop for groceries and other necessities, but big expenditures should be delayed. Financial clarity will come after the 28th when Mercury moves forward again, and that will be a good time to make your moves. Intuition is still very important in finances all month, but especially from the 24th to the 31st as Mercury 'camps out' on Neptune, the most spiritual of the planets. Take note of the dream life then too – there is financial guidance there. The dream life will get very active on the 15th and 16th as well.

Health is basically good, but needs a bit of attention this month. Detox regimes are beneficial.

April

Best Days Overall: 4, 5, 13, 14, 22, 23
Most Stressful Days Overall: 6, 7, 8, 19, 20, 26, 27
Best Days for Love: 2, 3, 6, 11, 12, 15, 21, 24, 26, 27
Best Days for Money: 2, 3, 4, 5, 13, 14, 15, 16, 22, 23
Best Days for Career: 2, 3, 6, 7, 8, 11, 12, 21

You're approaching a yearly career peak this month, beginning on the 20th. But Venus, your career planet, is having her solstice from the 22nd to the 25th. She pauses in the heavens (in her latitudinal motion) and then changes direction. She stays at the same degree of latitude those days. Thus a brief pause is in store for you too. Then a change of direction. A pause – a stillness – is always the prelude to action.

Health is wonderful now – especially until the 20th. Mars moves away from his stressful aspect and there is only one planet – Uranus – in stressful alignment with you. So energy is high and everything is possible. Progress should be swift this month too, with the planetary momentum overwhelmingly forward.

Finances are good too. Mercury moves forward all month. Until the 17th he is in spiritual Pisces, your 8th house – a good time to detox the financial life and de-clutter your environment. ('De-clog' might be a better description.) This will make room for the new and better that wants to come into your life. On the 17th Mercury moves into Aries, your 9th house. This shows expanded earnings. Your wealth goals are very high, and even if they aren't completely attained, this aspect still tends to prosperity. Financial decisions tend to be quick and decisive. And, generally, right.

The month ahead is successful. The ruler of your Horoscope crosses the Mid-heaven on the 20th and enters your 10th career house. You are above everyone in your world. You're in charge. People look up to you. You're a role model and a celebrity in your world. There is honour and recognition in store. You're successful as much because of your body, image and overall demeanour as for your professional achievements.

Health needs more attention after the 20th. There's nothing serious afoot, just a period of lower-than-usual energy. Enhance the health in the ways mentioned in the yearly report.

The Sun travels with your love planet from the 21st to the 23rd (and you'll probably feel the influence of this even before). This signals a change in the image and perhaps some experimenting with the body – testing its limits. But it also shows love. Singles have important romantic meetings. Those already in relationships are very close to the beloved now.

May

Best Days Overall: 1, 2, 3, 10, 11, 19, 20, 29, 30
Most Stressful Days Overall: 4, 5, 17, 18, 24, 25, 31
Best Days for Love: 2, 3, 4, 13, 14, 21, 24, 25, 31
Best Days for Money: 2, 3, 10, 11, 13, 14, 19, 20, 23, 24, 29, 30
Best Days for Career: 2, 3, 4, 5, 14, 21, 30, 31

Career is still the main headline this month. Your 10th house is chock-full of friendly planets – 40 per cent (and sometimes 50 per cent) of the planets are either there or moving through there this month. Your 4th house of home and family, by contrast, is empty; only the Moon moves through there on the 17th and 18th. Moreover, your family planet, Pluto, went into reverse on April 24. So issues at home are going to need time to resolve. You need to focus on the career. You're very successful this month – both personally and professionally. The Sun is still in your 10th house and while he is not the 'most elevated' planet this month, he is up there.

Venus starts to travel with Uranus, your love planet, from the 15th to the 19th, a romantic period. There can be business functions (socials) in that period as well. The spouse, partner or current love is helping your career and seems successful in his or her own right.

Health needs watching until the 21st. There's nothing serious here, just lower energy than usual. Make sure to get enough rest. Enhance the health in the ways mentioned in the yearly report. Saturn, your health planet, goes retrograde on the 2nd, so study all health regime changes and medications more carefully.

Finances are good this month. For a start, Mercury is moving very fast – faster than usual. Thus you have confidence and cover a lot of territory. It shows fast financial progress. In addition, Mercury is also in favourable signs and houses this month. Until the 6th he is in the 9th house – a very fortunate house (according to the Hindu astrologers, it is the most fortunate house). From the 6th to the 21st he is in your 10th house, at the top of the chart – another powerful position. Mercury is at his brightest here. And after the 21st he is in his own sign of Gemini, his natural home, his place of comfort. Until the 6th foreigners and foreign investments bring increase. From the 6th to the 21st you have the favour of bosses, parents and the authority figures in your life. Pay rises can happen. Your good career reputation brings earning opportunities. Mercury travels with Uranus on the 7th and 8th bringing unexpected money. From the 21st onwards friends and social connections are playing a big role in finances – they seem supportive.

June

Best Days Overall: 7, 8, 15, 16, 25, 26
Most Stressful Days Overall: 1, 13, 14, 20, 21, 27, 28, 29
Best Days for Love: 1, 9, 11, 17, 18, 20, 21, 27
Best Days for Money: 3, 4, 7, 8, 9, 10, 13, 14, 15, 16, 24, 25, 26
Best Days for Career: 1, 11, 20, 21, 27, 28, 29

Last month on the 15th the planetary power began to shift from the Western, social sector of your chart to the Eastern sector of self. This power shift gets stronger this month. The planets are moving towards you rather than away from you. Personal independence is growing day by day. Love, of course, is important – Uranus is still at the top of your chart. But now you are less dependent on others. You're thinking of your own interests – as you should. So if conditions irk you, make whatever changes need to be made. Your happiness is up to you.

Your 11th house of friends became powerful on May 21 and remains strong until June 21. So this is a social kind of month. But it is a detached kind of social life: it's more about friendship than romance. It's a social life with no strings attached. This is a good period to buy high-tech equipment and state-of-the-art gadgets (and you're probably doing this). It is also good to expand your overall knowledge of science, technology, astronomy and astrology.

The month ahead is spiritual too. Mars will spend the entire month in your 12th house. Mercury will join him on the 4th and the Sun on the 21st. With Mars, your planet of religion, in your spiritual 12th house, it is a very good time to explore the mystical traditions of your native religion. It also favours a more active kind of spirituality – the spirituality of good works.

Finances look good this month. Mercury is still moving faster than usual, moving through three signs and houses of your chart this month. Like last month it shows confidence and someone who makes fast financial progress. Until the 4th the social connections and the online world are important financially. From the 4th to the 27th the intuition once again becomes important. Beware of extreme moodiness in finances. If you have an important decision to make, sleep on it. Get quiet and peaceful, then make your decision. The end of the month seems the most prosperous period. Mercury crosses your Ascendant on the 27th and enters your own sign, signalling financial windfalls. Financial opportunity pursues you. The money people in your life seem devoted to you. Additionally, Mercury will start to make very nice aspects to Jupiter, the planet of abundance.

Your financial planet goes 'out of bounds' from the 1st to the 16th. This indicates some adventurous financial behaviour. You're willing (and perhaps you must) to go outside your normal haunts to attain your goals. There are no answers in the usual places; you must look beyond. You're thinking 'outside the box' financially.

Health is good this month.

July

Best Days Overall: 4, 5, 13, 14, 22, 23, 24, 31
Most Stressful Days Overall: 10, 11, 17, 18, 19, 25, 26
Best Days for Love: 1, 6, 10, 11, 15, 17, 18, 19, 20, 21, 25, 31
Best Days for Money: 4, 5, 6, 7, 13, 14, 21, 22, 23, 24, 29, 30, 31
Best Days for Career: 1, 10, 11, 20, 21, 25, 26, 31

The month ahead is happy and successful, this in spite of two eclipses happening. The only issue is that we are at maximum retrograde activity for the year. So things are slowing down in the world. The pace of life is slower. You have to deal with more glitches and delays.

The two eclipses are almost replays (but not quite) of the eclipses of January. The solar eclipse of the 2nd occurs in your 6th house of health and work. Thus, once again, there are job changes and changes in the conditions of work. If you hire others, there can be staff turnover now. The health regime changes in dramatic ways (and this will go on for the next few months). Pluto, your family planet, is affected by this eclipse, so there are dramas in the lives of family members, and especially with a parent or parent figure. Repairs might be needed in the home – hidden flaws come to light. Every solar eclipse impacts on your body, image and self-concept, and this one is no different. So, once again, you need to redefine yourself. You will be changing the way you think about yourself and the way you want others to think about you. You will present a 'new look' to the world over the next six months.

The lunar eclipse of the 16th occurs in your 12th house of spirituality, bringing major changes in your spiritual life. Keep in mind that there is a double hit here. The eclipse is in the 12th house and impacts on the ruler of that house, the Moon. So there are disturbances in spiritual and charitable organizations you're involved with. There are dramas in the lives of guru figures in your life. Your dream life is apt to be hyperactive and disturbing too. But don't give your dreams much weight at this time – they are 'psychic waste', not scenes of the future. The eclipse will prompt you to change your spiritual practice and attitudes. Perhaps even your teachers and teachings. You're in a spiritual course correction period, which is a good thing.

Yet, as we mentioned, the month ahead is happy. Your health is basically good. Your 1st house becomes very powerful from the 23rd onwards. You're in one of your yearly personal pleasure peaks. You have confidence and self-esteem. You look great. You are expressing the star that you are. Usually this is good for love, but love seems better before the 23rd than after. Perhaps the beloved sees you as too self-centred, too in love with yourself. You need to work harder on your relationship.

Your financial planet goes retrograde from the 7th onwards. So, although financial opportunities are coming your way, they need more homework and there can be delays. Patience is the keynote for the month ahead.

August

> Best Days Overall: 1, 9, 10, 19, 20, 28, 29
> Most Stressful Days Overall: 7, 8, 14, 15, 21, 22
> Best Days for Love: 1, 2, 9, 10, 11, 14, 15, 20, 21, 30, 31
> Best Days for Money: 1, 2, 3, 9, 10, 19, 20, 28, 29, 30, 31
> Best Days for Career: 1, 9, 10, 20, 21, 22, 30, 31

Retrograde activity is still high, but less so than last month (40 per cent of the planets are moving backward for most of the month). So the pace of life is still slow. However, again the month ahead is both happy and prosperous.

Last month the planetary power was at its maximum Eastern position. And this is the case now as well, so you are in a period of maximum personal independence. You have the support of the cosmos. This is the time to make those changes in your life that need to be made. This is the time to take responsibility for your own happiness. Your interests are just as important as anyone else's. Later on, as the planets shift to the West again, these changes will be more difficult.

You're still in the midst of one of your yearly personal pleasure peaks. So this is a time for enjoying all the physical and sensual pleasures – good food, good wine, massages and general pampering of the body. There is travel in store as well (this could have happened last month too). The physical appearance shines. You emanate a light.

Venus in your sign until the 21st brings happy career opportunities to you and adds beauty, grace and style to your image. Mars in your sign (he was there last month too) adds energy, courage and a 'can do' spirit. In spite of all this, love seems difficult. Like last month you need to work harder on your relationship. Also, your love planet Uranus will start to go into reverse on the 12th. Love should improve after the 23rd. Part of the problem in love is not the relationship per se but the stresses on the beloved. This complicates things. For singles the 29th and 30th bring happy romantic opportunities.

With your financial planet now moving forward again (from the 2nd), the month ahead is very prosperous. In fact it's one of the best financial months in your year. Mercury will be in your spiritual 12th house until the 11th. So be alert to intuition. On the 11th he will cross your Ascendant and enter your 1st house, bringing financial windfalls and opportunities. You look rich and you feel rich. People see you this way and you're probably dressing this way. On the 23rd, as the Sun moves into your money house, you begin a yearly financial peak. Mars, moves into your money house on the 18th, and this indicates business-related travel. Venus moves into the 2nd house on the 21st, signalling the financial favour of the authority figures in your life. And, if all this wasn't enough, the Moon will (unusually) visit the money house twice this month.

Health is excellent all month. You have the energy of ten people. There's nothing you can't accomplish once you set your mind to it.

September

Best Days Overall: 5, 6, 15, 16, 24, 25
Most Stressful Days Overall: 3, 4, 10, 11, 17, 18, 19, 30
Best Days for Love: 7, 8, 9, 10, 11, 17, 20, 26, 28, 29
Best Days for Money: 5, 6, 8, 9, 15, 16, 20, 21, 24, 25, 26, 27, 28, 29
Best Days for Career: 8, 9, 17, 18, 19, 20, 28, 29

The month ahead is still very prosperous. Your yearly financial peak continues until the 23rd. Mars, the ruler of your 9th house (who functions as a friend and beneficent planet) will be in your money house all month. This shows, like last month, business-related travel. But it also indicates financial good fortune and expansion. Whatever your financial status is in life, this is a period of increased earnings.

Love seems happy this month too. The beloved is feeling better. There is less stress on him or her and this helps things. Also, you seem more in harmony with him or her. Love and social opportunities are still happening as you pursue your career goals, but this is not a strong career period. The planetary power is now mostly below the horizon of your chart – in the night side. So this is a period (and next month too) for career preparation. Preparation is 90 per cent of success. If your preparation is good, the chances are that your actions and execution will also be good.

Your career planet, Venus, has her solstice (one of them) from the 15th to the 18th. She occupies the same degree of latitude and then reverses direction (in latitude). This is similar to what happens when the Sun has his twice-yearly solstices. This pause – a space – in career activity will lead to a change of direction.

Venus will be in your money house until the 14th, indicating (as mentioned last month), the financial favour of the 'higher ups' – the authority figures – in your life. But it also shows that you measure career success in monetary terms, not in terms of prestige or status. If you earn more you're more successful. If you earn less, you're less successful. Status has no real relevance. On the 14th Venus will move into your 3rd house of communication and intellectual interests. Thus good marketing and PR are important for the career. Your gift of the gab is a boost. Your knowledge is well received and appreciated by your superiors.

Your 3rd house becomes very powerful after the 23rd and this is excellent for students. They seem serious at school, focused on their studies, and this tends to success. Even if you're not a formal student, however, this is a good month to become one. A good time to attend classes, seminars, lectures and workshops (especially those that relate to finance and career). Good to catch up on your reading and build up your knowledge. A good month to study a foreign language too.

The job situation seems more turbulent after the 23rd. You need to work harder there. Relations with co-workers (or employees) seem more complicated.

Health is excellent.

October

Best Days Overall: 2, 3, 4, 12, 13, 21, 22, 30, 31
Most Stressful Days Overall: 1, 7, 8, 15, 16, 28, 29
Best Days for Love: 5, 7, 8, 10, 11, 14, 15, 19, 20, 23, 28, 29
Best Days for Money: 2, 3, 4, 10, 11, 12, 13, 19, 20, 21, 22, 23, 24, 28, 29, 30, 31
Best Days for Career: 10, 11, 15, 16, 19, 20, 28, 29

Your 4th house of home and family becomes ultra-powerful after the 23rd. The planetary power is now at its maximum lower position with 70 per cent (sometimes 80 per cent) of the planets on the night side of the chart. Figuratively speaking, you're in the midnight hour of your year. So, career can be downplayed. The focus needs to be on the home and family and your emotional wellness. Even Venus, your career planet, will be in your 4th house from the 8th onwards. Home and family *is* the career this month.

Career is still important, but is advanced in different ways. This is, as mentioned last month, a period of preparation for the next career push, which will happen next year. Preparation is just as important as actual execution. Without good preparation, execution will suffer. This is also a good time to pursue career goals in interior ways – by the methods of night rather than the methods of day. Visualize, dream, put yourself in the feeling of what you want to achieve. Live as much as possible in that feeling. When the time comes for overt action (next year), it will happen effortlessly and smoothly. When you visualize your career goals make a note of what comes up in your mind. What feelings arise? These are good clues as to what obstacles need to be overcome psychologically.

Health needs some attention from the 23rd onwards. As always, make sure to get enough rest. Enhance the health in the ways mentioned in the yearly report. It won't hurt to timetable in more massages or other health treatments.

Finance doesn't seem a big issue this month. Mars leaves the money house on the 4th and after that the house is basically empty. (Only the Moon will move through there on the 23rd and 24th.) This is most likely a good thing. Financial goals (the short-term ones at least) have been achieved now and you can focus on your intellectual interests and emotional wellness. Mercury spends most of the month in your 4th house (from the 3rd onwards). Thus you're spending more on the home and family and can earn from here as well. Family support should be good. Be careful of excessive moodiness in financial matters. In a good mood you're as rich as Croesus; in a bad mood you feel like a pauper. Make sure to be in a calm, serene mood before making important financial decisions. Sleep on things.

Love becomes more stressful after the 23rd. You and the beloved are not in synch. You see things in opposite ways. You seem more distant with each other – not necessarily just physically but psychologically too. It will be a challenge to bridge your differences, but if you can, your relationship will be stronger than ever. Singles – the unattached – don't seem much interested in love these days. This is a temporary situation that will pass in the coming months. The retrograde of the love planet is not helping matters.

November

Best Days Overall: 8, 9, 10, 18, 19, 26, 27
Most Stressful Days Overall: 3, 4, 5, 11, 12, 24, 25
Best Days for Love: 1, 3, 4, 5, 8, 9, 11, 18, 19, 20, 28, 29
Best Days for Money: 6, 7, 8, 9, 10, 16, 17, 18, 19, 20, 21, 24, 25, 26, 27
Best Days for Career: 8, 9, 11, 12, 18, 19, 29

Continue to focus on the home and family, and especially on your emotional wellness this month. Keep in mind last month's discussion. Your 4th house is still very powerful, until the 22nd. Mars will move into this house on the 19th and stay there for the rest of the month. This will be an excellent time for making repairs or home renovations. For some of you it is a good time to build a home.

Mars will make dynamic aspects with Uranus from the 22nd to the 25th. You, family members and the beloved should be more mindful on the physical plane.

Career is not a major focus this month, but in spite of this a happy career opportunity will arise between the 22nd and the 24th. There are good career opportunities for children and children figures too. It looks like a nice payday for them as well. Your career planet, Venus, spends most of the month (until the 26th) in your 5th house. Thus just following the 'path of bliss' will help the career. A lot of blockages in life come from worry. When you're having fun, worry tends to leave and the natural cosmic solutions to problems get revealed.

On the 22nd the Sun enters your 5th house and you begin another one of your yearly personal pleasure peaks. It's party time! Time to enjoy life. We don't need to give you any lectures about this, Leo – you know how to do this!

Finances are more complicated this month as your financial planet, Mercury, is retrograde from the 2nd to the 20th. If you have important financial decisions to make, wait until after the 20th. Financial judgement will be a lot better then. Mercury will spend the month in your 4th house (he was there last month too), so family support is good and you can earn money from home and through family connections. Mercury in the sign of Scorpio, which rules detox, shows that it's a good time to de-clutter and de-complicate your finances. Simplify. Get rid of extraneous bank or investment accounts. Eliminate waste. Get rid of possessions that you don't need or use. This will unclog the 'financial arteries'.

Health still needs watching until the 22nd, but improves afterwards. Pace yourself and make sure to get enough rest. Enhance the health in the ways mentioned in the yearly report.

Love is improving, but still needs more work. There is still distance between you and the beloved, and singles feel 'distant' from their social interests. This will change next month.

December

Best Days Overall: 6, 7, 15, 16, 24, 25
Most Stressful Days Overall: 1, 2, 8, 9, 21, 22, 28, 29
Best Days for Love: 1, 2, 8, 9, 17, 18, 26, 28, 29
Best Days for Money: 6, 7, 8, 15, 16, 17, 18, 25, 26
Best Days for Career: 8, 9, 17, 18, 28, 29

A happy month ahead. You work hard but you play hard too. You manage to have fun and to be productive.

A solar eclipse on the 26th occurs in your 6th house of health and work – this is the third eclipse this year in that house. So, there are job changes happening. This time they seem good. Jupiter will be in your 6th house from the 3rd onwards (and well into next year). Job changes should be welcomed. Big improvements are happening. Once again it is necessary to change your health regime. Sometimes these kinds of eclipses produce health scares, but your health is very good and any such scare will probably not amount to much. Children and children figures in your life are affected by this eclipse, so it is best if they take it easy over this period. If foreign travel can be avoided it should. They have had a prosperous past year and now (and for next year) the prosperity is even stronger. Every solar eclipse forces you to re-imagine and redefine yourself. This one is no different. Apparently you've been growing and more redefinitions of yourself are necessary. You're not some 'static' kind of person. You're growing and evolving, and your self-concept needs to reflect this.

The month ahead, eclipse notwithstanding, is happy. Health is good. You're having fun – especially until the 22nd. Prosperity is strong and many job opportunities are coming to you – good ones. If you are unemployed, this condition will not last long. You have five or six job opportunities to choose from. And even those of you already employed will have overtime or jobs on the side. One job is not enough for you these days, but you'll have plenty of energy to handle them.

The other headline this month is the improvement in your love life. Marriage is not advisable just yet – your love planet Uranus is still retrograde. But love is happy. Jupiter will be making very nice aspects to Uranus all month – especially from the 13th to the 17th. This indicates fun with the beloved. For singles it shows happy romantic meetings. Uranus is receiving very nice aspects from other planets too, not just Jupiter. The Sun will trine Uranus on the 23rd and 24th – another happy romantic and social period. On the 20th Venus will enter your 7th house for the second time this year. Again she will be in 'mutual reception' with your love planet, signalling good cooperation between them. Each is a guest in the house of the other. This indicates socializing with important people – the 'higher ups' in your life. You're meeting people socially who can help your career. Bosses, parents and parent figures are playing Cupid.

Virgo

♍

THE VIRGIN

Birthdays from
22nd August to
22nd September

Personality Profile

VIRGO AT A GLANCE

Element – Earth

Ruling Planet – Mercury
   Career Planet – Mercury
   Love Planet – Neptune
   Money Planet – Venus
   Planet of Home and Family Life – Jupiter
   Planet of Health and Work – Uranus
   Planet of Pleasure – Saturn
   Planet of Sexuality – Mars

Colours – earth tones, ochre, orange, yellow

Colour that promotes love, romance and social harmony – aqua blue

Colour that promotes earning power – jade green

Gems – agate, hyacinth

Metal – quicksilver

Scents – lavender, lilac, lily of the valley, storax

Quality – mutable (= flexibility)

Quality most needed for balance – a broader perspective

Strongest virtues – mental agility, analytical skills, ability to pay attention to detail, healing powers

Deepest needs – to be useful and productive

Characteristic to avoid – destructive criticism

Signs of greatest overall compatibility – Taurus, Capricorn

Signs of greatest overall incompatibility – Gemini, Sagittarius, Pisces

Sign most helpful to career – Gemini

Sign most helpful for emotional support – Sagittarius

Sign most helpful financially – Libra

Sign best for marriage and/or partnerships – Pisces

Sign most helpful for creative projects – Capricorn

Best Sign to have fun with – Capricorn

Signs most helpful in spiritual matters – Taurus, Leo

Best day of the week – Wednesday

Understanding a Virgo

The virgin is a particularly fitting symbol for those born under the sign of Virgo. If you meditate on the image of the virgin you will get a good understanding of the essence of the Virgo type. The virgin is, of course, a symbol of purity and innocence – not naïve, but pure. A virginal object has not been touched. A virgin field is land that is true to itself, the way it has always been. The same is true of virgin forest: it is pristine, unaltered.

Apply the idea of purity to the thought processes, emotional life, physical body and activities of the everyday world, and you see how Virgos approach life. Virgos desire the pure expression of the ideal in their mind, body and affairs. If they find impurities – the beginning of disorder, unhappiness and uneasiness – they will attempt to clear them away.

The secrets of good health are here revealed: 90 per cent of the art of staying well is maintaining a pure mind, a pure body and pure emotions. When you introduce more impurities than your mind and body can deal with, you will have what is known as 'dis-ease'. It is no wonder that Virgos make great doctors, nurses, healers and dieticians. They have an innate understanding of good health and they realize that good health is more than just physical. In all aspects of life, if you want a project to be successful it must be kept as pure as possible. This is the secret behind Virgo's awesome technical proficiency.

One could talk about Virgo's analytical powers – which are formidable. One could talk about their perfectionism and their almost superhuman attention to detail. But this would be to miss the point. All of these virtues are manifestations of a Virgo's desire for purity and perfection – a world without Virgos would have ruined itself long ago.

Virgos' apparent vices come from their inherent virtue. Their analytical powers, which should be used for healing, helping or perfecting a project in the world, sometimes get misapplied and turned against people. Their critical faculties, which should be used constructively to perfect a strategy or proposal, can sometimes be used destructively to harm or wound. Their urge to perfection can turn into worry and lack of confidence; their natural humility can become self-denial and self-abasement. When Virgos turn negative they are apt to turn their devastating criticism on themselves, sowing the seeds of self-destruction.

Finance

Virgos have all the attitudes that create wealth. They are hard-working, industrious, efficient, organized, thrifty, productive and eager to serve. A developed Virgo is every employer's dream. But until Virgos master some of the social graces of Libra they will not even come close to fulfilling their financial potential. Purity and perfectionism, if not handled correctly or gracefully, can be very trying to others. Friction in human relationships can be devastating not only to your pet projects but – indirectly – to your wallet as well.

Virgos are quite interested in their financial security. Being hard-working, they know the true value of money. They do not like to take risks with their money, preferring to save for their retirement or for a rainy day. Virgos usually make prudent, calculated investments that involve a minimum of risk. These investments and savings usually work out well, helping Virgos to achieve the financial security they seek. The rich or even not-so-rich Virgo also likes to help his or her friends in need.

Career and Public Image

Virgos reach their full potential when they can communicate their knowledge in such a way that others can understand it. In order to get their ideas across better, Virgos need to develop greater verbal skills and fewer judgemental ways of expressing themselves. Virgos look up to teachers and communicators; they like their bosses to be good communicators. Virgos will probably not respect a superior who is not their intellectual equal – no matter how much money or power that superior has. Virgos themselves like to be perceived by others as being educated and intellectual.

The natural humility of Virgos often inhibits them from fulfilling their great ambitions, from acquiring name and fame. Virgos should indulge in a little more self-promotion if they are going to reach their career goals. They need to push themselves with the same ardour that they would use to foster others.

At work Virgos like to stay active. They are willing to learn any type of job as long as it serves their ultimate goal of financial security. Virgos may change occupations several times before they find the one they really enjoy. Virgos work well with other people, are not afraid to work hard and always fulfil their responsibilities.

Love and Relationships

If you are an analyst or a critic you must, out of necessity, narrow your scope. You have to focus on a part and not the whole; this can create a temporary narrow-mindedness. Virgos do not like this kind of person. They like their partners to be broad-minded, with depth and vision. Virgos seek to get this broad-minded quality from their partners, since they sometimes lack it themselves.

Virgos are perfectionists in love just as they are in other areas of life. They need partners who are tolerant, open-minded and easy-going. If you are in love with a Virgo do not waste time on impractical romantic gestures. Do practical and useful things for him or her – this is what will be appreciated and what will be done for you.

Virgos express their love through pragmatic and useful gestures, so do not be put off because your Virgo partner does not say 'I love you' day-in and day-out. Virgos are not that type. If they love you, they will demonstrate it in practical ways. They will always be there for you; they will show an interest in your health and finances; they will fix your sink or repair your gadgets. Virgos deem these actions to be superior to sending flowers, chocolates or Valentine cards.

In love affairs Virgos are not particularly passionate or spontaneous. If you are in love with a Virgo, do not take this personally. It does not mean that you are not alluring enough or that your Virgo partner does not love or like you. It is just the way Virgos are. What they lack in passion they make up for in dedication and loyalty.

Home and Domestic Life

It goes without saying that the home of a Virgo will be spotless, sanitized and orderly. Everything will be in its proper place. For Virgos to find domestic bliss they need to ease up a bit in the home, to allow their partner and children more freedom and to be more generous and open-minded. Family members are not to be analysed under a microscope, they are individuals with their own virtues to express.

With these small difficulties resolved, Virgos like to stay in and entertain at home. They make good hosts and like to keep their guests happy at social gatherings. Virgos love children, but they are strict with them – at times – since they want to make sure their children are brought up with the correct sense of family values.

Horoscope for 2019

Major Trends

The year ahead is basically happy, with a few challenges thrown in just to keep things interesting!

Your 5th house of fun, children and creativity is easily the strongest in the Horoscope this year – and it will get even stronger after December 3. So the year ahead is creative and fun-filled. With you even fun has to have some purpose, some practical rationale, and this is the case this year. Fun just for the sake of fun is not your style. Learning to discipline and communicate properly with children will be an important focus.

Jupiter will spend almost all year in your 4th house of home and family. Often this indicates a move and an expansion of the family circle. Jupiter in the 4th house (and then, from early December, in your 5th house) often shows a pregnancy for those of childbearing age.

Neptune has been in your 7th house of love for many years, and will be there for many more. You need someone spiritual as a mate or love.

Uranus has been in your 8th house of regeneration for the past seven years, but now this year he is going to leave finally. The era of sexual experimentation is over with. By now you know what works for you and it's time to experiment in other areas – in your religious, philosophical and theological beliefs. This will be a long-term trend. There will be much change here in the coming years. These changes will impact well on your health.

This year, unusually, we will have five eclipses (normally there are only four). Of the five, four will impact on your spiritual life. So major changes and upheavals are going on; these also indicate dramatic changes in the spiritual or charitable organizations you're involved with.

Your most important areas of interest this year are home and family (until December 3); children, fun and creativity; love and romance; sex, personal transformation and occult studies (until March 7); and religion, philosophy, theology and foreign travel (from March 7 onwards).

Your paths of greatest fulfilment this year are home and family (until December 3); children, fun and creativity (from December 3 onwards); and friends, groups and group activities.

Health

(Please note that this is an astrological perspective on health and not a medical one. In days of yore there was no difference, both of these perspectives were identical. But now there could be quite a difference. For a medical perspective, please consult your doctor or health practitioner.)

Overall health and energy is much better than it was in 2016 and 2017. And, come December 3, it will be even better than last year. Most of the long-term planets are in harmonious aspect with you, with only two – Jupiter and Neptune – making stressful aspects. (And, from December 3 even Jupiter will start to make positive aspects.)

Of course, there will be periods in the year where health and energy are less easy than usual and perhaps even stressful. However, these are not trends for the year, only the temporary effect of the short-term planets. When they pass, health and energy will return to their norms.

Health is normally always important for a Virgo, but this year less so than usual. Your 6th house of health is basically empty – only short-term planets will move through there and their effect is temporary. With the way your chart is this year, an empty 6th house is a good thing. You can more or less take good health for granted, with no need to focus overly on it.

Good though your health is you can make it even better. Give more attention to the following – the vulnerable areas of your Horoscope (the reflexology points are shown in the chart above):

- The small intestine. This is always important for Virgo as your sign rules this organ. However, you always pay attention to diet, and you tend to be on the case.

- The ankles and calves are another important area for Virgo. Uranus, your health planet, rules these. Regular ankle and calf massage should be part of your health regime. The ankles tend to need more support when exercising.
- The head, face and scalp. These have gained in importance over the past seven years, as your health planet has been in Aries. After March 7 however, they will become rather less of an issue. Until then, continue to massage the scalp and face on a regular basis. Craniosacral therapy is also good for the head.
- The musculature. As with the head and face, the muscles wane in importance after March 7. In the meantime vigorous exercise is good. After March 7, gentler exercises will suffice.
- The adrenals. Like the muscles, head and face, these have been important while Uranus has been in Aries and will be less so after March 7. As always avoid anger and fear, the twin emotions that stress the adrenals. Ginseng is said to be good for them.

Important foot reflexology points for the year ahead

Try to massage all of the foot on a regular basis – the top of the foot as well as the bottom – but pay extra attention to the points highlighted on the chart. When you massage, be aware of 'sore spots' as these need special attention. It's also a very good idea to massage the ankles especially, and below them.

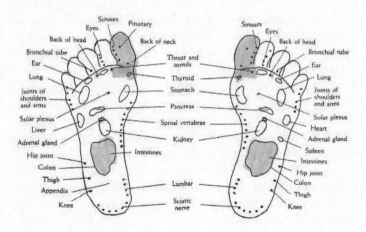

- The neck and throat. These gain in importance after March 7 as your health planet moves into Taurus, the sign that rules these areas. Regular neck massage should become part of your health regime for the next seven years. Craniosacral therapy is good for the neck too.

Since these are the most vulnerable areas this year, problems, if they happened (God forbid), would most likely begin here. Thus keeping them healthy and fit is sound preventive medicine. Usually problems can be averted completely. But even in cases where they can't (due to karma) they can be mitigated to a large extent. They will not be as severe as they could be.

Uranus's move into Taurus, your 9th house, shows that your personal philosophy of life – your theology (or lack of it) – is playing a big role in your overall health. Health problems (along with all other problems) are only masks for theological problems. Underneath all the medical and psychological verbiage lies a theological deficiency, some misconception about the nature of the Divine. In the coming years you will see this. The best cure for error (the main pathology of the philosophical mind) is light. It will be good to invoke it regularly.

Your philosophy of health and disease, your philosophy of what the body is, also is important. The current prevailing philosophy is not adequate and will need to be amended.

The health planet in the 9th house shows the power of prayer (a bit different from meditation) as a valid healing force. You get to learn this over the next seven years.

Home and Family

With Jupiter in your 4th house of home and family this year, this is a major focus. Basically it shows happiness and success here. As we mentioned earlier, the family circle is enlarged. Generally this happens through birth or marriage, but not always. Sometimes you meet people who are 'like' family to you (and they were probably family members in past incarnations). They give you the unconditional support that would usually come from the family.

If you are of childbearing age (and this applies to members of your family too) fertility is much stronger than usual. The family as a whole prospers this year and next. There is good family support these days.

Jupiter in the 4th house often signals a move – a relocation. But this need not be taken too literally. Often the home is renovated or enlarged and it is 'as if' you have moved. Sometimes expensive items are bought for the home, making the present home happier and better. Sometimes people buy additional homes or they have access to an additional home. There is good fortune in the purchase or sale of a home.

Jupiter in the 4th house gives other messages as well. It shows that the year ahead is one of great psychological progress. Important psychological breakthroughs will happen. Those of you undergoing therapy will make great strides. And even if you're not undergoing any official kind of therapy, your psychological understanding will increase.

Dealing with children and children figures in your life seems like the main challenge this year. It seems like a burden, but you will handle it. Children need limits and some discipline – not cruelty, but an understanding of what is and is not permissible. Sometimes tough love is needed, but it should never be overdone. Tough love at an early age – when behaviour is more correctable – will often prevent serious problems later on in life. Educating the children also seems like a challenge.

A parent or parent figure is prospering this year and very involved in your domestic life – it seems like in a good way. He or she is doing more travelling this year but is not likely to move. (There's nothing against it however.)

Siblings and sibling figures are also prospering this year. They're having a banner financial year. They are feeling a need for a change of residence, but it is more likely to happen next year.

Children and children figures have been emotionally volatile these past seven years but they appear calmer, especially after March 7.

Grandchildren (if you have them), or those who play that role in your life, are restless this year. They might not physically move, but they will be staying in different places for long periods of time. They are more rebellious these days too. They want to explore their personal freedom. Many are testing the limits of their bodies.

If you're planning any home renovations, all this year will be good for such work. If you're beautifying the home – redecorating in a cosmetic kind of way - January 7 to February 8 and November 1 to December 22 are good times.

Finance and Career

Money doesn't seem a big issue this year. The money house is empty and only short-term planets will move through there temporarily. (The Moon will move there, briefly, every month.) But these are not long-term trends. It's not an especially strong financial year and the tendency will be to the status quo. You have more freedom in shaping the financial life, but lack the interest and motivation (usually because you're more or less content with things as they are).

Money is important, but it's not everything. And it is certainly not the purpose of life, as some have made it. Love, children, creativity, family and personal happiness are much more important than money this year. Keep in mind that the 2nd house is only one of the twelve houses - a small part of the total picture.

As we mentioned earlier, there is good family support for you this year. There is good fortune in buying or selling a home. Residential real estate, restaurants, the food business and hotels seem like interesting investments this year. You have a good feeling for them. A family business would be attractive too.

With Venus as your financial planet you have a natural affinity for the beauty industry - fashion, cosmetics, jewellery, art, antiques, interior design - things and products that beautify people and life. And, of course, the health field (your natural interest) is always good.

Venus is a fast-moving planet. In any given year she will move through all the signs and houses of your chart and make aspects (connections) to every one of your planets. (This year she is moving about a third faster than usual too.) Thus there are many short-term trends in finance that depend on where she is and the aspects she receives (or makes). These are best dealt with in the monthly reports.

Venus's fast motion this year is a positive financial signal. It shows confidence. It shows someone who makes fast progress. It shows stronger earning power. But, as we've said, there is a lack of interest.

This is not an especially strong career year for you either. Your 4th house of home and family is much stronger than your 10th career house (which is basically empty). And though you tend to be ambitious by nature, this year you are less so than usual.

Mercury is your career planet and he moves even faster than Venus. So, there are many short-term career trends that depend on where Mercury is and the aspects he receives and makes, which again are best discussed in the monthly reports.

Love and Social Life

The love and social trends haven't changed much over previous years. Neptune has been in your 7th house for some time now and will be there for many more years to come. The love life is becoming more spiritualized – more idealistic – and this is an ongoing process. The transit of a planet like Neptune is not really an 'event' but a process, a long series of events with a certain goal in mind.

So, as in previous years (and it is good to repeat things for the sake of newer readers), you're attracting spiritual-type people into your social sphere. In fact, these connections are a big part of your spiritual growth.

If you've been going to the usual bars and clubs looking for love, you're wasting your time. You might find sex or a night's entertainment, but not love. For love you need to go to spiritual seminars and lectures, to charity events, or events put on by altruistic organizations. You need to meet people who are on your spiritual wavelength.

For those of you already in a relationship (and most of you are), the challenge is to balance your home and family interests with your love interests. The current love or spouse doesn't seem in synch with your family. More work will be needed here. Also there are all kinds of revelations about the current love that don't sit well with the family (especially one of the parent figures).

The same is more or less true for singles. The family doesn't seem to approve of the people you're dating. Also family ties and responsibilities are distracting you from your social life. This will pass by the end of the year, but in the meantime it's a challenge.

Singles are searching for 'ideal love' and don't seem to brook compromise. The problem is that while some humans have a greater capacity for love than others, few can live up to your idealized desires. So, even the best of relationships carries some degree of disappointment.

There is a serious romantic relationship for singles this year. There is someone there in your house of love. A spiritual, artistic, inspired kind of person – perhaps a musician, a poet, a dancer, a spiritual channel or minister type. These are the kinds of people who allure you.

Love information and guidance will come to you in dreams (and you need to pay attention) or through psychics, astrologers, tarot readers, mediums or spiritual channels. If there is confusion here it would be beneficial to consult with people such as these.

With good spiritual compatibility almost every problem in a relationship can be worked out. Nothing is impossible to spirit. But without it, almost nothing can work out.

Last year was a banner love and social year. Many of you married or got involved in serious relationships – relationships that were like a marriage. For most of this year the love life is OK. Not spectacular but OK. But by the end of the year – after December 3 – it starts to sparkle. Next year will be even better.

The spouse, partner or current love is having a very strong career year and there is much success happening. This could be a distraction for him or her, in terms of your relationship. He or she seems focused on his or her own interests and this could also be a problem.

Self-improvement

We mentioned earlier that there is great – dramatic – change happening in your spiritual life, in your spiritual practice, teachings and teachers. Four of the five eclipses this year impact on the spiritual life. Generally people have misguided notions of what the spiritual life is all about and are many superstitions involved. These notions will get tested and many will have to be revised. Often spiritual practice changes because of interior revelation – the whole object of spiritual practice. Thus change happens. Some of you will be moving from one spiritual group to the next until some new bombshell happens that causes change. Gurus and guru figures in your life will also be having personal kinds of dramas – and often this produces change in teachers and teachings. There are many scenarios of what can happen. But the end result will be a new spiritual path, a new way or approach.

We've discussed the spiritual implications of Neptune in your 7th house in past reports. Since this trend is still very much in effect, we should repeat this for the sake of newer readers. On the surface this transit shows a desire for 'ideal' love, which we have discussed above. But there is a much deeper agenda happening here. The cosmos is guiding you, little by little, to the realization of spiritual love – the real ideal. No human being can ever completely fulfil this ideal – not in our present stage of evolution. But once contact is made with the 'Inner Lover' – the Divine – all one's love needs are fulfilled. All means *all*. Whatever the need is, the Divine will fulfil it. Whether you are in a relationship or not, you will feel basically the same. You will always feel loved. In a relationship you will experience certain pleasures. Out of a relationship you will experience other pleasures. But it won't matter much. You won't have this pressing need to be in a relationship. You will never feel lonely. Love is only a thought away. A turn of your attention. This won't happen overnight but as a gradual process.

With Neptune in your 7th house it is important to surrender the love life to the Divine – and do it sincerely – and let that handle things. If this is done properly miracles start to happen. A good affirmation is: 'I cast the burden of my love life on the God within and I go free.' Repeat it over and over until you start to feel it.

Uranus in your 9th house of religion, philosophy and theology after March 7 shows that your religious and philosophical beliefs will get challenged. Many will be exploded (Uranus likes drama and explosions); many will need to be revised. The challenges are likely to come from the scientific world. By the time Uranus is finished with you in seven years' time, you will have a whole new philosophy of life – and a much better one. This change in philosophy will impact on every other area of life in a positive way. So many of our hindrances stem from philosophical or theological errors. Truth, indeed, sets one free.

Month-by-month Forecasts

January

Best Days Overall: 5, 6, 15, 16, 23, 24
Most Stressful Days Overall: 2, 3, 10, 11, 17, 18, 30, 31
Best Days for Love: 1, 10, 11, 12, 13, 19, 20, 21, 22, 27, 28, 30, 31
Best Days for Money: 1, 2, 3, 12, 13, 21, 22, 25, 26, 30, 31
Best Days for Career: 4, 5, 15, 16, 17, 18, 25

The month ahead looks happy, even with two eclipses happening. They will just add some spice – some excitement – to the month. The eclipses seem kind to you (but if they hit some sensitive point in your personal Natal chart, cast especially for you, you will certainly feel it).

You're in one of your yearly personal pleasure periods, which began last month on the 22nd. This is a time to relax, drop your cares and enjoy the thrill of life. Personal creativity is very strong – and very good. Those involved in the creative arts should have a productive month.

The solar eclipse of the 6th (in America it happens on the 5th) occurs in your 5th house and impacts on the children and children figures in your life. They have personal dramas. Some of these dramas can be quite normal, but they produce major change – puberty, sexual awakening, going off to college, etc. Still it won't hurt for them to take it easy over this time and avoid stressful, daredevil activities. A parent or parent figure has some financial crisis and is forced to make dramatic changes. The money people in your life are having family dramas.

Every solar eclipse affects your spiritual life and this one is no different. You go through these things twice a year (this year it will be four times) and by now you know how to handle them. The spiritual life needs periodic course corrections and the eclipses give you the opportunity to make them. There are shake-ups and disturbances in a spiritual or charitable organization you're involved with, and gurus and guru figures have personal dramas. You are making important changes to your spiritual practice, teachers and teachings.

The lunar eclipse of the 21st brings more spiritual changes as it occurs in your spiritual 12th house. The dream life is apt to be more active this period – and probably negative. Don't pay too much attention. It is just psychic waste stirred up by the eclipse. Every lunar eclipse tests your friendships and this one is no different. Sometimes the friendship itself is flawed, but not always. Sometimes your friends are going through personal life-changing events that affect the relationship. High-tech gadgetry and equipment are likely to be more temperamental this period. Often repairs or replacements are needed.

Health is OK this month. On the 20th, as your spiritual planet the Sun moves into your 6th house of health you'll benefit from spiritual healing. If you feel under the weather see a spiritual healer.

February

Best Days Overall: 1, 2, 11, 12, 19, 20, 28
Most Stressful Days Overall: 6, 7, 13, 14, 26, 27
Best Days for Love: 6, 7, 9, 11, 15, 16, 19, 20, 24, 25, 28
Best Days for Money: 9, 10, 11, 17, 18, 19, 20, 21, 22, 26, 27, 28
Best Days for Career: 3, 4, 13, 14, 15, 16, 24, 25

Love started to improve on January 5 and will get even better this month. On the 10th, Mercury, the ruler of your Horoscope – and a very important planet – moves into your 7th house. Then on the 19th the Sun moves into your house of love and stays there for the rest of the month. You are in a yearly love and social peak.

The two most spiritual planets in your chart occupy the 7th house this month – Neptune, the generic spiritual planet, and the Sun, the ruler of your spiritual house. This gives us many messages. Spiritual compatibility has been important in love for some years now and this month becomes even more important. With spiritual compatibility the knottiest problems can be worked out, but without it, very little can be solved. Love has been idealistic for many years, but now even more so. Singles are searching for the 'perfect love'. This month they will come close (but the really perfect love is the Divine Love that is unconditional and which doesn't depend on human beings). Love is ultra-romantic this month – dreamily romantic. Perhaps it is an illusion but it's a pleasant illusion. (A little illusion makes life tolerable.) The 18th and 19th are particularly strong romantic days.

Love is not found at the bars and clubs. Love and love opportunities happen in more spiritual-type venues – in yoga or meditation classes, at spiritual lectures or charity events, as you pursue your spiritual goals and with people involved in your spiritual life.

There is a dark side to this transit too. Both the Sun and Neptune rule the 'revelation of hidden things' – and sometimes this is not so pleasant. These planets are not causing scandal per se, just revealing what is – good, bad or indifferent. An impersonal light is shining on the love and social life.

Mars travels with Uranus from the 11th to the 14th. This is a very dynamic aspect. Be more mindful on the physical plane. Sometimes surgery is recommended under this kind of aspect. (It doesn't mean that you need it – get a second opinion.)

Health in general is more stressful from the 19th onwards. So make sure, as always, to get enough rest. Head, face and scalp massage is still beneficial, but this will change next month.

Your financial planet, Venus, will move into Capricorn on the 3rd. The financial judgement is sound and trustworthy. You're conservative in money matters, but not too much so. A well-hedged speculation could work. This is a good month to set up budgets and long-term savings and investment plans.

March

    Best Days Overall: 1, 2, 10, 11, 19, 20, 27, 28, 29
    Most Stressful Days Overall: 5, 6, 7, 13, 14, 25, 26
    Best Days for Love: 3, 4, 5, 6, 7, 15, 16, 23, 24
    Best Days for Money: 3, 4, 8, 9, 15, 16, 17, 18, 21, 22, 23, 24, 25, 26
    Best Days for Career: 5, 6, 7, 13, 14, 15, 16, 23, 24

All the planets are in the Western, social sector of your chart this month, which is highly unusual. Only the Moon will be in the Eastern sector, from the 13th to the 25th. Your 7th house of love is chock-full of planets, while your 1st house of self is empty: you are totally 'other oriented' this month. It's as if your own needs are non-existent – not a factor in things. Your personal popularity is at its peak. And you are still in the midst of a yearly love and social peak. So, 'go with the flow', as the saying goes. It's good every now and then to take a vacation from yourself and your interests. (Many psychological pathologies arise from an unbalanced focus on the self.) The time will come where you can focus on yourself, but not right now. Let others have their way, so long as it isn't destructive. Good will come to you through your social relationships, rather than through personal initiative.

Love, like last month, is spiritual and idealistic. It is in spiritual-type venues that love and love opportunities happen.

Health, like last month, is delicate until the 20th. Your health planet, Uranus, finally moves into your 9th house on the 7th. The head, face and scalp are now less important, and the focus should be more on the neck and throat. Regular neck massage will be important for the next seven years. Venus in your 6th house of health and work signals that more focus is needed on the kidneys and hips, with regular hip massage. But this is a short-term need that will pass by the 26th.

Uranus's move also shows job changes. There will be opportunities to work in foreign lands or with foreign companies. This will be a trend for many years. Your religious and philosophical beliefs will get tested with Uranus's move – especially your beliefs about health and healing. Many of these beliefs are little more than superstition.

Your money house is empty this month, with only the Moon moving through there on the 23rd and 24th. Thus finance is not a major interest. I read this as a good thing. It shows contentment. Your financial planet Venus in your 6th house until the 26th indicates that money is earned the old-fashioned way, through work and productive service. On the 26th Venus moves into Pisces, her strongest, most exalted position. This shows enhanced earnings, a fabulous financial intuition and the financial graces of your social contacts. Often with this kind of transit there are opportunities for partnerships or joint ventures.

April

Best Days Overall: 6, 7, 8, 15, 16, 24, 25
Most Stressful Days Overall: 1, 2, 3, 9, 10, 22, 23, 29, 30
Best Days for Love: 1, 2, 3, 11, 12, 19, 20, 21, 29, 30
Best Days for Money: 2, 3, 4, 5, 11, 12, 13, 14, 17, 18, 21, 22, 23
Best Days for Career: 2, 3, 9, 10, 13, 14, 22, 23

All the planets, with the exception of the Moon (and then only for part of the time) are still in the Western, social sector of your chart. Your 1st house is still empty (only the Moon visits on the 17th and 18th). So, like last month, this is a very social month. Your way is not the best way. Your interests come after the interests of others. Self-will doesn't get you very far these days; it is the grace and favour of others that bring you good. With Mercury, the ruler of your Horoscope, in your 7th house, you're very much like a Libra these days! You learn about yourself through your relationships. Like last month your personal popularity is very strong. Your devotion to others is appreciated.

Your financial planet Venus has her solstice from the 22nd to the 25th. She occupies the same degree of latitude during that period. Her motion is 'paused'. She is 'camped out' on one point and then she changes direction (in latitude). So a pause in your financial life and then a change of direction is in order.

Venus will be in your 7th house until the 20th, in Pisces (like last month), her sign of greatest exaltation. This shows 'exalted' earning power and, like last month, solid financial intuition. The financial intuition is unusually strong from the 9th to the 11th as Venus travels with Neptune: keep a note of your dreams. It is also a powerful love period.

Venus moves into your 8th house of regeneration on the 20th. This is especially good for paying down debt (or for taking on debt – depending on your need). It is good for tax and insurance planning and, for those of you of appropriate age, estate planning. Putting other people first also involves putting their financial interests first. This doesn't mean that you harm your financial interests, you just keep them in the background. Your job is to make other people rich these days. The karmic law will take care of your personal financial needs. The financial planet in Aries indicates someone who can jump into financial deals too quickly – too impulsively. When your intuition is spot on these things work out. But if it is off, you can get hurt. Sleep on things before making important financial decisions.

Health is improving this month. If you want to enhance it further, give extra attention to the neck and throat. Spiritual therapies are especially powerful from the 21st to the 23rd.

May

Best Days Overall: 4, 5, 13, 14, 21, 22, 31
Most Stressful Days Overall: 6, 7, 19, 20, 26, 27
Best Days for Love: 2, 3, 8, 9, 14, 17, 18, 21, 26, 27, 31
Best Days for Money: 2, 3, 10, 11, 14, 15, 16, 19, 20, 21, 29, 30, 31
Best Days for Career: 2, 3, 6, 7, 13, 14, 23, 24

Mars, the ruler of your 8th house of regeneration, went 'out of bounds' on April 21 and will remain so for the entire month ahead. This gives various messages. You seem more experimental sexually, doing things outside your personal 'norm' or with people outside your normal sphere. The spouse, partner or current love is forced to go outside the normal boundaries in their financial life. There are no answers for him or her in the usual places, so they search elsewhere. Since Mars is going out of bounds in your 10th house of career, it is likely that career demands are also pulling you out of your normal comfort zone.

Health is good until the 21st but still needs watching. The good news is that Virgo *always* keeps an eye on health. Mars, Neptune and Jupiter are in stressful alignment with you. On the 21st the Sun and Mercury come into stressful alignment. (Mars, though, will move into a harmonious alignment with you on the 16th.) So, as always, make sure to get enough rest. Enhance the health in the ways mentioned in the yearly report.

Career is the main headline this month. Mars has been in your house of career since April 1 and is there until the 16th of this month. This shows much frenetic activity in the career. There can be surgery or near-death kinds of experiences in the lives of bosses, parents or parent figures. Sometimes your company or industry has a near-death kind of experience. On the 21st both the Sun and Mercury move into your 10th house and you begin a yearly career peak. Your main challenge will be to balance the demands of career with the demands of the home and family. With most of the planets above the horizon this month, give more attention to the career whenever possible. The Sun's move into your 10th house shows that you can further the career by being involved with charities or altruistic activities. Your spiritual practice and understanding will help the career. Career guidance can come in dreams or through psychics, spiritual channels or tarot readers. Mercury's move into your 10th house shows personal elevation and success.

Love needs more work this month. It could be that your career focus is distracting you from your social life or not sitting well with the spouse, partner or current love. Family members might not be getting on with the beloved either. This has been a problem all year, but seems more intense this month.

June

Best Days Overall: 1, 9, 10, 18, 19, 27, 28, 29
Most Stressful Days Overall: 2, 3, 15, 16, 23, 24, 30
Best Days for Love: 1, 5, 6, 11, 13, 14, 20, 21, 23, 24
Best Days for Money: 1, 7, 8, 11, 12, 15, 16, 20, 21, 25, 26
Best Days for Career: 2, 3, 4, 13, 14, 24, 30

An active and successful month ahead. Career is even stronger than it was last month, as Venus moves into your 10th house on the 9th. Pay rises, official or unofficial, are likely. You have the financial favour of bosses, parents and parent figures. Venus, your financial planet, at the top of your chart shows that finance is high on the agenda. Additionally, planets are always stronger in their 'high noon' position (the Mid-heaven) than in other places. So your career success translates into financial success. (This is not always the case, but certainly is this month.) Money can come to you through trading, buying, selling or retailing. Your good communication skills also help the bottom line.

Continue to pay attention to health, and rest and relax more until the 21st. Enhance the health in the ways mentioned in the yearly report. Try to schedule in more massages or health treatments too. The career is very demanding and you need to meet these demands, but rather than over-work, drop the trivia from your life.

Health and energy will improve dramatically after the 21st, as the Sun moves into harmonious aspect with you. Both the love life and your social life will improve then too. The 15th and 16th bring a happy romantic meeting. Those already in relationships will have happy social experiences and more romance within the relationship. It will be

a good time to be involved with groups and organizations after the 21st
– especially of the spiritual type. The only complication with love is the
retrograde of your love planet Neptune after the 21st. Enjoy the love
life for what it is; don't project too far into the future. The retrograde
of your love planet will slow down the social life but won't stop it.
Children and children figures will have a very active love and social life
this month.

Mars is still 'out of bounds' until the 12th. He then 'returns to the
fold', so the spouse, partner or current love returns to his or her normal
financial sphere, and the sex life becomes more conventional.

Mercury, who rules you and your career, goes 'out of bounds' from
the 1st to the 16th. Thus your career is pulling you into unfamiliar
places.

Retrograde activity is increasing this month. After the 21st 40 per
cent of the planets will be retrograde – a high percentage. Next month
the percentage will be at its maximum for the year, with half of the
planets moving backward. But we're approaching that point now and
the pace of life slows down.

July

Best Days Overall: 6, 7, 15, 16, 25, 26
Most Stressful Days Overall: 1, 13, 14, 20, 21, 27, 28
Best Days for Love: 1, 2, 3, 10, 11, 20, 21, 29, 30, 31
Best Days for Money: 1, 4, 5, 8, 9, 10, 11, 13, 14, 20, 21, 22, 23,
    24, 31
Best Days for Career: 1, 4, 5, 14, 21, 27, 28, 29, 30

Retrograde activity is at its maximum for the year this month. From the
7th onwards, 50 per cent of the planets are in retrograde motion, as we
mentioned in June's report – a very high percentage. So things happen
with delayed reactions, including the eclipse phenomena.

We have two eclipses this month and, happily, their effects are relatively mild for you. It won't hurt to take things a bit easier though; they
might not be so kind to the people around you.

The solar eclipse of the 2nd occurs in your 11th house of friends,
bringing dramas in their lives and testing certain friendships. It will

impact on your computers, smart phones and other high-tech equipment too. (Sometimes such gadgets need repair or replacement.) Children and children figures in your life have love and social challenges. Parents or parent figures have to make important financial changes. As with every solar eclipse there are changes in the spiritual life – changes in teachings, teachers and attitudes. It is time for a course correction here (which is a healthy thing). There are dramas in the lives of gurus and guru figures, and shake-ups in organizations that you belong to – both spiritual and secular ones.

The lunar eclipse of the 16th also affects your high-tech equipment – it is almost a repeat of the solar eclipse in this matter. Make sure your anti-virus, anti-hacking software is up-to-date and that your important files are properly backed up. Again there are dramas in the lives of your friends and shake-ups in professional or trade organizations you belong to. This eclipse occurs in your 5th house, so children and children figures in your life are affected. They should relax and take it easy over this period. Again a parent or parent figure has to make a financial course correction. This eclipse impacts on Pluto, the ruler of your 3rd house, so drive more carefully; cars and phones get tested. Students can make important educational changes under this eclipse. There are shake-ups in the neighbourhood and in their schools.

The month ahead is a very spiritual kind of month, especially after the 23rd. Those on a spiritual path will make good progress. Those not on a path will have all kinds of synchronistic and ESP (extrasensory perception) experiences that might just put them on the path.

August

Best Days Overall: 2, 3, 11, 12, 21, 22, 30, 31
Most Stressful Days Overall: 9, 10, 16, 17, 23, 24, 25
Best Days for Love: 1, 7, 8, 9, 10, 16, 17, 20, 21, 26, 27, 30, 31
Best Days for Money: 1, 4, 5, 9, 10, 19, 20, 21, 28, 29, 30, 31
Best Days for Career: 8, 19, 20, 23, 24, 25, 30

On June 9 the planetary power began shifting from the Western, social sector of your chart to the Eastern sector of self. Thus, little by little, personal independence has been increasing and this month (and next month too) your personal independence will be at its maximum for the year. There is more personal power. You don't need to adapt to situations or give in to other people. You can, and should, have your way. Make the changes that need to be made. Take responsibility for your own happiness. You've had many months of developing your social skills. Now it's time to develop more personal initiative.

The month ahead is happy and prosperous. It starts off slowly as the planetary power is mostly in your 12th house of spirituality. Things are happening in your life, but they happen on the invisible, interior level. This is a period for spiritual breakthroughs. A hyperactive dream life is normal with these aspects. Enhanced ESP abilities likewise. There is a need for more solitude too – a need for peace and quiet.

On the 18th Mars moves into your 1st house. This increases personal independence even further. This transit is great for weight loss or detox regimes. Athletes perform at their personal best. On the 21st Venus, your financial planet, moves into your sign. On the 23rd the Sun, your spiritual planet, moves into your sign, and on the 29th Mercury joins the party. It is one of your yearly personal pleasure peaks. Time to pamper the body and enjoy all the physical delights. Time to reward the body for its faithful, sterling service.

With all the power in your own sign, the personal appearance shines. There is more charisma (from the Sun), beauty and grace (from Venus) and sex appeal (from Mars). The opposite sex takes notice, yet love is more challenging. It could be that the current love is feeling stressed and this complicates things. But it can also be that you and the beloved are psychologically distant from each other. You are in opposite signs. You see things in opposite ways. The challenge will be to bridge your differences.

Venus's move into your sign on the 21st brings financial windfalls and opportunity. Before that – until the 21st – follow intuition. The danger is overspending, but this changes after the 21st.

Health is excellent all month, but especially after the 23rd. Mars in your sign suggests a need to be more patient and to watch the temper. Temper can cause physical conflicts, accidents and injury.

September

Best Days Overall: 7, 8, 9, 17, 18, 19, 26, 27
Most Stressful Days Overall: 5, 6, 12, 13, 14, 20, 21
Best Days for Love: 3, 4, 8, 9, 12, 13, 14, 20, 22, 23, 28, 29
Best Days for Money: 1, 2, 5, 6, 8, 9, 15, 16, 20, 24, 25, 28, 29
Best Days for Career: 8, 9, 20, 21, 28, 29

Another happy and prosperous month ahead, Virgo. Health – another form of wealth – is excellent all month. Mars will spend the month in your sign, giving energy, courage and a 'can do' spirit. With retrograde activity lessening you should see faster progress to your goals.

Since August 18 we've had a rare Grand Trine in the Earth signs. This is still in effect this month too, although it is less exact. This is a comfortable aspect for you (Earth is your native element). It indicates good management ability, a down-to-earth outlook on life and an enhanced ability to make 'dreams' real. It tends to prosperity. With your financial planet, Venus, still in your sign until the 14th this is even stronger. Earning power is strong. Financial judgement is good. You get value for money. Financial opportunities seek you out. The money people in your life seem very supportive and provide opportunities.

On the 14th Venus moves into your money house – her own sign and house – a comfortable place for her. This too is a nice financial signal. On the 23rd the Sun moves into your money house and you begin a yearly financial peak. A period of peak earnings. The focus is on finance – as it should be. This is a great period to get your financial house in order. The new Moon of the 5th, which occurs in your money house, will help you in this. It will clarify the finances and bring you all the information you need as the month unfolds.

Venus has her solstice from the 15th to the 18th. She occupies the same degree of latitude over that period. She pauses in her motion and then changes direction. So don't be alarmed about a financial pause or change of direction. It's all to the good.

Like last month, personal appearance is unusually good. But love is challenging. The problem is not in attracting the opposite sex, it's about handling the actual relationship. For singles the focus is more on the self and the personal needs (which is right and proper) and not so much on others. For those already in a relationship the problem is bridging the differences with the beloved. You still see things in opposite ways and have opposite opinions. In addition, Neptune, your love planet, has been retrograde since June 21. So the spouse, partner or current love lacks direction and is not sure what he or she wants.

October

Best Days Overall: 5, 6, 15, 16, 23, 24
Most Stressful Days Overall: 2, 3, 4, 10, 11, 17, 18, 30, 31
Best Days for Love: 1, 10, 11, 19, 20, 28, 29
Best Days for Money: 2, 3, 4, 10, 11, 12, 13, 19, 20, 21, 22, 26, 27, 28, 29, 30, 31
Best Days for Career: 10, 11, 17, 18, 19, 20, 28, 29

Finance is the main headline this month. Your money house is chock-full of planets. This means that money and financial opportunity can come to you in many ways and through many people. It shows good 'cosmic' support for your financial goals. You're still in the midst of a yearly financial peak until the 23rd.

The Sun in the money house until the 23rd signals good financial intuition. But this transit also favours industries that cater to youth, entertainment and music. Venus is in the money house until the 8th, which favours the beauty industry. It also shows the importance of social connections in finance – who you know could be more important than how much you have. Mercury has been in your 2nd house since September 14, indicating the financial favour of bosses, elders, parents and parent figures. It also shows your personal focus on finance.

Career is not a major focus these days. On August 29 the planetary power began to shift to the lower half of your Horoscope – the night side – and this is the present situation. Your 10th house of career is empty (only the Moon moves through there on the 17th and 18th). Your 4th house of home and family, by contrast, is strong and will get even stronger in the coming months. So the focus is more on home, family and your emotional wellness. Career is in a preparatory stage now. This is just as important as your overt career moves. Good preparation will lead to good outward actions. On the 3rd, your career planet, Mercury, moves into your 3rd house and stays there for the rest of the month. Thus it appears a good time to brush up on your reading and take classes that relate to your career. Good knowledge and good communication skills will help the career later on down the road.

Love is much improved over last month. From the 3rd onwards Mercury (your ruling planet) is making very nice aspects to Neptune, your love planet. Thus there is harmony with the beloved. The 14th to the 16th is an especially strong romantic period. For singles it shows a romantic meeting. For those already attached it shows harmony with the beloved. Love will be happy from the 23rd onwards.

Health is good this month but you could be making changes to your health regime. Be more mindful on the physical plane (and at work) from the 5th to the 7th.

November

Best Days Overall: 1, 2, 11, 12, 20, 21, 28, 29, 30
Most Stressful Days Overall: 6, 7, 13, 14, 26, 27
Best Days for Love: 6, 7, 8, 9, 16, 17, 18, 19, 24, 25, 29
Best Days for Money: 8, 9, 10, 18, 19, 22, 23, 26, 27, 29
Best Days for Career: 6, 7, 13, 14, 16, 17, 24, 25

There is less focus on finance this month. On the 19th, as Mars leaves the money house, the money house will be empty. Financial goals (the short-term ones at least) have been achieved and so it's time to focus on other things. Until the 19th it would be good to use spare cash to pay down debt. This period is also good to detox the financial life as well – eliminate waste and redundancies. Get rid of possessions that you don't need or use. Prosper by cutting needless expense.

You're entering the midnight hour of your year. The deepest part of the night. This is a time for building up your internal energies for the next day – which will happen in a few months' time. A good night's sleep is the prelude for a good day. The activities of night are just as important – though different – as the activities of day.

The month ahead looks prosperous. Venus will be in your 4th house until the 26th. This indicates good family support (especially from the

22nd to the 24th). You're probably spending more on the home. A good period to buy objects of beauty for the home or to redecorate. Family and family connections are playing a big role in the financial life. On the 26th Venus will enter your 5th house, bringing 'happy money'. A time to enjoy the wealth that you have. As you enjoy your life, financial opportunities will come to you. Well-hedged, well-thought-out speculations could work this period. However, it's probably best to avoid risky casino-type speculations. Your financial planet in Capricorn signals sound financial judgement: a good time to set up disciplined savings and investment plans. If you follow the plan (and it takes discipline) your long-term wealth will be assured.

Health is good until the 22nd, but afterwards will need watching. Surgery or some procedure could be recommended between the 22nd and 25th but get other opinions. Be more mindful on the physical plane over that period. The spouse, partner or current love has some financial disturbance. There could be some disturbance at the workplace too.

The Sun's move into your 4th house on the 22nd shows that your spiritual understanding will help you on the emotional level. This is a very good period (and next month too) for psychological therapies. As old memories arise just observe them without judgement. Though you shouldn't try to rewrite history, you will probably interpret old events in a different, better way now.

December

Best Days Overall: 8, 9, 17, 18, 26, 27
Most Stressful Days Overall: 3, 4, 5, 11, 12, 24, 25, 31
Best Days for Love: 3, 4, 5, 8, 9, 13, 14, 17, 18, 21, 22, 28, 29, 31
Best Days for Money: 8, 9, 17, 18, 19, 20, 26, 28, 29
Best Days for Career: 6, 7, 11, 12, 15, 16, 25

In general at this time of the year there are more parties, but for you there will be more than the norm. Jupiter moves into your 5th house on the 3rd; Venus will be there until the 20th and the Sun will enter on the 22nd. You are entering a yearly (and, for some of you, a lifetime) personal pleasure peak. A very happy month ahead.

Your 4th house of home and family is still strong until the 22nd. So there is much focus – as there should be – on the family and the emotional wellness. Even your career planet, Mercury, will be in your 4th house from the 9th to the 29th – most of the month. Thus, your family *is* the career this month – your mission. The message of the Horoscope is get into emotional harmony, get the family situation right, and the career will fall into place very naturally. Good emotional health will result in good physical health too – especially from the 13th to the 17th. Jobseekers have an excellent job opportunity over that period too.

There will be another solar eclipse in your 5th house on the 26th. This will be the third one this year in this house. Again it impacts on the children and children figures in your life. They are having personal kinds of dramas. Since this eclipse affects Jupiter, your family planet, the home is affected. Repairs might be necessary. A parent or parent figure is once again forced to make dramatic financial changes. And, for the fourth time this year, there are spiritual changes – changes in practice, teachings and teachers. There are also shake-ups in charities or spiritual organizations you're involved with, and – once again – there are dramas in the lives of gurus or guru figures in your life.

Health needs more attention until the 22nd. Make sure to get enough rest, and enhance the health in the ways mentioned in the yearly report. After the 22nd the health is super.

Venus, your financial planet, is still in your 5th house until the 20th. So money is earned in happy ways and is spent on happy things. You enjoy the wealth that you have. You probably spend more on children or the children figures in your life, but can earn from them as well. On the 20th Venus enters your 6th house, signalling earning through work and productive service. Probably you are spending on high-tech gadgetry or technology upgrades. This seems like a good investment, as technology is important for earnings.

Love is happy this month – but better after the 22nd than before. Neptune, the love planet, started to move forward on November 27, and will be moving forward for many more months. He is also receiving mostly positive aspects this month. The Moon will visit your 7th house of love twice this month too, adding to the social energy.

Libra

THE SCALES

Birthdays from
23rd September to
22nd October

Personality Profile

LIBRA AT A GLANCE

Element – Air

Ruling Planet – Venus
   Career Planet – Moon
   Love Planet – Mars
   Money Planet – Pluto
   Planet of Communications – Jupiter
   Planet of Health and Work – Neptune
   Planet of Home and Family Life – Saturn
   Planet of Spirituality and Good Fortune – Mercury

Colours – blue, jade green

Colours that promote love, romance and social harmony – carmine, red, scarlet

Colours that promote earning power – burgundy, red-violet, violet

Gems – carnelian, chrysolite, coral, emerald, jade, opal, quartz, white marble

Metal – copper

Scents – almond, rose, vanilla, violet

Quality – cardinal (= activity)

Qualities most needed for balance – a sense of self, self-reliance, independence

Strongest virtues – social grace, charm, tact, diplomacy

Deepest needs – love, romance, social harmony

Characteristic to avoid – violating what is right in order to be socially accepted

Signs of greatest overall compatibility – Gemini, Aquarius

Signs of greatest overall incompatibility – Aries, Cancer, Capricorn

Sign most helpful to career – Cancer

Sign most helpful for emotional support – Capricorn

Sign most helpful financially – Scorpio

Sign best for marriage and/or partnerships – Aries

Sign most helpful for creative projects – Aquarius

Best Sign to have fun with – Aquarius

Signs most helpful in spiritual matters – Gemini, Virgo

Best day of the week – Friday

Understanding a Libra

In the sign of Libra the universal mind – the soul – expresses its genius for relationships, that is, its power to harmonize diverse elements in a unified, organic way. Libra is the soul's power to express beauty in all of its forms. And where is beauty if not within relationships? Beauty does not exist in isolation. Beauty arises out of comparison – out of the just relationship between different parts. Without a fair and harmonious relationship there is no beauty, whether it in art, manners, ideas or the social or political forum.

There are two faculties humans have that exalt them above the animal kingdom: their rational faculty (expressed in the signs of Gemini and Aquarius) and their aesthetic faculty, exemplified by Libra. Without an aesthetic sense we would be little more than intelligent barbarians. Libra is the civilizing instinct or urge of the soul.

Beauty is the essence of what Librans are all about. They are here to beautify the world. Discussing Librans' social grace, their sense of balance and fair play, their ability to see and love another person's point of view would be to miss their central asset: their desire for beauty.

No one – no matter how alone he or she seems to be – exists in isolation. The universe is one vast collaboration of beings. Librans, more than most, understand this and understand the spiritual laws that make relationships bearable and enjoyable.

A Libran is always the unconscious (and in some cases conscious) civilizer, harmonizer and artist. This is a Libran's deepest urge and greatest genius. Librans love instinctively to bring people together, and they are uniquely qualified to do so. They have a knack for seeing what unites people – the things that attract and bind rather than separate individuals.

Finance

In financial matters Librans can seem frivolous and illogical to others. This is because Librans appear to be more concerned with earning money for others than for themselves. But there is a logic to this financial attitude. Librans know that everything and everyone is connected and that it is impossible to help another to prosper without also prospering yourself. Since enhancing their partner's income and position tends to strengthen their relationship, Librans choose to do so. What could be more fun than building a relationship? You will rarely find a Libra enriching him- or herself at someone else's expense.

Scorpio is the ruler of Libra's solar 2nd house of money, giving Libra unusual insight into financial matters – and the power to focus on these matters in a way that disguises a seeming indifference. In fact, many other signs come to Librans for financial advice and guidance.

Given their social grace, Librans often spend great sums of money on entertaining and organizing social events. They also like to help others when they are in need. Librans would go out of their way to help a friend in dire straits, even if they have to borrow from others to do so. However, Librans are also very careful to pay back any debts they owe, and like to make sure they never have to be reminded to do so.

Career and Public Image

Publicly, Librans like to appear as nurturers. Their friends and acquaintances are their family and they wield political power in parental ways. They also like bosses who are paternal or maternal.

The sign of Cancer is on Libra's 10th career house cusp; the Moon is Libra's career planet. The Moon is by far the speediest, most changeable planet in the horoscope. It alone among all the planets travels through the entire zodiac – all twelve signs and houses – every month. This is important for the way in which Librans approach their careers, and also to what they need to do to maximize their career potential. The Moon is the planet of moods and feelings – Librans need a career in which their emotions have free expression. This is why so many Librans are involved in the creative arts. Libra's ambitions wax and wane with the Moon. They tend to wield power according to their mood.

The Moon 'rules' the masses – and that is why Libra's highest goal is to achieve a mass kind of acclaim and popularity. Librans who achieve fame cultivate the public as other people cultivate a lover or friend. Librans can be very flexible – and often fickle – in their career and ambitions. On the other hand, they can achieve their ends in a great variety of ways. They are not stuck in one attitude or with one way of doing things.

Love and Relationships

Librans express their true genius in love. In love you could not find a partner more romantic, more seductive or more fair. If there is one thing that is sure to destroy a relationship – sure to block your love from flowing – it is injustice or imbalance between lover and beloved. If one party is giving too much or taking too much, resentment is sure to surface at some time or other. Librans are careful about this. If anything, Librans might err on the side of giving more, but never giving less.

If you are in love with a Libra, make sure you keep the aura of romance alive. Do all the little things – candle-lit dinners, travel to exotic locales, flowers and small gifts. Give things that are beautiful, not necessarily expensive. Send cards. Ring regularly even if you have nothing in particular to say. The niceties are very important to a Libra. Your relationship is a work of art: make it beautiful and your Libran lover will appreciate it. If you are creative about it, he or she will appreciate it even more; for this is how your Libra will behave towards you.

Librans like their partners to be aggressive and even a bit self-willed. They know that these are qualities they sometimes lack and so they like their partners to have them. In relationships, however, Librans can be very aggressive – but always in a subtle and charming way! Librans are determined in their efforts to charm the object of their desire – and this determination can be very pleasant if you are on the receiving end.

Home and Domestic Life

Since Librans are such social creatures, they do not particularly like mundane domestic duties. They like a well-organized home – clean and neat with everything needful present – but housework is a chore and a burden, one of the unpleasant tasks in life that must be done, the quicker the better. If a Libra has enough money – and sometimes even if not – he or she will prefer to pay someone else to take care of the daily household chores. However, Librans like gardening; they love to have flowers and plants in the home.

A Libra's home is modern, and furnished in excellent taste. You will find many paintings and sculptures there. Since Librans like to be with friends and family, they enjoy entertaining at home and they make great hosts.

Capricorn is on the cusp of Libra's 4th solar house of home and family. Saturn, the planet of law, order, limits and discipline, rules Libra's domestic affairs. If Librans want their home life to be supportive and happy they need to develop some of the virtues of Saturn – order, organization and discipline. Librans, being so creative and so intensely in need of harmony, can tend to be too lax in the home and too permissive with their children. Too much of this is not always good; children need freedom but they also need limits.

Horoscope for 2019

Major Trends

A challenging and hyperactive year ahead, Libra. Keep in mind that the universe never gives us more than we can handle. If the challenges are given, it means – by definition – that we are able to handle them. The family situation is most challenging this year. Family obligations seem onerous. The good news is that it will get easier at the end of the year.

Health will need watching in the year ahead. Details later.

In spite of all the challenges this year, there is much good news too. Uranus is moving out of your 7th house of love on March 7, where he has been for the past seven years, destabilizing the love life and bringing many a divorce and break up. The love and social life will start to become more stable. More on this later on.

Uranus's move into your 8th house of regeneration in March shows more sexual experimentation. The spouse, partner or current love becomes financially experimental.

Jupiter spends almost all year in your 3rd house of communication and intellectual interests, which is very good news for students. It shows success in their studies – perhaps even honours. It is an excellent aspect for writers, bloggers, teachers, journalists, and sales and marketing people too. If you are in these fields the year ahead is successful.

Jupiter will move into your 4th house of home and family on December 3, bringing more family harmony and easing much of the stress in this area. Often it brings moves and the expansion of the family circle.

While the romantic life is becoming more stable, friendships seem unstable and many will get tested in the year ahead. We have five eclipses this year (usually there are four), and four out of the five will impact on your friendships.

Neptune has been in your 6th house of health and work for many years now and he will be there for many more to come. This shows someone who is going deeper into spiritual healing. More on this later.

The most important areas of interest this year are communication and intellectual interests (until December 2); home and family; health and work; love and romance (until March 7); and sex and personal transformation (from March 7 onwards).

Your paths of greatest fulfilment this year are career; communication and intellectual interests (until December 3); and home and family (from December 3 onwards).

Health

(Please note that this is an astrological perspective on health and not a medical one. In days of yore there was no difference, both of these perspectives were identical. But now there could be quite a difference. For a medical perspective, please consult your doctor or health practitioner.)

Health, as we mentioned above, needs keeping an eye on this year. You begin your year with three powerful long-term planets in stressful alignment with you, and you will end the year in the same way. In between, from March 7 to December 3, there will be two long-term planets stressing you – and they are strong ones, Saturn and Pluto. So health needs more attention this year. You can't just take it for granted. It needs some effort on your part. The good news is that your 6th house of health is strong and you seem willing to make the effort. This is a positive.

The first line of defence, as regular readers know, is to maintain high energy levels. Low energy is the primal disease. Everything else proceeds from that. So make sure to get enough rest. Don't allow your energy to get depleted. Keep your focus on the really important things in your life and don't waste time on trivia. Hard choices need to be made.

There is more good news. You can enhance your health and prevent problems developing by giving more attention to the following – the vulnerable areas of the Horoscope (the reflexology points are shown in the chart above):

- The heart has grown in importance over the past eleven years, and became even more important last year. Most spiritual healers agree that the root cause for heart problems is worry and anxiety. So avoid these emotions (not so easy, as they are considered so normal). Cultivate faith rather than worry.
- The kidneys and hips. These are always important for Libra (Libra rules these areas). Regular hip massage should be a part of your normal health regime. A herbal kidney cleanse every now and then would be a good idea – especially if you feel under the weather.
- The feet. These too are always important for Libra, and for some years have become even more so. Your health planet, Neptune, has been in Pisces for many years now and both Neptune and Pisces

Important foot reflexology points for the year ahead

Massage all of the foot on a regular basis – the top of the foot as well as the bottom – but pay extra attention to the points highlighted on the chart. When you massage, be aware of 'sore spots' as these need special attention. It's also a good idea to massage the ankles and below them.

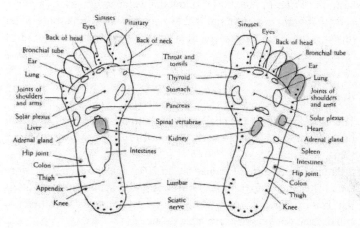

rule the feet. So regular foot massage – see our chart above – should be part of your normal health regime. The good thing about foot massage is that it not only strengthens the feet but the entire body as well, as if you're giving the whole body a massage – including your internal organs. Wear shoes that fit correctly and that don't upset your balance. Comfort is more important than style. Keep the feet warm in the winter.

Since these are the vulnerable areas, problems, if they happen (God forbid) would most likely begin here. Thus keeping these areas healthy and fit is sound preventive medicine. Most of the time problems can be prevented, but even when they can't, they can be softened to a great degree. They need not be devastating.

Neptune as your health planet shows that you respond well to spiritual-type therapies such as meditation, reiki, the laying on of hands and the manipulation of subtle energies. If you feel under the weather, see a spiritual healer.

Your health planet in a water sign (and this has been the case for many years) indicates a special connection to the considerable healing powers of the Water element. It is good to be near large bodies of water such as oceans, rivers and lakes. Good to soak or swim in them too. Swimming and water sports are good exercises these days. Natural water is always best, but at a pinch you can take long soaks in your bathtub. When in the shower allow the water to hit any area of the body that bothers you. It's probably a good idea to drink more water this year too. The Water element is weak in your Horoscope and this can tend to dehydration.

Home and Family

This is an important and challenging area in the year ahead. Your 4th house is easily the most powerful in your Horoscope. An area of major focus.

Saturn moved into this house late in 2017 and has been there since then. This shows extra family burdens and responsibilities. Things that you can't avoid. You have to 'bear down' and deal with them. If you do, you will find help available to you.

But Saturn's presence here is only part of the picture. Three out of the five eclipses this year occur in your 4th house, so there is much family disturbance – even chaos – happening these days. This will require even more of your attention. Often an eclipse here signals a need for repairs in the home as hidden flaws are revealed. Often it shows explosions within the family circle – dramas in the lives of family members, especially a parent or parent figure. You're dealing with all kinds of home and family emergencies this year. Have no fear, you can handle it. It's just good to understand what's going on.

Your financial planet, Pluto, has been in your 4th house since 2008 – a long time. This gives many messages. You're spending more money on the home and family, but can earn from here as well. Family and family connections are playing a big role in earnings. Often it shows someone who is earning from home, and many of you have set up home offices. The home is as much a place of business as it is a home. We will cover this more fully later on.

Saturn in the 4th house shows a tendency to depression. Be careful about this. It often shows a tendency to repress one's true feelings. One doesn't feel safe in expressing them and so the tendency is to repress them. We will deal with this issue later on.

This aspect would also indicate a feeling of 'disappointment' with the family. One is involved with them (family members, a parent figure) out of a sense of duty, rather than from love. It's a feeling of someone who 'grits their teeth' and does what has to be done.

There is also a feeling of 'lack of space' – being over-crowded – in the home. But a move is not in the cards just yet. Make do with the space you have – a little creativity can solve the problem.

Things will change later on in the year – after December 3 – as benevolent Jupiter moves into your 4th house. The family situation will get happier. Many of you could decide to move when this happens, but a move is more likely next year. Communication with the family will improve too.

Major repairs or renovations can happen any time this year, but if you have some free will in the matter, after December 3 is best. If you're redecorating in a cosmetic kind of way, or buying objects of beauty for the home, February 3 to March 1 and November 25 to the end of the year are good times.

A parent or parent figure seems over-controlling and demanding – difficult to handle. But he or she also seems very involved in your finances, and this complicates things. He or she does seem helpful financially, but in a controlling kind of way. He or she also seems pessimistic, seeing the dark side of everything, which can be very difficult.

Siblings and sibling figures in your life are prospering, but a move is more likely next year than this.

Children and children figures seem unsettled these days. They can have multiple moves in the coming years.

Finance and Career

You're ending a very strong financial year. By now most of your short-term financial goals have been achieved and you're more or less content with things as they are. This would tend to the status quo.

However, Saturn is travelling very close to your financial planet Pluto this year. This would indicate taking on more financial responsibilities (and they seem related to the family). This can create a feeling of lack even when one is prospering. It's just a feeling. There's a need to reorganize the finances this year, to restructure them and shift things around a bit. If you do this, you will find that you have all the resources that you need.

Your financial planet has been in your 4th house of home and family for many years now, and he will remain there for many more. So, as we mentioned, you're spending more money on the home and family, but you can earn from here as well. Family and family connections are playing a huge role in earnings. This position favours residential real estate, furniture makers, interior designers, landscaping, house-cleaning services and industries that cater to the homeowner and family. It also favours restaurants, the food industry, hotels and motels. These are interesting as jobs, businesses or investments (there are many public companies involved in these things).

It favours your family business, but also any business with a family atmosphere – that is run like a family.

Your financial planet in conservative Capricorn, travelling with Saturn, signals excellent financial judgement. There is an astuteness here. You know how to get value for your money. You have a good sense of where an investment will be many years down the road. In Wall Street terminology, you are a 'value investor' rather than a speculator or 'momentum investor'. As investments you would favour the large, traditional blue chip companies that comprise the DOW, FTSE or S&P 500 listings. You like the tried and true. Companies that have stood the test of time.

You are in a good period (and especially since last year) for setting up long-term investment and savings plans. You have a good feeling for 'disciplined savings'. It's also a good time to set up budgets – you seem willing to abide by them.

You're in a cycle for building long-term wealth – slowly, steadily, methodically and organically. The quick buck, the 'can't miss' investment, is not for you.

Saturn travelling with Pluto teaches you how to build secure wealth.

This is not an especially strong career year. Your 4th house of home and family is much stronger and more active than your 10th house of career (which is basically empty). Also, the lower half of the Horoscope will dominate all year. There will be periods when the upper (day) side of your chart is stronger, but it will never really dominate. The focus is on the home, family and emotional well-being. Some years are like that.

Your career planet, the Moon, is the fastest moving of all the planets. Where the other fast-moving planets might take approximately a year to move through your whole chart, the Moon will do so every month. So there are a lot of short-term career trends that are best dealt with in the monthly reports.

A solar eclipse on July 2 occurs in your 10th house, which will create some change and disturbance. It can bring changes in your industry, its hierarchy or your company, and in the rules of the game.

Though home and family is most important this year, the presence of the Moon's North Node in your 10th house shows that it will be good to give the career some focus. Don't ignore it completely. Your career will give you a sense of fulfilment.

Love and Social Life

Love and social activities are always important to you, Libra – as many a Libra has said to me, 'Relationship is what life is all about.' But this year, after March 7, they are a little less important. Everything is a matter of degree.

As we mentioned, you've had Uranus – a dynamic and volatile planet – moving through your 7th house for the past seven years. This has not only caused divorces and break-ups, but you are in a completely different social circle than you were seven years ago. This was his purpose. And, most likely your social circle is better and happier than it was in 2012. Before the cosmos can improve things, before it can answer your prayers, sometimes it has to shake things up.

The love life is much calmer and more stable than it has been. There is a better chance for a romantic relationship to last.

Your 7th house of love will be basically empty after March 7. This tends to the status quo. If you're already in a relationship, it will most likely continue. Those who are unattached will most likely remain unattached.

Mars is your love planet and he is relatively fast moving; this year he will move through seven signs and houses of your Horoscope. So, there will be many short-term trends in love depending on where Mars is at any given time and the aspects he receives and makes. These are best discussed in the monthly reports.

Love might be stable, but the sex life seems very active. Uranus moves into your 8th house of regeneration in March, and will stay there for another seven years. So, this is a long-term trend. Uranus in the 8th house indicates much sexual experimentation happening. So long as it isn't destructive, it's a good thing. It is through experimentation that we gain real knowledge of ourselves. In your case, all the rule books and 'how to's' get thrown out and you learn what works for you personally. Every person is unique. Every person is wired up in a unique way. What works for one doesn't work for another, and this applies to sex too.

The spouse, partner or current love becomes financially experimental. He or she is willing to try new approaches, new strategies and new kinds of investments. Earnings will tend to be unstable, but the financial life will be exciting. Singles will meet these kinds of people.

Friendships, as we mentioned, will get tested all year. Most likely it is not your fault or the fault of the relationship. There are many eclipses impacting on your friends and they will be going through personal, life-changing dramas.

The marriage of the parents or parent figures is stressful this year, but will improve after December 3. Siblings and sibling figures are having a status quo kind of love year. If they are married they will stay married and if they're single they will stay single. The same is true for children and children figures in your life.

Self-improvement

Spiritual Neptune, your health planet, has been in Pisces for many years. So, many of the trends that we've written about in past years are still very much in effect. For the sake of newer readers, we should however recap a bit. In the health report we mostly dealt with the purely physical side of health. But there is a lot more to it. The physical body is only the place where disease winds up, it never begins there. Always (without exception) disease has its origin on the more subtle levels – the worlds of thought and feeling (and the various subdivisions of those worlds). Spiritual disconnection – disconnection from the Divine within, is really the root cause of all sickness. It 'short circuits', or creates a separation in the life force, which lowers overall energy and makes a person vulnerable to disease. But in your case it is much more dramatic.

The message of your Horoscope is 'get right spiritually and good health will naturally follow'.

It is always a good idea to stay 'prayed up' and in a state of grace. But with you it's an actual health issue.

The cosmos is calling you – and has been for many years now – to explore the spiritual dimensions of health. Many of you are already involved in this and are going deeper and deeper into it – it's a huge subject and there's always more to learn. Read all you can on it; attend classes and seminars. Most importantly, apply what you've learned. You will learn things not written in any book.

With Neptune involved in health, intuition becomes very important. Things that always worked for you might, in a given instance, not work. Conversely, things that never worked, in a given instance could work. It is the intuition of the moment that matters.

Saturn has been in your 4th house since December 2017. Thus, as we mentioned earlier, there is a tendency to repress the emotions. Spiritually speaking, the cosmos is giving you the opportunity to have more control over the emotions and moods. And, by the time Saturn leaves your 4th house next year, you will have achieved this. But there is legitimate control and there is repression – they are two different things. Repression rarely lasts, and it has serious consequences, healthwise and in other ways. You can't repress a strong emotion for too long. Eventually it will express itself, usually in destructive and unbalanced ways. So, there is a need for a healthy way to release your true feelings without doing damage to yourself or others. Negative feelings and emotions should be considered 'psychic waste'. We don't need to over-analyse them, but just to get them out of the system, out of the astral body. There are many safe ways to do this. Some are outlined in my book *A Technique For Meditation** but there are other ways too. See how much better you feel when the negative feelings are released. You will be amazed. Also see how solutions to your problems come to you. They were always there but you couldn't access them because of the repressed feelings. Your prayer and meditative practice will also go much better.

Month-by-month Forecasts

January

Best Days Overall: 7, 8, 17, 18, 25, 26
Most Stressful Days Overall: 5, 6, 12, 13, 19, 20
Best Days for Love: 1, 2, 12, 13, 21, 22, 30, 31
Best Days for Money: 1, 2, 3, 5, 6, 12, 13, 15, 16, 21, 22, 23, 24, 27, 28
Best Days for Career: 5, 6, 16, 19, 20, 25

Health needs some attention this month, and especially around the period of the solar eclipse of the 6th (in America it's on the 5th). Make sure, as always, to get enough rest – always the most important thing. At least 60 per cent of the planets (and sometimes 70 per cent) are in

---

* Mantra Books, 2011.

stressful alignment with you, so, if possible, spend more time at a health spa or schedule more massages or health treatments. Enhance the health in the ways mentioned in the yearly report. Try not to spread yourself too thin. Keep your focus on the really important things in your life and delegate wherever possible.

The solar eclipse occurs in your 4th house of home and family, and is the first of three eclipses that will occur here this year. It's probably the strongest too, since it impacts on Saturn, your family planet – a double hit. So there are shake-ups in the family and the family circle. There are dramas in the lives of family members – and especially parents or parent figures. Hidden flaws in the home get revealed so that you can make the necessary corrections. Siblings and sibling figures have financial shake-ups and are forced to make changes in this area. Since the Sun rules your 11th house there are dramas in the lives of friends and friendships get tested. High-tech equipment can be erratic too – often repairs or replacements are necessary.

A lunar eclipse on the 21st is kinder to you, although it won't hurt to have an easier relaxed schedule at this time. (If it happens to hit a sensitive point in your personal horoscope – cast especially for you and your exact time of birth – its effects can be strong indeed.) This eclipse tests friendships and high-tech equipment – just as we saw in the previous eclipse. Since the Moon (the eclipsed planet) is your career planet, it shows career changes happening. There are various scenarios here. Sometimes there are shake-ups in your company – in the company hierarchy. Sometimes there are shake-ups in your industry. And, sometimes, people actually change the career. Once again a parent or parent figure has a personal crisis.

Love seems happy and active this month. Mars, your love planet, is in his own sign and house – where he is comfortable and powerful. From the 9th onwards Venus, your ruling planet, makes beautiful aspects with Mars, signalling harmony in love. For singles it shows happy love opportunities.

The month ahead is prosperous too. The Sun travels with your money planet Pluto from the 10th to the 12th: a nice financial period. From the 21st to the 23rd Venus travels with Jupiter – another nice financial period, and also wonderful for love.

February

> Best Days Overall: 3, 4, 5, 13, 14, 21, 22
> Most Stressful Days Overall: 1, 2, 8, 9, 10, 15, 16, 28
> Best Days for Love: 8, 9, 10, 11, 19, 20, 28
> Best Days for Money: 1, 2, 9, 10, 11, 12, 17, 18, 19, 20, 24, 25, 26, 27, 28
> Best Days for Career: 3, 4, 14, 15, 16, 24

Health and energy started to improve after January 20 and it improves further after the 14th of this month. But still it needs watching. Respect your energy levels and don't fritter it away on unimportant things. Enhance the health in the ways mentioned in the yearly report. The good news here is that health becomes a focus from the 10th onwards. Spiritual healing is especially powerful on the 18th and 19th.

You entered one of your yearly personal pleasure peaks on January 20, and this continues until the 19th. Time to enjoy your life and express your personal creativity (Libra is very creative). Children and children figures in your life are having a great social month. If they are of appropriate age and single there are romantic opportunities in store.

Venus enters your 4th house on the 3rd and stays there for the whole month, showing a focus on home and family (this focus was even stronger last month). History and psychology are unusually interesting now. Your moods impact dramatically on your physical appearance, so do your best to keep your feelings positive.

Career is not a big issue this month. Most of the planets are in the night side (the lower half) of your chart. Your 10th house of career is empty (only the Moon moves through there this month, on the 15th and 16th) while your 4th house of home and family is chock-full of planets. So continue to focus on the home, family and your emotional wellness. Your yearly career push is not too far off. In the meantime it is good to put the psychological infrastructure in place.

Though career is not a big issue, a 'super full Moon' on the 19th brings success and opportunity. (The full Moon occurs when the Moon is at her perigee, her closest distance to Earth.) Career activities will go better from the 4th to the 19th as the Moon waxes.

The 22nd and 23rd, when Venus travels with Pluto, bring earnings opportunities to you. The power in your 6th house of health and work from the 19th onwards brings opportunities for jobseekers. Children and children figures have a strong financial period from the 19th onwards.

Mars, your love planet, and Uranus travel together from the 11th to the 14th, which is a very dynamic aspect. The current love, children and children figures in your life should take it easy and be more mindful on the physical plane. There could be disturbances in the love life over that period too.

March

  Best Days Overall: 3, 4, 13, 14, 21, 22, 30, 31
  Most Stressful Days Overall: 1, 2, 8, 9, 15, 16, 27, 28, 29
  Best Days for Love: 1, 2, 3, 4, 8, 9, 10, 11, 15, 16, 19, 20, 23, 24, 28, 29
  Best Days for Money: 1, 2, 8, 9, 10, 11, 17, 18, 19, 20, 23, 24, 25, 26, 28, 29
  Best Days for Career: 8, 9, 15, 16, 17, 18, 25, 26

It's good that you're focusing on health this month, Libra. Your 6th house is easily the strongest in the Horoscope. With two long-term planets still in stressful alignment with you (and the Sun will also be in stressful alignment with you after the 20th), health should be a focus. A lot of confusion about health matters will get clarified by the new Moon of the 6th. It not only occurs in your 6th house but also right on Neptune, your health planet. So all the knowledge and information you need about your health will come to you as the month progresses.

Mars, your love planet, moved into your 8th house of regeneration on February 14 and remains there all this month. Uranus finally moves into your 8th house on the 7th of this month, and will spend the next seven years there. So, love is very sexual this month. This is how love is shown and how you feel loved. For singles the sexual magnetism of a possible partner is most likely the biggest attraction. Uranus in your 8th house shows much sexual experimentation as well. But, as most of you know, a good relationship needs more than good sex to succeed. This will be more clearly seen later on.

The good news, as was mentioned in the yearly report, is that love is becoming more stable now. It has a greater chance for longevity now that Uranus has left your house of love for good. On the 20th, as the Sun enters your 7th house, you begin a yearly love and social peak. Being involved with friends and groups – professional and trade organizations and the like – is good for love. The online world is also good for love. Friends like to play Cupid.

Children and children figures in your life need to learn emotional stability. They seem restless and temperamental. They can have multiple moves this year, and in the coming years.

Your 6th house of health contains very spiritual planets this month. It contains Neptune, the generic spiritual planet, and also Mercury, your actual spiritual planet. So there is much progress in spiritual healing this month. The 15th and 16th (as the Sun travels with Neptune) and the 24th to the 31st (as Mercury camps out on Neptune) are particularly good for spiritual healing.

Career is still not a major focus, though this will begin to change next month. The new Moon of the 6th and the full Moon of the 20th (which is almost a super full Moon) will be good career days. You will also have more enthusiasm for the career from the 6th to the 20th as the Moon waxes.

One lone planet occupies the Eastern half of your chart. All the rest are in the Western, social sector. So personal independence is at its weakest these days. On the other hand, personal independence isn't needed at the moment; the focus is on others and their needs.

April

Best Days Overall: 9, 10, 17, 18, 26, 27
Most Stressful Days Overall: 4, 5, 11, 12, 24, 25
Best Days for Love: 2, 3, 4, 5, 9, 10, 11, 12, 17, 18, 21, 26, 27
Best Days for Money: 4, 5, 7, 8, 13, 14, 15, 16, 19, 20, 22, 23, 24, 25
Best Days for Career: 4, 5, 11, 12, 13, 14, 24

The planetary power is still overwhelmingly in the Western, social sector of the chart. Even the ruler of your Horoscope, Venus, will enter her maximum Western position on the 20th. Your 7th house of love is still very powerful and you are still in the midst of a yearly love and social peak. So the month ahead (like last month) is all about others. Relationship is everything these days. Where some signs would chafe at this (Aries and Leo for example), for you, Libra, this is the most comfortable thing in the world. You're in your element exercising your genius.

Health needs more care this month. The social demands are strong, but don't allow yourself to get over-tired. Work steadily and pace yourself. Enhance the health in the ways mentioned in the yearly report. Health will improve after the 20th but will still need watching.

This month after the 20th, the upper, day side of your chart is becoming stronger. Dawn is breaking in your year. It is time to be up and about and focused on the outer world. Career is starting to become more important than it has been all year, and it's time to start working on it in overt, physical kinds of ways. The new Moon of the 5th, the full Moon of the 19th, and the Moon's perigee on the 16th are all strong career days. In general you'll have more enthusiasm for career matters from the 5th to the 19th as the Moon grows fuller than when she shrinks and wanes from the 20th to the 30th.

Venus travels with Neptune, your work and health planet, from the 9th and 11th. This will bring happy job opportunities even if you're employed. It will bring intuition, an enhanced dream life, and spiritual-type experiences.

There are interesting things happening in love this month. Mercury and Mars are in 'mutual reception'. Each is a guest in the house of the other. This shows cooperation. Thus love (Mars) and foreigners and foreign lands (Mercury) are cooperating with each other. It also indicates good romantic prospects at your place of worship or at educational functions.

Your love planet Mars goes 'out of bounds' on the 21st. This reinforces what we've just said. You're outside your normal sphere in your search for love. Or love, a relationship, pulls you outside your normal sphere. Possibly in foreign or exotic places. A love or social opportunity happens suddenly and unexpectedly for children or children figures in your life between the 21st and 23rd.

May

Best Days Overall: 6, 7, 15, 16, 24, 25
Most Stressful Days Overall: 1, 2, 3, 8, 9, 21, 22, 29, 30
Best Days for Love: 1, 2, 3, 6, 7, 14, 17, 21, 26, 27, 29, 30, 31
Best Days for Money: 2, 3, 4, 5, 10, 11, 13, 14, 17, 18, 19, 20, 21, 22, 29, 30, 31
Best Days for Career: 4, 5, 8, 9, 13, 14, 24

The upper, day side of your Horoscope is as strong as it will be all year now, although it is only dominant from the 1st to the 14th and on the 29th and 30th. From the 15th to the 29th the upper and lower halves are equal in strength. Still, you should focus more on your outer goals. You won't be able to totally focus on the career, but you will be able more than you have been. The duties and responsibilities of the family can't be ignored however.

Mars, your love planet, crosses the Mid-heaven and enters your 10th career house on the 16th. This gives many messages. Your love life is very high on the agenda. Love is the actual career (regardless of what your worldly career happens to be). The spouse, partner or current love is successful in his or her own right and is supporting your career. Your social grace – your likeability – is important, and perhaps *as* important as your professional skills. You further your career goals through social means. Much of your socializing is career-related.

Mars is still 'out of bounds' all this month. So, you are still outside your normal sphere socially and in love.

Finance isn't a big issue this month. Your money house is basically empty, with only the Moon moving through there on the 17th and 18th. In spite of this there is prosperity. Pluto, your financial planet is very well aspected. Earnings are increasing, but there are delays and glitches – Pluto is retrograde.

Venus travels with Uranus from the 17th to the 19th, signalling that you're ready for some adventure. You want to do something different and have perhaps some 'exotic' kind of fun. You might want to test the limits of the body. If so, do it mindfully and safely.

The power in the 8th house until the 21st shows that the spouse, partner or current love is having a strong financial month. You seem very involved in this. It is also a more sexually active kind of period. Whatever your age and stage, libido is higher than usual. As our regular readers know, power in the 8th house is good for detox regimes of all kinds and on all levels. It is good for de-cluttering your life, for simplifying things, for getting rid of what you don't use or need. The cosmos wants to shower its wealth upon us, but if there's no room, it can't do it. We have to empty ourselves to receive things.

June

Best Days Overall: 2, 3, 11, 12, 20, 21, 30
Most Stressful Days Overall: 5, 6, 18, 19, 25, 26
Best Days for Love: 1, 4, 5, 11, 13, 14, 20, 21, 23, 24, 25, 26
Best Days for Money: 1, 7, 8, 9, 10, 13, 14, 15, 16, 18, 19, 25, 26, 28, 29
Best Days for Career: 2, 3, 5, 6, 11, 12, 22

Your 9th house of religion, philosophy and foreign travel became powerful on May 21 and is still very strong until the 21st of this month. A strong 9th house generally spells happiness. The Hindu astrologers consider the 9th house the most fortunate of all the houses. The horizons are expanded. There is optimism. Travel opportunities are happening – also educational opportunities. College students seem more successful than usual. This inner expansion – this expansion of the mind – leads to career success after the 21st. It is a natural progression.

Your 10th house of career becomes very strong after the 21st. But your 4th family house is also strong. So, you are working to be successful in the world and successful at home. Not an easy thing to do. One time you will shift one way, another time the other way. Like a see-saw. Mars, your love planet, remains in the career house all month, and you should review last month's discussion of this. It is still relevant. Mars in the 10th house also shows a need to be more aggressive in the career – to fend off competitors or other hostile forces. You do this in a charming kind of way. Charming, but not less effective.

The Sun's move into your 10th house on the 21st shows that friends are succeeding and providing opportunity. (It reinforces the social dimension of the career that we discussed last month.) Mercury's move through your 10th house from the 4th to the 27th shows career-related travel. It shows that being involved in charities or altruistic kinds of activities are helping the career. It shows expanding career horizons.

Health is more stressful this month, especially after the 21st. So, as always, make sure to get enough rest. Handle your responsibilities, but let lesser things go. Enhance the health in the ways mentioned in the yearly report. Spiritual-type therapies are always good for you, but especially this month.

Career is going well but finances are more stressed this month – especially after the 21st. Pluto, your financial planet, receives stressful aspects and he is retrograde to boot. So finances are a bit sluggish. Things will improve next month, but in the meantime you need to go the extra mile in financial matters. You have to work harder. Avoid major purchases or investments at the moment.

Usually career success brings financial success, but at this time the financial success will happen later on. Often there is a need to make some financial sacrifice in order to advance the career. This might be one of those times.

July

Best Days Overall: 1, 8, 9, 17, 18, 19, 27, 28
Most Stressful Days Overall: 2, 3, 15, 16, 22, 23, 24, 29, 30
Best Days for Love: 1, 4, 10, 11, 13, 14, 20, 21, 22, 23, 24, 31
Best Days for Money: 4, 5, 6, 7, 10, 11, 13, 14, 15, 16, 22, 23, 24, 25, 26, 31
Best Days for Career: 2, 3, 10, 11, 21, 29, 30, 31

Health is stressed this month and two powerful eclipses – which affect you strongly – are not helping. Pay more attention to health, especially around the eclipse periods. Let go of trivia and focus on essentials. Rest and relax more. Get more massages and health treatments. Enhance the health in the ways mentioned in the yearly reports. The good news is that health will improve dramatically after the 23rd. So, you just have to get past the stresses earlier in the month.

The solar eclipse of the 2nd occurs in your 10th house, indicating career changes and shake-ups. Often there are shake-ups in your company or industry. Sometimes bosses, parents or parent figures – the 'higher ups' in your life – experience personal, life-changing dramas. Sometimes the career itself changes. There are also dramas in the lives of friends. Your high-tech equipment – software and computers – get tested. Make sure files are backed up, and that anti-virus, anti-hacking software is up to date.

The lunar eclipse of the 16th occurs in your 4th house of home and family, and as the eclipsed planet rules your career, this too brings career changes. It is almost (but not quite) a replay of the solar eclipse at the beginning of the month. Again there are shake-ups in your company or industry, and the authority figures in your life have personal kinds of dramas – parents and parent figures likewise. There are dramas at home and in the lives of family members. Repairs might be needed in the home. Is that water heater or microwave defective? Is there a leak in one of the pipes? It's now that you find out about it so that repairs and corrections can be made. This eclipse impacts on Pluto, your financial planet. So there is a need to make financial changes. (But give these things more thought. They can also have a delayed reaction as Pluto is retrograde.) The events of the eclipse will force these things.

Your love planet, Mars, spends the month in your 11th house. Thus love and love opportunities can happen through friends and through involvement with groups and organizations. Online activities can also lead to romance. Love seems happy. Friends like to play Cupid. And, in many cases, someone you thought of as a friend becomes more than that. Mars will make dynamic aspects with Uranus from the 9th to the 12th. Both you and the beloved need to be more mindful on the physical plane. The beloved can be erratic this period. Be more patient.

August

> Best Days Overall: 4, 5, 14, 15, 23, 24, 25
> Most Stressful Days Overall: 11, 12, 19, 20, 26, 27
> Best Days for Love: 1, 9, 10, 19, 20, 21, 30, 31
> Best Days for Money: 1, 2, 3, 7, 8, 9, 10, 11, 12, 19, 20, 21, 22, 28, 29, 30, 31
> Best Days for Career: 1, 9, 10, 20, 26, 27, 30

Career is starting to taper off this month, but still looks good. Two new Moons (in itself a rarity) – one of them a super new Moon, on the 1st – give the career some extra 'oomph'. The full Moon of the 15th also brings career success. In general you have more enthusiasm and drive for the career from the 1st to the 15th and on the 30th and 31st as the Moon waxes. Mercury in your 10th house until the 11th shows career-related travel (abroad) or much dealing with foreign countries. It also signals that being involved in charities and altruistic causes will help the career.

Your 11th house became powerful on July 23 and is still powerful until the 23rd of this month. So it is a social kind of month. Very good aspects to get involved with groups and professional organizations (and until the 18th this can bring romantic opportunities for singles). It is also a good period to expand your knowledge of science, astrology and technology.

The good news is that health is much improved over last month. After the 11th only two planets (excluding the Moon, whose transits are temporary) are in stressful alignment with you. Getting through last month was a major achievement and a nice pat on the back is well deserved. You could be making changes to your health regime from the 18th onwards, but research things more carefully. The job situation seems hectic, and perhaps troubled, after that date.

Finances are also much improved. Your financial planet Pluto is still retrograde, but he is not receiving stressful aspects. After the 23rd the aspects he receives will be positive. So prosperity is growing – improving – day-by-day. (Next month will be even better.)

There will be a rare Grand Trine in the Earth signs from the 18th onwards, meaning that the overall energy on the planet is practical and down to earth. Airy ideas are not much respected – only practical results.

The planetary power has begun to shift from the Western, social sector to the Eastern sector of the self. This began last month on the 3rd and is getting even stronger this month. You are in a period of independence – not so comfortable for a Libra. Personal initiative is more important now than your social genius. It is time to take responsibility for your own happiness. If conditions are irksome, you don't need to question your friends about what to do; make the changes that need to be made. The planetary power flows towards you and supports you. Your way is best for you right now. Relationships are always important to you, but you need to get comfortable in your own skin.

September

Best Days Overall: 1, 2, 10, 11, 20, 21, 28, 29
Most Stressful Days Overall: 7, 8, 9, 15, 16, 22, 23
Best Days for Love: 7, 8, 9, 15, 16, 17, 18, 19, 20, 26, 27, 28, 29
Best Days for Money: 3, 4, 5, 6, 8, 9, 15, 16, 18, 19, 24, 25, 26, 27, 30
Best Days for Career: 7, 8, 18, 19, 22, 23, 28

Last month, on the 18th, your 12th house of spirituality became very strong, and it remains so until the 23rd. So this is a good period to pursue more solitude. (Libra will never be happy with solitude, but sometimes, for brief periods, it is called for.) It will be good to spend more time on your spiritual practice and to focus on spiritual growth. Good to study the sacred texts of your religion. Good to be involved in charities and altruistic activities – causes that you believe in. For those on the spiritual path there are breakthroughs occurring, and these are most joyous when they happen. Peak experiences are more likely now than at other times of the year. All kinds of synchronistic, supernatural-type experiences will happen. The Invisible world is letting you know that it's around. Even love is more spiritual these days. Mars, your love planet, will spend the month in your spiritual 12th house. (He moved in there on August 18.) There are many messages here. The Horoscope is saying, get right spiritually, get in right alignment with the Divine, and the love life will take care of itself. Surrendering the love life to the Divine (in a heartfelt and sincere way) will solve the most difficult love and social situations. Love can be found in spiritual venues – meditation seminars or spiritual lectures, charity events or prayer meetings – these kinds of places. The bars and clubs are a waste of time this month.

We still have a Grand Trine in the Earth signs all month, so review our discussion of this last month. Stay practical. This Grand Trine is very positive for finance. Pluto is still moving backward, so there can be delays and glitches, but he is receiving very positive aspects. From the 5th to the 7th Venus makes beautiful aspects to him. From the 8th to the 10th Mercury comes into harmonious alignment. And from the 12th to the 13th the Sun joins the party. These are all nice paydays and will bring financial opportunities (but not a smooth ride). Finances get more delicate after the 23rd. You'll just have to work harder for earnings.

You are entering your maximum period for personal independence, which will last into next month too. Time to have things your way. You know what's best for you, so make the changes that need to be made. Later on it will be more difficult to do.

October

Best Days Overall: 7, 8, 17, 18, 26, 27
Most Stressful Days Overall: 5, 6, 12, 13, 19, 20
Best Days for Love: 7, 10, 11, 12, 13, 17, 18, 19, 20, 26, 27, 28, 29
Best Days for Money: 1, 2, 3, 4, 5, 6, 12, 13, 15, 16, 21, 22, 23, 24, 28, 29, 30, 31
Best Days for Career: 7, 8, 17, 18, 19, 20, 28

A happy and prosperous month, Libra. Enjoy!

Last month on the 14th, both Mercury and Venus entered your sign. Mercury brought travel opportunities, and spiritual techniques to enhance the appearance. Venus brought beauty, grace, charm and a sense of style (you always have this, but at the moment it is even stronger than usual). When the Sun entered your sign on September

23, you began a yearly personal pleasure peak. A time to enjoy the good life and to reward the body for its faithful service to you. A very good time to get the body and image the way you want them to be. Very good now to buy clothing or personal accessories, as your choices will be good.

Your personal pleasure peak continues until the 23rd. Mars, your love planet, enters your 1st house on the 4th and will be there all month. This is wonderful for love. It shows that love is pursuing you, instead of you having to look for love. Love opportunities come to you with little effort on your part – just go about your daily business. Those already in relationships will find the beloved more attentive and devoted. When Mars enters your sign he will be having his solstice (from the 4th to the 11th). He will pause in the Heavens – camp out in the same degree of latitude – and then change direction (in his latitudinal motion). This indicates a turning point in your love life. A pause and then a change of direction.

There are a lot of positive developments happening in your financial life as well. Pluto, your financial planet, starts to move forward again on the 3rd, which should bring financial clarity and better judgement. Long-stalled deals start to move forward. On the 3rd Mercury enters your money house, signalling financial increase (he rules your 9th house of expansion). He also brings the gift of financial intuition. On the 8th Venus, the ruler of your Horoscope, moves into your money house. The ruler of your Horoscope is always friendly and always fortunate. This transit shows a personal focus on finance – and focus is 90 per cent of the battle. You spend on yourself and look like a prospering person. On the 23rd the Sun enters your money house and you begin a yearly financial peak. Friends seem very supportive. You have their financial favour. Best of all, Pluto will be receiving harmonious aspects from the 23rd onwards. The new Moon of the 28th occurs in your money house and this will clarify financial issues well into next month. All the information you need to make correct decisions will be coming to you – naturally and normally. Your financial questions will be answered. Jobseekers will have wonderful opportunities from the 8th onwards (although these opportunities will need studying closely: Neptune, your work planet, is still retrograde).

November

Best Days Overall: 3, 4, 5, 13, 14, 22, 23
Most Stressful Days Overall: 1, 2, 8, 9, 10, 16, 17, 28, 29, 30
Best Days for Love: 3, 4, 5, 8, 9, 10, 17, 18, 19, 26, 29
Best Days for Money: 1, 2, 8, 9, 10, 11, 12, 18, 19, 20, 21, 24, 25, 26, 27, 28, 29, 30
Best Days for Career: 6, 7, 16, 17, 26

Health was good last month and is good in the month ahead too. Neptune, your health and work planet, starts to move forward again on the 27th, so after that it will be safer to make changes in your health regime.

You're still in the midst of a yearly financial peak until the 22nd. And finances should be good even afterwards. Mars moves into your money house on the 19th and spends the rest of the month there. Thus you have the financial favour of the spouse, partner or current love – and also of your social connections. Often this aspect brings opportunities for business partnerships or joint ventures. Investors often profit from mergers in their portfolio. Venus, your ruling planet, travels with Jupiter from the 22nd to the 24th – a very fortunate and fun kind of aspect. It will bring financial increase and perhaps new communication equipment – or even a car. It shows success for students. There are happy travel opportunities happening too.

On the 22nd the Sun enters your 3rd house of communication and intellectual interests and stays there for the rest of the month. This too is wonderful for students; they are focused on their studies and seem successful. This will be a great period to catch up on your reading and expand your knowledge base. Attend classes, workshops or seminars in subjects that interest you.

Love is basically happy this month. Mars remains in your sign until the 19th, and you're having love on your own terms. The spouse, partner or current love is still very devoted to you. Singles don't have to do anything special to attract love. It finds them. Mars will make dynamic aspects with Uranus from the 22nd to the 24th. The beloved, children and children figures in your life will need to be more mindful on the physical plane. They need to avoid conflict as much as possible. Be more patient with them this period; they seem restless and rebellious.

Venus will go 'out of bounds' from the 15th to the 30th. So, you are outside your normal comfort zone this period. Perhaps your reading or intellectual interests are outside your normal tastes. Perhaps siblings or sibling figures are pulling you away from your usual haunts.

On October 4, the planetary power shifted from the upper half to the lower half of your Horoscope – from the day side to the night side. So it is time to let go of career (you won't ignore it completely) and focus on the home, family and your emotional wellness. Now is the time for career preparation – preparing for the next career push, which will happen next year.

December

Best Days Overall: 1, 2, 11, 12, 19, 20, 28, 29
Most Stressful Days Overall: 6, 7, 13, 14, 26, 27
Best Days for Love: 3, 4, 5, 6, 7, 8, 9, 13, 14, 17, 18, 21, 22, 28, 29, 31
Best Days for Money: 8, 9, 17, 18, 21, 22, 26, 27
Best Days for Career: 6, 7, 13, 14, 15, 16, 26

The 4th house of home and family has been powerful all year – but not very happy. However, it becomes very powerful this month (and much happier). Jupiter moves into your 4th house on the 3rd. All the work, effort and extra responsibilities of the past two years are starting to pay off. Good things are happening. First of all, your emotional life is much more optimistic than it has been. Your moods are a bit brighter (and next year you will see even more improvement). Family support is better. The family circle starts to expand. Siblings and sibling figures are prospering and having wonderful financial opportunities.

The only issue now – and it is a big issue – is health. There are many planets – long-term ones – that are in stressful alignment with you. By now you know the drill. Rest more. Delegate as much as possible. Work steadily and pace yourself. Keep your focus on the real essentials in your life and let go of the non-essentials. Tough choices will have to be made. What is essential? What is non-essential? Enhance the health in the ways mentioned in the yearly report. Try to spend more time at the health spa, and schedule more massages and health treatments. The solar eclipse of the 26th affects you strongly, so be sure to take a nice relaxed schedule over that period.

The solar eclipse of the 26th is the 3rd eclipse in your 4th house this year. Home and family have been taking a pounding. None of this was punishment, the purpose was only to force changes that would improve things. So, once again, hidden flaws in the home are revealed so that they can be corrected. Family members (and especially a parent or parent figure) have personal dramas. Emotions at home run high, so be more patient. There are dramas in the lives of friends and with computer and technical equipment. (Make sure files are backed up and that anti-virus, anti-hacking software is still up to date.) Siblings and sibling figures are also affected (Jupiter is impacted by this eclipse). They have personal dramas and need to make financial changes. These financial changes will be good as they are in a prosperity period now. Students make important changes to their educational plans. They may be changing schools. There are shake-ups and disturbances here.

Love is more materialistic these days. Singles are attracted to the wealthy – the good providers. Material gifts turn you on. This is how you show love and how you feel loved. The sexual magnetism is perhaps of equal importance. The ideal this month will be those who have both – good sexual chemistry and good earning power. Love opportunities happen as you pursue your financial goals and with people involved in your finances.

Scorpio

♏︎

THE SCORPION

Birthdays from
23rd October to
22nd November

Personality Profile

SCORPIO AT A GLANCE

Element – Water

Ruling Planet – Pluto
  Co-ruling Planet – Mars
  Career Planet – Sun
  Love Planet – Venus
  Money Planet – Jupiter
  Planet of Health and Work – Mars
  Planet of Home and Family Life – Uranus

Colour – red-violet

Colour that promotes love, romance and social harmony – green

Colour that promotes earning power – blue

Gems – bloodstone, malachite, topaz

Metals – iron, radium, steel

Scents – cherry blossom, coconut, sandalwood, watermelon

Quality – fixed (= stability)

Quality most needed for balance – a wider view of things

Strongest virtues – loyalty, concentration, determination, courage, depth

Deepest needs – to penetrate and transform

Characteristics to avoid – jealousy, vindictiveness, fanaticism

Signs of greatest overall compatibility – Cancer, Pisces

Signs of greatest overall incompatibility – Taurus, Leo, Aquarius

Sign most helpful to career – Leo

Sign most helpful for emotional support – Aquarius

Sign most helpful financially – Sagittarius

Sign best for marriage and/or partnerships – Taurus

Sign most helpful for creative projects – Pisces

Best Sign to have fun with – Pisces

Signs most helpful in spiritual matters – Cancer, Libra

Best day of the week – Tuesday

Understanding a Scorpio

One symbol of the sign of Scorpio is the phoenix. If you meditate upon the legend of the phoenix you will begin to understand the Scorpio character – his or her powers and abilities, interests and deepest urges.

The phoenix of mythology was a bird that could recreate and reproduce itself. It did so in a most intriguing way: it would seek a fire – usually in a religious temple – fly into it, consume itself in the flames and then emerge a new bird. If this is not the ultimate, most profound transformation, then what is?

Transformation is what Scorpios are all about – in their minds, bodies, affairs and relationships (Scorpios are also society's transformers). To change something in a natural, not an artificial way, involves a transformation from within. This type of change is radical change as opposed to a mere cosmetic make-over. Some people think that change means altering just their appearance, but this is not the kind of thing that interests a Scorpio. Scorpios seek deep, fundamental change. Since real change always proceeds from within, a Scorpio is very interested in – and usually accustomed to – the inner, intimate and philosophical side of life.

Scorpios are people of depth and intellect. If you want to interest them you must present them with more than just a superficial image. You and your interests, projects or business deals must have real substance to them in order to stimulate a Scorpio. If they haven't, he or she will find you out – and that will be the end of the story.

If we observe life – the processes of growth and decay – we see the transformational powers of Scorpio at work all the time. The caterpillar changes itself into a butterfly; the infant grows into a child and then an adult. To Scorpios this definite and perpetual transformation is not something to be feared. They see it as a normal part of life. This acceptance of transformation gives Scorpios the key to understanding the true meaning of life.

Scorpios' understanding of life (including life's weaknesses) makes them powerful warriors – in all senses of the word. Add to this their depth, patience and endurance and you have a powerful personality. Scorpios have good, long memories and can at times be quite vindictive – they can wait years to get their revenge. As a friend, though, there is no one more loyal and true than a Scorpio. Few are willing to make the sacrifices that a Scorpio will make for a true friend.

The results of a transformation are quite obvious, although the process of transformation is invisible and secret. This is why Scorpios are considered secretive in nature. A seed will not grow properly if you keep digging it up and exposing it to the light of day. It must stay buried – invisible – until it starts to grow. In the same manner, Scorpios fear revealing too much about themselves or their hopes to other people. However, they will be more than happy to let you see the finished product – but only when it is completely unwrapped. On the other hand, Scorpios like knowing everyone else's secrets as much as they dislike anyone knowing theirs.

Finance

Love, birth, life as well as death are Nature's most potent transformations; Scorpios are interested in all of these. In our society, money is a transforming power, too, and a Scorpio is interested in money for that reason. To a Scorpio money is power, money causes change, money controls. The power of money fascinates them. But Scorpios can be too materialistic if they are not careful. They can be overly awed by the power of money, to a point where they think that money rules the world.

Even the term 'plutocrat' comes from Pluto, the ruler of the sign of Scorpio. Scorpios will – in one way or another – achieve the financial status they strive for. When they do so they are careful in the way they handle their wealth. Part of this financial carefulness is really a kind of honesty, for Scorpios are usually involved with other people's money – as accountants, lawyers, stockbrokers or corporate managers – and when you handle other people's money you have to be more cautious than when you handle your own.

In order to fulfil their financial goals, Scorpios have important lessons to learn. They need to develop qualities that do not come naturally to them, such as breadth of vision, optimism, faith, trust and, above all, generosity. They need to see the wealth in Nature and in life, as well as in its more obvious forms of money and power. When they develop generosity their financial potential reaches great heights, for

Jupiter, the Lord of Opulence and Good Fortune, is Scorpio's money planet.

Career and Public Image

Scorpio's greatest aspiration in life is to be considered by society as a source of light and life. They want to be leaders, to be stars. But they follow a very different road than do Leos, the other stars of the zodiac. A Scorpio arrives at the goal secretly, without ostentation; a Leo pursues it openly. Scorpios seek the glamour and fun of the rich and famous in a restrained, discreet way.

Scorpios are by nature introverted and tend to avoid the limelight. But if they want to attain their highest career goals they need to open up a bit and to express themselves more. They need to stop hiding their light under a bushel and let it shine. Above all, they need to let go of any vindictiveness and small-mindedness. All their gifts and insights were given to them for one important reason – to serve life and to increase the joy of living for others.

Love and Relationships

Scorpio is another zodiac sign that likes committed clearly defined, structured relationships. They are cautious about marriage, but when they do commit to a relationship they tend to be faithful – and heaven help the mate caught or even suspected of infidelity! The jealousy of the Scorpio is legendary. They can be so intense in their jealousy that even the thought or intention of infidelity will be detected and is likely to cause as much of a storm as if the deed had actually been done.

Scorpios tend to settle down with those who are wealthier than they are. They usually have enough intensity for two, so in their partners they seek someone pleasant, hard-working, amiable, stable and easy-going. They want someone they can lean on, someone loyal behind them as they fight the battles of life. To a Scorpio a partner, be it a lover or a friend, is a real partner – not an adversary. Most of all a Scorpio is looking for an ally, not a competitor.

If you are in love with a Scorpio you will need a lot of patience. It takes a long time to get to know Scorpios, because they do not reveal themselves readily. But if you persist and your motives are honourable, you will gradually be allowed into a Scorpio's inner chambers of the mind and heart.

Home and Domestic Life

Uranus is ruler of Scorpio's 4th solar house of home and family. Uranus is the planet of science, technology, changes and democracy. This tells us a lot about a Scorpio's conduct in the home and what he or she needs in order to have a happy, harmonious home life.

Scorpios can sometimes bring their passion, intensity and wilfulness into the home and family, which is not always the place for these qualities. These traits are good for the warrior and the transformer, but not so good for the nurturer and family member. Because of this (and also because of their need for change and transformation) the Scorpio may be prone to sudden changes of residence. If not carefully constrained, the sometimes inflexible Scorpio can produce turmoil and sudden upheavals within the family.

Scorpios need to develop some of the virtues of Aquarius in order to cope better with domestic matters. There is a need to build a team spirit at home, to treat family activities as truly group activities – family members should all have a say in what does and does not get done. For at times a Scorpio can be most dictatorial. When a Scorpio gets dictatorial it is much worse than if a Leo or Capricorn (the two other power signs in the zodiac) does. For the dictatorship of a Scorpio is applied with more zeal, passion, intensity and concentration than is true of either a Leo or Capricorn. Obviously this can be unbearable to family members – especially if they are sensitive types.

In order for a Scorpio to get the full benefit of the emotional support that a family can give, he or she needs to let go of conservatism and be a bit more experimental, to explore new techniques in childrearing, be more democratic with family members and to try to manage things by consensus rather than by autocratic edict.

Horoscope for 2019

Major Trends

Last year was very prosperous, Scorpio, and the year ahead seems even more prosperous. Jupiter, your financial planet will spend almost all year in your money house. More on this later.

Your 3rd house of communication and intellectual interests is easily the strongest in your Horoscope this year. Also the most challenging. Students will have to work harder on their studies. They need to 'knuckle down'. Siblings and sibling figures in your life seem stressed. Sales and marketing projects are fraught with delays and have more challenges attached. Things will improve here later on in the year, as Jupiter moves into your 3rd house on December 3. In the meantime, put in the extra effort.

Neptune has been in your 5th house for many years and will be there for many more to come. Children and children figures in your life are becoming more spiritual – and if not, they have to be careful about drugs and alcohol. Your tastes in amusements are more refined and spiritual these days. The fine arts appeal to you. Personal creativity is very inspired. When you're relaxed and having fun, you have good connection with spirit.

The major headline this year is Uranus's move from your 6th career house (where he's been for the past seven years) into your 7th house. This is going to have a profound impact on your love life and current relationship. The social life becomes more unstable – but also more fun and more exciting. More details later.

There are a lot of shake-ups in your career this year. Much more than usual. We have five eclipses this year (usually there are four) and of the five, four impact directly on the career. More on this later.

Your most important interests in the year ahead are finance (until December 3); communication and intellectual interests; children, fun and creativity; health and work (until March 7); and love, romance and social activities (after March 7).

Your paths of greatest fulfilment this year are finance (until December 3); communication and intellectual interests (from December 3 onwards); and religion, philosophy, theology and foreign travel.

Health

(Please note that this is an astrological perspective on health and not a medical one. In days of yore there was no difference, both of these perspectives were identical. But now there could be quite a difference. For a medical perspective, please consult your doctor or health practitioner.)

Health and energy are good this year. As the year begins there are no long-term planets in stressful alignment with you. And after March 7 (as Uranus moves into Taurus) there will be only one in stressful alignment. All the others are either making harmonious aspects or leaving you alone. Of course, there will be periods where health and energy are less easy than usual (and we will discuss them in the monthly reports). These come from the transits of the short-term planets. They are temporary and not trends for the year. When they pass, health and energy return to their normal ease.

Your 6th house of health has been powerful for the past seven years, but after March 7, it will basically be empty. (Only short-term planets

Important foot reflexology points for the year ahead

Try to massage all of the foot on a regular basis – the top of the foot as well as the bottom – but pay extra attention to the points highlighted on the chart. When you massage, be aware of 'sore spots' as these need special attention. It's also a good idea to massage the ankles, and especially below them.

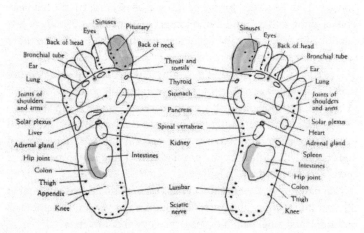

will move through there.) This I read as a good sign. Health is good and you have no need to overly focus here.

For the past seven years you've been experimental in health matters. The cosmos was urging you to learn how you function, to learn what works for you personally, to learn how you are 'wired up'. By now these lessons have been learned and there's no need for further experimentation.

With Uranus in your health house, many of you were attracted to alternative medicine. And even those who stayed with orthodox medicine have been attracted to the new, experimental, cutting-edge technologies in that system. These urges are less intense this year.

Your health is good, but you can make it even better. Give more attention to the following areas – the vulnerable areas of your Horoscope (the reflexology points are shown in the chart above):

- The head, face and scalp. These are always important for Scorpio; Mars, the ruler of these areas, is your health planet. So face and scalp massage should be an integral part of your health regime. Craniosacral therapy is also excellent for the head.
- The musculature. This too is always important for Scorpio as the muscles are also ruled by Mars. You don't need to be a body builder or fitness expert, just have good muscle tone. Weak or flabby muscles can knock the spine and skeleton out of alignment and this will cause all kinds of other problems. So vigorous exercise (according to your age and stage in life) is important.
- The adrenals are another important area for Scorpio. The important thing here is to avoid anger and fear, the two emotions that stress the adrenals. Ginseng is said to be good for them.
- The colon, bladder and sexual organs – another important area, ruled by your sign, Scorpio. So safe sex and sexual moderation are always important. A herbal colon cleanse every now and then is also a good idea.
- The ankles and calves. These have only become important over the past seven years while Uranus, the planet that rules them, has been in your 6th house. They are still important until March 7, so continue to massage these areas and give the ankles more support when exercising.

Good emotional health has been very important over the last few years. This is a good thing in its own right, but for the past seven years it has been a health issue. It starts to become less important after March 7. Good family relations likewise.

Your health planet, Mars, will move through eight signs and houses of your chart this year. So, there are many short-term health trends based on where Mars is and the aspects he receives. These are best dealt with in the monthly reports.

Home and Family

Your 4th house of home and family is not a house of power this year, and this tends to the status quo. Though you can afford to move or renovate, and have the freedom to do these things, there is no driving urge for this.

Your family planet Uranus has been in the sign of Aries for the past seven years, so family life has been active and aggressive. Passions have been running high. The home has become as much a health spa and sports centre as a home. This is starting to change this year. Uranus in Taurus is much more stable. Moods and emotions should be more stable.

Uranus in your 7th house of love (after March 7) shows various things. For a start, it shows more entertaining from home and more socializing with the family – family events and gatherings. It also shows the 'beautification' of the home. The home is not just a home but a place of beauty and the main social centre. You will be doing more redecorating and buying objects of beauty for the home. With some people I've seen, the home is like a museum or art gallery. You might not go this far, but you will be focused more on its appearance.

You also tend to favour more rural, less busy settings. Previously you liked the 'action spots'. You perhaps start to favour expensive and very heavy kinds of furniture. Solid pieces.

If you're planning a major renovation, August 13–23 would be a good time. If you're redecorating or buying objects of beauty for the home, January 20 to February 19, March 1 to March 26, and August 21 to August 30 are good times.

A parent or parent figure could move – and not just once either. He or she could be staying in different places for long periods of time. He or she will have multiple moves in the coming years. One of them has beautiful job offers this year, and if there have been health problems there is good news on that front.

Siblings and sibling figures are having stressful financial times these days, but prosperity will happen later in the year – after December 3. They have probably moved multiple times in the past seven years, but now they are starting to settle down. They seem emotionally more stable too – especially after March 7.

Children and children figures in your life should go easy on any alcohol or drugs, as they can overreact to these things. They seem very idealistic these days. There are job changes in store this year, but it looks stable on the home front.

Finance and Career

A very prosperous year ahead, Scorpio. Enjoy. Your financial planet, Jupiter, will spend most of the year in your money house. He will be in his own sign and house and thus he will function more powerfully on your behalf. This spells increased earning power.

Assets you own will increase in value – and substantially. All kinds of happy opportunities will come to you. Your financial horizons – your limits as to what you think is achievable – are greatly expanded.

Jupiter in Sagittarius shows someone who earns easily and who spends easily. So, you're both a big spender (perhaps an impulse spender) and big earner. There are some pitfalls here. Jupiter in Sagittarius likes the 'quick buck' – fast money. This can make you vulnerable to scammers. Be wary of these 'get rich quick' schemes.

Jupiter in Sagittarius denotes happy-go-lucky finances. There is a vast confidence and optimism about financial matters, which is probably why you prosper so much. There is a strong belief in wealth and in the earning abilities. As one metaphysical writer puts it, 'your faith is your fortune'.

Jupiter in Sagittarius can be speculative, but this year is less favourable for speculations than last year was. Tone this down.

You always have a good affinity for publishing, the travel business, airlines, international shipping and transportation, and for-profit colleges. This year even more so than usual. People involved in these industries can be playing an important role in earnings. There is also a strong affinity for foreign companies and foreign investments. Foreigners are probably playing a big role in finances too.

It looks like there will be a lot of business travel this year – probably to foreign countries.

By the end of the year, when Jupiter moves on to your 3rd house in early December, most financial goals (at least the short-term ones) will be fulfilled. You can now spend more time pursuing intellectual interests, broadening your knowledge base. You have the financial freedom to do so now.

The financial planet in the 3rd house favours trading, buying, selling and retailing. It favours telecommunications (both local and long distance), transportation (local and long distance) and media companies (print media primarily). Whatever you are doing, good sales, marketing, PR and good use of the media will be important. People need to know about your product or service.

One of the good things with Jupiter's move into your 3rd house is that he will be in the sign of Capricorn. This enhances the financial judgement. You will not be reckless with money. You will take a slower, more methodical approach to wealth. Conservative investments will be more appealing. You will think more long term about wealth. It's a good aspect for disciplined savings and investment regimes. Wealth will be more secure because of this.

There is strong prosperity this year, as we mentioned, but next year, as Jupiter moves ever closer to Pluto, will also be prosperous.

This is not an especially strong career year, however. There will never be a time where the day side (the upper half) of your chart is truly dominant. There will be periods where it is stronger than usual (and we'll cover this in the monthly reports), but the day side will never dominate. Thus the year ahead is more about emotional wellness and home and family issues. Being in emotional harmony is more important than career success. (If you can have both, all the better.) Also keep in mind that your 10th house of career is basically empty this year. Only short-term planets will move through there.

Still, as we mentioned there are many changes happening here. Four of the five eclipses this year impact on your career, bringing changes in your company or industry. Government regulations can change the rules of the game. There can be management shake-ups in your company. Bosses, parents and parent figures – authority figures in your life – can experience life-changing dramas that impact on the career. In many cases the actual career path will change. A change of career would not be a surprise.

Love and Social Life

As we mentioned, on March 7 Uranus will move into your 7th house and will be there for the next seven or so years. This has profound implications for your relationships.

If you are in a marriage or serious relationship, you will need to work a lot harder on it. I've seen relationships survive a Uranus transit but it's never easy. It will be important to give the spouse, partner or current love as much space as possible, so long as it isn't destructive. He or she seems more rebellious these days so you need to learn how to deal with this.

If you are single, it is probably best not to marry for a while. Your Horoscope favours serial love affairs rather than long-term commitments. Your tastes in love are also different these days. You're attracted to unconventional kinds of people – technical geeks, programmers, inventors, scientists, astrologers and astronomers. Plain run-of-the-mill types are not very interesting. It is the exotic that appeals to you. The problem is that these kinds of relationships are rarely stable.

There is a lot of good in this transit too. It makes things very exciting. Love can happen at any time, in any place – often when you least expect it, and from surprising sources. These things are fun while they last, but the stability of them is questionable. A lightning flash illuminates a dark night but tends to disappear very quickly. Don't try to trap the lightning, just enjoy it for what it is. More flashes will come.

By the time Uranus is finished with you in 2026 or so, you will be in completely different social circumstances, and probably in a new circle of friends.

Scorpio is a sign that likes stability, so this transit can be uncomfortable. However, this is the cosmic lesson of the transit – learning to be comfortable with social change.

Uranus is the planet of science, technology and the online world. So online activities – social media and dating sites – are likely venues for romance. Love will probably be conducted more online than offline as well.

Uranus is also your family planet. Thus, as we mentioned, you're entertaining more from home and with family. Family and family connections can be a source of romance for singles. They like to play Cupid these days. Attending a family gathering can also lead to romance.

Uranus makes nice aspects to your ruling planet Pluto after March 7. So love seems happy. You seem to enjoy the instability. Instability is the price we pay for more freedom. One thing is certain. The love life will not be dull. It will be a constant soap opera.

Self-improvement

We have just discussed some of the challenges happening in love. First, is being able to deal with the instability. Even with long-term relationships, you won't know what to expect from the beloved from day-to-day or moment-to-moment. It's as if you are dealing with a new situation constantly. You can't take the relationship for granted. You sort of have to woo the beloved every day. Complacency is deadly. The instability is something to embrace. It gives both of you more freedom. One of the things that can be done to make the relationship easier is to do wild, unconventional things together as a couple. Avoid the routine and mundane. Strike out on new paths. Travel to really exotic kinds of places and indulge in off-beat activities. This will introduce more change and excitement into the relationship.

Learn to be comfortable with sudden social changes too. Everything might be 'up in the air', and that's OK. Trust that everything will work out eventually, one way or another.

Spiritual Neptune has been in your 5th house for many years now. This, as we said before, shows a desire for more refined entertainment. You will gravitate to more spiritually oriented videos, music and films. Also, as we mentioned, the children and children figures in your life are becoming more spiritual, and this is having an effect on you. I've seen many cases like this. The parents are secular and worldly, but the children embrace either a religious or mystical path. Now the parents have to adjust to this.

For those of you involved in music or the arts, this is a wonderful transit. Your creativity is very much inspired these days. It is hitting a whole new level.

For those of you already on a spiritual path, there is much forward progress this year. Venus, your spiritual planet, is moving unusually fast, and this tends towards confidence and fast progress.

With Venus as your spiritual planet, love solves all things. Stay in the feeling of love and you contact the Divine rather easily. This is when you feel closest. (Not only that, but it will ease the strains on your love life as well.) Love, love, love as they say, and everything will turn out all right.

Month-by-month Forecasts

January

Best Days Overall: 1, 10, 11, 19, 20, 27, 28
Most Stressful Days Overall: 7, 8, 15, 16, 21, 22, 27, 28
Best Days for Love: 1, 12, 13, 15, 16, 21, 22, 30, 31
Best Days for Money: 2, 3, 12, 13, 21, 22, 30, 31
Best Days for Career: 5, 6, 16, 21, 22, 25

You begin your year in a period of personal independence. But this will not last long. By the 24th the Western, social sector of your chart will start to dominate. So, if there are changes to be made, make them straightaway at the beginning of the month.

Venus, your love planet (and the generic love planet) is in your sign until the 7th. Love is happy and on your terms. It seeks you out rather than vice versa. On the 7th Venus will move into your money house and starts to travel with Jupiter. The conjunction with Jupiter will be most exact from the 21st to the 23rd. This is a powerful period for both love and finance and brings a nice payday. Singles will meet interesting love opportunities. There are happy social experiences.

We have two eclipses this month to make things more exciting – to provide some drama. The solar eclipse of the 6th (in America it's on the 5th) occurs in your 3rd house and impacts on the ruler of the 3rd house, Saturn. So drive more carefully – more defensively – that period. Students have shake-ups in their schools and make important changes to their educational plans. They could also change schools. Siblings, sibling figures and neighbours experience personal dramas and should reduce their schedule over this period. Communication equipment will get tested and might need replacement. The money people in your life have to make important financial changes. Every solar eclipse impacts on your career, as the Sun is your career planet. Thus there are career changes afoot. There can be shake ups in your company or industry. There are personal dramas in the lives of bosses, parents, parent figures and authority figures in your life.

The lunar eclipse of the 21st also impacts on your career as it occurs in your career 10th house. So again, course corrections in the career are happening. In some cases the actual career will change. In other cases, you will approach things differently. This eclipse affects you more strongly than the previous one, so take it nice and easy and avoid risk taking and daredevil-type activities. Every lunar eclipse impacts on 9th house activities (the Moon is ruler of your 9th house). So, this eclipse affects college-level students. It brings changes in their educational plans and courses – maybe even changes of colleges. There are shake-ups in your place of worship and dramas in the lives of worship leaders. It's not advisable to travel over this time, but if you must, try to schedule your trip around the eclipse period.

More attention to health is needed from the 20th onwards. Make sure to get enough rest and enhance the health in the ways mentioned in the yearly report.

February

Best Days Overall: 6, 7, 15, 16, 24, 25
Most Stressful Days Overall: 3, 4, 5, 11, 12, 17, 18
Best Days for Love: 11, 12, 19, 20, 28
Best Days for Money: 9, 10, 17, 18, 26, 27
Best Days for Career: 3, 4, 14, 17, 18, 24

On January 20 the planetary powers entered their maximum lower position in your Horoscope. The night side of your chart is overwhelmingly dominant, with at least 80 per cent (and sometimes 90 per cent) of the planets below the horizon. Your 4th house of home and family is powerful, while your 10th house of career is empty (only the Moon will move through there on the 17th and 18th). So we have a clear message. Career is in a preparation stage now. Give your attention to the home, family and your emotional wellness. If these are in order, your career push, which will happen later on in the year, will be strong and healthy. Even your career planet, the Sun, spends most of the month (until the 19th) in your 4th house. So home and family *is* the career – *is* the mission – right now.

Mars makes dynamic aspects with your family planet Uranus from the 11th to the 14th. This can bring repairs or renovations in the home. A parent or parent figure seems more temperamental and restless. He or she should try to relax more over that period. More mindfulness on the physical plane is needed.

Mars, your health planet, moves into your 7th house of love on the 14th and stays there for the rest of the month. This can complicate the love life. The spouse, partner or current love can be more impatient and perhaps critical. He or she is prone to anger or irritation. Try to avoid power struggles in your relationship. There's no need to make matters worse than they need to be. For singles, this tends to show aggressiveness in love. You go after what you want with great courage. You're attracted to health professionals, people involved in your health and to athletes and military types. Your love planet, Venus, spends most of the month in your 3rd house – from the 3rd onwards. So love is close to home; it can be found in your neighbourhood and perhaps with neighbours. When Venus travels with Saturn on the 17th and 18th there are social opportunities with a neighbour or at school. There is even better romantic opportunities on the 22nd and 23rd.

Jobseekers find opportunities through social contacts from the 14th onwards.

Finances are very good this month. You're in a prosperous year. Your financial plant Jupiter is receiving helpful aspects. After the 19th the finances will need more work, but prosperity will happen.

Health still needs watching until the 19th. Enhance the health in the ways mentioned in the yearly report. On the 14th, as Mars your health planet moves into Taurus, enhance the health through neck massage. Craniosacral therapy will also be beneficial.

March

Best Days Overall: 5, 6, 7, 15, 16, 23, 24
Most Stressful Days Overall: 3, 4, 10, 11, 17, 18, 30, 31
Best Days for Love: 3, 4, 10, 11, 15, 16, 23, 24
Best Days for Money: 8, 9, 17, 18, 25, 26
Best Days for Career: 8, 9, 17, 18, 25, 26

The planetary power is now firmly – decisively – in the Western, social sector of your chart. Personal independence is much weaker now, as it should be. The focus is more on others and their needs. You're taking a brief vacation from yourself – a healthy thing to do every now and then. The love and social life does need more of your attention now. Mars will be in your 7th house all month, and on the 7th Uranus moves in too and will remain there for the next seven years. The whole social sphere becomes more unstable. A current relationship will need a lot more work to hold together.

In spite of all the social challenges – and these will all work out – the month ahead is happy. On February 19 the Sun entered your 5th house of fun, creativity and children and you entered one of your yearly personal pleasure peaks (you will have another one later in the year). Women of childbearing age are unusually fertile now – especially on the 15th and 16th. And though career is not a major focus right now, your leisure activities can bring career opportunities. In some cases you're entertaining clients or prospective customers, showing them a good time. In other cases you make important contacts at the theatre or resort – some place of entertainment. Children and children figures in your life are more ambitious this month too.

Finances need more work. Like last month, prosperity is happening, but you're earning it. Finances will get much easier after the 20th. Health is basically good this month. Even the stressful aspects of Mars and Uranus will not have much effect. The short-term planets are supporting you. You can enhance your already good health through neck massage and craniosacral therapy – as well as by the ways mentioned in the yearly report.

On the 26th your love planet, Venus, moves into your 5th house, where she will be in her sign of exaltation – Pisces. So the social magnetism is very powerful. Singles are attracting the opposite sex, but perhaps the wrong kinds of people – non-serious people. However, with the love planet in the 5th house this might not be a concern. Love is about fun and you're probably not thinking seriously. Instability doesn't concern you right now.

The Sun's move into your 6th house of health and work is good for jobseekers. You're in the mood for work and employers pick up on this. Your good work ethic also impresses superiors.

April

Best Days Overall: 1, 2, 3, 11, 12, 19, 20, 29, 30
Most Stressful Days Overall: 6, 7, 8, 13, 14, 26, 27
Best Days for Love: 2, 3, 6, 7, 8, 11, 12, 21
Best Days for Money: 4, 5, 13, 14, 22, 23
Best Days for Career: 4, 5, 13, 14, 24

Love is very exciting this month, but highly unstable. You don't seem to mind, however, and you don't seem that serious about it until the 20th. Instability is fun. Love opportunities happen suddenly and out of the blue. Anything can happen at any time. On the 20th, as the Sun enters your 7th house of love, you begin a yearly love and social peak. Singles are not likely to marry but they will have romance and romantic opportunities. A very happy romantic opportunity happens between the 9th and the 11th. But it seems like fun and games. Venus travels with Neptune.

On the 20th, Venus enters your 6th house. Thus love opportunities happen at work or as you pursue your health goals. Health professionals are alluring. Venus in Aries indicates a love-at-first-sight, impulsive kind of energy. The tendency is to leap before you look. It saves courtship time, but can lead to mistakes.

Venus, your love planet, has her solstice from the 22nd to the 25th. She pauses in the Heavens. She camps out at the same degree of latitude and then changes direction. And so it is in your love life. A change of direction is happening.

Mars, your health and work planet, goes 'out of bounds' from the 21st onwards (and will remain out of bounds all of next month and well into June). Thus your work can be taking you outside your normal sphere. In health matters too you are outside your normal comfort zone. Jobseekers need to look 'outside the box' during this period; those who employ others likewise.

The Sun's entry into your 7th house on the 20th shows that you are mixing with high and mighty people, people of power and prestige, people above you in status. A lot of your socializing seems career-related – and it's a good idea to attend these functions. This is a valid way to promote your career. This aspect often brings an office romance (or the opportunity for such a liaison).

Health is good this month but needs more attention after the 20th. There is nothing serious afoot, only lower-than-usual energy. Enhance the health in the ways mentioned in the yearly report, but also give more attention to the arms, shoulders and respiratory system. Arm and shoulder massage and plain old fresh air will enhance the health.

Finances are good this month – especially until the 20th. But Jupiter, your financial planet, goes retrograde on the 10th. Earnings are happening but more slowly, and there are glitches and delays.

May

Best Days Overall: 8, 9, 17, 18, 26, 27
Most Stressful Days Overall: 4, 5, 10, 11, 24, 25, 31
Best Days for Love: 2, 3, 4, 5, 14, 21, 31
Best Days for Money: 2, 3, 10, 11, 19, 20, 29, 30
Best Days for Career: 4, 5, 10, 11, 13, 14, 24

Health still needs attention until the 21st. Arm and shoulder massage and fresh air – breathing exercises – are helpful until the 16th. After then, pay more attention to your diet. Often simple dietary changes can relieve many problems. Health will improve after the 21st. Your health planet Mars will be 'out of bounds' all month, so you're exploring therapies that are outside your normal experience. There are no remedies to be found in the usual places, so you must look elsewhere.

Your financial planet, Jupiter, is still retrograde this month (and, in general, retrograde activity is increasing this month), so earnings are happening more slowly than usual. After the 21st there are more financial challenges to deal with. You just have to work harder to achieve your goals. There are financial disagreements with parents, parent figures and bosses after the 21st and you seem temporarily out of favour with them. You will have to find the middle ground.

Love is still unstable, but happy this month. You're still in the midst of a yearly love and social peak until the 21st – and you might even feel it afterwards too. Venus, your love planet, will be in your 7th house from the 5th onwards. While marriage is not advisable these days, you can still enjoy love for what it is. It can disappear tomorrow, but even so, there are many fish in the sea. Like last month you're mixing with people of power and prestige. In fact, power and prestige are romantic turn-ons these days. Your social connections help the career (which is becoming more important this month). Your love planet travels with Uranus from the 17th to the 19th, signalling sudden romantic meetings or sudden social invitations. The spouse, partner or current love is more temperamental (and rebellious) this period. Tread lightly and be more patient. He or she has an interesting career opportunity.

On the 21st the Sun, your career planet, enters your 8th house of regeneration – your favourite house – and stays there for the rest of the month. Personal finances might be slower than usual, but the finances of the spouse, partner or current love are excellent. He or she makes up the slack.

The 8th house is a Scorpio house. Scorpio is its natural ruler. So this month is wonderful for detox regimes, taking on or paying down debt (according to your need), dealing with tax and insurance issues and, for those of you of appropriate age, doing estate planning.

June

Best Days Overall: 5, 6, 13, 14, 23, 24
Most Stressful Days Overall: 1, 7, 8, 20, 21, 27, 28, 29
Best Days for Love: 1, 11, 20, 21, 27, 28, 29
Best Days for Money: 7, 8, 15, 16, 25, 26
Best Days for Career: 2, 3, 7, 8, 11, 12, 22

Your 8th house is still strong until the 21st. So, in addition to the things we wrote of last month, it is a good time to indulge in your favourite pastimes – occult studies, ruminating on death and rebirth, and in sexual indulgence. Your already legendary libido is even stronger now. Whatever your age or stage in life, libido is stronger than ever.

It is also good to de-clutter your life. De-clutter is the more popular word, but I like 'simplify'. Simplicity is wealth. Keep what you need for your happiness and let go of everything else. Extraneous things are distractions. These things 'clog the arteries' – the regular flow of supply from the cosmos is impeded. Get rid of them and the blood flow (the cosmic supply) is restored to normal.

The planetary power is now mostly on the day side of your Horoscope, the upper half. So career is becoming more important now. You haven't yet reached your 'noon-time' peak – this will happen in the next two months – but you're making progress. You pursue your career in overt, physical ways.

Finances are still a bit rocky, until the 21st, but you will see improvement afterwards. Your financial planet Jupiter is still moving backward, but the main problem is the stressful aspects he receives. By the 21st these stressful aspects will be over with. In the meantime, shop for groceries or other necessities, of course, but not for the big-ticket things. You're still in a period of gaining clarity in your finances. This is the most important thing. Jupiter will start to move forward soon (on August 11) and that will be the time to execute your plans.

Health is excellent this month – especially after the 21st. You have all the energy you need to achieve whatever you set your mind to. There will be only one long-term planet in stressful alignment with you – Uranus. But all the other planets are either in harmony with you or leaving you alone.

Health may be good, but ego and self-esteem are another story. The ruler of your Horoscope, Pluto, receives stressful aspects from the 21st onwards. Self-confidence could be better. However, your ruling planet is retrograde to boot and very near Saturn – so it could be good to take a lower personal profile. Shine by all means, but quietly.

July

Best Days Overall: 2, 3, 10, 11, 20, 21, 29, 30
Most Stressful Days Overall: 4, 5, 17, 18, 19, 25, 26, 31
Best Days for Love: 1, 10, 11, 20, 21, 25, 26, 31
Best Days for Money: 4, 5, 13, 14, 22, 23, 24, 31
Best Days for Career: 2, 3, 4, 5, 10, 11, 21, 31

Your self-esteem and self-confidence have been weaker than usual due to planetary stress, as we discussed last month. A lunar eclipse on the 16th exacerbates things. At times like this it is good to remember who you are – a child of the Divine, a child of the universe.

We have two eclipses this month. The first is a solar eclipse on the 2nd which occurs in your 9th house. This one affects you relatively mildly, but it won't hurt to reduce your schedule a little. It affects college students, who will be making changes in their educational plans or changing schools. Often this happens because of some disruption or disturbance at the college – and there are many scenarios as to what exactly happens. The institutions can change rules or policies. There can be shake-ups in the administration. Course or graduation requirements can change. There are also shake-ups in your place of worship and dramas in the lives of rabbis, ministers, priests and imams. With your 9th house very strong until the 23rd, foreign travel is very attractive, but you don't want to be en route during the eclipse period. This eclipse, as does every solar eclipse, signals career changes. These will probably be good, as you enter a yearly career peak on the 23rd. The eclipse will clear out obstructions on your pathway. There can be shake-ups in your company or industry. Bosses (and parents or parent figures) experience personal life-changing dramas.

The lunar eclipse of the 16th occurs in your 3rd house of communication and intellectual interests, and so it affects all students. They can

change schools or educational plans. There are shake-ups and disturbances at their educational establishments. There are dramas in the
lives of siblings, sibling figures and neighbours. (There can be disturbances in the neighbourhood as well.) The money people in your life
have to make important financial changes. This eclipse, as mentioned
earlier, impacts Pluto, the ruler of your Horoscope. So, take it easy this
period. Avoid risk-taking activities. Avoid unnecessary travel. The
events of the eclipse (and the general stressful aspects Pluto's receiving) will force a redefinition of yourself – your image and self-concept.
You need to define yourself for yourself, otherwise others will do it and
it won't be so pleasant. Because the eclipsed planet, the Moon, rules
your 9th house there are more disturbances in your place of worship
and in the lives of worship leaders. (It is almost a repeat of the solar
eclipse in this respect.)

August

Best Days Overall: 7, 8, 16, 17, 26, 27
Most Stressful Days Overall: 1, 14, 15, 21, 22, 28, 29
Best Days for Love: 1, 9, 10, 20, 21, 22, 30, 31
Best Days for Money: 1, 9, 10, 19, 20, 28, 29
Best Days for Career: 1, 9, 10, 20, 28, 29, 30

On July 23 the Sun entered your 10th house and you began a yearly
career peak. But even before that, on July 1, Mars entered the house of
career. So the career has been hectic, active, and requiring much
energy and attention. You've been fending off rivals and competitors.
Your good work ethic has become very important. Your yearly career
peak continues until the 23rd, although Mars will leave your 10th
house on the 18th. At least the workload lightens a bit. Still, the month
ahead is very successful. Your career planet, the Sun, is very strong in
his own sign and house: another signal of success.

Health has been an issue since July 23. The good news is that with
Mars, your health planet, at the top of the chart, you're paying attention here. Without good health, career success is meaningless. So, rest
and relax more – as always. Don't waste energy on trivial distractions.
Focus on what's really important. Enhance the health in the ways

mentioned in the yearly report, but also give more attention to the heart until the 18th, and to the small intestine afterwards. Look at the reflex points to the heart and small intestine shown in the yearly report (page 236) and massage them regularly.

There are many positive financial developments happening. Your financial planet, Jupiter, starts moving forward on the 11th. And perhaps more importantly, he is receiving beautiful aspects until the 23rd. So the month ahead is prosperous. It is safe to make those delayed major purchases or investments after the 11th. There is greater financial clarity now. Finances become more challenging after the 23rd, but it won't affect your overall prosperity. These are short-term stresses caused by the short-term planets. You'll just have to work a little harder.

Love seems happy this month too. The instability – a long-term trend – is still there, but you're having fun. Venus in Leo is a 'love at first sight' kind of energy. Love happens quickly. Venus will be in your 10th house of career until the 21st so you find love opportunities as you pursue your career goals, and perhaps with people involved in your career. There can be an office romance too. You are turned on by successful people – people who have achieved things, people of high status and prestige. Your social grace is important careerwise and helps things along. Much of your socializing is career-related, and it will be beneficial to attend these 'working' social functions. On the 21st, Venus will move into Virgo – not her best position. She is not very comfortable there. If you can avoid hyper-criticism and perfectionism (two of the problems with Venus in Virgo), love should be OK.

September

   Best Days Overall: 3, 4, 12, 13, 14, 22, 23, 30
   Most Stressful Days Overall: 10, 11, 17, 18, 19, 24, 25
   Best Days for Love: 8, 9, 17, 18, 19, 20, 28, 29
   Best Days for Money: 5, 6, 15, 16, 24, 25
   Best Days for Career: 7, 8, 18, 19, 24, 25, 28

As of last month, the planetary power shifted from the social Western sector to the Eastern sector of self. Personal independence is getting stronger day by day. You can have your way – and you should. The only problem, with Pluto retrograde, is being clear on what your way really is. Now is the time to pay attention to your own interests and desires. Your personal happiness, so long as it isn't destructive, is precious to the cosmos and the planets are supporting this.

Health is good this month. This should be considered another form of wealth. There is only one planet, Uranus, in stressful aspect with you. (The Moon will occasionally make stressful aspects but of very short duration.) You can enhance the health even more by giving more attention to the small intestine and through abdominal massage. And through the ways mentioned in the yearly report.

Jobseekers should look online or through social contacts for job opportunities. The opportunities are there. Finances are still a bit stormy – they need more effort – until the 23rd, but afterwards they will flow rather easily and abundantly. A good financial month, Scorpio, after the 23rd.

Venus, your love planet, will have her solstice from the 15th to the 18th. She will camp out on the same degree of latitude, so it seems like a pause. She is stationary in her latitudinal motion. Then she will change direction. So it will be in your love and social life. Venus will be in your 11th house of friends until the 14th. So the love attitudes and needs have changed from previous months. You're looking for friendship with your beloved. You prefer a relationship of equals. You're not trying to 'date up' or 'marry up'. The only issue now – as we saw last month – is that Venus is weak in the sign of Virgo. Your social magnetism is not up to its usual standard. And, the tendency will be to 'too much head' and not enough heart. This will change after the 14th as Venus enters romantic Libra, her own sign and house. Here she is powerful. She is at home and operates at full power. Venus in your 12th house indicates a need for spiritual compatibility with the beloved. You don't need to agree on every point but you should at least be on the same page and support each other's growth. Love can be found in spiritual-type settings from the 14th onwards – at meditation seminars, spiritual lectures, charity events, prayer meetings. There is a happy romantic meeting between the 5th and the 7th, as Venus makes beautiful aspects to Pluto, the ruler of your chart. Try to avoid any over-analysis and criticism.

October

Best Days Overall: 1, 10, 11, 19, 20, 28, 29
Most Stressful Days Overall: 7, 8, 15, 16, 21, 22
Best Days for Love: 10, 11, 15, 16, 19, 20, 28, 29
Best Days for Money: 2, 3, 4, 12, 13, 21, 22, 30, 31
Best Days for Career: 7, 8, 17, 18, 21, 22, 28

A happy and prosperous month ahead, Scorpio. Enjoy. Pluto starts moving forward on the 3rd, bringing more self-confidence and self-esteem. The planetary power is entering its maximum Eastern position, so personal independence is near the maximum for the year. (It will be strong next month too.) So now is the time to have things your way and to make the necessary changes in conditions that irk you. It is time to have life on your terms. If you are happy others will eventually come around. Love is happy this month, but still very unstable. Venus moves into your own sign on the 8th and stays there for the rest of the month ahead. So, you look good. You dress stylishly. You have flair and panache. Love pursues you. The current love is very devoted to you. You come first – they put you ahead of their own interests.

Prosperity looks good too. Your financial planet Jupiter is moving forward and receiving good aspects. Not only that, the Moon visits your money house twice this month too. In your chart the Moon is very beneficent – she is the ruler of your important 9th house. Next month will be even more prosperous.

Health is excellent all month. Like last month there is only one planet (with the exception of the Moon's fleeting transits) that is in stressful alignment with you. Mars, your health planet, will move into your spiritual 12th house on the 4th and stay there for the rest of the month. This shows that you will get good health results from spiritual healing and spiritual techniques. If you like, you can enhance the health even further through hip massage and paying more attention to the kidneys.

The month ahead is very spiritual. Your 12th house became strong on September 23 and is strong until the 23rd of this month. Your career planet in the 12th house indicates that you further the career through involvement with charities and altruistic activities. But it also shows that your spiritual understanding helps the career. Another way to read this is that your spiritual growth *is* the career at this time. This is your mission.

On the 23rd, as the Sun enters your own sign, career opportunities – and happy ones – come to you almost unbidden. They pursue you. Parents, parent figures, bosses and authority figures are devoted to you and favourably disposed. You look successful and dress that way too. Others see you as successful. Venus in your sign gives beauty and grace. The Sun gives charisma and star quality – a different kind of beauty – an energetic beauty.

November

Best Days Overall: 6, 7, 16, 17, 24, 25
Most Stressful Days Overall: 3, 4, 5, 11, 12, 18, 19, 24
Best Days for Love: 8, 9, 11, 12, 18, 19, 29
Best Days for Money: 8, 9, 10, 18, 19, 26, 27
Best Days for Career: 6, 7, 16, 17, 18, 19, 26

Another happy and prosperous month Scorpio. Last month on the 23rd you began a yearly personal pleasure peak – the second one this year. This continues until the 22nd. Self-esteem and self-confidence are excellent. The personal appearance shines. More energy tends to improve the appearance. This is an excellent period in which to get the body and image the way you want them to be. It also a good time to pamper the body, rewarding it for its years of selfless service. It's a good practice to spend time thanking the body – and each of the individual organs – for their service, and especially the parts that might be bothering you. This simple practice will make you feel better.

Venus spends most of the month in your money house. Jupiter has been there all year. The two bountiful planets of the zodiac in the money house – that spells prosperity. On the 22nd the Sun will enter there too and you begin a yearly financial peak. Venus in the money house shows the financial support of the spouse, partner or current love, and the importance of your social contacts. They all seem supportive. Since Venus is your love planet, this aspect can indicate a business partnership or joint venture. (This seems especially likely from the 22nd to the 24th – this period is good for both love and money.) Singles are likely to meet romantic partners. The only issue – as has been the case since March – is the stability of these relationships. Nevertheless it is fun. Wealth is a romantic allure until the 26th. You gravitate to the good providers. Material gifts excite love. This is how you show love and how you feel loved.

Venus in Sagittarius is a 'love at first sight' energy. You don't waste time. And the people you meet are like this as well. On the 26th Venus moves into Capricorn, your 3rd house. This will change things. Now you are more cautious in love. You want to test it. Wealth is less important than ease of communication. You're attracted to intellectuals and to people with the gift of the gab. The mind is just as important as the physical chemistry now. Until the 26th love opportunities happen as you pursue your financial goals and with people involved in your finances. After the 26th you find love in more educational-type settings – at lectures, seminars, bookstores and libraries.

Venus will be 'out of bounds' from the 15th to the 30th. Thus in love issues you're going outside your usual norms. It could be that your partner pulls you outside your usual sphere, or your search for a partner takes you outside your sphere.

Mars enters your sign on the 29th, and while this gives energy and courage, it can also induce rush and impatience. Anger can also be a problem. Be aware of this.

December

Best Days Overall: 3, 4, 5, 13, 14, 21, 22, 31
Most Stressful Days Overall: 1, 2, 8, 9, 15, 16, 28, 29
Best Days for Love: 8, 9, 17, 18, 28, 29
Best Days for Money: 8, 17, 24, 25, 26
Best Days for Career: 6, 7, 15, 16, 26

On November 19 the planetary power shifted from the upper half of your Horoscope to the lower half – from the day side to the night side. At least 80 per cent of the planets are now in the night side. It is evening in your year. You are a night person these days. Career can be downplayed now. It is more about preparation now than overt activity. Now is the time to focus on the home, family and your emotional well-being. This is the infrastructure upon which a successful career is based. It is, in its way, just as important as your career – because this is what supports it.

You're still very much in a prosperity period. The Sun is still in your 2nd money house until the 22nd. You have the financial favour of bosses, parents and parent figures. Your good career reputation brings earnings and earnings opportunities to you. Your mission this month (until the 22nd) is finance.

Jupiter, your financial planet, has spent the year in your money house. So you are richer now than when the year began. Jupiter leaves the money house on the 3rd and enters your 3rd house. This signals earnings will now come from sales, marketing, advertising, PR and through good use of the media. It's important now to get the word out about your product or service. The money people in your life get even richer: 'To those who have, more shall be added.' On the 22nd, the Sun joins Jupiter in your 3rd house and this house becomes very powerful. Students will do well in school and are focused on their studies. Those who write or teach for a living will be earning more. Siblings, sibling figures and neighbours start to prosper – they've had a rough year and have earned some respite.

A solar eclipse on the 26th occurs in your 3rd house – this is the third eclipse this year in this house and it impacts on Jupiter, your financial planet. So, important financial changes are happening. You need to make a course correction here. Strategy and tactics need to change. And since the Sun is your career planet, there are career changes afoot too. By now you should be used to it – this is the third solar eclipse of the year. There are more changes, disruptions and shake-ups in your company or industry. Bosses, parents and parent figures have personal life-changing dramas, and the same is true for siblings, sibling figures and neighbours. Students at all levels make important changes to their educational plans. Happily this eclipse doesn't affect you personally too much, but it won't hurt to take things a bit easier at this time.

Health is good.

Sagittarius

THE ARCHER

Birthdays from
23rd November to
20th December

Personality Profile

SAGITTARIUS AT A GLANCE

Element – Fire

Ruling Planet – Jupiter
  Career Planet – Mercury
  Love Planet – Mercury
  Money Planet – Saturn
  Planet of Health and Work – Venus
  Planet of Home and Family Life – Neptune
  Planet of Spirituality – Pluto

Colours – blue, dark blue

Colours that promote love, romance and social harmony – yellow, yellow-orange

Colours that promote earning power – black, indigo

Gems – carbuncle, turquoise

Metal – tin

Scents – carnation, jasmine, myrrh

Quality – mutable (= flexibility)

Qualities most needed for balance – attention to detail, administrative and organizational skills

Strongest virtues – generosity, honesty, broad-mindedness, tremendous vision

Deepest need – to expand mentally

Characteristics to avoid – over-optimism, exaggeration, being too generous with other people's money

Signs of greatest overall compatibility – Aries, Leo

Signs of greatest overall incompatibility – Gemini, Virgo, Pisces

Sign most helpful to career – Virgo

Sign most helpful for emotional support – Pisces

Sign most helpful financially – Capricorn

Sign best for marriage and/or partnerships – Gemini

Sign most helpful for creative projects – Aries

Best Sign to have fun with – Aries

Signs most helpful in spiritual matters – Leo, Scorpio

Best day of the week – Thursday

Understanding a Sagittarius

If you look at the symbol of the archer you will gain a good, intuitive understanding of a person born under this astrological sign. The development of archery was humanity's first refinement of the power to hunt and wage war. The ability to shoot an arrow far beyond the ordinary range of a spear extended humanity's horizons, wealth, personal will and power.

Today, instead of using bows and arrows we project our power with fuels and mighty engines, but the essential reason for using these new powers remains the same. These powers represent our ability to extend our personal sphere of influence – and this is what Sagittarius is all about. Sagittarians are always seeking to expand their horizons, to cover more territory and increase their range and scope. This applies to all aspects of their lives: economic, social and intellectual.

Sagittarians are noted for the development of the mind – the higher intellect – which understands philosophical and spiritual concepts. This mind represents the higher part of the psychic nature and is motivated not by self-centred considerations but by the light and grace of a Higher Power. Thus, Sagittarians love higher education of all kinds. They might be bored with formal schooling but they love to study on their own and in their own way. A love of foreign travel and interest in places far away from home are also noteworthy characteristics of the Sagittarian type.

If you give some thought to all these Sagittarian attributes you will see that they spring from the inner Sagittarian desire to develop. To travel more is to know more, to know more is to be more, to cultivate the higher mind is to grow and to reach more. All these traits tend to broaden the intellectual – and indirectly, the economic and material – horizons of the Sagittarian.

The generosity of the Sagittarian is legendary. They feel that they are rich, that they are lucky, that they can attain any financial goal – and so they feel that they can afford to be generous. Sagittarians do not carry the burdens of want and limitation which stop most other people from giving generously. Another reason for their generosity is their religious and philosophical idealism, derived from the higher mind, which is by nature generous because it is unaffected by material circumstances. The act of giving also tends to enhance their emotional nature. Every act of giving seems to be enriching, and this is reward enough for the Sagittarian.

Finance

Sagittarians generally entice wealth. They either attract it or create it. They have the ideas, energy and talent to realize their vision of paradise on Earth. But mere wealth is not enough. Sagittarians want luxury – earning a comfortable living seems small and insignificant to them.

In order for Sagittarians to attain their true earning potential they must develop better managerial and organizational skills. They must learn to set limits, to arrive at their goals through a series of attainable sub-goals or objectives. It is very rare that a person goes from rags to riches overnight. But a long-drawn-out process is difficult for Sagittarians. Like Leos, they want to achieve wealth and success quickly and impressively. They must be aware, however, that this over-optimism can lead to unrealistic financial ventures and disappointing losses. Of course, no zodiac sign can bounce back as quickly as Sagittarius, but only needless heartache will be caused by this attitude. Sagittarians need to maintain their vision – never letting it go – but they must also work towards it in practical and efficient ways.

Career and Public Image

Sagittarians are big thinkers. They want it all: money, fame, glamour, prestige, public acclaim and a place in history. They often go after all these goals. Some attain them, some do not – much depends on each individual's personal horoscope. But if Sagittarians want to attain public and professional status they must understand that these things are not conferred to enhance one's ego but as rewards for the amount of service that one does for the whole of humanity. If and when they figure out ways to serve more, Sagittarians can rise to the top.

The ego of the Sagittarian is gigantic – and perhaps rightly so. They have much to be proud of. If they want public acclaim, however, they will have to learn to tone down the ego a bit, to become more humble and self-effacing, without falling into the trap of self-denial and self-abasement. They must also learn to master the details of life, which can sometimes elude them.

At their jobs Sagittarians are hard workers who like to please their bosses and co-workers. They are dependable, trustworthy and enjoy a challenge. Sagittarians are friendly to work with and helpful to their colleagues. They usually contribute intelligent ideas or new methods that improve the work environment for everyone. Sagittarians always look for challenging positions and careers that develop their intellect, even if they have to work very hard in order to succeed. They also work well under the supervision of others, although by nature they would rather be the supervisors and increase their sphere of influence. Sagittarians excel at professions that allow them to be in contact with many different people and to travel to new and exciting locations.

Love and Relationships

Sagittarians love freedom for themselves and will readily grant it to their partners. They like their relationships to be fluid and ever-changing. Sagittarians tend to be fickle in love and to change their minds about their partners quite frequently.

Sagittarians feel threatened by a clearly defined, well-structured relationship, as they feel this limits their freedom. The Sagittarian tends to marry more than once in life.

Sagittarians in love are passionate, generous, open, benevolent and very active. They demonstrate their affections very openly. However, just like an Aries they tend to be egocentric in the way they relate to their partners. Sagittarians should develop the ability to see others' points of view, not just their own. They need to develop some objectivity and cool intellectual clarity in their relationships so that they can develop better two-way communication with their partners. Sagittarians tend to be overly idealistic about their partners and about love in general. A cool and rational attitude will help them to perceive reality more clearly and enable them to avoid disappointment.

Home and Domestic Life

Sagittarians tend to grant a lot of freedom to their family. They like big homes and many children and are one of the most fertile signs of the zodiac. However, when it comes to their children Sagittarians generally err on the side of allowing them too much freedom. Sometimes their children get the idea that there are no limits. However, allowing freedom in the home is basically a positive thing – so long as some measure of balance is maintained – for it enables all family members to develop as they should.

Horoscope for 2019

Major Trends

Jupiter, your ruling planet, will be in your own sign for almost all of the year ahead. This is not only a prosperity signal, but also one of happiness. You are even more Sagittarius-like than usual, displaying even more of your true nature. There is more foreign travel and more of the good life. Optimism, always strong in you, is even stronger these days.

Prosperity is strong all year, but will get even more so after December 3 as Jupiter moves into your money house. Next year will also be prosperous. More on this later.

Neptune has been in your 4th house for many years now, and will be there for many more. So, your emotional body, your feeling body, is becoming more sensitive and spiritualized. Perhaps even too sensitive. Family members are under strong spiritual influences.

Uranus makes a major move this year from your 5th house to your 6th house, on March 7. For the next seven years, Uranus will remain in your house of health and work, signalling many job changes and changes in the health regime. More on this later.

Last year was a very strong spiritual year. By now you have absorbed the lessons and need not focus too much here.

We will have five eclipses this year (usually there are four). Of the five, four impact on your 9th house of travel, legal issues, higher education, religion and theology. So there are a lot of shake-ups going on here. Your religious and theological beliefs get tested. College-level students can change schools, courses and educational plans.

Your most important interests in the year ahead are the body, image and personal pleasure (until December 3); finance; home and family; children, creativity and fun (until March 7); and health and work (from March 7 onwards).

Your paths of greatest fulfilment this year are sex, personal transformation and occult studies; the body and image (until December 3); and finance (from December 3 onwards).

Health

(Please note that this is an astrological perspective on health and not a medical one. In days of yore there was no difference, both of these perspectives were identical. But now there could be quite a difference. For a medical perspective, please consult your doctor or health practitioner.)

Health looks excellent this year, Sagittarius. There is one long-term planet (Neptune) in stressful alignment with you; all the others are either in harmony with you or leaving you alone. Health and energy therefore should be wonderful. If you have any pre-existing conditions, you should see relief and improvements here.

Keep in mind that, in spite of your good health, there will be periods in the year where health is less easy than usual. These periods come from the transits of the short-term planets. Their effects are temporary and don't show trends for the year. When the planets move on, health and energy recover to their normal ease.

Good though your health is, you can make it even better. Give more attention to the following – the vulnerable areas of your Horoscope (the reflexology points are shown in the chart above):

- The liver and thighs are always important for Sagittarius, as your sign rules these areas. Regular thigh massage should be part of your normal regime, and a herbal liver cleanse every now and then – especially if you feel under the weather – might be a good idea.
- The neck and throat are also always important for you, and regular neck massage should also be part of your health regime. Tension tends to collect there and needs to be released. Craniosacral therapy will also be helpful for the neck.

- The ankles and calves become important this year, from March 7 onwards. (They were important briefly last year too.) Calves and ankles should be regularly massaged. Give the ankles more support when exercising.

These are the most vulnerable areas this year and problems, if they happened, would most likely begin here. So, keeping them healthy and fit is sound preventive medicine. Most of the time problems can be prevented. And, even in cases where they can't be totally prevented (due to strong karmic momentums), they can be softened to a great degree. They need not be devastating.

Uranus's move into your 6th house of health has very important health implications, as we said. It signals more experimentation in health. You're more willing to try out new and untested kinds of therapies, diets and programmes. In fact, the newer they are the more they attract you. Generally it shows a gravitation to alternative therapies. But even if you stay with conventional medicine, it is the new, cutting-edge technologies that are alluring.

Important foot reflexology points for the year ahead

Try to massage all of the foot on a regular basis – the top of the foot as well as the bottom – but pay extra attention to the points highlighted on the chart. When you massage, be aware of 'sore spots' as these need special attention. Make sure you massage the ankles especially, and below them.

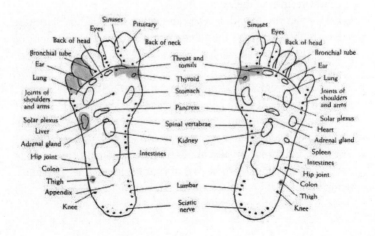

One of the dangers with Uranus in the 6th house is overdoing a good thing. It's great to be open to the new, great to be experimental, but sometimes people become 'health faddists' – running from one miracle diet or therapy to the next without doing their homework. Some people prefer to be 'trendy' than right. And this kind of behaviour can be quite expensive.

But this position has one very strong positive. It shows a recognition that you are wired up in a unique way. Your body operates uniquely. What works for others might not work for you. And, conversely, what works for you might not work for others. The next seven years are about learning about yourself, learning how you function, learning what works for you. This is perhaps one of the most important things a person can learn and it only happens through personal experimentation – trial and error. Every person has to learn this sooner or later; for you it's happening now and over the next few years.

Uranus rules your 3rd house of the lower mental body, the intellect, which would indicate the importance of good mental health in overall health. Good health for you also means good mental health – a sound mind and sound faculties. The main pathology of the mind is error. Error will not only cause all kinds of pain and suffering in the outer affairs, due to bad judgement and bad decisions, but if held long enough will manifest as some kind of physical pathology. Intellectual purity is good in its own right, but with you it's a health issue as well.

Home and Family

This has been an important area for many years and the trend continues. A move is not advisable this year – it is more likely next year. The main problem seems to be conflict with the family – and especially with one of the parents or parent figures in your life. They seem to obstruct you from what you really want to be doing, travelling and enjoying your life. Perhaps they feel you are too frivolous. You will have to work harder on your family relationships this year. With some effort and creativity, harmony can be restored.

For women of childbearing age, there is enhanced fertility this year.

With Neptune as your family planet (and occupying your 4th house of home and family to boot), you favour homes that are near water –

homes next to the sea, rivers or lakes. It would favour installing a swimming pool in the home too.

Neptune, as our regular readers know, is the most spiritual of all the planets. This gives many messages. The family is becoming more spiritual and idealistic. And, their spirituality could be in conflict with you. It would also show that they are more emotionally sensitive – more easily hurt. The brash, in-your-face honesty of the Sagittarius could be seen as cruelty by them (even though you don't mean it that way). Be more alert here. Watch your voice tone and body language. Little things can set them off.

This position would also show that your spiritual understanding and growth is vital in handling and understanding the family. Also in understanding your own emotions.

In areas involving the home – buying, selling, renovating, repairing or redecorating – intuition seems just as important as the cold rational facts. The facts should be noted, but follow intuition.

The home is becoming as much a spiritual centre as a home. It is easy to imagine spiritual lectures, meditation groups or prayer circles happening in your home. You and the family are idealistic at home. There would be a tendency to invite the homeless or other unfortunates to stay. This is laudable, but again follow intuition. Not all these people are good.

If you're planning to renovate or do major repairs to the home, May 16 to July 1 and November 19 onwards are good times. If you're redecorating or buying objects of beauty for the home, March 26 to April 20, July 3 to July 27 and October 8 to November 1 are good times.

A parent or parent figure (not the one you're having problems with) can move this year. He or she seems very devoted to you, and is having a prosperous year.

Siblings and sibling figures in your life can have multiple moves this year and in the coming years. Their finances improve after December 3. Emotionally they seem unstable, however, and need to be careful of wild and sudden mood swings.

Children and children figures are experimenting financially and can have extreme ups and downs. A move, though, is not likely. Their social lives become more stable.

Finance and Career

You've been in a strong prosperity cycle for over three years now, and it continues. In 2016 and 2017 your financial planet, Saturn, was in your sign. In 2018 he moved into his natural home, your money house, where he is most comfortable and powerful. Saturn will remain there for 2019. Jupiter, as we mentioned, will be in your sign almost all year, and is the planet of abundance and expansion. So we get a picture of someone living 'high on the hog' – living to a higher standard than usual and with the earnings to support that life.

Your money house is easily the most powerful in your chart this year. This is another signal for prosperity. It shows focus. It shows fire in the belly – a willingness to overcome all the various challenges that arise. I feel this focus is more important than just easy aspects.

What I like about your present aspects is that the financial judgement is sound. In 2016 and 2017, with Saturn in your own sign, you could have been more reckless and speculative. Since last year, as your financial planet moved into his own sign, there has been more conservatism and caution with finances. Now, being a Sagittarius, you are always speculative and risk-taking, but now much less so. You're able to take risks when necessary but you're not wild in that department. Every investment – even the seemingly safe – carries some degree of risk; the issue is the degree of risk that one is willing to take. Sagittarius has a high risk tolerance, but since last year, less so.

All your normal financial strengths and affinities are magnified this year. Book publishing, the travel business, airlines, long-distance transportation and for-profit colleges are interesting and tend to be profitable. Commercial real estate, traditional blue-chip companies listed on the DOW, FTSE or S&P 500 indices, are also attractive.

You're more involved in money management these days, and this is a good thing. Managing what you have properly seems just as important as increasing earnings.

Later in the year – after December 3 – Jupiter will move into your money house. This increases the prosperity further and it shows it will go on well into next year.

There are three eclipses that occur in your money house this year. We will cover them more fully in the monthly reports, but they indicate dramatic changes happening in the financial life – changes in investments, banks, stockbrokers or in the lives of people or companies involved with your finances. Because the year is so prosperous, I read this as a need to adjust to the prosperity. Too much of a good thing can be just as disruptive as too little. (It's a good problem to have though.)

Uranus's move into your 6th house of work in March signals job changes happening, and a very unstable job situation over the next seven years. Sometimes these changes can be within the present company, sometimes not. The conditions of work will also dramatically change. If you employ others there is employee turnover.

Though finance is very important to you this year, the year ahead is not an especially strong career year. Your 10th house is basically empty. Only short-term planets will move through there this year and their effects are transitory. The night side of your Horoscope is very strong as well. *All* the long-term planets are in the lower half of your chart. So, while the upper half will get stronger after May 23, it will never be dominant. Finance, family and emotional wellness are much more important this year. You'd rather have money (and the feeling of harmony) than status or prestige. Earning more in a backroom job is preferable to earning less in more prominent position.

Your career planet Mercury is a very fast-moving planet, as our regular readers know. Thus there will be many short-term career trends that depend on where Mercury is and the aspects he receives at any given time. These are best dealt with in the monthly reports.

Love and Social Life

Your 7th house of love hasn't been a house of power for some years now. It doesn't seem a major focus. This tends, as our regular readers know, to the status quo. Those who are married will tend to stay married, and singles will tend to stay single. This doesn't mean that marriage is forbidden. It shows lack of interest. There's nothing special pulling you in that direction.

However, we do see big improvements in your love and social life – this began last year. In 2016 and 2017 stern Saturn was in your sign. While this was good financially and for business, it was not especially good for love. You came across as too cold, too aloof (even though you're not that kind of person). This was Saturn's influence on you. Last year Saturn moved out of your sign and more of your warm and ebullient self could come through. This year Jupiter is in your sign and you become a 'hot' item. Bubbly, effervescent, jovial, friendly. This will make for greater popularity in general. And, in the case of those of you who are married, more harmony in the marriage.

Those working on (or in) the second or third marriage also have a stable kind of year. Those working on the fourth marriage, however, have very nice opportunities. Serious love is on the cards.

The two planets that rule love in your chart – Venus, the generic ruler, and Mercury, the actual ruler in your Horoscope – will visit your sign twice this year. This is unusual. They usually visit a sign only once. So there will be romantic opportunities for sure. But marriage? Probably not.

Mercury, your love planet, is a very fast-moving planet with many modes of motion. In a given year he will move through all the signs and houses of your chart and make aspects (good and bad) to all the planets in your chart. So there are many short-term love trends that depend on where Mercury is and the aspects he receives. These are best dealt with in the monthly reports.

Parents and parent figure, siblings and sibling figures in your life have stable love years. Likewise children.

Love is important, but these days you have other fish to fry.

Mercury is both your love planet and your career planet. Thus, in general, you're attracted to intellectual types, people with the gift of the gab, people with whom you can share ideas. Not only that but you like successful people, people who have achieved something, people who can help you careerwise.

Communication is how you show love and how you feel loved. If someone is talking to you, calling you regularly, sharing with you, you feel loved. The 'silent treatment' is devastating.

In general you find love opportunities in educational-type settings, at lectures, seminars, school events, bookstores and libraries. Also as you pursue your career goals or with people involved in your career. (This will change month to month, and sometimes several times a month.)

Self-improvement

Neptune in your 4th house will show a hyperactive dream life. The dreams will be vivid, in Technicolor, and you'll feel that you're actually participating. Many of them will be prophetic. Many will be revelations into your psychological condition and family relationships. Pay attention here – especially to the vivid ones. Since the 4th house rules the past, many of your dreams will be revelations of past incarnations. These are surfacing for therapeutic purposes. Some of you will be pulled to past-life regressions. You find it very fascinating these days.

Your spiritual planet, Pluto, has been in your money house for many years now and will be there for many more years to come. This shows various things. You're exploring deeper into the spiritual dimensions of wealth. Sagittarians have an instinctive understanding of these things, but now it is getting deeper. This tendency is further reinforced by the fact that your financial planet, Saturn, is travelling very close to Pluto almost all year. Natural money is a wonderful thing and should be appreciated, but 'miracle money' is much more interesting – and more fun. You are in a period for experiencing more 'miracle money', money that doesn't come from your expected channels. Wealth, from the spiritual perspective, is infinite. The only limit is a person's capacity to receive. If one goes to the ocean (and the spiritual supply is like an ocean) with a tea cup, that's what you get. Go to the same ocean with a barrel and you will receive much more. The ocean doesn't care. The other interesting thing is that the Ocean of Supply doesn't have favourites. Wealth, spiritually speaking, is equally present everywhere. Right where you are.

Jupiter in your 1st house signals the good life – fine restaurants, foods and wines. While this is certainly pleasurable, if you're not careful you can put on the pounds. Weight is an issue this year, Sagittarius. Indulge and enjoy, but don't overdo it.

Uranus in your 6th house of health shows a need (and an ability) to learn how you function, as we discussed earlier. It's a very important trend that will lead to better health down the road. The rule books are based on averages, but you are not average. You're unique and special, wired up in a unique and special way. Learn yourself for yourself.

Month-by-month Forecasts

January

Best Days Overall: 2, 3, 12, 13, 21, 22, 30, 31
Most Stressful Days Overall: 10, 11, 17, 18, 23, 24
Best Days for Love: 1, 4, 5, 12, 13, 15, 16, 17, 18, 21, 22, 25, 30, 31
Best Days for Money: 2, 3, 5, 6, 12, 13, 15, 16, 21, 22, 23, 24
Best Days for Career: 4, 5, 15, 16, 23, 24, 25

Two eclipses this month will only add some drama and excitement to a basically happy and prosperous month.

The solar eclipse of the 6th (in America it happens on the 5th) causes financial shake-ups and course corrections. It not only occurs in your money house but also impacts on the financial planet, Saturn. A double hit. Your financial thinking and strategy are amiss and the events of the eclipse will show you why. Generally these changes happen through some financial disturbance or shock. Things are not the way you thought they were. But now you can make corrections and they will be good. You're still in the midst of a yearly financial peak until the 20th. So earnings are good. Since the Sun rules your 9th house, this eclipse (like every solar eclipse) affects college-level students. They make important educational changes. Sometimes they change courses; sometimes they change colleges. There are shake-ups and disturbances in the college. There are also shake-ups in your place of worship and dramas in the lives of worship leaders. Sagittarians love to travel, but best to avoid it this period. (It would be good to avoid it over the lunar eclipse period too.)

The lunar eclipse of the 21st occurs in your 9th house and is almost, but not quite, a replay of earlier solar eclipse. Thus there are shake-ups in your place of worship and dramas in the lives of worship leaders. Students are forced to change their educational plans. Foreign travel (especially if it is not essential) is not advisable. Both eclipses this month impact on your personal religion and personal philosophy of life. They will test your beliefs – a good thing, but not always pleasant. Some beliefs should be discarded, some should be moderated.

Since Moon rules your 8th house of regeneration, the lunar eclipse will force the spouse, partner or current love to make important financial changes. His or her strategy and thinking have been unrealistic, as the events of the eclipse will show. Often there are confrontations with death – generally on the psychological level. Sometimes there are dreams or memories of it. Sometimes events in the news trigger these things. This is to give you a better understanding of death, so that you will live better. Fear of death is one of the great obstacles to our goals.

Health is good this month. There is only one planet in stressful aspect with you (excluding the Moon, whose transits are short term).

Love is also happy.

February

Best Days Overall: 8, 9, 10, 17, 18, 26, 27
Most Stressful Days Overall: 6, 7, 13, 14, 19, 20
Best Days for Love: 11, 12, 19, 20, 28
Best Days for Money: 1, 2, 9, 10, 11, 12, 17, 18, 19, 20, 26, 27, 28
Best Days for Career: 3, 4, 15, 16, 19, 20, 24, 25

Health is still good this month, but after the 19th needs more attention being paid to it. Mars moving into your 6th house on the 14th shows a need for more physical exercise and good muscle tone. Head and scalp massage will be good. Your health planet, Venus, moves into your money house on the 3rd and spends the rest of the month there. Thus, good health for you also means good financial health. Probably you spend more on health and health products this month, but you can also earn from this field. The health planet in Capricorn shows a need to keep the spine and skeleton in alignment. Regular back and knee massage will be good. If you feel under the weather a visit to a chiropractor or osteopath might be a good idea. Good dental health is important too. With your health planet in conservative Capricorn you're more conservative in health matters, with a tendency to conventional, orthodox medicine. Even if you opted for alternative therapies you would prefer the old traditional ones – the ones that have stood the test of time. More important than all the above is the need to maintain high energy levels. Make sure to get enough rest.

Your 3rd house became powerful on January 20 and is still powerful until the 19th. This is good for students at all levels; it shows focus on their studies. It is also good for sales and marketing people, teachers and writers. The communication skills are much enhanced.

Love is a lot happier this year now that Saturn is out of your sign. And with Jupiter now in the 1st house you are more like your bubbly Sagittarian self – you exude warmth and optimism and people gravitate to this. Your love planet Mercury is in your 3rd house until the 10th. He is making nice aspects with Jupiter and love seems happy and harmonious. Things become trickier after the 10th as Mercury moves into Pisces and an adverse aspect with Jupiter. You will have to work harder on your relationship. The beloved (and those in your social circle) are more sensitive and easily hurt these days, so be more mindful about this. Your love planet in the 4th house indicates more socializing with the family and from home. The home becomes the social centre. Family members like to play Cupid (and many a marriage has happened in this way). The only problem here is moodiness in love. Your mood determines everything. In a good mood you are loving and tender, but in a bad mood, those around you had better look out! Those involved romantically with Sagittarius need to understand this.

Mercury is not only your love planet but also your career planet, and his position in your 4th house shows that home and family is your career, your mission, this month. This is the focus.

March

Best Days Overall: 8, 9, 17, 18, 25, 26
Most Stressful Days Overall: 5, 6, 7, 13, 14, 19, 20
Best Days for Love: 3, 4, 5, 6, 7, 13, 14, 15, 16, 23, 24, 25, 26
Best Days for Money: 1, 2, 8, 9, 10, 11, 17, 18, 19, 20, 25, 26, 27, 28, 29
Best Days for Career: 5, 6, 7, 15, 16, 19, 20, 23, 24

It is midnight in your year. The night side of your Horoscope is at its maximum strength. All the planets are below the horizon this month and only the Moon will move through the upper half of your chart in March, from the 13th to the 25th. Your 4th house of home and family is easily the strongest in your chart, while your 10th house of career is empty, apart from the Moon's transit on the 19th and 20th. So you're a night person these days. The activities of night are the most powerful and rewarding. Night is for internal activity – recharging the body and renewing the cells, dreaming and reviewing the past, preparing for the next day, which – figuratively speaking – will happen later in the year.

Like last month, even your career planet, Mercury, is in the 4th house. Home, family and emotional wellness are the real career this month. Outer career goals are best dealt with by the methods of night – dreaming, creative visualization, and getting into the 'mood and feeling' of what you want to achieve. If this is done properly, when the time comes to act, the actions will be powerful. With your career planet retrograde from the 5th to the 25th everything we are saying here is magnified. There is not much you can do careerwise right now. Career issues will be resolved by time rather than by any overt effort on your part. So focus on the family.

Health is a major issue this month. It's nothing serious, however, just a temporary period of lower energy. So, as always, make sure to get enough rest. Mars is still in your 6th health house all month, so physical exercise is important – each according to their age and stage in life. Head and face massage and craniosacral therapy will be beneficial. Your health planet spends most of the month in Aquarius, so massage the ankles and calves. Uranus's move into your 6th house on the 7th also points to the importance of the ankles and calves. You're starting to become more experimental in health matters. On the 26th Venus moves into your 4th house and the sign of Pisces, indicating the importance of good emotional health. The feet become more important then too. Foot massage and spiritual-type therapies will be helpful.

Health will improve after the 20th but will still need watching.

Your love planet Mercury is retrograde for most of the month, and your 7th house is basically empty (only the Moon moves through there on the 13th and 14th). So love is not a big issue this month. Love is more or less on hold. Like last month, Mercury spends the month in your 4th house, making the home the social centre. There is more socializing with the family and with people who are like family to you. Moodiness in love is still an issue, as we discussed last month.

April

Best Days Overall: 4, 5, 13, 14, 22, 23
Most Stressful Days Overall: 1, 2, 3, 9, 10, 15, 16, 29, 30
Best Days for Love: 2, 3, 9, 10, 11, 12, 13, 14, 21, 22, 23
Best Days for Money: 4, 5, 7, 8, 13, 14, 15, 16, 22, 23, 24, 25
Best Days for Career: 2, 3, 13, 14, 15, 16, 22, 23

Last month was a time for making psychological progress – for psycho-logical-type breakthroughs. This happened even to those not in conventional therapy. Nature took care of it. The month ahead is about enjoying the fruits of these breakthroughs – there's more fun in life. More joy. More relaxation and creativity.

Your 5th house of fun, creativity and children became powerful on March 20, and is even more powerful this month. You are in the midst of one of your yearly personal pleasure peaks. Joy itself is a powerful healing force, as you will learn after the 20th. Happiness is really a spiritual choice. It is not dependent on outer conditions.

Health is much improved over last month. By the 20th you are super-charged with energy. Your health planet, Venus, is still in Pisces until the 20th, so foot massage and spiritual-healing techniques are power-ful. Good emotional health is also very important. In the unlikely event of a health problem, restore harmony within the family as quickly as you can. Get into emotional balance quickly (meditation will be a help). Spiritual healing is especially potent from the 9th to the 11th. After the 20th, as your health planet moves into Aries, physical exercise, head and face massage and craniosacral therapy will be good. On the 20th the Sun enters your health house, so chest massage will also be beneficial.

The job situation has been unstable since last month. Job changes are likely in the coming year (and for many years to come). But with the Sun in your 6th house of work you have good job opportunities – possi-bly in foreign lands or with foreign companies.

Love is smoother this month than last, but it doesn't seem serious. You're more interested in amusement than serious committed love. Love is just another form of entertainment this month. On the other hand, why not have fun? As long as you don't have unrealistic expec-tations, there's no harm done.

You're in a prosperous period this year, but this month finances are temporarily rocky. You need to work harder than usual to achieve your financial goals. This will change after the 20th. Earnings should increase and come much easier then.

On March 26 the planetary power shifted from the Eastern sector of self to the Western, social sector. Personal independence is lessened. On the 10th, Jupiter, the ruler of your Horoscope, begins to move backward, which also weakens self-confidence and independence. Yet, this can be good. You don't need to be in charge. Let others have their way. Adapt to conditions as best you can. The time will come – later in the year – when change will be easier to impose.

May

Best Days Overall: 1, 2, 3, 10, 11, 19, 20, 29, 30
Most Stressful Days Overall: 6, 7, 13, 14, 26, 27
Best Days for Love: 2, 3, 6, 7, 13, 14, 21, 23, 24, 31
Best Days for Money: 2, 3, 4, 5, 10, 11, 13, 14, 19, 20, 21, 22, 29, 30, 31
Best Days for Career: 2, 3, 13, 14, 23, 24

Mars has been in your 7th house since April 1 and will be here until the 16th. This shows a 'fun' orientation to love as we mentioned last month. But it can also show power struggles in love – conflict. So be careful about this. (In India, if the astrologer sees Mars in the 7th house he advises against a marriage happening.)

Mars, your planet of children, fun and creativity, went 'out of bounds' on last month, and will remain 'out of bounds' for the whole month ahead. This gives many messages. The children or children figures in your life are venturing outside their normal haunts. In your creative life you're exploring things outside your comfort zone, trying out new things. You're also being experimental in your leisure tastes.

Love is the main headline this month. Mars, as we mentioned, is in your 7th house until the 16th. On the 21st, the Sun and your love planet, Mercury, enter the 7th house and you begin a yearly love and social peak. There will be many romantic opportunities for singles, and even those in relationships will have a more active social life – there will be more parties, weddings and gatherings. The only issue now is the opposition these planets make to Jupiter, the ruler of your Horoscope. This signals that you and the beloved are at opposite sides of the heavens. You see things in opposite ways and have opposite interpretations of things. The challenge will be to bridge your differences. If you can do this your current or new relationship will end up stronger than ever. In astrology, one's opposite is the natural marriage partner. He or she is considered one's 'complement'. He or she is strong where you are weak; you are strong where he or she is weak. But there needs to be respect for the other's position. Somewhere there is middle ground.

Mercury, your love planet, goes 'out of bounds' from the 28th onwards, indicating that love matters are going outside your normal areas. There are no answers to be found in the usual places so you must look beyond them. It can also be that a relationship – the needs of the partner – take you out of your normal sphere.

Health needs keeping an eye on after the 21st. It's not a serious issue, just a period of low energy caused by the short-term planets. So, as always, rest more. You benefit from experimental therapies on the 17th and 18th. Head and face massage and craniosacral therapy are good until the 15th. Physical exercise is important that period too. After the 15th neck massage is good – craniosacral therapy is good for the neck as well.

June

Best Days Overall: 7, 8, 15, 16, 25, 26
Most Stressful Days Overall: 2, 3, 9, 10, 23, 24, 30
Best Days for Love: 1, 2, 3, 4, 11, 13, 14, 20, 21, 24, 30
Best Days for Money: 1, 7, 8, 9, 10, 15, 16, 18, 19, 25, 26, 28, 29
Best Days for Career: 3, 4, 9, 10, 13, 14, 24

The planetary power is now at its maximum Western position – the sector of others. Your 1st house of self is strong, but your 7th house of love is much stronger. So, take a vacation from yourself for a while and focus more on others and their needs. This is a time to hone and perfect your social skills, as these are what bring you your good. Personal initiative and independence is a wonderful thing, but not right now. Let others have their way so long as it isn't destructive. Your way is probably not the best way these days.

You're still in the midst of a yearly love and social peak until the 21st. The social life is very active and singles have many romantic opportunities. But the same problem that we discussed last month is still in effect. There is a need to reconcile opposites – a need to bridge differences with the beloved or the new love interest. If you can find middle ground, love can be happy. If not, it's just going to lead to conflict. The new Moon of the 3rd occurs in your 7th house and will help clarify love and social issues as the month progresses. Your love questions will get answered.

Health still needs attention until the 21st. Make sure you get enough rest and don't burn the candle at both ends. Neck massage and cranio-sacral therapy are still beneficial until the 9th. After that, try arm and shoulder massage. Tension tends to collect in the shoulders and needs to be released. If you feel under the weather, get out in the fresh air and do some deep breathing. Fresh air is a healing tonic from the 9th onwards.

You're in a prosperity year, have no fear, but this month, especially after the 21st, finances seems rocky. Your financial planet, Saturn, went retrograde on May 2 and will be retrograde for many more months to come. But more important than that is the stressful aspect Saturn receives after the 21st (and even before). He is under pressure. Financial goals happen with challenges and difficulties. It's not a smooth ride. Even good things come in more complicated ways. This is just a temporary bump in the road, however; by the end of next month the difficulties in finances will resolve themselves.

On the 9th, the planetary power begins to shift from the lower half of your chart to the upper half – from the night side to the day side. Dawn is breaking in your year. It is time to be up and about and focus on your outer career goals.

July

Best Days Overall: 4, 5, 13, 14, 22, 23, 24, 31
Most Stressful Days Overall: 1, 6, 7, 20, 21, 27, 28
Best Days for Love: 1, 4, 5, 10, 11, 14, 20, 21, 27, 28, 29, 30, 31
Best Days for Money: 4, 5, 6, 7, 13, 14, 15, 16, 22, 23, 24, 25, 26, 31
Best Days for Career: 4, 5, 6, 7, 14, 21, 29, 30

Health is much, much improved this month. In fact it is excellent. After the 3rd there is only one planet in stressful aspect with you – Neptune. The Moon will occasionally make stressful aspects, but these are of short duration (and she will make kind aspects to you as well – also of short duration). So you have plenty of energy to handle the challenges of the two eclipses that happen this month.

The solar eclipse of the 2nd occurs in your 8th house of regeneration. This has many messages. The spouse, partner or current love has to make dramatic financial changes, possibly involving insurance, taxes and estates. Those of you of appropriate age can be making changes to wills. There can be encounters with death (ruled by the 8th house). These are generally of a psychological nature, rather than actual physical encounters, and signal a need to understand death on a deeper level. Those of you who already have this understanding will not be bothered much. Though you love travel – and there are happy travel opportunities coming to you – it's best to avoid it during this period (certainly unnecessary travel). If you must travel, schedule your journey around the eclipse period. Every solar eclipse affects college students, so there is a need for them to refine and change their educational plans. There are shake-ups in your place of worship and dramas in the lives of worship leaders. Your personal religion and personal philosophy of life will get tested (this happened in January too). Some of your beliefs will have to be discarded, while some will be amended.

The lunar eclipse of the 16th occurs in your money house. So you and the spouse, partner or current love have to make important financial changes. The events of the eclipse will show you where your thinking and planning have been amiss. Once again there can be dramas involving taxes, insurance and estates. Once again those of appropriate age can be changing their will. Since the Moon rules your 8th house, there can be more confrontations (psychological confrontations) with death. In a sense the eclipse repeats the one earlier in the month. This eclipse affects Pluto, your spiritual planet. Thus you will make changes to your spiritual practice. Teachers and teachings can change. There are upheavals in spiritual or charitable organizations you're involved with and dramas in the lives of gurus and guru figures.

Keep in mind that these events need not happen on the actual day of the eclipse. They can happen over the next six months.

August

Best Days Overall: 1, 9, 10, 19, 20, 28, 29
Most Stressful Days Overall: 2, 3, 16, 17, 23, 24, 25, 30, 31
Best Days for Love: 1, 8, 9, 10, 19, 20, 21, 23, 24, 25, 30, 31
Best Days for Money: 1, 2, 3, 9, 10, 11, 12, 19, 20, 21, 22, 28, 29, 30, 31
Best Days for Career: 2, 3, 8, 19, 20, 30, 31

Health is excellent until the 23rd, but afterwards needs more attention. Now that the eclipses are over with it is safer to travel, and many of you will – perhaps even multiple times. Your 9th house of religion, philosophy and travel has been ultra-powerful since July 23 and will remain so until the 23rd of this month.

This is a good month for college students. They seem focused on their studies and seem successful. It is wonderful month for religious and philosophical breakthroughs too. Sagittarius is very interested in these things in general, but this month more than usual. A good, juicy theological discussion is more alluring than a night out on the town.

Your 10th house of career becomes powerful from the 18th onwards, and especially after the 23rd, and you enter a yearly career peak. This is where the focus needs to be. You can't completely ignore home and family, but you can best serve your family's interests by succeeding in the outer world. The kids' soccer match can wait; that deal you're working on will benefit the children more. (It is interesting that the children and children figures in your life understand this and support your career goals.)

As we said, health becomes more delicate after the 23rd. You're working very hard in your career and it seems very hectic. Mars in your 10th house is showing this. So you need to make sure to get enough rest. Inessentials should be dropped (mentally and physically). Keep focused on the really important things. Until the 21st chest massage is beneficial. Look up the reflex to the heart in the yearly report (page 266) and massage it regularly. After the 21st abdominal massage will be good, and the reflex to the small intestine should be massaged. The feet can be more sensitive this month too. So foot massage is good.

Love seems happy until the 29th. Your love planet Mercury is moving speedily, which shows good confidence and fast progress. You cover a lot of social territory. Until the 11th sexual magnetism is the main allure; after the 11th you like good times and a fun-loving spirit. Foreigners, religious people and highly educated people attract you. You like people you can learn from. However, after the 29th your attention is caught by power people – people who have achieved something in life and who can help you careerwise. You're meeting these kinds of people now.

Finance is much improved over last month. Saturn is still retrograde but earnings are growing – especially after the 23rd. It might be happening more slowly, but it is happening.

September

Best Days Overall: 5, 6, 15, 16, 24, 25
Most Stressful Days Overall: 12, 13, 14, 20, 21, 26, 27
Best Days for Love: 8, 9, 20, 21, 28, 29
Best Days for Money: 5, 6, 7, 8, 9, 15, 16, 17, 18, 19, 24, 25, 26, 27
Best Days for Career: 8, 9, 20, 21, 26, 27, 28, 29

You're still in a very successful period and much progress is happening in your career. But health still needs watching until the 23rd. Tough choices need to be made. You can't do everything. You have to distinguish the essential from the non-essential and act accordingly. You need to carve out time for rest. Until the 14th give more attention to the small intestine – look up the reflex point in the yearly report (page 266) and massage it on both feet. Try to schedule more massages and health treatments. After the 14th hip massage will be good. In addition, look up the reflex to the kidneys in the yearly report and massage that point on both feet. Work to maintain social harmony too. Problems with friends or with the beloved can be a root cause for health problems. Your health and work planet, Venus, will have her solstice from the 15th to the 18th. She occupies the same degree of latitude during that period – and from that perspective she is stationary, paused in the heavens. Then she reverses direction (in latitude). So a pause and a change of direction are happening, in both work and health matters.

Finances are good this month (especially until the 23rd). Saturn will start moving forward on the 18th after many months of retrograde motion. The financial confidence and clarity returns. He also receives very nice aspects until the 23rd. After the 23rd finances become more challenging. You just have to work harder to achieve your goals. You have to go the extra mile.

Mars will spend the month in your 10th house of career, indicating frenetic activity. Yet, it seems like fun too. It shows that children and children figures in your life are succeeding too and they seem supportive of your career goals.

By the 23rd the short-term career goals have been achieved and you can start to enjoy the fruits of career success – the social life and friendships that come with it. This is a great period to be involved with friends, groups and group activities. You won't see the bottom line effects of this for a while, but it's all fun. This is also a great period to expand your knowledge of science, technology, astrology and astronomy. Most likely you will be spending a lot of time online.

The planetary power is now shifting to the Eastern sector of your chart, the sector of self. Jupiter is moving forward as well, so self-confidence, self-esteem and personal independence are getting stronger day by day. Other people are important, but you don't need their consent for your happiness. Happiness is up to you. You can start taking the initiative more here.

October

Best Days Overall: 2, 3, 4, 12, 13, 21, 22, 30, 31
Most Stressful Days Overall: 10, 11, 17, 18, 23, 24
Best Days for Love: 10, 11, 17, 18, 19, 20, 28, 29
Best Days for Money: 2, 3, 4, 5, 6, 12, 13, 15, 16, 21, 22, 23, 24, 30, 31
Best Days for Career: 10, 11, 19, 20, 23, 24, 28, 29

The power in your 11th house until the 23rd shows that parents, parent figures and bosses are having a strong financial month. It also shows a strong social month for you, although it is more about friendships than romance, but it's happy. Like last month, it is a good time to increase your knowledge of technology, science, astronomy and astrology. Many people have their Horoscopes done when the 11th house is strong.

Finances are still stormy but they improve day by day. By the 23rd earnings will be stronger and come much more easily. Saturn is moving forward and he is in his own sign and house. He functions powerfully on your behalf. Financial judgement is sound.

A lot of interesting things are happening spiritually. On the 3rd, Pluto, your spiritual planet, starts moving forward, and day by day your spiritual 12th house gets stronger and stronger. So this is a month for spiritual progress and internal growth, especially after the 23rd. The new Moon of the 28th occurs in your spiritual 12th house as well, helping to clarify many spiritual issues for you. Your questions will get answered – normally and naturally – well into next month and the next new Moon.

With your love and career planet Mercury in your 12th house from the 3rd onwards, and with Venus there from the 8th onwards, the message of the Horoscope is, get right spiritually and health, career and love will take care of themselves. Everything will fall into place.

The career planet in the 12th house signals that you can further the career (and probably make important contacts) as you get involved in charities and altruistic causes. Also, your spiritual understanding and intuition will help the career. Career guidance will come in dreams and visions and through astrologers, psychics, tarot readers, spiritual channels or ministers.

Mercury will oppose Uranus from the 5th to the 8th, which can create dramas or shake-ups in love and in the career. Parents, parent figures and bosses should be more mindful on the physical plane. Likewise the beloved. The Sun will oppose Uranus on the 27th and 28th. Avoid foreign travel at that time. There are disturbances in your place of worship or educational establishment.

Health is excellent this month. By the 4th, as Mars moves out of his stressful alignment with you, only the Moon (and then only occasionally) will make a stressful aspect with you. So health and energy are good.

November

Best Days Overall: 8, 9, 10, 18, 19, 26, 27
Most Stressful Days Overall: 6, 7, 13, 14, 20, 21
Best Days for Love: 6, 7, 8, 9, 13, 14, 16, 17, 18, 19, 24, 25, 29
Best Days for Money: 1, 2, 8, 9, 10, 11, 12, 18, 19, 20, 21, 26, 27, 28, 29, 30
Best Days for Career: 6, 7, 16, 17, 20, 21, 24, 25

Mercury's retrograde from the 2nd to the 20th this month complicates both the career and the love life. Important decisions on either subject shouldn't be taken during this time. Your job is to attain clarity. Career is becoming less and less important this month: by the 20th, the planetary power will have shifted to the lower half of your Horoscope – the night side. The Sun is setting in your year. The activities of night, rather than those of day are becoming more important.

The month ahead is basically happy and prosperous. Jupiter, the ruler of your Horoscope, has been in your own sign all year. Venus will be there until the 26th, and on the 20th the Sun will enter your sign and you begin a yearly personal pleasure peak. Personal independence, self-confidence and self-esteem are very strong now. (Next month they will be even stronger.) Happy travel and educational opportunities are coming to you. Venus in your sign brings job opportunities as well – good ones. Venus will travel with Jupiter from the 22nd to the 24th.

This is wonderful for love and for the personal appearance. There is much personal happiness on those days. You look good. Health is good. Finances are good. But love is complicated because of Mercury's retrograde. The issues are not your fault. The social confidence is not what it should be. The spouse, partner or current love lacks direction these days. Time, and time alone, will resolve things. You will see big improvements next month.

Health, as we said, is good this month. There is only one planet (with the exception of the Moon) in stressful aspect with you. Venus, your health planet, is in your sign until the 26th. You look healthy and feel healthy. The state of your health does more for your personal appearance than hosts of lotions and potions. Good health is the best cosmetic and outfit this month.

Your financial planet Saturn is moving forward, and after the 19th has only one planet in stressful aspect to him. All the others (with the exception of the Moon, whose effects are temporary) are making nice aspects to him. So prosperity is happening. On the 26th Venus moves into your money house and stays there for the rest of the month. This shows money from work – perhaps from overtime or second jobs.

Mars will oppose Uranus from the 22nd to the 25th. This is a dynamic kind of aspect. Watch the temper. Drive more defensively. Children figures need to be more mindful on the physical plane.

December

Best Days Overall: 6, 7, 15, 16, 24, 25
Most Stressful Days Overall: 3, 4, 5, 11, 12, 17, 18, 31
Best Days for Love: 6, 7, 8, 9, 11, 12, 15, 16, 17, 18, 25, 28, 29
Best Days for Money: 8, 9, 17, 18, 26, 27
Best Days for Career: 6, 7, 15, 16, 17, 18, 25

The past year has been prosperous – and you certainly have lived that way – but now it will become even more prosperous and this will carry on well into next year. Jupiter, the ruler of your Horoscope, moves into your 2nd money house on the 3rd. This is a double financial blessing. Jupiter brings prosperity in his own right, but here he enters as ruler of the Horoscope, always friendly, always helpful, always fortunate. In addition, it shows personal focus. You're not delegating financial issues but taking the reins in your own hands. You will dress in more extravagant and expensive ways and people will see you as a money person.

Even a solar eclipse on the 26th will not dim your prosperity, despite the fact it occurs in the money house and impacts on Jupiter (so affects you strongly). Take it easy during that period. Though it forces important financial changes and course corrections, prosperity remains intact. You were probably underestimating your financial potential. It is greater than you think.

This is not an especially great period for travel – and this is the time of year when people are travelling. Best to schedule visits around the eclipse period. Once again, for the fourth time this year, college-level students are forced to make changes to their educational plans. There are shake-ups at schools and in the place of worship. There are dramas in the lives of religious figures and professors. You are forced to redefine your self – your image and self-concept. You are creating a new 'look' – a new presentation to the world. You want others to see you in a different way. This will go on for some more months. Sometimes an eclipse impacting the ruler of the Horoscope brings a detox of the body – especially if you haven't been careful in dietary matters. But health is good this month. Only one planet, Neptune, is in stressful alignment with you. (The Moon will make occasional stressful aspects but of very short duration.)

On the 22nd, as the Sun enters the money house, you begin a yearly financial peak. Earnings will increase and well-hedged, well-thought-out speculations seem successful.

Personal independence is at its maximum now, so take responsibility for your own happiness. Make the changes that need to be made. You have the support of the cosmos.

Love is happy this month. Your love planet Mercury is in your own sign from the 9th to the 29th. There's not much you need to do to attract love. It finds you. And, you have it on your terms. Those in a relationship will find the significant other very devoted – very attentive.

Capricorn

♑

THE GOAT

Birthdays from
21st December to
19th January

Personality Profile

CAPRICORN AT A GLANCE

Element – Earth

Ruling Planet – Saturn
  Career Planet – Venus
  Love Planet – Moon
  Money Planet – Uranus
  Planet of Communications – Neptune
  Planet of Health and Work – Mercury
  Planet of Home and Family Life – Mars
  Planet of Spirituality – Jupiter

Colours – black, indigo

Colours that promote love, romance and social harmony – puce, silver

Colour that promotes earning power – ultramarine blue

Gem – black onyx

Metal – lead

Scents – magnolia, pine, sweet pea, wintergreen

Quality – cardinal (= activity)

Qualities most needed for balance – warmth, spontaneity, a sense of fun

Strongest virtues – sense of duty, organization, perseverance, patience, ability to take the long-term view

Deepest needs – to manage, take charge and administrate

Characteristics to avoid – pessimism, depression, undue materialism and undue conservatism

Signs of greatest overall compatibility – Taurus, Virgo

Signs of greatest overall incompatibility – Aries, Cancer, Libra

Sign most helpful to career – Libra

Sign most helpful for emotional support – Aries

Sign most helpful financially – Aquarius

Sign best for marriage and/or partnerships – Cancer

Sign most helpful for creative projects – Taurus

Best Sign to have fun with – Taurus

Signs most helpful in spiritual matters – Virgo, Sagittarius

Best day of the week – Saturday

Understanding a Capricorn

The virtues of Capricorns are such that there will always be people for and against them. Many admire them, many dislike them. Why? It seems to be because of Capricorn's power urges. A well-developed Capricorn has his or her eyes set on the heights of power, prestige and authority. In the sign of Capricorn, ambition is not a fatal flaw, but rather the highest virtue.

Capricorns are not frightened by the resentment their authority may sometimes breed. In Capricorn's cool, calculated, organized mind all the dangers are already factored into the equation – the unpopularity, the animosity, the misunderstandings, even the outright slander – and a plan is always in place for dealing with these things in the most efficient way. To the Capricorn, situations that would terrify an ordinary mind are merely problems to be managed, bumps on the road to ever-growing power, effectiveness and prestige.

Some people attribute pessimism to the Capricorn sign, but this is a bit deceptive. It is true that Capricorns like to take into account the negative side of things. It is also true that they love to imagine the worst possible scenario in every undertaking. Other people might find such analyses depressing, but Capricorns only do these things so that they can formulate a way out – an escape route.

Capricorns will argue with success. They will show you that you are not doing as well as you think you are. Capricorns do this to themselves as well as to others. They do not mean to discourage you but rather to root out any impediments to your greater success. A Capricorn boss or supervisor feels that no matter how good the performance there is always room for improvement. This explains why Capricorn supervisors are difficult to handle and even infuriating at times. Their actions are, however, quite often effective – they can get their subordinates to improve and become better at their jobs.

Capricorn is a born manager and administrator. Leo is better at being king or queen, but Capricorn is better at being prime minister – the person actually wielding power.

Capricorn is interested in the virtues that last, in the things that will stand the test of time and trials of circumstance. Temporary fads and fashions mean little to a Capricorn – except as things to be used for profit or power. Capricorns apply this attitude to business, love, to their thinking and even to their philosophy and religion.

Finance

Capricorns generally attain wealth and they usually earn it. They are willing to work long and hard for what they want. They are quite amenable to foregoing a short-term gain in favour of long-term bene-fits. Financially, they come into their own later in life.

However, if Capricorns are to attain their financial goals they must shed some of their strong conservatism. Perhaps this is the least desir-able trait of the Capricorn. They can resist anything new merely because it is new and untried. They are afraid of experimentation. Capricorns need to be willing to take a few risks. They should be more eager to market new products or explore different managerial tech-niques. Otherwise, progress will leave them behind. If necessary, Capricorns must be ready to change with the times, to discard old methods that no longer work.

Very often this experimentation will mean that Capricorns have to break with existing authority. They might even consider changing their present position or starting their own ventures. If so, they should be willing to accept all the risks and just get on with it. Only then will a Capricorn be on the road to highest financial gains.

Career and Public Image

A Capricorn's ambition and quest for power are evident. It is perhaps the most ambitious sign of the zodiac – and usually the most success-ful in a worldly sense. However, there are lessons Capricorns need to learn in order to fulfil their highest aspirations.

Intelligence, hard work, cool efficiency and organization will take them a certain distance, but will not carry them to the very top. Capricorns need to cultivate their social graces, to develop a social style, along with charm and an ability to get along with people. They need to bring beauty into their lives and to cultivate the right social contacts. They must learn to wield power gracefully, so that people love them for it – a very delicate art. They also need to learn how to bring people together in order to fulfil certain objectives. In short, Capricorns require some of the gifts – the social graces – of Libra to get to the top.

Once they have learned this, Capricorns will be successful in their careers. They are ambitious hard workers who are not afraid of putting in the required time and effort. Capricorns take their time in getting the job done – in order to do it well – and they like moving up the corporate ladder slowly but surely. Being so driven by success, Capricorns are generally liked by their bosses, who respect and trust them.

Love and Relationships

Like Scorpio and Pisces, Capricorn is a difficult sign to get to know. They are deep, introverted and like to keep their own counsel. Capricorns do not like to reveal their innermost thoughts. If you are in love with a Capricorn, be patient and take your time. Little by little you will get to understand him or her.

Capricorns have a deep romantic nature, but they do not show it straightaway. They are cool, matter of fact and not especially emotional. They will often show their love in practical ways.

It takes time for a Capricorn – male or female – to fall in love. They are not the love-at-first-sight kind. If a Capricorn is involved with a Leo or Aries, these Fire types will be totally mystified – to them the Capricorn will seem cold, unfeeling, unaffectionate and not very spontaneous. Of course none of this is true; it is just that Capricorn likes to take things slowly. They like to be sure of their ground before making any demonstrations of love or commitment.

Even in love affairs Capricorns are deliberate. They need more time to make decisions than is true of the other signs of the zodiac, but given this time they become just as passionate. Capricorns like a relationship to be structured, committed, well regulated, well defined, predictable and even routine. They prefer partners who are nurturers, and they in turn like to nurture their partners. This is their basic psychology. Whether such a relationship is good for them is another issue altogether. Capricorns have enough routine in their lives as it is. They might be better off in relationships that are a bit more stimulating, changeable and fluctuating.

Home and Domestic Life

The home of a Capricorn – as with a Virgo – is going to be tidy and well organized. Capricorns tend to manage their families in the same way they manage their businesses. Capricorns are often so career-driven that they find little time for the home and family. They should try to get more actively involved in their family and domestic life. Capricorns do, however, take their children very seriously and are very proud parents – particularly should their children grow up to become respected members of society.

Horoscope for 2019

Major Trends

Last year, Saturn moved into your sign and he will still be here for the rest of the year ahead. Normally a Saturn transit is considered difficult. But for you, no. It is much easier to handle. Saturn is the ruler of your Horoscope – a friendly planet. And now you are even more Capricornish than usual. All the strengths and weaknesses of your sign are magnified these days. On the positive side, you're more organized, more down to earth, more patient and methodical than usual. Your management skills are stronger than ever. On the negative side, you can be too cold, aloof and distant. You can be more pessimistic than usual too. Capricorn always likes to look at the dark side so they can figure out an escape route. These days you might be overdoing it. Lighten up a bit.

You've been in a strong spiritual period for some years now. In 2016 and 2017, Saturn was in your spiritual 12th house. Last year, you had a bit of a break, but this year Jupiter will occupy your 12th house almost all year. So the year ahead brings spiritual progress and breakthroughs, and a renewed interest in spiritual things. This will increase even more later in the year when Jupiter, your spiritual planet, moves into your own sign.

Uranus has been in your 4th house of home and family for the past seven years. Last year he began to flirt with your 5th house and this year, on March 7, he enters there for the long haul. Your emotional life becomes more stable and settled, but children and children figures in your life become more of a challenge. They seem more rebellious and unsettled.

Neptune will be in your 3rd house of communication, as he has been for many years. Your taste in reading is becoming more refined. You gravitate to spiritual and artistic kinds of books and magazines.

This year we have five eclipses (usually there are four), and four of the five will impact on your 8th house of regeneration. Thus there is much dealing with death and near-death kinds of experiences. Usually these are psychological confrontations with death. These eclipses also indicate that the spouse, partner or current love is forced to make dramatic financial changes. We will deal with this more fully in the monthly reports.

Your most important interests this year are the body and image; communication and intellectual interests; home and family (until March 7); children, fun and creativity (from March 7 onwards); and spirituality (until December 3).

Your paths of greatest fulfilment will be love and romance; spirituality (until December 3); and the body and image (from December 3 onwards).

Health

(Please note that this is an astrological perspective on health and not a medical one. In days of yore there was no difference, both of these perspectives were identical. But now there could be quite a difference. For a medical perspective, please consult your doctor or health practitioner.)

Health should be good this year. The one long-term planet that was stressing you out – Uranus – is moving away from his stressful aspect and into a harmonious one from March. Saturn is in your sign and while for most people this would be stressful, for you it's not. Saturn is your friend and helper. He will strengthen the body.

Your 6th house of health is empty this year – only short-term planets move through there and their influence is temporary. This I read as a good signal. You have no need to overly focus on health. You kind of take it for granted. There's no need to fix something that's not broken.

There will be periods in the year when health is less easy than usual – perhaps even stressful. These come from the temporary transits of the short-term planets and are not trends for the year. When they pass your normally good health and energy return.

Good though your health is, you can make it even better. Give more attention to the following – the vulnerable areas of your Horoscope (the reflexology points are shown in the chart above):

- The heart. The heart beat seems slower than usual, so massage the reflexology point regularly. The important thing with the heart is to avoid worry and anxiety (you are very prone to this) and to develop more faith and confidence. It's OK to look at the dark side of things, but look at them with faith that these things can be overcome.
- The spine, knees, teeth, skin and overall skeletal alignment are always important for Capricorn as these areas are ruled by your sign. So, regular back and knee massage should be a part of your regular health regime. There are chairs, mats and other gadgets that massage the back automatically, and it might be worth investing in one of these. Regular visits to the chiropractor or

Important foot reflexology points for the year ahead

Try to massage all of the foot on a regular basis – the top of the foot as well as the bottom – but pay extra attention to the points highlighted on the chart. When you massage, be aware of 'sore spots' as these need special attention. It's also a good idea to massage the ankles and below them.

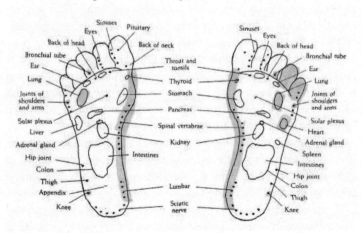

osteopath are also a good idea. The vertebrae need to be kept in alignment. Good posture will reduce back problems – so therapies such as the Alexander technique, yoga and Pilates are good. Regular dental check-ups and good dental hygiene are always important for you too, and if you're out in the sun use a good sunscreen. Give the knees more support when exercising.

- The lungs, arms, shoulders and respiratory system. These too are always important for Capricorn. Arms and shoulders should be regularly massaged – especially the shoulders. Tension tends to collect there and needs to be released.

Since these are the most vulnerable areas, any problems would most likely begin here. So keeping them healthy and fit is sound preventive medicine. Most of the time problems can be averted. Even in cases where they can't be completely prevented (karma plays a big role here), they can be lessened to a great degree. They need not be devastating.

Your health planet, Mercury, is a very fast-moving planet. Only the Moon moves faster than him. In a given year he will move through all the sectors of your chart and make aspects to all of your planets, so there are many short-term health trends that depend on where Mercury is and the aspects he receives. These are best dealt with in the monthly reports.

Saturn and Pluto spend the whole year in your sign. This signals good fortune in weight loss or detox regimes. It tends to leanness. Jupiter, on the other hand, tends to overweight. This will only be an issue after December 3 when Jupiter moves into your sign. The feeling I get is of someone who over-indulges at times and then diets – back and forth. But until December 3 this will not be an issue.

Home and Family

This has been an important area for the past seven years. With Uranus in your 4th house the whole family situation was unstable. There were probably break-ups or near break-ups in the family circle. Probably there were multiple moves or multiple renovations of the home. Your moods (and those of the family) were prone to change at the drop of a hat. You never knew where you stood with a parent or parent figure from day to day (even from hour to hour). The same was true for family members. Happily, most of this is over. Uranus is getting ready to leave your 4th house and enter your 5th. Much of the craziness is abated.

A move is not likely this year – though it could happen before March 7. And by now you have learned to deal with the volatile emotions of the family.

Uranus in your 5th house of fun, creativity and children can show sudden or unexpected pregnancies for those of childbearing age. This is especially so after December 3 as Jupiter moves into your sign. Dealing with children in general is more challenging, as we have mentioned. They're much more rebellious and freedom-loving these days. So long as it isn't destructive, give them as much space as possible. (Capricorn always likes to be in control, but with the children, temper this.)

If you're planning major repairs or renovations to the home, January 1 to March 31, May 16 to July 1 and November 19 to the end of the year are good times. If you're redecorating or otherwise beautifying the home (or buying objects of beauty for the home), January 7 to March 1, April 20 to May 15, and July 27 to September 14 are good times.

The marriages of parents and parent figures in your life were severely tested these past seven years. Separations or divorce would not have been surprising. This year, however, things are becoming more stable for the parents and parent figures socially. One of the parent figures is having a very successful year and is making important financial changes. The other parent or parent figure can have a move after December 3.

Siblings and sibling figures are having a stable kind of year. Children and children figures might not actually move but will travel a lot and live in different places for long periods of time. They need to explore their personal freedom. They are very restless – ready for change.

Finance and Career

The year ahead will be prosperous. It might start off slowly, but as the year progresses, finances will keep improving.

Capricorn is always interested in finance, but with an empty money house this year, it is not as important as it usually is. Normally an empty money house would show a quiet, stable year, but this year we see some important changes. Uranus, your financial planet, makes a major move on March 7 out of your 4th house and into your 5th, moving from the sign of Aries into Taurus. So there are important financial developments happening. For the past seven years you've been a bit of a risk-taker, more involved with start-ups and new enterprises. You've spent money on the home and family and probably earned through family or family connections. Now things will be different.

The financial planet in Taurus is definitely a more comfortable position for you. There is more conservatism in your financial attitudes, and this is more in line with your conservative nature. There will still be risk-taking – every investment has some degree of risk – but this will be toned down. If you do speculate, you seem more successful these days.

The financial planet in Taurus favours rural real estate, agriculture, farming, the beef industry, copper and the copper industry. People in these industries can be important in your financial life.

Uranus's move into your 5th house gives other messages too. You're spending more on the children and children figures in your life. But they can also be sources of income. In some cases they are financially supportive in direct ways, and sometimes through their connections or advice. And, in many cases, they inspire, or give ideas that are wealth-producing. This aspect also favours the entertainment industry and industries that cater to the youth market.

The financial planet in the 5th house is considered fortunate for finances. It shows luck in speculations, though you will be more cautious about this. It shows 'happy money' – money that is earned in happy ways, perhaps at a resort, party or place of entertainment. It shows that money is spent in happy and enjoyable ways, on leisure and fun activities. It shows someone who is enjoying the wealth that he or she has. The act of earning is pleasurable.

Uranus as your financial planet shows an affinity for technology and the online world. It shows that the good use of technology is vital in earning power – regardless of what you're actually doing.

On December 3 Jupiter will move into your sign and start to make very nice aspects to your financial planet. December will be a very strong financial month. You will not only be earning more but you will be living more extravagantly. Your financial intuition will get much sharper too. Intuition is always logical, but only when seen in hindsight. It is only in the moment that it seems illogical.

Capricorn is always ambitious, but with your empty career house, you are less so than usual this year. Also you should keep in mind that almost all of the long-term planets are in the night side of your chart – the bottom half. And, after December 3 *all* the long-term planets will be there. So, while the upper half of the chart (the day side) will get stronger at times, it will never be dominant. This is a year for focusing on your emotional wellness, your physical body and image and on family interests.

Venus is your career planet and, as our regular readers know, she is a fast-moving planet. Indeed, this year she moves even faster than usual. So there will be many short-term career trends this year that depend on where Venus is and the aspects she receives. These are best dealt with in the monthly reports.

Venus's speedy motion shows career confidence and someone who covers a lot of ground. But this is not a major focus this year. Career will most likely be stable.

Love and Social Life

The love and social life are not a major focus this year. Not only is your 7th house empty but so is your 11th house of friends. Only short-term planets will move through there. This tends to the status quo, as regular readers know. You have much freedom in love, but the drive is not there. Generally it shows a contentment with things as they are.

Three eclipses impact on the love life this year (usually it's only two). We have two lunar eclipses (which always affect love), and one solar eclipse that occurs in your 7th house of love. You've survived these things many times, but they do disturb the current relationship. Good relationships will survive, but flawed ones are in danger.

This year is more about personal independence and personal desires and goals. Your 1st house of the self is easily the strongest in your Horoscope. So, the focus is more on the self than on relationships or others. (During the year this will change at times, but only temporarily.) This self-centredness (even though it is basically good) is generally not good for relationships. There is a feeling of 'I don't need anybody' and 'I'll go my own way.'

It is good to get your body and image into shape. Good to create the conditions of your own happiness. Good to be independent. But more focus should be given to others and to the love life. The North Node of the Moon spends the whole year in your 7th house. This shows that it is an area of fulfilment – probably a fulfilment that you don't suspect.

Saturn in your own sign could also be a problem in love. As we mentioned, it makes you more of a Capricorn than usual. While this is a great aspect for business and management, it's not so great for love. You could be coming across as too cold, too business-like, too aloof, too brusque. Your heart is not coming through to others. Make it a project to project love and warmth to others.

Singles are unlikely to marry this year. However, with Uranus in your 5th house there will be plenty of opportunities for love affairs. But these are strictly entertainment. These are not with people you would consider marriage material.

Those of you in or working on the second marriage have a stable kind of year. Those working on the third or fourth marriage have good opportunities this year, and even better ones next year. Romance is in the stars for you.

The Moon, fastest-moving of all the planets, is your love planet. She moves through your whole chart every month and makes aspects (good or bad) to every planet in your chart. So, there are a lot of short-term trends in love that are best discussed in the monthly reports.

In general we can say that love will go best at the new and full Moons – periods where the lunar energy is very strong. Also you will have more social magnetism and enthusiasm when the Moon is waxing (growing) than when she is waning (getting smaller).

Self-improvement

The year ahead is very spiritual, as we mentioned. Jupiter will be in your 12th house for almost all the year, so this is a year for internal growth – for spiritual breakthroughs. These happen in secret, away from the crowd, in the solitary places of meditation. Secret though they be, they produce profound change – first in you, then in your family, your community, your country and eventually the world. Some have referred to these as 'aha' moments – 'eureka' moments – peak experiences. You will have a goodly share of these in the year to come. The dream life will be hyperactive – much more active than usual – and attention should be paid to those dreams. Extrasensory perception (ESP) and synchronistic experiences will increase this year. Your 'sixth sense' is greatly strengthened and more active.

Your spiritual planet, Jupiter, crosses your Ascendant and enters your 1st house on December 3. This signals many things. For a start, a guru or spiritual teacher is coming into your life. It looks like a close association. But this also shows that your spiritual understanding will help you deal with the issues of your body, image and personal appearance. It's been an important focus all year. Spiritual techniques will be revealed that help the process.

You have the image of a business or corporate person this year, but with Jupiter in your sign you will also have the image of someone with heart, someone altruistic. It's not just business.

Jupiter in your 12th house favours the mystical teachings of your native religion. Every religion has its mystical side. It would be good for you to explore that.

Capricorn students who are below college level will do better in parochial or art-centred schools than in regular schools. The main danger for them in school is 'dreaminess'. They can go off to 'other worlds' when they should be paying attention to the teacher.

Siblings and sibling figures in your life are more spiritual these days. They should be involved in some spiritual discipline. If not they could be prone to alcohol or drug abuse. Drugs and alcohol are not good things for them as their bodies are more refined now and could over-react to these things.

With Neptune in your 3rd house (as he has been for many years), those of you involved in teaching, sales or marketing should make more use of films and videos. Your message will come across better.

Month-by-month Forecasts

January

> Best Days Overall: 5, 6, 15, 16, 23, 24
> Most Stressful Days Overall: 12, 13, 19, 20, 25, 26
> Best Days for Love: 1, 5, 6, 12, 13, 16, 19, 20, 21, 22, 25, 30, 31
> Best Days for Money: 2, 3, 4, 7, 8, 12, 13, 14, 21, 22, 31
> Best Days for Career: 1, 12, 13, 21, 22, 25, 26, 30, 31

You begin your year with the planetary power mostly in the Eastern sector of your chart. Thus you are in a period of maximum personal independence. Time to focus on your interests and personal happiness. This is not selfish or evil; it's just the cycle you're in. Basically, the month ahead is happy and prosperous, though two eclipses will complicate things a bit.

The solar eclipse of the 6th (in America it's on the 5th) affects you very strongly. It not only occurs in your own sign, but also impacts the ruler of your Horoscope, Saturn. So a relaxed, stress-free schedule is called for over this period. Spend some quiet time at home. Things that can be rescheduled should be rescheduled. This eclipse will force a redefinition of your self – your self-concept and image. You have to redefine yourself for yourself or others will do it for you and it won't be so pleasant. In the coming months you will adopt a new look – a new image – that reflects your internal redefinition.

Since the Sun (the eclipsed planet) rules your 8th house of regeneration, the eclipse brings important financial changes for the spouse, partner or current love. Financial thinking and strategy have been amiss, as the events of the eclipse will show. An eclipse often brings the 'X factor' not envisioned in our calculations. There can be encounters with death too – usually on the psychological level. This is to give you a better understanding of death and to help you lose your fear of it. There can be dramas with insurance and tax issues. Those of you of appropriate age will be making changes to wills.

The lunar eclipse of the 21st occurs in your 8th house and again brings financial changes to the spouse, partner or current love. More course corrections are necessary. It also forces a redefinition of the beloved's self-concept and image. In the coming months he or she will be changing his or her 'look', the manner of dress, etc., to reflect this new definition of self. He or she can be having personal dramas too. The marriage or current relationship gets tested. Long-repressed grievances and imperfections come up for cleansing. Good relationships survive these things. (You go through this twice a year, and by now you know how to handle it.) The flawed ones can be in danger. Again there are more psychological encounters with death.

Despite the drama there is prosperity this month. On the 20th, the Sun enters your money house and you begin a yearly financial peak.

February

Best Days Overall: 1, 2, 11, 12, 19, 20, 28
Most Stressful Days Overall: 8, 9, 10, 15, 16, 21, 22
Best Days for Love: 3, 4, 11, 14, 15, 16, 19, 20, 24, 28
Best Days for Money: 3, 4, 5, 9, 10, 17, 18, 26, 27
Best Days for Career: 11, 19, 20, 21, 22, 28

You're still in the midst of a yearly financial peak until the 19th. The Sun in the money house shows a good ability to make, pay down or refinance debt. It is a good time for attracting outside investors to your projects – and they seem available. It is also good for tax and insurance planning. For those of you of appropriate age it is good for estate planning. Mercury, your planet of health and work, in the money house until the 10th indicates money from work, from foreign investments and perhaps foreigners. You could be spending more on health at this time, but can earn from here as well. Mercury in Aquarius is his most exalted position. He is powerful in this sign. Mars travels with your financial planet, Uranus, from the 11th to the 14th. This can show some expense at home, but also shows good financial support from the family (a parent or parent figure especially), or from family connections.

When Mars leaves your 4th house on the 14th, health improves. You can enhance the health further through calf and ankle massage until the 10th, and through foot massage after then. You respond very well to spiritual-healing techniques from the 10th onwards.

Though Spring, when the Sun moves into Aries, is considered the best starting energy of the year, the month ahead might be even better. All the planets are moving forward. Your personal solar cycle is waxing (growing) as you have just had your birthday, and the Universal solar cycle is also waxing. The 4th to the 19th would be the optimum time to launch a new product, project or business, as this is when the Moon is also waxing.

Venus moves into your sign on the 3rd and spends the rest of the month there. This is a happy transit. It brings more fun into the life. You tend to be overly sober and serious these days, and Venus will lighten things up a bit. She brings beauty, grace and charm to the image and opportunities for love affairs (not serious love). On the 17th and 18th she travels with Saturn, the ruler of your Horoscope, bringing an opportunity for a love affair. This transit can also bring a happy career opportunity. But career is not that important right now, with at least 80 per cent (and sometimes 90 per cent) of the planets in the night side (the lower half) of your chart. You are a night person these days. This period is for night-time activities – preparing for the next day, resting, building emotional harmony and wellness.

Love is not a big issue right now. Your 7th house of love is empty (only the Moon moves through there on the 15th and 16th). Love would tend to the status quo.

March

Best Days Overall: 1, 2, 10, 11, 19, 20, 27, 28, 29
Most Stressful Days Overall: 8, 9, 15, 16, 21, 22
Best Days for Love: 3, 4, 8, 9, 15, 16, 17, 18, 23, 24, 25, 26
Best Days for Money: 1, 3, 4, 8, 9, 10, 17, 18, 19, 25, 26, 27, 30, 31
Best Days for Career: 3, 4, 15, 16, 21, 22, 23, 24

Very nice developments are happening in health and finance this month. Uranus's move into Taurus, your 5th house, on the 7th further improves the health. It also shows positive financial changes. The financial planet in Taurus is more conservative and thoughtful in financial matters. While he was in Aries over the past several years, you were more speculative and risk-taking. This will change now.

Capricorn always has good financial judgement, but now it gets even better. You seem more comfortable financially – more in tune with the way that you earn. The financial planet in the 5th house can be speculative – but not as wild as Uranus in Aries. It shows a more controlled kind of speculation, speculation that is more thought out and well hedged. It also shows 'happy money' – money that is earned in enjoyable ways. It shows spending on happy things – leisure pursuits and perhaps on the children and children figures in your life.

Your 3rd house of communication and intellectual pursuits is where the power is this month – especially until the 20th. This is a wonderful aspect for students. They are focused on their studies and their minds are sharp. It shows success. It is a wonderful aspect for teachers, writers, sales and marketing people too. The communication skills are enhanced and they should be more successful. The money people in your life get even richer this period.

Venus spends most of the month in your money house – until the 26th. She will also be in 'mutual reception' with your financial planet Uranus from the 7th to the 26th. Each is a guest in the house of the other. So there is good cooperation between the two planets. This is a good financial signal. Speculations will tend to be favourable. You have the financial favour both of children and children figures, and of parents, parent figures and bosses. Your good career reputation brings earnings and earnings opportunities.

Health needs some attention after the 20th, but any problem is mild compared to those of the past and is just a temporary low in the energy levels. Enhance the health through foot massage and spiritual techniques. If you feel under the weather see a spiritual-type healer.

Mercury is retrograde from the 5th to the 28th so avoid making dramatic changes to the health regime over that period. And if you must travel, allow more time to get to and from your destination.

The new Moon of the 6th occurs right on Neptune. For singles this indicates a romantic opportunity in the neighbourhood or with a neighbour. It could also happen at a lecture or seminar. The full Moon of 21st (in America it occurs on the 20th) is almost a 'super Moon' – she is very near her closest distance to earth, her perigee. Another good day for romance.

April

Best Days Overall: 6, 7, 8, 15, 16, 24, 25
Most Stressful Days Overall: 4, 5, 11, 12, 17, 18
Best Days for Love: 2, 3, 4, 5, 11, 12, 13, 14, 21, 24
Best Days for Money: 4, 5, 6, 13, 14, 15, 22, 23, 24, 26, 27
Best Days for Career: 2, 3, 11, 12, 17, 18, 21

Health needs watching until the 20th, although you will see big improvement afterwards. In the meantime enhance the health through foot massage and spiritual techniques until the 17th, and through head, face and scalp massage from the 17th onwards. Craniosacral therapy and physical exercise are also good after the 17th.

The power this month (and it began on March 20) is in your 4th house of home and family, despite Uranus's departure from there last month. The night side of your chart is dominant now and even your career planet, Venus, will be in your 4th house from the 20th. So, you work on the career by the methods of night – by visualization and controlled dreaming. Get into the mood and feeling of what you want to achieve. If this is done, the overt actions – which will happen later on – will go well. The career planet in the 4th house shows that home and family, and especially your emotional wellness, are the real career – the real mission – from the 20th onwards. Preparation is just as important as the actual doing.

Your health planet, Mercury, in the 4th house from the 17th onwards shows the importance of emotional wellness. Good health for you means more than just 'no symptoms' – it means a healthy family life and healthy moods and feelings. With so much power in your family house the cosmos will help you in your quest for right feeling. Old memories – perhaps old traumas – will arise and you'll be able to resolve them from your present state of consciousness. You won't be rewriting history; you'll be reinterpreting it in a better way.

The Sun moves into your 5th house on the 20th and you enter a yearly personal pleasure peak. When emotional wellness happens, when there is harmony at home, the reward of fun, leisure and enhanced creativity happens naturally. So it is a period for doing things that you enjoy. Whether you are on vacation or not, there are always ways you can inject fun into your life. The Sun will travel with your financial planet from the 21st to the 23rd. This is a good financial transit and indicates 'sudden' money – money that comes unexpectedly. There would be luck in speculations too. This transit signals good financial cooperation with the spouse, partner or current love, too.

Your career planet, Venus, has her solstice from the 22nd to the 25th. She occupies the same degree of latitude that period. She is paused in one place and then she changes direction. So your career pauses and then changes direction. It is a happy pause.

May

Best Days Overall: 4, 5, 13, 14, 21, 22, 31
Most Stressful Days Overall: 1, 2, 3, 8, 9, 15, 16, 29, 30
Best Days for Love: 2, 3, 4, 5, 8, 9, 13, 14, 21, 23, 24, 31
Best Days for Money: 2, 3, 4, 10, 11, 13, 19, 20, 21, 24, 25, 29, 30, 31
Best Days for Career: 2, 3, 14, 15, 16, 21, 31

A happy and prosperous month ahead, Capricorn. Enjoy. You're still in the midst of a yearly personal pleasure peak until the 21st. Fun seems frivolous to Capricorn, yet it is part of life and just as important in its way as work. It relaxes the mind and allows solutions to reveal themselves. It's a different order of responsibility. When done properly it assists responsibility. By the 21st, as the Sun enters your 6th house however, you're partied out and ready for work.

Though your money house is empty this month – only the Moon moves through there on the 24th and 25th – the month ahead looks prosperous. Your financial planet receives nice aspects – in fact there are no discordant aspects to it at all. (Only the Moon – and only occasionally – will make challenging aspects to Uranus.) So earning power is strong and there are no impediments to it. Mercury will travel with Uranus on the 7th and 8th. This brings financial increase and perhaps a job opportunity. Venus travels with Uranus from the 17th to the 19th, bringing luck in speculations and the financial favour of children, children figures, parents, parent figures and bosses.

Health is excellent this month – about as excellent as it will be all year. After the 6th the only possible adverse aspects you have to contend with are Saturn and Pluto in your own sign. And, because Saturn is your planetary ruler, he is actually helpful to you. You can enhance the health further through physical exercise, face and scalp massage until the 6th. From the 6th to the 21st enhance the health through neck massage. After the 21st arm and shoulder massage will be good, as will fresh air.

Love is more complicated this month, with Mars's move into your 7th house on the 16th. This tends to power struggles and conflicts in relationships, so try to avoid these. The spouse, partner or current love can be more irritable and impatient. No need to make matters worse than they need to be. Since Mars is your family planet this signals more socializing from home and with the family. Family and family connections are playing a role in romance – especially for singles. Singles are attracted to people with strong family values and with whom there is an easy emotional intimacy.

Mars, your family planet, went 'out of bounds' on April 21 and will be this way for the entire month. So family members are going outside their normal boundaries these days – especially a parent or parent figure. In your emotional life, too, you are visiting strange and unfamiliar places.

Mercury will be 'out of bounds' from the 28th onwards, indicating that your job or your health goals can take you out of your normal sphere.

June

Best Days Overall: 1, 9, 10, 18, 19, 27, 28, 29
Most Stressful Days Overall: 5, 6, 11, 12, 25, 26
Best Days for Love: 1, 2, 3, 5, 6, 11, 12, 20, 21, 22
Best Days for Money: 1, 7, 8, 9, 15, 16, 17, 18, 20, 21, 25, 26, 27
Best Days for Career: 1, 11, 12, 20, 21

Your 6th house of health and work became powerful on May 21 and remains strong until the 21st of this month. There is a good focus on your health, which will stand you in good stead towards the end of the month, when health will need more attention (after the 21st). This is also a very nice month for jobseekers – there are multiple job opportunities. Even those of you already employed have opportunities for overtime or second jobs. It is a good period for those who employ others as well. Good applicants are applying for vacancies.

Health, as we have said, becomes more stressful and complicated after the 21st. Good health is not just about 'no symptoms' but about good social and emotional health. If you can maintain harmony in your marriage or relationship and keep the moods positive and constructive, 90 per cent of the battle is won. You'll probably go through with good health. Another important thing is to get enough rest.

The planetary power is now in the Western, social sector of your chart, approaching the maximum Western position. Thus personal independence, self-esteem and self-confidence are at a low point. Peer pressure is very strong, and this might not be a bad thing – as long as it isn't destructive. Others should have their way right now. But with your own 1st house still very strong, this might be difficult for you to accept. Try to achieve your goals through cooperation and consensus now, rather than by direct action.

Love is the main headline this month. Mars will be in your 7th house of love all month. And on the 21st, the Sun enters this house and you begin a yearly love and social peak. The social life is active, perhaps even hectic. You are more aggressive in love these days. Singles go after what they want very directly. Wealth is a romantic turn-on. Those already in relationships will find that their beloved is having a strong financial month, from the 21st onwards. Love and social opportunities happen in many ways this month. Mercury in your 7th house indicates an attraction to foreigners, religious people and highly educated types. Romance can happen in foreign lands, your place of worship or at a school function. Family and family connections seem important socially – like last month. Family members like to play Cupid. A family event can lead to romance. With the Sun in your 7th house, social opportunities can even happen at funerals or wakes, or as you call to pay your respects to the bereaved.

Finances are still very good. Your financial planet Uranus receives no stressful aspects until the 27th. (Only the Moon will occasionally by in stressful alignment.) So Uranus can function unimpeded this month, and thus is strong on your behalf.

July

Best Days Overall: 6, 7, 15, 16, 25, 26
Most Stressful Days Overall: 2, 3, 8, 9, 22, 23, 24, 29, 30
Best Days for Love: 1, 2, 3, 10, 11, 20, 21, 29, 30, 31
Best Days for Money: 4, 5, 6, 13, 14, 15, 17, 18, 19, 22, 23, 24, 25, 31
Best Days for Career: 1, 8, 9, 10, 11, 20, 21, 31

A hectic and stormy kind of month this month, but you'll get through it. The cosmos never gives us more than we can handle. If it's given, we can handle it. There are two issues of concern. The first is that health is stressed. The second is the two eclipses this month – both of which affect you strongly. You need to be sure to get enough rest anyway, but especially around the eclipse periods.

The solar eclipse of the 2nd occurs in your 7th house of love and tests the marriage or current relationship. Some of this testing might not be your fault. The beloved is having personal and financial dramas and this could impact on your relationship. Be more patient with him or her. The beloved is once again being forced to redefine him or herself, to redefine the way he or she thinks of him or herself (this happened back in January too). This redefinition will result over the coming months in changes to his or her wardrobe, hairstyle and overall image. (And this will happen again on the lunar eclipse of the 16th.) Every solar eclipse brings confrontations with death (psychological confrontations normally), and this one is no exception. These confrontations are love letters from the Divine to make you focus on your mission in life – the reason you were born.

The lunar eclipse of the 16th occurs in your own sign and impacts on Pluto, your planet of friends. So there are social upheavals here too – both with friends and the beloved. Friendships and the current love relationship get tested. Dirty laundry – old repressed grievances, real or imagined – comes up for cleansing. Good relationships survive these things, but shakier ones are in danger. Since this eclipse occurs in your sign, you once again need to redefine yourself, your self-concept and the image you want to project to the world (as you did in January). This is basically a healthy thing and should be done periodically. We are

ever-growing, ever-changing beings and our self-concept should
reflect this. Here it is sort of forced on you. The eclipse's impact on
Pluto shows that high-tech equipment – computers, software and
gadgets – get tested. If there are hidden flaws, now is when you find
out about them.

Health improves this month after the 23rd, but finances become
more stormy. Uranus receives stressful aspects and you need to work
harder to achieve your financial goals. It's not a good idea to indulge in
speculative investments at this time.

August

Best Days Overall: 2, 3, 11, 12, 21, 22, 30, 31
Most Stressful Days Overall: 4, 5, 19, 20, 26, 27
Best Days for Love: 1, 9, 10, 20, 21, 26, 27, 30, 31
Best Days for Money: 1, 2, 9, 10, 11, 14, 15, 19, 20, 21, 28, 29,
    30
Best Days for Career: 1, 4, 5, 9, 10, 20, 21, 30, 31

On July 3 the planetary power shifted decisively from the lower, night
side of your Horoscope to the upper, day side. Career is becoming ever
more important. Home and family issues can be downplayed now.
Focus on the career and serve your family by being successful in the
outer world. Your career planet, Venus, is in your 8th house of regeneration until the 21st. So this is a good time to detox the career and
outer goals. Get rid of any extraneous issues and focus on the essence.
After the 21st, as Venus moves into your 9th house, career-related
travel is signalled. Your willingness to travel helps the career. Good to
accept educational opportunities related to the career too.

From the 18th onwards there will be a rare Grand Trine in the Earth
signs – your native element. You are very comfortable with this. Your
strong practical nature is appreciated and enhanced. Likewise your
strong management skills. Along with this, there will be wonderful
aspects to your financial planet from the 18th onwards. So prosperity
is strong. The only issue financially is the retrograde of your financial
planet on the 12th. You will have increased earnings but perhaps they
will come more slowly than usual. However, Uranus's retrograde, a

process that will go on for many months, is the time to get financial clarity. The financial landscape is not the way you think. If you must make major purchases or investments now, study them more and resolve all doubts first.

Health is much, much improved over last month. Health is good but if you want to enhance it further be more careful in dietary matters until the 11th. After the 11th chest massage will be powerful. Give more attention to the heart. From the 29th to the end of the month give more attention to the small intestine.

Mercury will be in your 7th house until the 11th. This shows an attraction to health professionals and to people involved in your health. The workplace is also a social centre and there are opportunities for office romances. The 'super new Moon' (it occurs when the Moon is at its closest to Earth) of the 1st is a powerful romantic day. The new Moon of the 30th (a regular new Moon) will also be good for romance. In general your social energy is stronger from the 1st to the 15th and on the 30th and 31st – when the Moon, your love planet, is waxing.

September

Best Days Overall: 7, 8, 9, 17, 18, 19, 26, 27
Most Stressful Days Overall: 1, 2, 15, 16, 22, 23, 28, 29
Best Days for Love: 7, 8, 9, 18, 19, 20, 22, 23, 28, 29
Best Days for Money: 5, 6, 7, 10, 11, 15, 16, 17, 24, 25, 26
Best Days for Career: 1, 2, 8, 9, 20, 28, 29

We still have a Grand Trine in the Earth signs this month: a very positive signal for health and finance. You have sound managerial judgement. You always have a sense for what works on the ground but now it is even stronger. A good month to make managerial decisions.

Your 9th house became powerful on August 18 and remains so this month until the 23rd. This is a happy and optimistic period. Your horizons expand – in the career, at work and with the family. For the spouse, partner or current love it is a good period to catch up on reading, to take courses in subjects that interest him or her and to catch up on correspondence. Those of you in college have a successful month. If you are involved in legal issues there is good fortune too. Foreign lands call to you and happy travel opportunities come. A strong 9th house signals an interest in religion, philosophy and theology. Many problems that appear to be financial or health or relationship issues are really theological problems in disguise. This is why theological or philosophical breakthroughs – which are likely now – are so important. The Hindu astrologers consider the 9th house the most beneficent of houses for this reason.

Your 10th house of career becomes strong this month, beginning on the 14th as both Mercury and Venus enter. On the 23rd the Sun enters and you begin a yearly career peak. It looks very successful as the planets there are beneficent ones. The Sun's entry into the 10th house can bring instances of surgery or near-death experiences for bosses, parents or parent figures. (They may not actually have surgery but it could be recommended to them.)

The prelude to career success happens from the 15th to the 18th as your career planet Venus has her second solstice. She camps out in the same degree of latitude during that period so she seems motionless. She is pausing and then changing direction. So there is a pause in the career and then a change of direction.

Health becomes more delicate after the 23rd. Nothing really serious, just a period of lower-than-normal energy. Things you did without effort before the 23rd are now more difficult to do. So, make sure to get enough rest. This is always most important. Enhance the health through hip massage after the 14th. The buttocks should also be massaged. Look up the kidney reflexology point in the chart in the yearly report (page 296) and massage it.

Your financial planet Uranus is still moving backward, but until the 14th he receives good aspects. Finances might happen slower than normal, but earnings are good. After the 14th Uranus does not receive as many positive aspects as before, so there could be a drop off in earnings. Continue to work for financial clarity. Avoid making major purchases or investments as far as possible.

October

Best Days Overall: 5, 6, 15, 16, 23, 24
Most Stressful Days Overall: 12, 13, 19, 20, 26, 27
Best Days for Love: 7, 8, 10, 11, 17, 18, 19, 20, 28, 29
Best Days for Money: 2, 3, 4, 5, 7, 8, 12, 13, 14, 15, 21, 22, 23, 30, 31
Best Days for Career: 10, 11, 19, 20, 26, 27, 28, 29

A very hectic but successful month ahead. Health needs watching, especially until the 23rd. You're not going to avoid the demands of the career, which seem very strong now (Mars in your 10th house from the 4th onwards is showing this). But you can schedule more rest periods into your day and work more steadily. You may have to drop lesser things from your schedule and this often entails tough choices. You can and should schedule more massages and health treatments into your diary. Until the 3rd enhance the health with hip massage and pay more attention to the kidneys. After the 3rd give more attention to the colon and bladder (look up the reflexology points in the chart included in the yearly report, page 296). Safe sex and sexual moderation is important after the 3rd, and detox regimes also seem called for.

Career is the main headline this month. You're still very much in a yearly career peak and much progress is being made. You have help in the career, but you're earning your success – like a true Capricorn. The good news here is that the family seems supportive. Your success is akin to a family project. The family as a whole seems elevated in status.

Finances are reasonable until the 23rd. Uranus is still retrograde but his aspects are not bad. After the 23rd it's a different story, however. Finances seem stressed and you have more challenges. You and the beloved are not in financial agreement. Business partners, children and children figures likewise. These are not disasters; it just means that more work and challenge are involved. If you put in the extra work you will prosper. The key words here are 'extra work'.

The good news is that health improves after the 23rd. Detox regimes are still powerful.

Though love and romance don't seem like priorities, the month ahead – especially after the 23rd – is very social. But it is more about friendships, groups and group activities than romance. Your 7th house of love is basically empty, with only the Moon moving through there on the 19th and 20th. This tends to the status quo. However the Moon, your love planet, will travel with Jupiter twice this month – double her usual time. So there are romantic opportunities for singles. These seem to be found in spiritual-type settings, in the yoga studio, at a meditation seminar or spiritual lecture, charity event or prayer meeting. Also you attract more spiritual-type people this month (especially on the 2nd, 3rd, 4th, 30th and 31st).

November

Best Days Overall: 1, 2, 11, 12, 20, 21, 28, 29, 30
Most Stressful Days Overall: 8, 9, 10, 16, 17, 22, 23
Best Days for Love: 6, 7, 8, 9, 16, 17, 18, 19, 26, 29
Best Days for Money: 1, 3, 4, 5, 8, 9, 10, 11, 18, 19, 20, 26, 27, 28
Best Days for Career: 8, 9, 18, 19, 22, 23, 29

Mars is still at the top of your chart in your 10th house until the 19th, so the career is still hectic. You need to be aggressive there as you seem to be fending off competition – either personal or in the industry. The family is still supporting the career, so there is no problem in letting go of family issues at the moment. You seem in conflict with a parent or parent figure (this was the case last month too), but this will resolve itself after the 19th. The family as a whole is elevated in status.

Your career planet, Venus, is 'out of bounds' from the 15th onwards. This indicates that your career is taking you outside your normal haunts. It could also be that you're pursuing career goals in unconventional ways. Venus spends most of the month in your spiritual 12th house and you further your career through involvement with charities and altruistic causes. Venus travels with Jupiter from the 22nd to the 24th and this brings career elevation and success to you. It also brings success in your spiritual practice. On the 26th Venus enters your sign for the second time this year, bringing happy career opportunities and the favour of parents, parent figures and bosses.

The planetary power is now mostly in the Eastern sector of the self. Saturn, the ruler of your Horoscope, is moving forward as well, so personal independence and initiative are getting stronger day by day. You have confidence and good self-esteem. You no longer need to adapt to others or put others first. You can and should create your own happiness. Now, and for the next few months, make the changes that need to be made and create the conditions for your own happiness. The world will eventually assent to it.

Your 11th house of friends is still strong until the 22nd. So it is still a social kind of time. Romance doesn't seem a big issue, but friendships, groups and group activities are. Many people have their Horoscopes done when their 11th house is powerful, and when interest in science, technology, astrology and astronomy is strong.

Health is much improved over last month. It is good right now and after the 19th will get even better. Your health planet Mercury spends the month (mostly in retrograde motion) in Scorpio. So like last month enhance the health through detox regimes and pay more attention to the colon and bladder. Safe sex and sexual moderation are still important.

Mars will oppose Uranus from the 22nd to the 23rd. This is a dynamic kind of aspect and there can be short-term financial turmoil – perhaps a sudden expense at home. There is a financial disagreement with one of the parents or parent figures. Family members should be more mindful on the physical plane during that period.

December

Best Days Overall: 8, 9, 17, 18, 26, 27
Most Stressful Days Overall: 6, 7, 13, 14, 19, 20
Best Days for Love: 6, 7, 8, 9, 13, 14, 15, 16, 17, 18, 26, 28, 29
Best Days for Money: 1, 2, 8, 17, 26, 28, 29
Best Days for Career: 8, 9, 17, 18, 19, 20, 28, 29

A very interesting and basically happy month ahead, Capricorn. Saturn and Pluto are travelling together closely – closer than they have been all year. Some of you could be contemplating cosmetic-type surgery. There is a closeness with friends. Perhaps a new friend is coming into the picture. Jupiter moves into your own sign on the 3rd and this will initiate a multi-year cycle of prosperity. More importantly, Jupiter will help you 'lighten up' a bit. You've been much too serious over the past two years and this has probably affected the love life. Jupiter brings some joy and optimism.

There is another solar eclipse in your sign on the 26th so, although health and energy are good this month, it would be advisable to reduce your schedule during the eclipse period – a few days before and after it. Again, for the third time this year, you are forced to redefine yourself – your image and self-concept. Sometimes this kind of eclipse brings a detox of the body (not to be confused with disease). This is especially likely if you haven't been careful in dietary matters. This eclipse impacts on Jupiter, your spiritual planet. Thus there are important spiritual changes happening – changes in teachers, teachings, attitudes and practice. There are dramas in the lives of gurus and guru figures and shake-ups in spiritual or charitable organizations that you're involved with. As with every solar eclipse, this one brings important financial changes with the spouse, partner or current love. It brings tax, insurance and estate dramas, and more changes to wills. Apparently the will is not written in stone. This is the third time you've made changes. And again, as with every solar eclipse, there are psychological confrontations with death. You need to go deeper in your understanding.

The past year was very spiritual, with Jupiter in your 12th house. And this spiritual focus will continue this month – and well into 2020. In fact, people will see you as a spiritual, philanthropic kind of person. You have that image.

Finances are excellent all month but especially after the 22nd. And self-esteem, self-confidence and personal independence are even stronger than last month. By all means, take the bull by the horns and create the conditions for your happiness. If conditions irk you, change them to your liking.

The combination of an eclipse in your 1st house with many planets there as well (70 per cent of them are either there or moving through there this month – a huge percentage) makes this an excellent month to get your body and image the way you want them to be. You enjoy the good life well into 2020, but especially in the month ahead.

Health is good, but you can make it even better with detox regimes until the 4th, thigh massage from the 4th to the 24th, and with back and knee massage from the 24th onwards.

Aquarius

~~~

THE WATER-BEARER

Birthdays from
20th January to
18th February

Personality Profile

AQUARIUS AT A GLANCE

Element – Air

Ruling Planet – Uranus
   Career Planet – Pluto
   Love Planet – Sun
   Money Planet – Neptune
   Planet of Health and Work – Moon
   Planet of Home and Family Life – Venus
   Planet of Spirituality – Saturn

Colours – electric blue, grey, ultramarine blue

Colours that promote love, romance and social harmony – gold, orange

Colour that promotes earning power – aqua

Gems – black pearl, obsidian, opal, sapphire

Metal – lead

Scents – azalea, gardenia

Quality – fixed (= stability)

Qualities most needed for balance – warmth, feeling and emotion

Strongest virtues – great intellectual power, the ability to communicate and to form and understand abstract concepts, love for the new and avant-garde

Deepest needs – to know and to bring in the new

Characteristics to avoid – coldness, rebelliousness for its own sake, fixed ideas

Signs of greatest overall compatibility – Gemini, Libra

Signs of greatest overall incompatibility – Taurus, Leo, Scorpio

Sign most helpful to career – Scorpio

Sign most helpful for emotional support – Taurus

Sign most helpful financially – Pisces

Sign best for marriage and/or partnerships – Leo

Sign most helpful for creative projects – Gemini

Best Sign to have fun with – Gemini

Signs most helpful in spiritual matters – Libra, Capricorn

Best day of the week – Saturday

Understanding an Aquarius

In the Aquarius-born, intellectual faculties are perhaps the most highly developed of any sign in the zodiac. Aquarians are clear, scientific thinkers who can think abstractly and formulate laws, theories and clear concepts from masses of observed facts. Geminis might be very good at gathering information, but Aquarians take this a step further, excelling at interpreting the information gathered.

Practical people – men and women of the world – mistakenly consider abstract thinking as impractical. The realm of abstract thought does take us out of the physical world, but the discoveries made in this realm often have tremendous practical consequences. All real scientific inventions and breakthroughs come from this abstract realm.

Aquarians are ideally suited to explore these abstract dimensions. Those who have explored these regions know that there is little feeling or emotion there. In fact, emotions are a hindrance to functioning in these dimensions; thus Aquarians seem – at times – cold and emotionless to others. It is not that Aquarians haven't got feelings and deep emotions, it is just that too much feeling clouds their ability to think and invent. The concept of 'too much feeling' cannot be tolerated or even understood by some of the other signs. Nevertheless, this Aquarian objectivity is ideal for science, communication and friendship.

Aquarians are very friendly people, but they do not make a big show about it. They do the right thing by their friends, even if sometimes they do it without passion or excitement.

Aquarians have a deep passion for clear thinking. Second in importance, but related, is their passion for breaking with the establishment and traditional authority. Aquarians delight in this, because for them rebellion is like a great game or challenge. Very often they will rebel strictly for the fun of rebelling, regardless of whether the authority they defy is right or wrong. Right or wrong has little to do with the rebellious actions of an Aquarian, because to a true Aquarian authority and power must be challenged as a matter of principle.

Where Capricorn or Taurus will err on the side of tradition and the status quo, an Aquarian will err on the side of the new. Without this virtue it is doubtful whether any progress would be made in the world.

The conservative-minded would obstruct progress. Originality and invention imply an ability to break barriers; every new discovery represents the toppling of an impediment to thought. Aquarians are very interested in breaking barriers and making walls tumble – scientifically, socially and politically. Other zodiac signs, such as Capricorn, also have scientific talents. But Aquarians are particularly excellent in the social sciences and humanities.

Finance

In financial matters Aquarians tend to be idealistic and humanitarian – to the point of self-sacrifice. They are usually generous contributors to social and political causes. When they contribute it differs from a Capricorn or Taurus. A Capricorn or Taurus may expect some favour or return for a gift; an Aquarian contributes selflessly.

Aquarians tend to be as cool and rational about money as they are about most things in life. Money is something they need and they set about acquiring it scientifically. No need for fuss; they get on with it in the most rational and scientific ways available.

Money to the Aquarian is especially nice for what it can do, not for the status it may bring (as is the case for other signs). Aquarians are neither big spenders nor penny-pinchers and use their finances in practical ways, for example to facilitate progress for themselves, their families, or even for strangers.

However, if Aquarians want to reach their fullest financial potential they will have to explore their intuitive nature. If they follow only their financial theories – or what they believe to be theoretically correct – they may suffer some losses and disappointments. Instead, Aquarians should call on their intuition, which knows without thinking. For Aquarians, intuition is the short-cut to financial success.

Career and Public Image

Aquarians like to be perceived not only as the breakers of barriers but also as the transformers of society and the world. They long to be seen in this light and to play this role. They also look up to and respect other people in this position and even expect their superiors to act this way.

Aquarians prefer jobs that have a bit of idealism attached to them – careers with a philosophical basis. Aquarians need to be creative at work, to have access to new techniques and methods. They like to keep busy and enjoy getting down to business straightaway, without wasting any time. They are often the quickest workers and usually have suggestions for improvements that will benefit their employers. Aquarians are also very helpful with their co-workers and welcome responsibility, preferring this to having to take orders from others.

If Aquarians want to reach their highest career goals they have to develop more emotional sensitivity, depth of feeling and passion. They need to learn to narrow their focus on the essentials and concentrate more on the job in hand. Aquarians need 'a fire in the belly' – a consuming passion and desire – in order to rise to the very top. Once this passion exists they will succeed easily in whatever they attempt.

Love and Relationships

Aquarians are good at friendships, but a bit weak when it comes to love. Of course they fall in love, but their lovers always get the impression that they are more best friends than paramours.

Like Capricorns, they are cool customers. They are not prone to displays of passion or to outward demonstrations of their affections. In fact, they feel uncomfortable when their other half hugs and touches them too much. This does not mean that they do not love their partners. They do, only they show it in other ways. Curiously enough, in relationships they tend to attract the very things that they feel uncomfortable with. They seem to attract hot, passionate, romantic, demonstrative people. Perhaps they know instinctively that these people have qualities they lack and so seek them out. In any event, these relationships do seem to work, Aquarian coolness calming the more passionate partner while the fires of passion warm the cold-blooded Aquarian.

The qualities Aquarians need to develop in their love life are warmth, generosity, passion and fun. Aquarians love relationships of the mind. Here they excel. If the intellectual factor is missing in a relationship an Aquarian will soon become bored or feel unfulfilled.

Home and Domestic Life

In family and domestic matters Aquarians can have a tendency to be too non-conformist, changeable and unstable, as willing to break the barriers of family constraints as they are those of other areas of life.

Even so, Aquarians are very sociable people. They like to have a nice home where they can entertain family and friends. Their house is usually decorated in a modern style and full of state-of-the-art appliances and gadgets – an environment Aquarians find absolutely necessary.

If their home life is to be healthy and fulfilling Aquarians need to inject it with a quality of stability – yes, even some conservatism. They need at least one area of life to be enduring and steady; this area is usually their home and family life.

Venus, the generic planet of love, rules the Aquarian's 4th solar house of home and family, which means that when it comes to the family and child-rearing, theories, cool thinking and intellect are not always enough. Aquarians need to bring love into the equation in order to have a great domestic life.

Horoscope for 2019

Major Trends

Spirituality has been important for many, many years now. Your 12th house has been strong since 2008. Last year the 12th house got even stronger and this year – after December 3 – it gets stronger still. It is easily the strongest house in your Horoscope this year. So the year ahead is very spiritual. It is a year for inner growth. This will not only increase your general well-being, but will create more prosperity. Neptune, the most spiritual of all the planets, is still in your 2nd money house, and will be for many years to come. More on this later.

Jupiter spends most of the year in your 11th house of friends. This is a very happy transit for you. It shows an active social life. It shows new and significant friends coming into the picture. Your naturally good networking and technology skills are enhanced further. Perhaps most importantly, it urges you to do the things that you most love to do. It reinforces your natural strengths. Later in the year, as Jupiter moves into your 12th house, you will be making more spiritual-type friends.

Friendships are active and happy this year, but love seems more turbulent. However, it doesn't seem a big issue for most of you. In addition, four out of the five eclipses this year will impact on your love life. More on this later.

Uranus, your ruling planet, is making a major move out of Aries and into Taurus. Last year he flirted with the sign of Taurus; this year he moves in for the long term – for the next seven years. This has big implications for the home and the family, and shows a move away from intellectual development to emotional development. There will be a great interest in psychology in the coming years.

You're coming out of a very strong and successful career year. This year career doesn't seem that important. The career goals have been achieved and now the focus is more on friendships. More details later.

Your areas of greatest interest this year will be finance; communication and intellectual interests (until March 7); home and family (from March 7 onwards); friends, groups and group activities (until December 3); and spirituality.

Your paths of greatest fulfilment this year will be health and work; friends, groups and group activities (until December 3); and spirituality (after December 3).

Health

(Please note that this is an astrological perspective on health and not a medical one. In days of yore there was no difference, both of these perspectives were identical. But now there could be quite a difference. For a medical perspective, please consult your doctor or health practitioner.)

Health and energy look very good this year. Until March 7, there are no long-term planets arrayed against you. After March 7 there will be only one. All the other long-term planets are either in harmonious alignment or leaving you alone.

So, the energy levels are high and the body is disease-resistant. Of course there will be periods in the year (when the short-term planets make stressful aspects) where health and energy are less easy and perhaps even stressful. But these are temporary things, not trends for the year. When the short-term planets move on (their effect is brief) your naturally good health and energy return.

Good though your health is, you can make it even better. Give more attention to the following – the vulnerable areas of your Horoscope (the reflexology points are shown in the chart above):

- The stomach and breasts. These are always important to Aquarius as the Moon is your health planet and rules these areas. When massaging the feet make sure to massage the top as well as the bottom of the feet. The top part, below the toes, reflexes to the breasts. Diet is always an important issue for you. What you eat is important, but *how* you eat is just as important. The act of eating should be elevated from mere animal appetite to an act of worship – a ritual if you will. Food should be blessed. Grace (in your own words) should be said before and after meals. If possible, have nice soothing music playing in the background. To elevate the act of eating literally changes the molecular structure of the food (as

Important foot reflexology points for the year ahead

Try to massage all of the foot on a regular basis – the top of the foot as well as the bottom – but pay extra attention to the points highlighted on the chart. When you massage, be aware of 'sore spots' as these need special attention. It's also a good idea to massage the ankles especially, and below them.

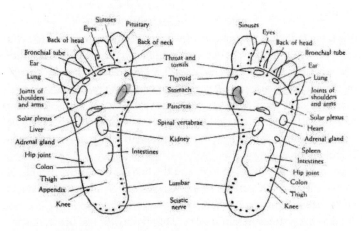

Masaru Emoto has shown)* and, more importantly, changes the body chemistry and the digestive system. You will get only the highest and best from the food you eat and it will digest better.

• The ankles and calves are also always important for Aquarius as your sign rules these areas. Ankle and calf massage should be a regular part of your health regime. Also good to give the ankles more support when exercising.

Your health planet, the Moon, is the fastest of all the planets. Where the other fast-moving planets will move through your Horoscope in a year or less, the Moon will move through it every month. In any given month she will make aspects (good and bad) to all of the planets in your Horoscope. So health will depend largely on where the Moon is at any given time and the kind of aspects she receives. The good news is that even under stressful aspects, the effect will be short term. These short-term trends are best dealt with in the monthly reports.

In general we can say that health and energy will be strongest at the new and full Moon – when she is most powerful. Also when the Moon is waxing (growing larger). The waning Moon (when she grows smaller) is good for detox regimes of all kinds.

Uranus's move into Taurus, your 4th house of home and family, on March 7 shows that your personal appearance is more or less determined by your mood and emotional state. This is true, to a degree, for everyone, but for you it's dramatic. Staying in a good mood, in a good state, will do more for your looks than hosts of lotions and potions.

Generally your health planet gets eclipsed twice a year. Thus twice every year you have opportunities for course corrections in your health regime. The body is a dynamic, ever-changing thing. Its needs change periodically, so these course corrections, these changes, are good. This year though there will be another eclipse that impacts on health. This is a solar eclipse on July 2 that occurs in your 6th house of health. So there will be more course corrections than usual this year. Often these eclipses can produce 'health scares' – but health is basically good this

---

* *The Hidden Messages in Water.* It is wonderful how he has confirmed what the ancients have known for thousands of years. This is why almost every religion has rituals for eating. In the past these things couldn't be proven, now they can.

year and they are unlikely to be more than that. Just a scare, not a reality.

With the Moon as your health planet, your emotional state not only affects your personal appearance, but your overall health as well. So again, do your best to stay in good emotional health – in emotional harmony. It won't be easy, but with meditation it can be done.

Home and Family

Home and family issues haven't been important for many years. However, this starts to change this year as Uranus, the ruler of your Horoscope, moves into your 4th house on March 7. He will be there, as we mentioned, for the next seven or so years. A long-term trend.

The good news here is that Uranus in the family house signals great personal focus here. Family is now ultra-important and this focus tends to bring success. You seem willing to do whatever it takes – deal with any challenge or difficulty – to ensure success.

The challenge here is that now the whole family and home situation becomes highly unstable. There can be break-ups – or near break-ups – in the family unit. There can be many 'emotional explosions'. Family members can have swift and sudden mood changes – bewilderingly swift. You never know where you stand with them (and especially one of the parent figures) from day to day and even hour to hour. It's as if your history or relationship doesn't exist and you have to build anew every day.

Since Uranus rules you, it could be that your presence, your demeanour, your overall presentation is sparking these reactions. (Perhaps this is the excuse they give.) Some personality issue in you is triggering them off. (It might not be a flaw – just the way that they perceive it.)

Your own moods can be more unstable these days too. Keep in mind that emotional stability and emotional harmony is very important healthwise, so you will want to get some control over this.

There are other messages here too. There is a need to constantly upgrade the physical home. Every time you think you've got the ideal – got things the way you want them – a new idea comes and you start to upgrade and change again. You upgrade the home the way some people upgrade their software and computers. It is an ongoing thing.

There can be moves – multiple moves – in the year ahead and in the coming years. You seem unsettled in your domestic tastes. Sometimes these are not literal moves, just upgrades and renovations. Sometimes both happen.

The marriage of a parent or parent figure becomes very unstable from March 7 onwards. It will get tested. Survival of the marriage is 'iffy'. One of the parents or parent figures is prospering this year and you're more or less in harmony with him or her. You're trying with the other parent or parent figure; you seem very devoted to him or her, but it's more complicated. This parent or parent figure wants more freedom, and will probably travel around a lot and live in different places for long periods of time. It might not be a formal move though, just a more nomadic lifestyle.

Siblings and sibling figures in your life have had their marriages tested over the past seven years. Divorce most likely happened. This year, the love life settles down. Romance can happen. But the home and family life seems stable.

Children and children figures have a stable kind of family year.

Renovations in the home can happen any time this year – and probably multiple times. If you have choice in the matter, February 14 to March 31 and August 18 to October 4 are the best times. If you're redecorating or buying objects of beauty for the home, May 15 to June 9, August 21 to September 14 and November 26 to December 20 are good times.

Finance and Career

Looks like a prosperous year ahead. You'll probably have to work harder than last year, but if you put in the effort there is prosperity. Last year you had the financial favour of friends. This year less so. Still, like last year the 'higher ups' in your life are still favourable to your financial goals. Money comes through your good career reputation and perhaps from pay rises – official or unofficial.

Friends will become more supportive after December 3. In the meantime you'll have to come to some sort of compromise with them.

Neptune is your financial planet, and, as we have mentioned has been occupying your money house for some years now – a great positive for finance. Neptune is in his own sign and house, and is comfortable and acting with power. This tends to increase earning power.

Neptune as the financial planet favours industries involving water – water utilities, water-bottling companies, shipping, shipbuilders, the fishing industry and seafood. It also favours oil, natural gas, retirement homes, hospices and certain pharmaceutical industries, such as the makers of anaesthetics and mood enhances. Alcohol too comes under Neptune. All these are favourable as jobs, businesses or investments. People in these industries can play a huge role in your finances.

Neptune, as our regular readers know, is the most spiritual of the planets. Thus intuition is probably the most important factor in earnings. The financial intuition is good and trustworthy.

Financial information will come to you in dreams and hunches, through psychics, tarot readers, astrologers, ministers or spiritual channels. Generally from outside the normal financial press – outside the mainstream.

The year ahead is basically prosperous, as we said. But there will be periods where earnings are less easy than usual and perhaps even stressful. These come from the transiting short-term planets and the effects are temporary. When they pass the normally good earning power returns.

Neptune as the financial planet shows that there is a lot of 'hidden activity' in your financial life and with the people involved in your finances. Thus major purchases and investments should be studied more carefully. Things are not as they seem. There can be scandals or unpleasant revelations involving the money people in your life.

Career is less important this year. You had much success and advancement last year and this year there's not much need to focus here. You will most likely hold on to the advances you made last year, but not necessarily go further. The focus is not there. Still, after a good year, the status quo should be considered good.

Pluto, your career planet, has been in your spiritual 12th house for many years now and will be there for many more. This gives many messages. You advance your career through being involved in charities and altruistic activities. Bosses and authority figures seem more altruistic these days (or they try to portray themselves that way). Your spiritual growth and understanding helps the career.

Love and Social Life

Your 7th house of love is not a house of power this year, so romance doesn't seem a big issue in 2019. Some years are like that. Generally it tends to the status quo. It shows contentment with things as they are and no special need to make dramatic changes.

However this year is a bit different. Four of the five eclipses that happen this year will impact on your love life, indicating shake-ups and change. You might feel content with things as they are, but the eclipses will force changes.

Generally the eclipses bring up old, repressed grievances – the psychic baggage that has been swept under the rug, which produces a crisis in a relationship. Generally this is a healing crisis. If the relationship is basically sound the crisis will improve things, once the dust settles. But if the relationship is flawed to begin with, it can dissolve.

Often eclipses bring change in the marital status. It can work both ways. Those who are married can decide to divorce, while singles can decide to marry – but it probably won't happen this year. It brings a course correction (and this year there are four) in the love life.

The good thing about the eclipses is that it forces you to pay more attention to love. With your empty 7th house this year, lack of attention can be the cause of the problem. Start paying more attention and the problems will get settled.

Sometimes the shakeups are not the fault of the relationship. In many cases the spouse, partner or current love is having personal life-changing dramas brought on by the eclipses, and these test the relationship.

While the love life seems troubled – prone to shake-ups – the area of friendships seems very happy. Jupiter, as we mentioned, will be in your 11th house of friends almost all year. Jupiter in his own sign and house is very comfortable here and operating at peak power. So you're making new friends – and good ones. You are meeting all kinds of new people. Your circle of friends expands. You seem more involved (more than usual) with professional and trade organizations. In other words, you're being a true Aquarian.

With the Sun as your love planet, there are many short-term trends in love that depend on where the Sun is and the aspects he receives. He is a fast-moving planet, changing signs every thirty days. In the course of a year he will move through every sector of your chart and affect every planet in your chart. These short-term trends are best dealt with in the monthly reports.

Self-improvement

Spirituality is really the story of the year ahead. Your 12th house of spirituality is easily the strongest in the Horoscope. And it becomes even stronger after December 3 when Jupiter moves into it. So the year ahead is about spiritual growth and practice. If you are right spiritually you will have career and financial success as happy side effects.

Your career planet Pluto has been in your 12th house for many years now – since 2008. On the mundane level, this shows that being involved in spiritual and altruistic kinds of activity boosts the career, as we said earlier. It shows a need for a spiritual-type career and favours non-profit organizations or charities. There is great satisfaction in these things. In many cases, Aquarius, you will opt for a spiritual-type of career – in ministry, astrology, healing and the like. Sometimes you will pursue a worldly career and work for some altruistic cause or charity on the side. There is a need to merge these areas.

In some cases, it would show that your spiritual practice, your internal growth, *is* the career – *is* the cosmic mission. We have written of this in past reports but the trends are still very much in effect (and even stronger than in past years). Saturn, your spiritual planet, and Pluto, your career planet, travel together this year. One merges into the other.

How can spiritual practice be a career? The world would laugh at this. Yet, it is viable. One spiritual breakthrough by a lone meditator, far from the glare of the media and the world, can change the world. Some new insight comes, some new inner discovery, some solution is seen and the world is forever changed. Eventually, it becomes public.

Your spiritual understanding and growth will not only help the career but increase your earnings as well. This should not be the motivation, but it will be a wonderful side effect. Spiritual Neptune has been in your money house for many years and will be there for many more years to come. Many fear to follow the spiritual path because of financial reasons. But this is not the case here. Your spiritual path will be financially rewarding. You will never lack. The need of the hour will always be fulfilled.

Continue to read all you can on the spiritual dimensions of wealth. By now you've reached a good state of understanding, but there's always more to learn. Refuse to acknowledge any source of supply except the Divine. But what about my job? My parents? My husband? My wife? My rich uncle? These are only the vehicles the Divine uses to supply you. They are never the actual source or cause.

You seem very generous in your charitable giving these days. And this is also part of the spiritual law of supply. Wealth is measured in what we give. Give more and you receive more. (This is opposite to the material perspective.)

If you find yourself in financial difficulties 'cast the burden' of it on the Divine. The solution to career and financial problems are spiritual in nature. First consult there and then take the appropriate actions.

Three eclipses occur in your 12th house this year, bringing shake-ups and changes in your spiritual practice, attitudes and teachings. Generally this happens because of inner growth – inner revelation. It is basically a good thing, but not always pleasant while it's happening. We will discuss these more fully in the monthly reports.

Month-by-month Forecasts

January

Best Days Overall: 7, 8, 17, 18, 25, 26
Most Stressful Days Overall: 15, 16, 21, 22, 27, 28
Best Days for Love: 1, 5, 6, 12, 13, 16, 21, 22, 25, 30, 31
Best Days for Money: 1, 2, 3, 10, 11, 12, 13, 19, 20, 21, 22, 27, 28
Best Days for Career: 1, 5, 6, 15, 16, 23, 24, 27, 28

The Eastern sector of your chart is unusually strong now – probably stronger than it will ever be this year. *All* the planets are in the East, the sector of self, this month. The only exception is the Moon, which will be in the Western, social half from the 15th to the 26th. So you are in a period of maximum personal independence. Self-esteem and self-confidence are strong. It's a kind of 'me first' type of month. You are expected to create your own happiness and to make the changes that need to be made in your life. You can't blame others now. It's up to you.

Two eclipses this month will hasten the changes that need to be made. The solar eclipse of the 6th (in America it's on the 5th) occurs in your 12th house and impacts on the ruler of that house, Saturn: a double hit on the affairs of the 12th house. So this eclipse is announcing major spiritual changes – changes in teachings, teachers and practice. Your current regime gets tested and the flaws will be revealed by the eclipse so that you can make adjustments. There are shakeups in spiritual or charitable organizations that you're involved with, and dramas in the lives of gurus and guru figures. Every solar eclipse impacts on the love life and current relationship, and this one is no different. So the marriage or relationship gets tested. Good relationships will survive these things (such testings happen twice a year every year, although this year it's four times), but the flawed ones are in danger. Old, repressed grievances – real or imagined – come up for cleansing. Often there are personal dramas in the life of the beloved that cause the stress. Be more patient with him or her this period.

The lunar eclipse of the 21st has more of an impact on you than the solar eclipse. Those of you born early in the sign of Aquarius (January 20–22) will feel this most intensely, but all of you will feel it. This eclipse occurs in your 7th house of love and once again tests your relationship. You have a double hit on your love life this month. The beloved should take a more relaxed, easy-going schedule during both eclipse periods. Every lunar eclipse impacts on the health and job, because the Moon, the eclipsed planet, is your health and work planet. So job changes are afoot. This can be within your present company or with a new one. The conditions of work are changed. If you employ others there can be staff turnover or dramas in the lives of employees. Often there are health scares under this kind of eclipse, but your health looks very good and so these are not likely to be anything more than scares. In the next few months you will be making important changes to the diet or health regime.

February

Best Days Overall: 3, 4, 5, 13, 14, 21, 22
Most Stressful Days Overall: 11, 12, 17, 18, 24, 25
Best Days for Love: 3, 4, 11, 14, 17, 18, 19, 20, 24, 28
Best Days for Money: 9, 10, 17, 18, 26, 27
Best Days for Career: 1, 2, 11, 12, 19, 20, 24, 25, 28

Love was tested last month but still seems very good. Your love planet, the Sun, is in your own sign this month and love opportunities come to you with little effort. The spouse, partner or current love is very devoted to you. You're having love on your terms.

You're still in a period of strong personal independence. Not as strong as last month – Mars moves to the social West on the 14th – but still strong. So, take the initiative and make the changes that need to be made. Later on in the year it will be more difficult to do.

Health is excellent. Mars will move into a stressful alignment to you after the 14th, but he will be the only planet (with the exception of the Moon – whose stressful aspects are only occasional and short term) in stressful aspect. You can enhance the health further in the ways mentioned in the yearly report. The 'super full Moon' of the 19th (when the Moon is at perigee, her closest point to the Earth) really enhances health. Personal appearance shines that day.

On January 20, as the Sun entered your 1st house, you began a yearly personal pleasure peak, which continues until the 19th. This is a great period to reward the body for its faithful service and to get it in right shape.

The month ahead will be prosperous. Mercury enters the money house on the 10th, and the Sun enters on the 19th. You begin a yearly financial peak. Mercury in the money house shows luck in speculations and a good financial intuition. The Sun's presence there signals the financial favour of the beloved and social contacts. Often with the love planet in the money house there are opportunities for business partnerships or joint ventures. Important financial information will come in dreams and hunches, and through psychics, tarot readers, astrologers and spiritual channels. Often – especially for those of you who know how to read the signs – nature herself, through animals and insects, will deliver financial messages. Take note of the dream life on the 18th and 19th – it has financial significance.

Drive more defensively from the 11th to the 14th. This goes for siblings and sibling figures in your life as well. Mars and Uranus are travelling together.

Mars's move into your 4th house of home and family on the 14th is excellent for making repairs or renovations in the home. (Venus, your family planet, travels with Pluto most of the month – and is most close on the 22nd and 23rd. This reinforces the above.) A parent or parent figure has a very nice social experience. You can have a happy career opportunity.

March

Best Days Overall: 3, 4, 13, 14, 21, 22, 30, 31
Most Stressful Days Overall: 10, 11, 17, 18, 23, 24
Best Days for Love: 3, 4, 8, 9, 15, 16, 17, 18, 23, 24, 25, 26
Best Days for Money: 5, 6, 7, 8, 9, 15, 16, 17, 18, 23, 24, 25, 26
Best Days for Career: 1, 2, 10, 11, 19, 20, 23, 24, 27, 28, 29

Avoid speculations during Mercury's retrograde from the 5th to the 28th. Be more patient with children and children figures in your life as they seem to lack direction that period. You're still very much in a yearly financial peak until the 20th. It is even stronger than last month. The Sun travels with your financial planet Neptune on the 15th and 16th and will boost earnings. The current love and social contacts are very supportive. A partnership or joint venture opportunity is likely to come. Those of you who invest can profit from mergers in your portfolio.

Mercury will camp out – make a station – on your financial planet from the 24th to the 31st. This should bring luck in speculations – but be careful until the 28th. Those involved in the creative arts receive marketable artistic inspiration.

The lower half, the night side of your Horoscope, is dominant now. On the 7th, Uranus, the ruler of your Horoscope, enters your 4th house of family, where he will stay for the next seven years. Mars has been in your 4th house since February 14 and remains there all this month too. Your 10th house of career, by contrast, is empty. Only the Moon will visit there on the 23rd and 24th. So this is a time to focus on the home, family and your personal emotional health and wellness. With your family planet, Venus, and Uranus in 'mutual reception' (each is a guest in the house of the other), there is good cooperation with the family and much progress will be made. With Mars still in your 4th house this is a good month for renovations and repairs.

Love is happy this month. Venus is in your sign until the 26th, bringing beauty, grace and charm to the image. Personal appearance shines. The love planet in the money house until the 20th shows that wealth is a romantic allurement. The spiritual connection is important too. You like spiritual people, but they also need to be materially well-off. Romantic and social opportunities happen as you pursue your financial and spiritual goals, and with people involved in these things. On the 20th your love planet moves into Aries, signalling that you are more a 'love at first sight' kind of person now. You tend to leap before you look. Love is close to home and in the neighbourhood, and perhaps with neighbours. The gift of the gab turns you on. People who are easy to communicate with turn you on. Love and social opportunities happen in educational-type settings – in schools, lectures, seminars, workshops, libraries and bookstores.

April

Best Days Overall: 9, 10, 17, 18, 26, 27
Most Stressful Days Overall: 6, 7, 8, 13, 14, 19, 20
Best Days for Love: 2, 3, 4, 5, 11, 12, 13, 14, 21, 24
Best Days for Money: 1, 2, 3, 4, 5, 11, 12, 13, 14, 19, 20, 22, 23, 29, 30
Best Days for Career: 7, 8, 15, 16, 19, 20, 24, 25

There's a lot of change going on at home and with the family. Venus's solstice from the 22nd to the 25th suggests a need for a pause and change of direction. For this is what she is doing in the Heavens. You are in the midnight hour of your year, beginning the 20th. So career is not that big an issue. But Saturn's conjunction with Pluto, your career planet, this month suggests a need to further the career through involvement with charities and causes that you believe in. But it also favours furthering the career by inner, spiritual means – through visualization, meditation, getting into the mood (the psychological state) of where you want to be – rather than by overt physical actions. And, this is in harmony with power in your 4th house. You're in a preparation stage careerwise. You're building on the internal levels.

Health needs more attention from the 20th onwards. There is nothing serious afoot, only a period of lower-than-usual energy. This can make you more vulnerable to problems. So, as always, make sure to get enough rest. Enhance the health in the ways mentioned in the yearly report. The period when the moon is waning, from the 1st to the 5th and from 19th onwards, favours detox regimes.

Your 3rd house of communication and intellectual interests became powerful on March 20, and is still powerful (even more so) until the 20th of this month. This is a nice aspect for students below college level as it indicates focus on their studies. The mind is sharper and the communication skills are better than usual. When the 3rd house is strong we all become students. We read more, take classes and increase our knowledge base. The mind is active and yearns for exercise. Sometimes however it gets overactive and out of control. This can deplete energy and cause all kinds of nerve or sleep disorders. So use the mind, but turn it off when not in use. Meditation is a big help here.

Love is still happy this month. Your love planet travels with Uranus from the 21st to the 23rd, indicating romantic meetings for singles. But all of you will have more romance over that period, and probably happy social experiences. Love can still be found in the neighbourhood and in educational settings until the 20th. Good mental and intellectual compatibility is important to you. After the 20th, as the Sun moves into your 4th house, emotional intimacy becomes important. You show love by giving emotional support, and this is how you feel loved too. Often with the love planet in this position old flames from the past come back into the picture (or sometimes it is someone who reminds you of the old flame). This is generally to help resolve old issues, and to clear the way for future love.

May

Best Days Overall: 6, 7, 15, 16, 24, 25
Most Stressful Days Overall: 4, 5, 10, 11, 17, 18, 31
Best Days for Love: 2, 3, 4, 5, 10, 11, 13, 14, 21, 23, 24, 31
Best Days for Money: 2, 3, 8, 9, 10, 11, 17, 18, 19, 20, 26, 27, 29, 30
Best Days for Career: 4, 5, 13, 14, 17, 18, 21, 22, 31

Mars went 'out of bounds' on April 21 and will be this way all month (actually until June 12). So your intellectual tastes, your reading, is broadening out beyond your normal sphere. Perhaps you're attending lectures or classes in out of the way places and in out of the way subjects. Siblings and sibling figures in your life are also outside their normal haunts these days. Mercury, the generic intellectual planet, will also go 'out of bounds' this month, from the 28th onwards, and this reinforces the above. Children and children figures in your life are also outside their normal spheres.

Health still needs watching until the 21st. So, as always, make sure to get enough rest. When the Moon waxes and grows from the 4th to the 18th, it would be beneficial to add things that the body needs – vitamins, minerals or other supplements. The Moon's waning period – from the 1st to the 4th and from the 18th onwards – favours detox regimes: getting rid of things that don't belong in the body. Health will improve after the 21st – and it will be dramatic. Perhaps some pill, therapy or supplement will get the credit, but the reality is the shifting of the planetary energy in your favour.

Your 4th house of home and family is still powerful until the 21st, so continue to downplay the career and focus on the home, family and, most importantly, your emotional wellness.

On the 15th the planetary power begins to shift to the Western, social sector of your chart. So it is time to improve and perfect your social skills. Other people – their needs and interests – become more important. Personal independence is weakened now, by cosmic design. You get things through cooperation and consensus now rather than by direct action. Let other people have their way so long as it isn't destructive.

Finances are good this month, especially until the 21st. Your financial planet Neptune is receiving helpful aspects and earnings should be strong. After the 21st you will have to work harder to achieve your financial goals. However, if you put in the extra effort (the key word here) you will prosper. Avoid speculations after the 21st.

Your love planet remains in your 4th house until the 21st, so review our discussion of this from last month. It signals more socializing at home and with the family (this is especially so from the 17th to the 19th). Family and family connections like to play Cupid and make introductions. Try to live in the moment in love matters. The tendency is to try to recapture old experiences. The experience of the now is always to be preferred.

On the 21st the Sun moves on into your 5th house of fun, creativity and children and you begin one of your yearly personal pleasure peaks. Love is all about fun now rather than commitment or responsibility. It is another form of entertainment, like going to the movies or the theatre.

June

Best Days Overall: 2, 3, 11, 12, 20, 21, 30
Most Stressful Days Overall: 1, 7, 8, 13, 14, 27, 28, 29
Best Days for Love: 1, 2, 3, 7, 8, 11, 12, 20, 21, 22
Best Days for Money: 5, 6, 7, 8, 13, 14, 15, 16, 23, 24, 25, 26
Best Days for Career: 1, 9, 10, 13, 14, 18, 19, 27, 28, 29

The two intellectual planets in your chart, Mercury (the generic ruler) and Mars (the actual ruler), are both still 'out of bounds'. So review our discussion of this last month: the trend is still in effect. Mars returns to his normal path on the 12th and Mercury follows on the 16th.

Health is much improved over last month and is very good now. By the 9th, as Venus moves away from her stressful aspect, there will be only one long-term planet in stressful alignment with you, and this will be the situation until the 29th (Mercury moves into stressful alignment then). All the other planets are either making nice aspects or leaving you alone. Yet, you seem focused on health. Mars will be in your 6th house of health and work all month; Mercury joins him on the 4th and the Sun enters there on the 21st. Since your health is good, this focus probably involves lifestyle changes or preventive measures. Sometimes it can indicate hypochondria, or a tendency to magnify minor things into major issues. Be careful about this. Your health is basically good, and 'if it ain't broke, don't fix it'.

You're still in a yearly personal pleasure period – your second of the year – until the 21st. This is the time to explore the many joys of life. Joy is really a choice, a spiritual choice that we make. It is all around us and not dependent on physical conditions. Those of you on the spiritual path will understand what is being said here. Joy is not only a healing force in and of itself, but it relaxes the mind so that solutions to problems can come in. Sometimes the knottiest problem can be solved by watching a good movie or doing some fun, creative thing. When you turn your mind to the problem again, the solution comes to you. The anxiety and focus on the problem was blocking the solution.

Love is still about fun and entertainment. You're attracted to people who can show you a good time. You don't seem very serious about love, and you're probably attracting non-serious people too. Mercury's move into your 7th house on the 27th reinforces this. (Mercury rules your 5th house of fun.) His position favours love affairs rather than serious romance. On the 21st your love planet moves into your 6th house of work and you get a bit more serious. Emotional intimacy becomes important. Family values too. Love is expressed through practical service. The moonlit dinners on the beach are nice, but you like the person who can fix your computer.

July

Best Days Overall: 1, 8, 9, 17, 18, 19, 27, 28
Most Stressful Days Overall: 4, 5, 10, 11, 25, 26, 31
Best Days for Love: 1, 2, 3, 4, 5, 10, 11, 20, 21, 31
Best Days for Money: 2, 3, 4, 5, 10, 11, 13, 14, 20, 21, 22, 23, 24, 29, 30, 31
Best Days for Career: 6, 7, 10, 11, 15, 16, 25, 26

Two eclipses this month are almost (but not quite) repeats of the eclipses of January. Happily these do not affect you too much.

The solar eclipse of the 2nd occurs in your 6th house and announces job changes – either within your present place of employment or with another. There are disturbances at work. If you employ others there can be hirings and firings, and dramas in the personal lives of employees. The good news is that your 6th house is very strong and there are plenty of good job opportunities out there. This eclipse can produce health scares too, and over the next few months there can be dramatic changes to your health regime. Overall your health is good – your constitution is strong and disease resistant. So, there is probably nothing to the health scare. (This month though, especially after the 23rd, you'll have to keep an eye on your health.) Once again love gets tested, as the Sun, the eclipsed planet, is your love planet. So be more patient with the beloved over this period. He or she can be having personal dramas that have nothing to do with your relationship, but can impact on it.

The lunar eclipse of the 16th occurs in your 12th house of spiritual-ity – the second eclipse of the year in this house. So again, as in January, course corrections are needed in the spiritual life and practice. There are more shake-ups and disturbances – perhaps even crises – in spiritual and charitable organizations, and more dramas in the lives of guru or guru figures. Friends have financial shake-ups and need to make changes. This lunar eclipse announces job changes too (every lunar eclipse does) and, since it impacts on your career planet, Pluto, it can bring changes in the career as well. There are shake-ups in your company or industry. Bosses, parents, parent figures – authority figures in your life – are having personal dramas.

The eclipses are the major headline of the month, but a second high-light is the love life. Your 7th house of love becomes very powerful from the 23rd onwards, initiating a yearly love and social peak. The love life is very active. Singles have many romantic opportunities – perhaps too many. But because these planets in your 7th house are stressfully aligned to you, there is a need for more work to keep the relationship together. Singles have to work harder on their social life. The social life is active but a serious romance or marriage isn't likely. Next month seems better for love than now.

Reduce your schedule from the 9th to the 12th, and drive more care-fully at that time too. Be more patient with siblings and sibling figures as they seem stressed. Neighbours too.

August

Best Days Overall: 4, 5, 14, 15, 23, 24, 25
Most Stressful Days Overall: 1, 7, 8, 21, 22, 28, 29
Best Days for Love: 1, 9, 10, 20, 21, 28, 29, 30, 31
Best Days for Money: 1, 7, 8, 9, 10, 16, 17, 19, 20, 26, 27, 28, 29
Best Days for Career: 2, 3, 7, 8, 11, 12, 21, 22, 30, 31

You're in the midst of a yearly love and social peak until the 23rd. The social life is hyperactive right now; 40 per cent, sometimes 50 per cent of the planets are in your 7th house or moving through there this month – a big percentage. So you are mixing with many different kinds of people these days. But all of this seems exploratory; romance will actually be better after the 23rd than before. There will be more harmony. The 29th and 30th seem best for romance or a serious relationship. Until then you're more or less 'testing the waters'.

Health needs more attention this month – especially until the 23rd. As always make sure to get enough rest. This is always your number one priority healthwise. The waxing Moon, from the 1st to the 15th and the 30th and 31st, is the best period for adding things to the body – vitamins, minerals, supplements, etc., while the 15th to the 30th is good for getting rid of things that don't belong in the body – detox regimes. Enhance the health in the ways mentioned in the yearly report. Also give more attention to the heart until the 23rd. Chest massage and massaging the heart reflexology point (see the chart in the yearly report, page 326) will be beneficial. Health will improve dramatically after the 23rd.

By the 11th of this month the planetary power has shifted to the upper, day side of your Horoscope. It is morning in your year. Time to be up and about and focused on the activities of the day. Time to pursue outer objectives in physical, overt ways. Pluto, your career planet, has been retrograde since April 24 and is still moving backward this month. However, after the 23rd he starts to receive very positive kinds of aspects, so happy things are happening careerwise, albeit with a delayed reaction.

The element of Earth is very strong this month, especially after the 18th. People are 'down to earth' and interested in practical things.

Your high intelligence and ideas are probably not much appreciated now. Yet, they are needed. Too much Earth can stifle abstract thinking. If you're communicating ideas, make sure to emphasize their practical side.

Finances are stressed after the 23rd. This is a temporary condition caused by the short-term planets and is not a long-term trend. You just have to work harder to achieve your financial goals. The retrograde of your financial planet Neptune since June 21 further complicates things. Your mission – especially this month – is to gain mental clarity on your finances. This is 90 per cent of the battle.

September

Best Days Overall: 1, 2, 10, 11, 20, 21, 28, 29
Most Stressful Days Overall: 3, 4, 17, 18, 19, 24, 25, 30
Best Days for Love: 7, 8, 9, 20, 21, 24, 25, 28, 29
Best Days for Money: 3, 4, 5, 6, 12, 13, 14, 15, 16, 22, 23, 24, 25
Best Days for Career: 3, 4, 8, 9, 18, 19, 26, 27, 30

Health is much improved this month. It will get even better from the 14th onwards, as Mercury and Venus start making harmonious aspects to you. It further improves after the 23rd.

Your 8th house of regeneration gained strength on August 23 and is still very strong until the 23rd of this month, signalling a period for expanding by 'cutting back' – a seeming oxymoron, but true. When vines or trees are pruned and cut back, the fruit grows better. Extraneous branches divert energy from where it needs to go. Cutting back – some people call it detoxing or de-cluttering – is an 8th house activity. Simplification might be a better word. We simplify life and our environment by getting rid of what we don't use or need. You will be amazed at how much energy is released by this. So, go through your belongings and remove what you don't need or use – sell them or give them to charity. It is also good to take stock of the mental and emotional life in this way too. Ideas and feelings that are not helpful should be removed (meditation can accomplish this).

On a more mundane level, with power in the 8th house, the spouse, partner or current love is prospering. He or she is having a great financial month. It is a good month to either borrow or pay off debt – according to your need. Good for tax, insurance and estate planning too (for those of you of appropriate age). And, it is a period of high libido.

Career is important this month, but Pluto is still retrograde, and after the 14th he is receiving stressful aspects. So there are more challenges involved in the career. With extra work you'll succeed. The main problem is getting the right direction. This will happen next month. Career issues go much better before the 14th than afterwards.

Finances are still stressful. Your financial planet is still retrograde and is also receiving stressful aspects. So you just have to work harder to achieve your financial goals. Debt could be burdensome right now. You will see improvement after the 23rd.

Love is still happy. Sexual magnetism seems the most important attraction until the 23rd. Love opportunities could happen at funerals, wakes and as you pay condolence visits. They may also happen as you pursue your goals of personal reinvention and transformation.

On the 23rd, your love planet moves into your 9th house, and you tend now to be attracted to ministers, worship leaders, professors and highly educated people. Foreigners are also alluring. You like people you can learn from. College, religious functions and foreign lands are venues for romance. Philosophical differences are probably the main cause for marital break-ups, though this is not well known. Philosophical harmony – a similar world view – is very important in love.

October

Best Days Overall: 7, 8, 17, 18, 26, 27
Most Stressful Days Overall: 1, 15, 16, 21, 22, 28, 29
Best Days for Love: 7, 8, 10, 11, 17, 18, 19, 20, 21, 22, 28, 29
Best Days for Money: 1, 2, 3, 4, 10, 11, 12, 13, 19, 20, 21, 22, 28, 29, 30, 31
Best Days for Career: 1, 5, 6, 15, 16, 23, 24, 28, 29

A lot of positive things are happening in the career and there is a successful month ahead, Aquarius. For a start, your career planet Pluto moves forward on the 3rd, bringing more confidence and clarity about career issues now. Your 10th career house also becomes more power-ful day by day: on the 3rd Mercury moves there; on the 8th, Venus moves in; and on the 23rd, the Sun enters there. You begin a yearly career peak. Usually when career is important there is a neglect of the home and family. But here with your family planet, Venus, in the 10th house this won't happen. You have career support from the family. You have their encouragement. Your success is their success. Mercury in your 10th house shows the support of children and children figures in your life. They seem very involved here. Children, children figures and the family as a whole are elevated in status this month. The Sun in your 10th house signals the support of the current love and your social connections too. After the 23rd a lot of your socializing is career-re-lated. It's one of the ways you advance the career.

Health will need more watching from the 23rd onwards. The demands of the career are strong but you can't let it affect your health. Make sure to schedule some rest periods into your diary. Drop less important things to schedule in more massages or health treatments. Enhance the health in the ways mentioned in the yearly report. The Moon's waxing phase, from the 1st to the 13th and the 28th to the 31st, is best for adding things that the body needs – vitamins, minerals and the like. From the 13th to the 28th, however, as the Moon wanes, is good for detoxing.

Love is happy until the 23rd but afterwards gets more complicated. Until that date, the love planet is in your 9th house. So, like last month, you are attracted to foreigners, religious and highly educated types of people. Mentor types. Romantic opportunities happen at educational and religious-type functions. People at your place of worship like to make introductions. Romance can happen in foreign countries too. After the 23rd, however, you and the beloved seem on opposite sides of the fence, distant from each other. This doesn't necessarily mean physical distance, but mental and emotional distance. You see things in opposite ways and have opposite opinions about things. The chal-lenge will be to bridge your differences – easier said than done. If you can, you have a strong relationship. The 27th and 28th seem the most troubled time. Happily it is a short-term problem.

The Sun moves into your 10th house from the 23rd onwards, indi-cating an allurement for successful and powerful people – people who have achieved something in life – people who can help you careerwise. And, you're meeting these kinds of people. For singles this shows office romances. The opportunity will be there.

November

Best Days Overall: 3, 4, 5, 13, 14, 22, 23
Most Stressful Days Overall: 11, 12, 18, 19, 24, 25
Best Days for Love: 6, 7, 8, 9, 16, 17, 18, 19, 26, 29
Best Days for Money: 6, 7, 8, 9, 10, 16, 17, 18, 19, 24, 25, 26, 27
Best Days for Career: 1, 2, 11, 12, 20, 21, 24, 25, 28, 29, 30

Finances improved last month from the 23rd onwards and they are still good until the 22nd of this month. Neptune will finally move forward on the 27th and clarity and confidence are returning to the financial life. Before that, he is receiving good aspects until the 22nd. Mercury is retrograde from the 2nd to the 20th. Best to avoid speculations during that time (though you will be sorely tempted). After the 22nd there is some financial disagreement with the beloved. It is a short-term problem, however. Don't make important financial moves until after the 27th.

You're still in the midst of a yearly career peak until the 22nd so success is happening. Mars's move into your 10th house on the 19th indicates a need for aggressive action – perhaps there is some conflict with competitors. Siblings and sibling figures are involved in your career. Your good communication skills and knowledge are contributing to your success.

Your love planet will be in your 10th house of career until the 22nd so, like last month, you favour powerful people, people above you in status. You advance the career in social ways, by attending or perhaps hosting the right parties and gatherings. Your social grace – your likeability – is playing a big role in your career.

On the 22nd the love planet moves into your 11th house. So love opportunities happen online, on social networks and as you get involved with groups and professional organizations. The love planet is in fiery Sagittarius, and this is a 'love at first sight' kind of energy. You can jump into relationships very quickly, sometimes too quickly.

Friends might want to be more than that. Others will enjoy making introductions.

Health improves after the 22nd. Be more mindful on the physical plane between the 22nd and 25th. Drive more defensively, and see to it that your car is roadworthy. Communications can be erratic that period too. You and a sibling, sibling figure or neighbour are not getting on. (This will pass next month.)

Your family planet Venus travels with Jupiter from the 22nd to the 24th. A parent or parent figure prospers now. Children and children figures have romance or happy social experiences (much depends on their age).

On the 19th the planetary power shifts once more to the East – the sector of self. Personal independence begins to grow stronger day by day. It is easier now to have your way. The only issue is knowing what your way is: Uranus, the ruler of your Horoscope, is still retrograde.

December

Best Days Overall: 1, 2, 11, 12, 19, 20, 28, 29
Most Stressful Days Overall: 8, 9, 15, 16, 21, 22
Best Days for Love: 6, 7, 8, 9, 15, 16, 17, 18, 26, 28, 29
Best Days for Money: 3, 4, 5, 8, 13, 14, 17, 21, 22, 26, 31
Best Days for Career: 8, 9, 17, 18, 21, 22, 26, 27

For two years now, your spiritual life and practice has been about discipline – it has been an effort. You practised with teeth clenched and shoulders hunched. You bore down. A lot of this is good. It's the daily discipline, day in, day out, feeling good or feeling bad, that takes us to the goal. But now, an element of joy enters the picture. Benevolent, jovial Jupiter enters your 12th house on the 3rd and stays there well into next year. Your practice will become more joyful. You won't be doing it out of a sense of duty, but because you enjoy it. Progress will be a lot swifter. Because Jupiter rules your 11th house, the spiritual side of astrology will become interesting and will unfold for you. It is a valid spiritual path in the coming year.

Though we have another solar eclipse this month, the month ahead is happy. There are only two planets, excluding the Moon (whose effects are temporary), in stressful alignment with you after the 9th. So, health is relatively good. Jupiter's move into Capricorn brings financial increase too – especially from the 13th to the 17th. The planetary power is now almost all in the Eastern sector of the chart and personal independence is strong. You can have your way in life now – but you still need clarity on what your way is. Uranus is still moving backward.

The solar eclipse of the 26th occurs in your 12th house of spirituality, the third eclipse of the year in that house. So there are more spiritual changes happening – and good ones. Often these changes happen because of interior revelation and not because of disaster. When a new revelation happens it is normal to change the practice and teaching. But sometimes it happens because of a shocking event – a loving tap from above. Once again, there are shake-ups in a spiritual or charitable organization you're involved with. Gurus and guru figures have personal dramas. And, since Jupiter is impacted by this eclipse, your high-tech equipment – computers, software and gadgetry – gets tested. There are dramas in the lives of friends and friendships get tested. And, as we saw in January and July, the marriage or current relationship gets tested again. If your relationship has survived the eclipses of January and July, it will survive this one too. The beloved has personal dramas and more patience is needed.

Pisces

THE FISH

Birthdays from
19th February to
20th March

Personality Profile

PISCES AT A GLANCE

Element – Water

Ruling Planet – Neptune
   Career Planet – Jupiter
   Love Planet – Mercury
   Money Planet – Mars
   Planet of Health and Work – Sun
   Planet of Home and Family Life – Mercury
   Planet of Love Affairs, Creativity and Children – Moon

Colours – aqua, blue-green

Colours that promote love, romance and social harmony – earth tones,
   yellow, yellow-orange

Colours that promote earning power – red, scarlet

Gem – white diamond

Metal – tin

Scent – lotus

Quality – mutable (= flexibility)

Qualities most needed for balance – structure and the ability to handle form

Strongest virtues – psychic power, sensitivity, self-sacrifice, altruism

Deepest needs – spiritual illumination, liberation

Characteristics to avoid – escapism, keeping bad company, negative moods

Signs of greatest overall compatibility – Cancer, Scorpio

Signs of greatest overall incompatibility – Gemini, Virgo, Sagittarius

Sign most helpful to career – Sagittarius

Sign most helpful for emotional support – Gemini

Sign most helpful financially – Aries

Sign best for marriage and/or partnerships – Virgo

Sign most helpful for creative projects – Cancer

Best Sign to have fun with – Cancer

Signs most helpful in spiritual matters – Scorpio, Aquarius

Best day of the week – Thursday

Understanding a Pisces

If Pisces have one outstanding quality it is their belief in the invisible, spiritual and psychic side of things. This side of things is as real to them as the hard earth beneath their feet – so real, in fact, that they will often ignore the visible, tangible aspects of reality in order to focus on the invisible and so-called intangible ones.

Of all the signs of the zodiac, the intuitive and emotional faculties of the Pisces are the most highly developed. They are committed to living by their intuition and this can at times be infuriating to other people – especially those who are materially, scientifically or technically orientated. If you think that money, status and worldly success are the only goals in life, then you will never understand a Pisces.

Pisces have intellect, but to them intellect is only a means by which they can rationalize what they know intuitively. To an Aquarius or a Gemini the intellect is a tool with which to gain knowledge. To a well-developed Pisces it is a tool by which to express knowledge.

Pisces feel like fish in an infinite ocean of thought and feeling. This ocean has many depths, currents and undercurrents. They long for purer waters where the denizens are good, true and beautiful, but they are sometimes pulled to the lower, murkier depths. Pisces know that they do not generate thoughts but only tune in to thoughts that already exist; this is why they seek the purer waters. This ability to tune in to higher thoughts inspires them artistically and musically.

Since Pisces is so spiritually orientated – though many Pisces in the corporate world may hide this fact – we will deal with this aspect in greater detail, for otherwise it is difficult to understand the true Pisces personality.

There are four basic attitudes of the spirit. One is outright scepticism – the attitude of secular humanists. The second is an intellectual or emotional belief, where one worships a far-distant God-figure – the attitude of most modern church-going people. The third is not only belief but direct personal spiritual experience – this is the attitude of some 'born-again' religious people. The fourth is actual unity with the divinity, an intermingling with the spiritual world – this is the attitude of yoga. This fourth attitude is the deepest urge of a

Pisces, and a Pisces is uniquely qualified to pursue and perform this work.

Consciously or unconsciously, Pisces seek this union with the spiritual world. The belief in a greater reality makes Pisces very tolerant and understanding of others – perhaps even too tolerant. There are instances in their lives when they should say 'enough is enough' and be ready to defend their position and put up a fight. However, because of their qualities it takes a good deal to get them into that frame of mind.

Pisces basically want and aspire to be 'saints'. They do so in their own way and according to their own rules. Others should not try to impose their concept of saintliness on a Pisces, because he or she always tries to find it for him- or herself.

Finance

Money is generally not that important to Pisces. Of course they need it as much as anyone else, and many of them attain great wealth. But money is not generally a primary objective. Doing good, feeling good about oneself, peace of mind, the relief of pain and suffering – these are the things that matter most to a Pisces.

Pisces earn money intuitively and instinctively. They follow their hunches rather than their logic. They tend to be generous and perhaps overly charitable. Almost any kind of misfortune is enough to move a Pisces to give. Although this is one of their greatest virtues, Pisces should be more careful with their finances. They should try to be more choosy about the people to whom they lend money, so that they are not being taken advantage of. If they give money to charities they should follow it up to see that their contributions are put to good use. Even when Pisces are not rich, they still like to spend money on helping others. In this case they should really be careful, however: they must learn to say no sometimes and help themselves first.

Perhaps the biggest financial stumbling block for the Pisces is general passivity – a *laissez faire* attitude. In general Pisces like to go with the flow of events. When it comes to financial matters, especially, they need to be more aggressive. They need to make things happen, to create their own wealth. A passive attitude will only cause loss and missed opportunity. Worrying about financial security will not provide that security. Pisces need to go after what they want tenaciously.

Career and Public Image

Pisces like to be perceived by the public as people of spiritual or material wealth, of generosity and philanthropy. They look up to big-hearted, philanthropic types. They admire people engaged in large-scale undertakings and eventually would like to head up these big enterprises themselves. In short, they like to be connected with big organizations that are doing things in a big way.

If Pisces are to realize their full career and professional potential they need to travel more, educate themselves more and learn more about the actual world. In other words, they need some of the unflagging optimism of Sagittarius in order to reach the top.

Because of their caring and generous characteristics, Pisces often choose professions through which they can touch the lives of other people. That is why many Pisces become doctors, nurses, social workers or teachers. Sometimes it takes a while before Pisces realize what they really want to do professionally, but once they find a career that lets them manifest their interests and virtues they excel at it.

Love and Relationships

It is not surprising that someone as 'otherworldly' as the Pisces would like a partner who is practical and down to earth. Pisces prefer a partner who is on top of all the details of life, because they dislike details. Pisces seek this quality in both their romantic and professional partners. More than anything else this gives Pisces a feeling of being grounded, of being in touch with reality.

As expected, these kinds of relationships – though necessary – are sure to have many ups and downs. Misunderstandings will take place because the two attitudes are poles apart. If you are in love with a Pisces you will experience these fluctuations and will need a lot of patience to see things stabilize. Pisces are moody, intuitive, affectionate and difficult to get to know. Only time and the right attitude will yield Pisces' deepest secrets. However, when in love with a Pisces you will find that riding the waves is worth it because they are good, sensitive people who need and like to give love and affection.

When in love, Pisces like to fantasize. For them fantasy is 90 per cent of the fun of a relationship. They tend to idealize their partner, which can be good and bad at the same time. It is bad in that it is difficult for anyone to live up to the high ideals their Pisces lover sets.

Home and Domestic Life

In their family and domestic life Pisces have to resist the tendency to relate only by feelings and moods. It is unrealistic to expect that your partner and other family members will be as intuitive as you are. There's a need for more verbal communication between a Pisces and his or her family. A cool, unemotional exchange of ideas benefits everyone.

Some Pisces tend to like mobility and moving around. For them too much stability feels like a restriction on their freedom. They hate to be locked in one location for ever.

The sign of Gemini sits on the cusp of Pisces' 4th solar house of home and family. This shows that Pisces likes and needs a home environment that promotes intellectual and mental interests. They tend to treat their neighbours as family – or extended family. Some Pisceans can have a dual attitude towards the home and family – on the one hand they like the emotional support of the family, but on the other they dislike the obligations, restrictions and duties involved with it. For Pisces, finding a balance is the key to a happy family life.

Horoscope for 2019

Major Trends

With spiritual Neptune in your 1st house, as he has been for many years now (and he'll be there for many more to come), the main challenge is to keep your feet on the ground and not drift off to some dream space – especially when you're driving or doing worldly work. Stay in the body. Practise mindfulness. Focus on what you're doing. The body is becoming very refined and sensitized these days – and it has been going on for a long time. We'll discuss this further later on.

Jupiter will spend almost all year in your 10th house. So you're in a very powerful career year. There is much success happening this year.

Uranus has spent the past seven years in your money house, and he'll remain there until March 7. You've gone through huge financial changes and many extreme ups and downs (much more than the normal ups and downs). This is starting to stabilize this year. Earnings will be smoother. In March Uranus will enter your 3rd house, signalling multiple school changes for students below the college level over the next few years. Intellectual interests become a very unstable area. Your taste in reading is always spiritual, but soon science and technology will become more interesting.

Your 11th house of friends and groups has been powerful for many years: Pluto has been there since 2008. Last year Saturn entered this house. And, towards the end of the year – after December 3 – Jupiter will move there. The 11th house is easily the strongest house in your Horoscope this year. Thus the year ahead is very social.

Love and romance don't seem like big issues this year. The tendency will be to the status quo. More details later.

We will have five eclipses this year, instead of the more usual four. Of the five, four will impact on health and work. So there are job changes happening and changes in the health regime. More on this later. Three of the eclipses will impact on your friendships, bringing much turmoil here too.

Your strongest interests this year will be the body and image; finance (until March 7); communication and intellectual interests (from March 7 onwards); career (until December 3); and friends, groups and group activities.

Your paths of greatest fulfilment this year are children, fun and creativity; career (until December 3); and friends, groups and group activities (from December 3 onwards).

Health

(Please note that this is an astrological perspective on health and not a medical one. In days of yore there was no difference, both of these perspectives were identical. But now there could be quite a difference. For a medical perspective, please consult your doctor or health practitioner.)

Though you're making many changes to your health regime, and perhaps have a few health scares, health is good this year. As the year begins there is only one long-term planet in stressful aspect to you. All the others are either in harmonious alignment or leaving you alone. Moreover, by the end of the year – after December 3 – there will be no long-term planets stressing you out. All will be in harmonious aspect. So, health and energy are super these days and getting better as the year progresses.

Understand that there will be periods in the year where health is less easy than usual – perhaps even stressful. These are caused by the temporary transits of the short-term planets and are not trends for the year. When these transits pass your naturally good health returns.

If there have been long-term pre-existing conditions they are most likely to be in abeyance now and less troubling than they have been. Your greater energy gives you more resistance to them.

Your health is good, but you can make it even better. Give more attention to the following – the vulnerable areas of your Horoscope (the reflexology points are shown in the chart above):

Important foot reflexology points for the year ahead

Try to massage all of the foot on a regular basis – the top of the foot as well as the bottom – but pay extra attention to the points highlighted on the chart. When you massage, be aware of 'sore spots' as these need special attention. It's also a good idea to massage the ankles and below them.

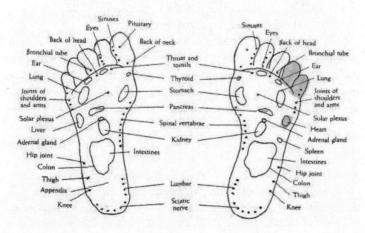

- The feet. These are always important for Pisces as Pisces rules the feet. Regular foot massage should be part of your normal health regime. Going to a professional reflexologer can get expensive, so it might be wise to invest in one of the many gadgets that massage the feet automatically as you're watching TV or at the computer (they are not too expensive). There are machines that give foot whirlpool baths too – these are also good. Keep the feet warm in the winter. Wear shoes that fit and don't knock you off balance. Better to be comfortable than stylish, but sometimes you can have both.
- The heart too is always important for Pisces. The Sun, your health planet, rules the heart. Worry and anxiety are said by spiritual healers to be the root cause of heart problems. So avoid these emotions. Replace them with faith.

Neptune, as we mentioned, has been in your 1st house for many years. While this gives glamour and beauty to the body, it also makes it much more sensitive. The body is being refined and spiritualized. A lot of what you feel in the body is not really you – you're picking up energies from the environment and from people you are in rapport with. Don't identify with these sensations. Just observe them. Think of the body as like a voltmeter or some other measuring device. It's just showing the environmental energies. Many unpleasant experiences can be avoided with this approach.

Year by year you're getting more control over the body. Year by year you're learning how spirit controls the body absolutely. Your ability to mould and shape the body is greatly increased.

Your health planet, the Sun, is a fast-moving planet that in a given year will move through all the signs and houses of your Horoscope, making aspects to all the planets in your Horoscope. So, there are many short-term health trends and changes to your health needs that are best discussed in the monthly reports.

Home and Family

Your 4th house of home and family is basically empty this year. Only short-term planets will move through there and their effects are temporary. This tends to the status quo. The cosmos neither pushes you one way nor another. You have much freedom in this department, but seem to lack interest. If family problems arise it is most likely due to your lack of attention (and will be solved by more attention). Career will be much more important than home and family issues this year.

Mercury is both your love planet and family planet. This shows various things. You like to socialize at home and with the family – and this is a big part of your social life. It indicates a need for a beautiful home. It need not be gaudy or grand, but it needs to have beauty. In some cases the home could be like an art gallery or museum – filled with beautiful paintings or objects. There would also be a need for books. Books and bookcases can be another form of decoration.

Mercury is a fast-moving planet – the fastest of all the planets, except for the Moon. During the year he will move through all the signs and houses in your chart (and often more than once) and make aspects to all the planets (good or bad). Thus there are many short-term family trends that depend on where Mercury is and the aspects he receives. These are better discussed in the monthly reports.

With Mercury as the family planet, family phenomena – the ups and downs of family life – tend to be short term. They come and they go.

One of the parents or parent figures in your life is prospering greatly this year (and his or her prosperity will get even stronger next year). He or she is travelling more this year and needs to watch the weight. If this parent or parent figure is of childbearing age, a pregnancy can happen. There is greater fertility now. There could have been a move last year – this year it is not likely. Another parent or parent figure is having a wonderful social year. If he or she is single there is romance. The social life is much more active than usual. A move would be more likely next year than now. This parent or parent figure is undergoing many profound spiritual changes – this is a long-term trend.

Siblings and sibling figures in your life seem very unsettled these days. Restless. Rebellious. There are family shake-ups and crises. A move could happen, but more likely they will travel around from place to place. The love life seems stressed.

Children and children figures are having a stable family year.

If you're planning major home renovations, March 31 to May 16 would be a good period. If you're redecorating or otherwise beautifying the home, June 9 to July 3 is a good time.

Finance and Career

As we mentioned, big shifts in the financial life are happening this year. You got a taste of it last year when Uranus temporarily left the money house. This year he moves out for the long term.

Uranus in your money house for the past seven years has made you more speculative and risk taking than usual. You favoured start-up companies. The newcomers. You favoured the technology and online worlds. Many of you were earning online. The financial life was exciting, money and opportunity happening at any time in any place, often in the darkest of times. It would happen suddenly and out of the blue. The financial highs were very high when they happened, but the crashes were painful. Extreme volatility would describe your finances over the last few years. Many of you changed brokers, banks and financial planners – perhaps multiple times. You were experimenting in your financial life. You threw out the rule books and learned what worked for you personally. Remember that the rule books deal with 'averages', but you are not average. You are unique. A law unto yourself. By now, you have learned these lessons and there is less of a need to experiment. You more or less know your strategy and approach now.

So, finances become less important after March 7. You're still a risk-taker, but less so than before. You're more settled in these matters.

Your financial planet is Mars. While he is not the fastest of the planets, he is still relatively quick-moving, and this year he moves through eight of your houses. So there will be many short-term financial trends that should be covered in the monthly reports.

With Mars as your financial planet, in this life your purpose is to develop financial courage. The conquest of financial fear is the most important thing. Better to take a financial hit and to conquer the fear than earn in supposedly safe and secure ways. There's nothing wrong with safety and security, but it won't lead to your highest financial potential. Mars favours sports and athletes and the companies that supply them. It favours the military and police departments and the companies that supply them. It favours the steel industry too.

When Uranus leaves your money house on March 7, your important short-term financial goals should have been achieved and you don't need to pay too much more attention here for the rest of the year.

The real headline this year is the career. It looks super. You are a hot item, Pisces. Jupiter, as we have mentioned, occupies your career house almost all year. Thus there are promotions and pay rises (official or unofficial). There is success, recognition and even honours. Your public and professional status is very much elevated. For many of you (it depends on your age) this will a lifetime high. For others, the older readers, it will be one of your lifetime highs.

It is not just about Jupiter moving through your 10th house. It is also that Jupiter is enormously powerful here – your career planet is in your career house, in his own sign and house. He is in his 'comfort zone' and is unusually powerful in this role. And, let's not forget that the Mid-heaven – the top of the chart – is a powerful position in its own right – regardless of the sign.

Even powerful Jupiter in the 10th house will not make the office clerk a managing director, but the clerk will rise above the present status. We always have to look at things in context. With an enlarged public and professional profile you attract happy career opportunities to yourself.

Short-term career goals are likely attained by the end of the year and your focus will shift to friendships and groups when your career planet moves into your 11th house on December 3. This is the fruit – the consequence – of career success. You meet new and significant people. You have better friends.

You have job changes – perhaps a few of them – in the coming year. As we mentioned, four out of the five eclipses impact on the job. These changes can be within your present company or with another one. It shows changes in the conditions of work and the workplace too. With career going so well, these job changes are likely to be positive.

Love and Social Life

Your 7th house of love and romance is not a house of power this year, as we mentioned. It is basically empty. Only short-term planets will move through there and the effects will be short-term. Not only that, but there no long-term planets in the Western, social sector of your chart either. So, love doesn't seem a major focus or priority this year. It tends to the status quo. Those who are married will likely stay married, and singles will likely stay single. Keep in mind that there's nothing against serious romance, but nothing especially favouring it either. You seem content with present situation and have no need to make major changes.

With the long-term planets in the Eastern half of your chart, you're in a more independent kind of phase. You're more interested in yourself and your personal goals. This tends to work against romance.

Your most active love and social period this year will be from August 23 to September 22.

Those of you working on the second marriage had great aspects and opportunity last year. This year is more stable. Those working on the third marriage have many opportunities this year. But serious romance is more likely at the end of the year – after December 3. Next year will also be good for romance.

Though love is stable this year, friendships are important – much more important than love. This is an active year for this: three eclipses happen in your 11th house this year. Thus there are many dramas with friends. Friendships will get tested and some will fall by the wayside. The good ones will remain. Much of this testing has nothing really to do with you and the relationship, they involve personal dramas in the lives of your friends. Because your 11th house is so strong, you are focused here; it is important to you and this will tend to bring success in spite of all the testing and challenges. We see at least three important friendships happening this year. This area will get a lot happier after December 3 when Jupiter moves into your 11th house. In fact you might see it as your mission to be there for your friends.

You are attracted to foreigners, highly educated and religious-type people this year. You make friends online, in foreign countries while travelling, and in educational or religious settings. Later in the year you will also be attracted by people of high professional and social status – people of achievement. And you will be meeting these kinds of people.

Mercury, a very fast-moving planet, is your love planet. As we mentioned, during the course of the year he moves through all the sectors of your Horoscope and make aspects with all the planets. So there are many short-term love trends that depend on where he is and the aspects he receives. These are best dealt with in the monthly reports.

Mercury will go retrograde three times this year, from March 5 to March 27, July 7 to August 1, and from November 2 to November 19.

These are times to review the love life, and to avoid making major decisions one way or another.

Self-improvement

Uranus is your spiritual planet. So his move out of Aries and into Taurus on March 7 shows important changes in the spiritual life. You tend to be spiritually experimental by nature, and in the past seven years more so than usual. Now with the spiritual planet in Taurus for most of this year, you become a bit more conservative. I presume that you have learned from your experimentation and can now settle into a more stable path.

In addition, over the past seven years you've made great progress in understanding the spiritual dimensions of wealth. And now you are more or less settled into your understanding.

In the past year you have been more of an activist in your spiritual life. You wanted to express your ideals in physical actions. Perhaps you were overly militant. Perhaps you wanted to force others into your mould (because you believed it was right). This trend quiets down now.

Uranus in your 3rd house of communication is a very nice transit for teachers, writers, journalists, bloggers, advertisers and PR people. You are more inspired and more intuitive in your work. Your work is more creative.

We have discussed some of the ramifications of spiritual Neptune, the ruler of your Horoscope, in your own house. The body becomes much more sensitive. You are more of a Pisces than usual. All the characteristics of your sign – positive and negative – are reinforced, stronger and more prominent. You have the image of a guru-like figure. Some of you will be a guru for many people, some for those in your sphere. Even children will be spiritual teachers for other children. You will be seen that way.

The body's sensitivity needs to be understood properly. It is a major eye opener when you see it and understand it. For example, if you are around people with heart problems, you can feel that in your own heart. It feels physical, but it's not. If you are around people with stomach problems you will feel them too. There is probably nothing wrong with you, but you could feel these energies. Some people have unnecessary and often dangerous medical procedures because of this. Think of your body as a psychic measuring tool, rather than just a lump of meat, a chemical factory or machine. If a meter picks up unusual energy it doesn't mean that something is wrong with the meter. The meter is doing its job.

Psychic sensitivity is a great blessing, but it can be painful at times. Make sure to be around positive, uplifting kinds of people.

The body has no will of its own. It has habits and appetites (we can call these karmic momentums) but no independent will. Sooner or later, it must take on the image that you give it. These days, you are learning this. Your results will be much quicker than usual. Mould the body in the way that suits you. Spirit will teach you.

Month-by-month Forecasts

January

Best Days Overall: 1, 10, 11, 19, 20, 27, 28
Most Stressful Days Overall: 2, 3, 17, 18, 23, 24, 30, 31
Best Days for Love: 1, 4, 5, 12, 13, 15, 16, 21, 22, 23, 24, 25, 30, 31
Best Days for Money: 2, 3, 12, 13, 21, 22, 30, 31
Best Days for Career: 2, 3, 12, 13, 21, 22, 30, 31

Your yearly career peak happened last month, but career is still strong now – and very successful. The planetary power is mostly above the horizon, on the day side of your chart. Your 10th house is strong, while your 4th house of home and family is empty. (Only the Moon will visit your 4th house on the 17th and 18th.) The family was supporting your career goals last month and is still supportive, until the 5th. So continue to focus on your career.

Two eclipses this month are relatively mild on you personally, still it won't hurt to take a more relaxed schedule anyway. (And if these eclipses hit a sensitive point in your personal Horoscope, cast for your exact date and time of birth, they can be powerful indeed.) The solar eclipse of the 6th (in America it happens on the 5th) occurs in your 11th house and affects the ruler of your 11th house, Saturn – a double hit on the affairs of this house. So friendships get tested. Flawed ones will tend to end or get de-emphasized. There will be personal dramas – life-changing kinds of dramas – in the lives of friends. Your high-tech equipment – computers, software, gadgetry – get tested. They seem erratic this period. Technology is a wonderful thing when it's working properly, but when it's not it's a nightmare. So make sure your files are backed up properly and your anti-virus, anti-hacking software is up to date. Parents, parent figures and bosses suffer financial disturbances and need to make changes. Since the Sun rules your 6th house, every solar eclipse affects the job and the health regime. So job changes are happening. There can be disturbances or upheavals at the workplace. If you employ others there are dramas in the lives of employees and perhaps staff turnover. Overall, your health is good, but you will be making important changes to your health regime in the coming months.

The lunar eclipse of the 21st occurs in your 6th house, again bringing job changes and disturbances at the workplace. This is almost a repeat of the earlier solar eclipse. There is a need to make important changes to your health regime – perhaps due to some health scare. Every lunar eclipse affects the children and children figures in your life and this one is no different. There are personal and financial dramas happening with them. They should definitely relax and take it easy over this period. Many Pisceans are involved in the creative arts. This eclipse will signal important changes in their creativity. It will start to take a new direction.

February

Best Days Overall: 6, 7, 15, 16, 24, 25
Most Stressful Days Overall: 13, 14, 19, 20, 26, 27
Best Days for Love: 3, 4, 11, 15, 16, 19, 20, 24, 25, 28
Best Days for Money: 8, 9, 10, 17, 18, 19, 26, 27, 28
Best Days for Career: 9, 10, 17, 18, 26, 27

A happy and prosperous month ahead, Pisces. Enjoy.

All the planets (with the exception of the Moon – and then for only part of the time) are in the independent Eastern sector of your chart.

This is highly unusual. Personal independence is unusually strong. Your personal happiness is important to the cosmos and it is supporting you. Self-esteem and self-confidence are also stronger than usual. Health and energy are good and you can do anything you set your mind to. If you're not happy, no use blaming others. Your happiness is up to you. Make the changes that need to be made; create the conditions that make you happy. You have the power now. With all the planets moving forward this month you will see fast progress to your goals.

The month ahead is very spiritual – your 12th house of spirituality is powerful until the 19th. But with Neptune's presence in your own sign, you will feel the spiritual influences even after the 19th.

Your health is good. After the 3rd there is only one long-term planet – Jupiter – in stressful alignment to you. And, even Jupiter's adverse aspects tend to be mild. Only the Moon (and only some of the time) will make stressful aspects. You can make the health even better with ankle and calf massage until the 19th, and with foot massage afterwards. Spiritual healing and spiritual techniques are always good for you, but this month even more so. If you feel under the weather (unlikely) see a spiritual-type healer.

Love is happy this month. On the 10th your love planet, Mercury, moves into your own sign, bringing happy love opportunities for singles and social opportunities for those already in relationships. There is more grace in the personal appearance too. The 18th and 19th, as your love planet travels with Neptune, are especially good romantic days. Nothing much you need to do – love will find you.

Your financial planet, Mars, has been in your money house since January 1 and is there until the 14th of this month. He is in his own sign and house and thus powerful on your behalf. Earnings are strong (with a few bumps in the road). Mars travels with Uranus from the 11th to the 14th. This brings sudden financial changes. Often it brings sudden, unexpected money or financial opportunity. Sometimes it brings a sudden, unexpected expense, but the money to cover it will also come in unexpected ways. The money people in your life can be having personal dramas at that time.

March

Best Days Overall: 5, 6, 7, 15, 16, 23, 24
Most Stressful Days Overall: 13, 14, 19, 20, 25, 26
Best Days for Love: 3, 4, 5, 6, 7, 15, 16, 19, 20, 23, 24
Best Days for Money: 1, 2, 8, 9, 10, 11, 17, 18, 19, 20, 25, 26, 28, 29
Best Days for Career: 8, 9, 17, 18, 25, 26

Another happy and prosperous month. When the Sun entered your 1st house on February 19 you began one of your yearly personal pleasure peaks. This continues until the 20th. So it is time to treat the body nicely – to give it some pampering – to reward it for the service it has given you all these years. Rarely do people thank their bodies. The body is an intelligence – an empire of trillions of cells. Just taking some time to acknowledge the body's service and thanking it and the individual organs (especially the ones that bother you) will do much to enhance both the health and the personal appearance.

This is an excellent month for jobseekers. Happy job opportunities will come with little effort on your part – you just have to accept or reject them. The 15th and 16th are especially strong for this. This period is also excellent for spiritual healing.

Love is still happy, but lacks direction. Your love planet is still in your sign, showing that love and love opportunities pursue you. Mercury's retrograde from the 5th to the 28th can slow things down but it won't stop love from happening. Social confidence is not what it should be at this time though. Happy romantic opportunities happen from the 24th to the 31st, as Mercury camps out on Neptune.

Health is excellent this month. Self-confidence and self-esteem are at yearly highs. Personal independence likewise. Like last month all the planets (with the exception of the Moon at times) are in the Eastern sector of the self. Your 1st house is chock-full of planets (and benefi-cent ones at that) while your 7th house is empty. (Only the Moon visits there, on the 19th and 20th.) It's a 'me first' kind of month. If you are not for you, who will be? Your happiness is your responsibility. Take the steps necessary to create things according to your specifications. If you create well you will see the results in the months to come. If there are mistakes, you'll have a chance to correct them when your next cycle of personal independence comes.

You can enhance your already good health through foot massage and spiritual techniques, which will be very effective until the 20th. After that, scalp and face massage, physical exercise and craniosacral therapy will be powerful.

A lot of nice things are happening financially this month. Uranus finally leaves your money house for good on the 7th. So, there will be more financial stability. The Sun enters the 2nd house on the 20th and you begin a yearly financial peak. Money comes from work – from your present job or overtime or second jobs. The health field looks like an interesting investment for those of you who invest. Mars, your financial planet, moved into your 3rd house on February 14 and he will be here for the entire month ahead. Mars in Taurus gives sound financial judgement and shows the importance of sales, marketing and good PR in earnings.

April

Best Days Overall: 1, 2, 3, 11, 12, 19, 20, 29, 30
Most Stressful Days Overall: 9, 10, 15, 16, 22, 23
Best Days for Love: 2, 3, 11, 12, 13, 14, 15, 16, 21, 22, 23
Best Days for Money: 4, 5, 9, 10, 13, 14, 17, 18, 22, 23, 26, 27
Best Days for Career: 4, 5, 13, 14, 22, 23

Your financial planet spends April in your 4th house of home and family. Thus you are probably spending more on the home this month. It is a good month for repairs or renovations in the home – if you need to make them. Family support is good. You spend on the home but can also earn from there as well. Family and family connections play an important role. Mars is in stressful aspect with Jupiter this month, so there can be financial disagreements with parents or parent figures. Career success this month can entail some financial sacrifice.

Earnings are still good this month, and you're still in the midst of a yearly financial peak until the 20th. Work is still the main source of income. Your work creates good luck. The Sun's nice aspects with

Jupiter on the 13th and 14th bring happy job opportunities and financial success. The career is boosted as well.

Health is still good, but a little less good than it was for the past few months. Now there are two planets in stressful alignment with you. This is not enough to cause problems, but you can feel it energetically. Enhance the health through scalp and face massage, and physical exercise until the 20th. After the 20th neck massage is beneficial. Craniosacral therapy would be good all month.

Love is better than last month, now that the love planet, Mercury, is moving forward. Love still pursues you until the 17th. Just go about your business and it will find you. On the 17th Mercury moves into your money house, indicating the financial favour of the current love and of your social contacts. They support your financial goals. Love opportunities happen as you pursue your financial goals and with people involved in your finances. The love planet in Aries signals a rashness to love. There is a tendency to jump into things too quickly. When this works out you save a lot of courtship time. But if your intuition is amiss, it can blow up in your face. But no matter; the love planet in Aries shows a need to develop fearlessness in love and social matters. As long as you overcome fear you have succeeded.

The planetary power is now below the horizon of your chart. The night side of your Horoscope now dominates the day side. You're having a successful career year, but now it's good to focus more on the home, family and your emotional well-being. Besides, Jupiter your career planet starts to reverse on the 10th, so many career issues need time to resolve themselves. You can safely downplay career for now.

May

Best Days Overall: 8, 9, 17, 18, 26, 27

Most Stressful Days Overall: 6, 7, 13, 14, 19, 20

Best Days for Love: 2, 3, 13, 14, 21, 23, 24, 31

Best Days for Money: 1, 2, 3, 6, 7, 10, 11, 17, 19, 20, 26, 27, 29, 30

Best Days for Career: 2, 3, 10, 11, 19, 20, 29, 30

The financial focus is gradually winding down. By the 15th of this month the money house will be empty. This I read as a good thing. Short-term financial goals have been more or less achieved and now you have the freedom to pursue other interests – intellectual, psychological and family interests. This is really the purpose of money. It is not an end in itself – though many behave that way – it is only the means by which we can grow as human beings; it buys freedom for self-development.

Your 3rd house of communication and intellectual interests became powerful on April 20 and is still powerful until the 21st. This is wonderful for students below college level. They are focused on their studies and are thus more successful. Also this energy enhances the intellectual and communication faculties. Information is more easily retained. Learning happens quicker. With a strong 3rd house all of us become students. The mind is hungry. There is a yearning for knowledge and information. People tend to talk more than usual too. So this is a good month for taking classes in subjects that interest you. It is also a good month for teaching about subjects that you know about.

Home, family and psychological interests become powerful after the 21st, as the Sun and Mercury enter your 4th house. Your career planet is still retrograde, so give your attention to the home and family. The 4th house (the opposite of the 10th house of career) is seen as its 'complement'. One goes with the other. One supports the other. The career is built on a good stable home and family base and a successful career should foster a more stable home and domestic life. Astrologically speaking, it's merely a question of which side to emphasize at a given time. Now is the time to build the psychological and emotional infrastructure – the foundation – upon which the career can be based. You won't be able to avoid the demands of career altogether, but you can shift more energy to the home – shift the emphasis.

Health needs more attention after the 21st. There is nothing serious afoot, just a period of lower energy. So, as always, make sure to get enough rest. Until the 21st enhance the health through neck massage and craniosacral therapy. After the 21st arm and shoulder massage will be good. Fresh air and right diet is also important.

Your financial planet Mars has been 'out of bounds' since April 21, and will remain so into June. So in finance you need to 'think outside the box' – you need to go beyond your normal sphere and activities to achieve your goals. On the 16th Mars enters your 5th house of fun, creativity and children. This is a happy financial transit. Money comes easily and is spent easily. There is luck in speculations. You spend on happy things and fun activities. There is a happy-go-lucky attitude to money.

June

Best Days Overall: 5, 6, 13, 14, 23, 24
Most Stressful Days Overall: 2, 3, 9, 10, 15, 16, 30
Best Days for Love: 1, 3, 4, 9, 10, 11, 13, 14, 20, 21, 24
Best Days for Money: 4, 5, 7, 8, 13, 14, 15, 16, 23, 24, 25, 26
Best Days for Career: 7, 8, 15, 16, 25, 26

The planetary power is still mostly below the horizon of your chart; your house of home and family is still powerful and your career planet is still retrograde. So, like last month, give more focus on the home and family and especially to your emotional well-being. Career issues need time to resolve – and they will resolve in a good way, eventually.

Health still needs watching until the 21st. As always the most important thing is to get enough rest. You need to maintain high energy levels, the first defence against disease. Diet is important all month. Likewise good emotional health. Problems in the family can be a root cause of health problems, so if, God forbid, there is a problem restore family harmony as quickly as you can. Until the 21st enhance the health with arm and shoulder massage and fresh air. After the 21st water-based therapies are good – soak in the bath or a natural spring. Spiritual-healing techniques become more powerful after the 21st as well. There will be big improvement in health after the 21st.

When the Sun, your health planet, enters your 5th house on the 21st you learn first-hand about the healing power of joy. Joy itself – just being happy – cures many ills. This transit also ushers in a yearly personal pleasure peak.

Your financial planet Mars remains 'out of bounds' until the 12th. So, like last month, you're going outside your normal sphere in search of earnings. It could also be that your business takes you outside your normal haunts. This seems to work though. There are no answers in the 'normal' places and you've needed to look elsewhere. The financial planet in the 5th house all month is a basically happy financial signal. You're earning in happy ways. Earning money is fun. You're spending (and perhaps overspending) on fun things. You're more speculative – but avoid this from the 13th to the 15th and from 18th to the 20th. Foreign travel too is not recommend between the 18th and the 20th. If you must travel, try to schedule your trip around these dates.

Love seems happy this month. As with finance, you're outside your normal social sphere. Your love planet is 'out of bounds' until the 16th and you are mixing with people outside your normal circle. But this seems the right thing these days. Love seems happy. Mercury moves fast this month, signalling social confidence. Singles are dating more and covering more territory. Mercury is in your 5th house from the 4th to the 27th, so you don't seem very serious about love. You just want fun. This aspect favours love affairs rather than serious committed love.

The message of the Horoscope this month is, relax, enjoy your life, stay happy and finance, love and health will take care of themselves.

July

Best Days Overall: 2, 3, 10, 11, 20, 21, 29, 30
Most Stressful Days Overall: 1, 6, 7, 13, 14, 27, 28
Best Days for Love: 1, 4, 5, 6, 7, 10, 11, 14, 20, 21, 29, 30, 31
Best Days for Money: 4, 5, 13, 14, 22, 23, 24, 31
Best Days for Career: 4, 5, 13, 14, 22, 23, 24, 31

Two eclipses this month give an almost repeat performance (but not quite) of the eclipses of January. Happily they seem basically kind to you. The solar eclipse of the 2nd occurs in your 5th house of children, fun and creativity. So children and children figures in your life are having both personal and financial dramas at this time. They should reduce their schedule over this period, for a few days before and after. Financial disturbances show a need for a change in their financial thinking and strategy. For you it shows job changes and disturbances at the workplace. There are dramas in the lives of co-workers and the conditions of work can change. This can also bring a health scare, but since your health is good, it is not likely to be more than that. Still, you will be making further changes to your health regime over the next few months.

The lunar eclipse of the 16th occurs in your 11th house (the second eclipse in that house this year). So friendships get tested and flawed ones may not survive. There are dramas, and in many cases, life-changing events in the lives of friends. High-tech equipment, computers, software and internet access get tested and can behave bizarrely. Hidden flaws are revealed so that you can correct them. As in January, make sure important files are backed up, and that anti-virus, anti-hacking software is up to date. Every lunar eclipse affects children and children figures in your life. Again, let them reduce their schedule over this period and stay out of harm's way. They are redefining themselves once again. They will update the way they think of themselves and the way they want others to think of them. So image and wardrobe updates are in store. Siblings and sibling figures are forced to make important financial changes.

Health is good this month. But if you like you can make it even better through right diet, good emotional health and water-based therapies, until the 23rd. After the 23rd massage the heart's reflexology point shown in the chart in the yearly report (page 357). Chest massage will also be good.

The solar eclipse brings dramas at the job and perhaps changes there, but there's no need to worry. Job opportunities are plentiful this month. The same is true for those of you who employ others. There are plenty of good applicants.

Your financial planet moves into your 6th house of work and health on the 1st and stays there for the rest of the month. Money is earned the old-fashioned way, through work. Those already employed are likely to have opportunities for overtime or second jobs. The children and children figures in your life have some financial shake-ups caused by the solar eclipse but the month ahead – especially after the 21st – seems prosperous for them.

August

Best Days Overall: 7, 8, 16, 17, 26, 27
Most Stressful Days Overall: 2, 3, 9, 10, 23, 24, 25, 30, 31
Best Days for Love: 1, 2, 3, 8, 9, 10, 19, 20, 21, 30, 31
Best Days for Money: 1, 9, 10, 19, 20, 21, 28, 29, 30, 31
Best Days for Career: 1, 9, 10, 19, 20, 28, 29

Though the Eastern sector of your chart is still very strong, the Western social sector is as strong as it will ever be this year. You never lose your sense of your self-interest these days, but it is good to develop your social skills. Personal independence is still strong, but not as strong as in the first few months of the year. In addition, with your 7th house becoming powerful after the 23rd, love becomes important. Too much self-interest and personal independence are not that great for love. Love is not only important for its own sake; after the 23rd it becomes a health issue too. Good health for you also means a healthy love life. Developing the social skills will also boost the bottom line after the 18th. Likeability seems a big factor in earnings.

Health is good until the 23rd but after that will need some attention paying to it. However, your intense focus on health until the 23rd (your 6th house is chock-full of planets) will stand you in good stead for afterwards. Health regimes and more attention is like depositing money in a health savings account. You build up more energy and resistance. Still, rest more after the 23rd. Don't burn the candle at both ends. Abdominal massage and massage of your small intestine reflex (see the reflexology chart in the yearly report, page 357).

With your 6th house so strong at the moment (it became strong on July 23), it is a good time to do all those boring, detailed tasks that you always put off doing. They will go better now – you're more in the mood for such work until the 23rd.

The love life is very active this month, but complicated. You and the current love are at opposite ends of the chart. You see things and interpret things in opposite ways. You have opposite opinions on things. Usually this is not pleasant, but if you can bridge your differences – see the merit in the other's perspective – your relationship can get even stronger. In astrology it is one's opposite that is the natural partner;

opposites are seen as complements. But you have to rise to a higher level to see this.

Your love planet moves speedily this month. Mercury moves through three signs and houses. He is at maximum speed. Thus you cover a lot of territory. Singles are dating more. There is social confidence. The only problem is that your love needs also change rapidly and it is difficult for the beloved to figure them out. Until the 11th you like fun and emotional intimacy. From the 11th to the 28th you like fun but you also like practical service. You're attracted to people who serve your practical interests. Until the 11th love opportunities happen at places of entertainment or through family connections. After the 11th love happens as you pursue your health goals – perhaps at the gym or the health centre – and with people involved in your health. On the 29th Mercury moves into Virgo, your 7th house, and love opportunities happen in the usual places, at parties and social gatherings. Be careful of hyper-criticism and hyper-perfectionism now.

September

Best Days Overall: 3, 4, 12, 13, 14, 22, 23, 30
Most Stressful Days Overall: 5, 6, 20, 21, 26, 27
Best Days for Love: 8, 9, 20, 21, 26, 27, 28, 29
Best Days for Money: 5, 6, 7, 8, 9, 15, 16, 17, 18, 19, 24, 25, 26, 27
Best Days for Career: 5, 6, 15, 16, 24, 25

The planetary power is still strongly in the Western, social sector this month. In fact it is at its maximum for the year. And your 7th house of love will never be stronger than now – not this year anyway. So let go (a bit) of your self-interest and develop the social skills. Your financial planet, Mars, spends the entire month in your house of love, so there are financial benefits to putting others first too. Your social skills are like money in the bank right now. And you may have to give in to others a bit for financial reasons.

With the financial planet in your 7th house for so long (since August 18), business partnerships or joint ventures are likely – the opportunities will come. Investors often earn through mergers in their portfolios.

The planetary power is now above the horizon of your chart. The trend began last month and now it is firmly established. Moreover, your career planet Jupiter started to move forward on August 11. This is beautiful timing. A lot of issues are resolved now. There is clarity about the career and you can start focusing on it. Career issues will go much easier after the 23rd. Until then you have to work at it, but now you are starting your yearly career push. It is daytime in your year.

Health still needs watching until the 23rd. As always the important thing is to not get overtired. Maintain high energy levels. Until the 23rd enhance the health through abdominal massage and the massage of the small intestine reflex (see page 357). After the 23rd, hip massage and massage of the kidney reflex will be beneficial. You respond well to detox regimes as well. You will see big improvements in health and energy after the 23rd.

The love planet in Virgo can make you too analytical, too head-oriented in love. Romance is only 10 per cent logic; 90 per cent is magic. Get more into the emotion of love. Avoid criticism or analysis in romantic moments. If you must criticize, keep it constructive. The time for analysis will come later on.

Pluto, the ruler of your 9th house of philosophy, religion and travel, receives very nice aspects this month. From the 5th to the 7th Venus makes a harmonious trine, as does Mercury from the 8th to the 10th, and the Sun from the 12th to the 14th. So, travel opportunities are likely to come and you might enjoy them. These aspects are wonderful for college students and signal success.

October

Best Days Overall: 1, 10, 11, 19, 20, 28, 29
Most Stressful Days Overall: 2, 3, 4, 17, 18, 23, 24, 30, 31
Best Days for Love: 10, 11, 19, 20, 23, 24, 28, 29
Best Days for Money: 2, 3, 4, 7, 12, 13, 17, 18, 21, 22, 26, 27, 30, 31
Best Days for Career: 2, 3, 4, 12, 13, 21, 22, 30, 31

Health is much improved over last month. By the 4th, as Mars moves away from his stressful aspect, there will be only one planet in stressful alignment with you – Jupiter. And his impact tends to be mild. Only the Moon – and then only occasionally – will make a stressful aspect. So, health is good. You have plenty of energy to achieve whatever you want to achieve. You can enhance the health even further through hip massage and massage of the kidney reflex until the 23rd. After the 23rd give more attention to the colon and bladder. The reflex points are shown in the chart on page 357. Detox regimes, safe sex and sexual moderation are important all month.

Your 8th house of regeneration became strong on September 23 and is strong until the 23rd of this month, giving many messages. It is a sexually active kind of period. Libido is at a high. It is good for projects involving personal transformation and reinvention. Good for occult studies too. It is a time to simplify your life, to expand by getting rid of whatever is unnecessary – whether it be possessions or mental and emotional patterns. This is a month for learning the art of the 'turna-round', the art of renewal. There are things in your life that might seem 'dead' or 'near dead' – these can be resurrected now. The ways will be revealed. This is what the 8th house is all about.

Your financial planet Mars enters the 8th house on the 4th and spends the rest of the month here. Thus you prosper by prospering others. The focus should be on the financial interest of others – the spouse, partner, friends and investors. To the degree that you succeed, your own prosperity will happen by the karmic law. This is a time for tax planning and becoming more tax efficient. Insurance planning also goes well. For those of you of appropriate age it is good for estate plan-ning. If you have good ideas this is a good month for recruiting outside investors. Borrowing, paying off or refinancing debt also goes well. You have good access to outside capital these days.

Mars has his solstice from the 4th to the 11th, just as he is changing signs moving from Virgo to Libra. He stays at the same degree of lati-tude that period. So, in effect, he 'pauses' in his latitudinal motion and then changes direction. It is a good pause, a cosmic pause, a healthy pause. So there will be a brief pause in your financial life and then a new direction (and it will be good).

Love is happy this month, especially after the 3rd. Sexual magnetism and chemistry seem the most important things in a relationship now, but don't neglect personal philosophy and religious compatibility either. These are equally important. The 14th to the 16th are especially powerful romantic days.

November

Best Days Overall: 6, 7, 16, 17, 24, 25
Most Stressful Days Overall: 13, 14, 20, 21, 26, 27
Best Days for Love: 6, 7, 8, 9, 16, 17, 18, 19, 20, 21, 24, 25, 29
Best Days for Money: 3, 4, 5, 8, 9, 10, 17, 18, 19, 26, 27
Best Days for Career: 8, 9, 10, 18, 19, 26, 27

A happy and successful month ahead. Enjoy.

Career has been successful all year, with varying degrees of intensity, but this month it gets even better. The Sun enters your 10th house on the 20th and you begin a yearly career peak. Your good work ethic impresses superiors.

Mars's move into your 9th house on the 19th shows prosperity. The 9th house is an expansive and beneficent house. Also Mars will be making very nice aspects to Neptune, the ruler of your Horoscope, from the 19th onwards. Earnings increase and happy financial opportunities come. Until the 19th Mars will be in your 8th house, so review our discussion of this last month. This is a time for cutting waste and financial redundancies. Do you have multiple bank accounts? Multiple pensions? Services that overlap each other? Consolidate them. Get rid of possessions that you don't need or use. Reduce the clutter and simplify the finances. You will see the benefits of this after the 19th.

Your love planet Mercury spends the month in your 9th house and in good aspect to you. So love is basically happy and harmonious. The only complication is Mercury's retrograde from the 2nd to the 20th. This won't stop love from happening but does slow things down. The passion and ardour are less than they should be. There is a lack of direction in the spouse, partner or current love. Your personal social confidence is not up to its usual standard. But this is a short-term issue and passes by the 20th. Love opportunities happen in foreign lands, at your place of worship, and at school or school functions.

Foreigners, religious and highly educated people are most alluring these days – especially if the sexual chemistry is strong. You have the aspects of someone who falls in love with the professor or minister this month. You like people you can learn from. You like mentor figures.

Health is wonderful until the 22nd, but afterwards needs a bit of attention. There is nothing serious afoot, only a period of lower energy. So make sure to get enough rest. Until the 20th detoxing is powerful. Like last month give more attention to the colon and bladder. After the 20th thigh massage is beneficial. It would also be good to massage the reflex to the liver (you can look this up in the chart shown in the yearly report, page 357). Heat therapies are potent from the 22nd onwards. Plain old sunshine is a healing tonic. Saunas, steam rooms and hot baths – as hot as you can take them – are good. Those of you who live in cold climates need to wrap up more.

December

Best Days Overall: 3, 4, 5, 13, 14, 21, 22, 31
Most Stressful Days Overall: 11, 12, 17, 18, 24, 25
Best Days for Love: 6, 7, 8, 9, 15, 16, 17, 18, 25, 28, 29
Best Days for Money: 3, 4, 5, 6, 7, 8, 13, 14, 17, 21, 22, 26, 31
Best Days for Career: 8, 17, 24, 25, 26

Health still needs watching until the 22nd. Try to rest more, massage the thighs and the liver reflex (shown on page 357) until the 22nd. After that the spine, back and knees become important and back and knee massage will be potent. However, you'll see improvement naturally after the 22nd. The overall planetary energy is more harmonious to you and the body will reflect that.

Career is the main headline this month. Not only are you in a yearly career peak (and for many of you it's been a lifetime peak), but a solar eclipse on the 26th impacts on Jupiter, your career planet, signalling important changes. My feeling is that your short-term career goals have been achieved and so a shift in attitude and direction is needed.

The solar eclipse of the 26th occurs in your 11th house (the third solar eclipse of the year and the third eclipse in this house), and almost replicates the solar eclipse of January. Since it impacts on your career planet and your work planet, the Sun, there are job and career changes happening. The conditions of work and career change. Friendships get tested once again and there are dramas in the lives of friends. There are shake-ups in professional or trade organizations you belong to. If you employ others there can be employee turnover now. Often this reflects not so much dissatisfaction with the job but dramas in their personal lives. Once again you will be making big changes to your health regime. A health scare can happen, but since your health is generally good it is not likely to be anything more than that. Once again your high-tech equipment – computers, software and gadgetry – get tested. They can behave erratically this period and sometimes they'll need repair, replacement or upgrading. Keep important files backed up and be extra vigilant about online security and viruses.

With Jupiter's move into your 11th house on the 3rd, career goals can now be most effectively pursued through networking and being more involved with groups and organizations. Good technology skills will foster the career.

Love is more complicated after the 9th. On the one hand the current love is supporting the career, but on the other he or she is not in agreement with you. You seem in conflict. This will resolve itself after the 29th. The love planet Mercury in the career house shows you furthering the career by social means. A lot of your socializing is career-related. Singles have opportunities for office romances. There is an attraction to successful people – people who have achieved things in life. Power is a romantic turn-on.